Black Ballots

Black Ballots

Voting Rights
in the South, 1944–1969

Steven F. Lawson

LEXINGTON BOOKS
Lanham • Boulder • New York • Oxford

LEXINGTON BOOKS

Published in the United States of America
by Lexington Books
4720 Boston Way, Lanham, Maryland 20706

12 Hid's Copse Road
Cumnor Hill, Oxford OX2 9JJ, England

Copyright © 1999 by Lexington Books
Originally published in 1976 by Columbia University Press.

British Library Cataloguing in Publication Information Available

Library of Congress Cataloging-in-Publication Data

Lawson, Steven F. 1945–
    Black ballots.
    Bibliography: p.
    1. Afro-American—Southern States—Politics and suffrage. I. Title.
JK 1929.A2L3   324'.15   76-18886
ISBN 0-7391-0087-4 (pbk. : alk. paper)

Printed in the United States of America

⊖™ The paper used in this publication meets the minimum requirements of American
National Standard for Information Sciences—Permanence of Paper for Printed Library
Materials, ANSI/NISO Z39.48–1992.

For William E. Leuchtenburg

Contents

Preface to the 1999 Edition

Black Ballots is reprinted as it was first published in 1976. The book is an example of contemporary history, and nearly all the events covered in it occurred during my lifetime. In 1944, the year before I was born, the Supreme Court outlawed the Democratic white primary in the South, and in 1965, following my junior year in college, Congress passed the Voting Rights Act. In between, the Civil Rights Movement successfully waged the struggle against white supremacy that resulted in the downfall of segregation and in the enfranchisement of the majority of African Americans. Although I did not participate directly in the movement, my own views were actively shaped by it. Not only supportive of the efforts to secure racial equality through lawsuits and legislation, I was especially drawn to the courage of the young people at the forefront of the sit-ins, freedom rides, and voter registration drives in the deep South. A quarter of a century later, my appreciation of what civil rights activists accomplished has only grown. In the face of personal violence and institutional resistance, African Americans and their white allies overthrew a deeply entrenched structure of racial apartheid designed to guarantee second-class citizenship for African Americans. The fact that the ballot has still not translated into economic equality for many blacks does not detract from the magnitude of the Civil Rights Movement's successes. Rather, it suggests the need for a renewed struggle and a revival of the imagination and dedication that brought about such significant change in the first place.

For those born after passage of the Voting Rights Act and who learn about the Civil Rights Movement chiefly through reading textbooks and viewing documentaries, the results may seem predestined and relatively easy to have achieved. Nothing could be further from the truth, and I hope *Black Ballots* conveys how difficult the fight was to make the nation live up to its democratic ideals. As I intended the book to show, the problem did not stem solely from prejudiced white southerners oppressing their black neighbors but also grew out of a political and constitutional system in which the national government reinforced racial inequality. In concentrating on the operation of the federal government in Washington, D.C., I attempted to show the role played by white northern officials in sustaining racial discrimination in the South. Until the mid 1940s the Supreme Court sanctioned devices to perpetuate black disfranchisement, and the occupants of both the White House and Congress refrained from taking the necessary measures to overcome discrimination. Only when the national government gradually reversed course in the two decades after 1944 did it become possible for African Americans to win their freedom. However, acknowledging the critical importance of Washington in shaping the outcome of the black freedom struggle does not thereby constitute a favorable moral judgment about those who held the power required to defeat Jim Crow. Indeed, as the history in the following pages demonstrates, government officials did not usually spring to action because they thought it was the right thing to do, but they responded mainly when forced to do so by African Americans exerting potent political pressure and precipitating unsettling crises.

Looking back, I consider *Black Ballots* a preliminary step in connecting the history of the Civil Rights Movement at the national and local levels. Its chapters detail the operation of the executive, legislative, and judicial branches in the nation's capital, but they also depict grassroots voter registration drives and political organizing. The book may be criticized for presenting a "top down" version of history that emphasizes the deliberations of white men in Washington, and, to a certain extent, that is a fair judgment. However, I think such an assessment underestimates the coverage given to local suffrage projects and such crucial episodes as the Mississippi Freedom Democratic Party challenge in 1964 that attracted the participation of southern black women and men. Nevertheless, in the years since the book first appeared, scholars have concentrated more heavily on the diverse histories of civil rights movements in local communities and states in the South. They have enriched our understanding of the ways in which ordinary citizens, women and men, organized themselves and mobilized resources in their own behalf.[1] In doing so, they have looked at the social, cultural, and political institutions of African-American communities and reminded us that southern blacks must appear at the center of civil rights history. At the same time, the story remains incomplete unless it examines the intersection of national and local undertakings, which *Black Ballots* sketched out and several other scholars have also addressed.[2]

This book traced only one aspect of the quest for black political emancipation—the restoration of the right to vote. The final chapter of the text only briefly discussed the implementation of the Voting Rights Act and not at all the efforts of black southerners to use the ballot to gain political office and influence public policy. I did write a sequel that explored these issues from the late 1960s and 1970s to the early 1980s, a period in which Congress extended the scope of the Voting Rights Act three times.[3] This era witnessed a shift in concern from the right to vote to the right to have fair representation. Civil rights advocates concentrated on challenging racial bias in electoral procedures that limited the power of African Americans and other minorities to select candidates. For the most part, the Supreme Court and Congress agreed with them by supporting election arrangements for municipal, state, and national offices that created majority-black legislative districts, thereby increasing the chances of minority candidates winning contests. In fact, since 1965, these electoral provisions have helped swell the number of southern black officeholders from less than 100 to around 5,000 in the mid-1990s.

However, the Supreme Court has recently threatened to reverse this progress. During the 1990s, the court has begun to question the degree to which race can be used as a criterion in drawing legislative districts to promote black political opportunities. In changing direction, the majority of justices seem to have ignored the fact that sophisticated forms of discrimination are as harmful as blatant ones. They have also departed from the legacy of the framers of the Voting Rights Act. These lawmakers recognized the novel schemes white southerners had devised over the past century to thwart black political advancement, and, consequently, they created a document flexible enough to remedy even the most subtle ways of hampering the black vote, including those that substantially reduce its potency. More than three decades after passage of the Voting Rights Act, African Americans hold onto the franchise, but issues affecting equitable representation and power sharing remain seriously contested.

These setbacks, as lamentable as they are, underline, once again, just how difficult it was for the Civil Rights Movement to accomplish as much as it did. The original preface to this book mentioned the travails of the Evers brothers, Medgar and Charles. The former was gunned down and killed in front of his home in Jackson, Mississippi, in 1963, and his assassin went free. Thirty years later, in a much different political climate in Mississippi, where two-thirds of the black electorate could vote and hundreds were holding office, the state reopened the case and convicted Medgar Evers' killer. In the interim, Charles Evers took up his brother's civil rights mantle, won election as mayor of Fayette, and became a powerful voice in the state's Democratic Party. No matter how many obstacles loom ahead, one must remember how much has changed in just a generation or so.

A final word on what has not been altered: the reader will quickly notice that the word "Negro" abounds throughout the text. At the time the book was written, it constituted standard scholarly usage, though it was becoming more frequent to write about "Blacks". "Afro-American" or "African-American" had not yet settled in as the conventional terms used today. Nonetheless, this current edition retains "Negro" as originally published. If the term sounds archaic, that, too, is a reflection of both the impact of African Americans on all aspects of American culture and the distance we as a nation have travelled since 1976. It cannot obscure, however, how far we still have to go to transform the aspirations and visions of black citizens into political and economic realities.

NOTES

1. Some of the most influential community and state studies include: William H. Chafe, *Civilities and Civil Rights: Greensboro, North Carolina and the Black Freedom Struggle* (New York: Oxford University Press, 1981); David R. Colburn, *Racial Change and Community Crisis: St. Augustine, Florida, 1877–1980* (New York: Columbia University Press, 1985); John Dittmer, *Local People: The Struggle for Civil Rights in Mississippi* (Urbana: University of Illinois Press, 1994); Adam Fairclough, *Race and Democracy: The Civil Rights Struggle in Louisiana, 1915–1972* (Athens: University of Georgia Press, 1995); Robert J. Norrell, *Reaping the Whirlwind: The Civil Rights Movement in Tuskegee* (New York: Vintage, 1986); Charles M. Payne, *I've Got the Light of Freedom: The Organizing Tradition and the Mississippi Freedom Struggle* (Berkeley: University of California Press, 1995). On women community activists specifically, see Sara Evans, *Personal Politics: The Roots of Women's Liberation in the Civil Rights and the New Left* (New York: Vintage, 1980); Vicki L. Crawford, Jacqueline Anne Rouse, and Barbara Woods, eds., *Women in the Civil Rights Movement: Trailblazers and Torchbearers, 1941–1965* (Brooklyn: Carlson Publishing, 1990); Cynthia Griggs Fleming, *Soon We Shall Not Cry: The Liberation of Ruby Doris Smith Robinson* (Lanham, Md.: Rowman & Littlefield, 1998); Belinda Robnett, *How Long? How Long? African-American Women in the Struggle for Civil Rights* (New York: Oxford University Press, 1997); Joanne Grant, *Ella Baker: Freedom Bound* (New York: John Wiley, 1998); Chana Kai Lee, *For Freedom's Sake: the Life of Fannie Lou Hamer* (Urbana: University of Illinois Press, 1999).

2. For example, see Taylor Branch, *Parting the Waters: America in the King Years, 1954–63* (New York: Simon & Schuster, 1988); Glenn T. Eskew, *But for Birmingham: The Local and National Movements in the Civil Rights Struggle* (Chapel Hill: University of North Carolina Press, 1997); David J. Garrow, *Protest at Selma: Martin Luther King, Jr., and the Voting Rights Act of 1965* (New Haven: Yale University Press, 1978); Richard Kluger, *Simple Justice: The History of Brown v. Board of Education and Black America's Struggle for Equality* (New York: Vintage, 1975).

3. *In Pursuit of Power: Southern Blacks and Electoral Politics, 1965–1982* (New York: Columbia University Press, 1985). See also my *Running for Freedom: Civil Rights and Black Politics in America Since 1941*, 2nd edition (New York: McGraw Hill, 1997).

Preface

In 1946 two black men recently discharged from the armed forces decided to apply for voting registration. What should have been a routine act for these veterans in a country just having defeated the battalions of fascism and racism caused quite a commotion. The place was Decatur, Mississippi, and these men found that their homeland had not changed very much. Their white neighbors blocked the entrance to the courthouse, and one of them snarled, "Who you niggers think you are?" The younger black replied, "We've grown up here. We have fought for this country and we should register." Unimpressed by this reasoning, the white man promised that there would be "trouble" if they persisted in trying to enroll.[1]

Medgar Evers and his brother Charles eventually did get to register and vote in Mississippi, but not without great personal sacrifice. Their contrasting fates revealed much about the struggle for the enfranchisement of blacks in the South over the last quarter of a century. On June 12, 1963 Medgar, the secretary of the Mississippi branch of the National Association for the Advancement of Colored People (NAACP), while walking up the driveway to his home in Jackson was gunned down from behind and killed by a sniper. Six years later, Charles was elected mayor of Fayette, the first black man to hold such a post in the state since Reconstruction.

This study explores the process by which a majority of southern black adults gained the right to vote. It shows how the legal and political institutions of the United States responded to Negro demands for enforcement of the Fifteenth

---

1. Charles Evers, *Evers* (New York: World, 1971), p. 92.

Amendment in the years since World War II. The courts interpreted the scope of the constitutional guarantee, Congress
enacted specific remedies to combat disfranchisement ruses,
and the executive implemented the powers conferred by the
legislature. But it took so much time, energy, and money to
eliminate the barriers in front of an unfettered suffrage. Enfranchisement occurred episodically in a piecemeal fashion,
and often it required a national crisis to precipitate a significant departure from past policies.

Until 1965, civil-rights advocates experimented with several
different approaches, most of which brought some gains but
basically left the problem unsolved. Thus, I have examined
court cases directed against specific abuses, for instance, the
white primary and poll tax, and I have detailed the passage of
various statutes that authorized the executive branch to wage
the franchise struggle in the South. By so doing, one can detail the forces that propelled policymakers and strategists to
correct previous failures.

As a vital element of this analysis, I have investigated the
role pressure groups played in securing blacks the right to cast
a ballot. To this end, I have focused on the philosophy, goals,
and methods of the leading civil-rights organizations, especially the NAACP and the Student Non Violent Coordinating
Committee (SNCC). Since the suffrage battle was waged on
several fronts, such agencies followed a rough division of
labor, performing those tasks—litigation, lobbying, and voter
registration drives—for which they were best suited. They
toiled valiantly to prick America's conscience, and tried to
work within the system to achieve meaningful political change
for southern blacks.

Yet more than moral fervor and legal arguments were
needed to convince Congress and the president to act. After
the Second World War, leaders of both political parties calculated that the influx of southern Negroes to the North, where
they had the opportunity to vote, created a new balance of
power in close elections. Consequently, candidates gained the
support of these blacks by endorsing legislation to help en-

franchise their family and friends remaining behind in Dixie. But once lawmakers joined the suffrage cause, they still faced the delicate task of translating their commitment into legislation. Hence the reformers encountered the obstacle of a Senate in which a southern minority aided by conservative Republicans and several northern Democrats could frustrate majority rule. Therefore, governmental leaders had to balance the requests made by civil rights lobbyists with the prospects of antagonizing powerful blocs in Congress.

It was logical that Washington furnished the main forum for settling the franchise problem. The elevation of Negroes in the South to the status of registered voters had to result from pressures outside that region. Charles V. Hamilton has pointed out, "In the process of political modernization, governments concentrate power in the center. Several countries on the European continent did this during the emergence of monarchical rule that followed centuries of feudalism." [2] Likewise, since most whites attempted to preserve the established racial order within the South, it was necessary that the central government crushed this powerful resistance to Negro political equality.

Extending the suffrage to blacks meant a readjustment of the boundaries within the federal system. Southern whites had been aided in perpetuating discrimination because control over voting qualifications was considered the prerogative of the states. Yet in theory the central government, particularly by virtue of the Fifteenth Amendment, had substantial power to safeguard the suffrage against racial bias. In practice, however, although Congress enacted statutes punishing bigoted interference with the right to vote, Washington argued that the responsibility for law enforcement rested with local officials. But many of these southern "peacekeepers" harassed and intimidated black citizens as they strived to exercise their constitutional rights. Without intense federal pressure, the

---

2. Charles V. Hamilton, "Blacks and the Crisis in Political Participation," *The Public Interest* XXIV (Winter 1974): 193.

states could effectively continue to exclude Negroes from the political process. The question of how far the national government could legitimately intervene not only brought Washington into conflict with the southern states, but also with the civil-rights proponents who did not share public policymakers' concerns about preserving the traditional demarcations of the federal system.

For all those interested in the civil rights battle, the right to vote was crucial. "Give us our ballot," Charles Evers had told a Mississippi registrar in 1946, because he perceived that by the way whites "guarded that ballot box, they let us know there was something mighty good in voting." [3] The suffragists argued, perhaps with a bit too much rhetorical flourish, that the franchise would provide the weapon to topple the barriers of discrimination. The ballot was expected to bring both material and psychological rewards. Once Negroes exercised their vote, they could help elect sheriffs who would be less likely to brutalize them; they would select officials who would see to it that ghetto streets were paved and cleaned; and ultimately they would use their ballots to dismantle the entire Jim Crow caste system. The opportunity for registration would be the first step toward liberating southern Negroes from centuries of mental oppression and in restoring the dignity that white Americans had tried to destroy. By 1969 part of this dream had come true, and blacks were gaining benefits from enrolling and going to the polls. As a symbolic gesture, Evers wrote, in a touching letter to his martyred brother, "Remember, Medgar, when that old Bilbo warned that rabble if they weren't careful they'd wake up to find those two little nigger boys representing them? Well, he wasn't far wrong. We are representing them, quite a few of them." [4]

3. Evers, *Evers,* pp. 92–96.
4. Ibid., p. 196.

Acknowledgments

WRITING THIS BOOK has been both a solitary and a communal experience. Of course the ultimate responsibility is my own, but along the way I have received the aid of many fine people. My friends and relatives who took an interest in what I was doing have my everlasting appreciation. Away from home, the archivists of the various libraries that I have visited eased my research trips with their patience and diligence. A number of people have shared their recollections on the subject of politics and civil rights, and I hope that they recognize their contributions.

The pages that follow particularly benefit from the suggestions made by former teachers and present colleagues. Professors Nathan Huggins, Kenneth Jackson, Charles V. Hamilton, and James S. Young of Columbia University originally read this study as a doctoral thesis and provided useful comments that strengthened the manuscript for publication. When John T. Elliff was at Barnard College, he generously made available to me his doctoral dissertation on the Justice Department and individual liberties, thereby giving me valuable insight into this crucial topic. At the University of South Florida, George Mayer found time in his busy schedule to improve both the content and style of this work; Darryl Paulson added his perspective as a political scientist; and Louis Pérez tested some of my assumptions and enlivened the walk from Mrs. Taylor's rooming house to the Library of Congress.

Several people had a hand in readying this book for print. Sharon Wilson typed the entire manuscript and Nancy Lee prepared early drafts of the chapters and handled correspondence. Both tolerated my last-minute, panic-stricken demands, deciphered my scrawl, and gave me encouraging words. At Columbia University Press Maria Caliandro helpfully answered my questions about editing, and Bernard Gronert, as executive editor, furnished assistance at every phase of the publication process.

Three people are very special to me. Mark Gelfand was always there when I needed him, whether nursing me through a bout with the flu in Independence, Missouri or taking notes for me at the Kennedy Library after I fractured my wrist. As lunchmate, research partner, interviewer, critic, and keeper of the faith, he helped make this book possible.

My gratitude also goes to William E. Leuchtenburg. Ample testimony of the high esteem in which Professor Leuchtenburg is held already appears in the acknowledgment pages of the numerous books that he initially sponsored as doctoral dissertations. He supervised this project from its conception, and I thank him for his concern and understanding. As a teacher and advisor, he performed beyond the call of duty. Although we sometimes drew different conclusions, Professor Leuchtenburg always insisted that I follow my own interpretive course. For this support and other reasons, I will always be indebted to him.

Finally, I wish to thank Steve Wrinn, my editor at Lexington Books/Rowman & Littlefield, for believing that *Black Ballots* should remain in print. I very much appreciate his vision and support.

1

The Strange Career of
Black Disfranchisement

FROM THE FOUNDING of this nation until its disruption in 1861, each decade had been marked by an expansion in voting rights. One recent historian who has traced this development concluded, "The almost total elimination of property as a qualification for voting . . . proved how successful had been the suffrage reform movement by the time of the Civil War." [1] Preparing for battle against each other, northerners and southerners shared at least one thing in common—pride in their democratic electoral system. Yet America had limited the franchise almost exclusively to white males. Women, Indians, and the majority of Negroes were not considered qualified to participate in the republican experiment. When Lee surrendered at Appomattox, Negroes living in five New England states, containing 6 percent of the total northern black population, were eligible to freely cast their ballots. [2] As the United States entered the second phase of its history, the country confronted the task of making political freedom a reality for all.

During Reconstruction most adult male southern Negroes were able to vote for the first time. The Military Reconstruction Acts of 1867 decreed that blacks must be permitted to take part in the framing of the new state constitutions and subsequently in the formation of the legislatures. Supervised by federal troops, approximately 700,000 blacks, most of whom were former slaves with no education and little knowledge of the workings of the political process, qualified as voters. John Hope Franklin, one of the most informed chroniclers of black history, has called this feature of the transition from slavery to freedom "the most revolutionary aspect of the reconstruction program." [3] The emancipated Negroes proved themselves capable of exercising the suffrage reasonably and held a variety of offices on the national, state, and local levels. Many historians today agree that black legislators in the South were not generally vindictive toward the former slaveholders, and that Negro politicians serving in the constitutional conventions and state legislatures promoted educational and economic benefits, as well as social reforms, for both races. [4]

While southern blacks were obtaining the right to vote, most of their northern brothers remained disfranchised. Only a few Negroes living above the Mason-Dixon line had been permitted to vote before the Civil War, and their status did not immediately change with the reunion of the country and the abolition of slavery. Between 1865 and 1868, northern white electors in Connecticut, Wisconsin, Kansas, Ohio, Michigan, and New York casting their ballots in referenda on the suffrage issue rejected the idea of extending the franchise to Negroes. A perusal of the election returns revealed that all of the states with a relatively large black population continued to support elections for whites only. [5]

Republican leaders were ahead of the rank and file. Fearful of a Democratic resurgence in the late 1860s, they advocated enfranchisement of northern blacks on the theory that the latter would reward their political benefactors. Calculation was camouflaged behind the rhetoric of principle and undercut by the painful awareness that some hitherto reliable white supporters above the Mason-Dixon line would desert the GOP if it pushed the suffrage issue. [6]

Like these short-term considerations, constitutional precedent encouraged the Republicans to take refuge in ambiguity. It offered no clear answer as to whether the vote was a right or a privilege, namely, an inherent attribute of citizenship or a reward conferred on the demonstrably worthy. In either case, the establishment of suffrage requirements had been left up to the states. So controversy was inevitable because an amendment conferring the franchise on all Negroes would involve a breach with tradition, while a more decentralized approach would be ineffective. As might have been expected, the radical wing supported provisions conferring universal suffrage on all males beyond the age of twenty-one and prohibiting state literacy, property, and registration requirements. The moderates, comprising a majority of the party, did not want to disturb state power to determine suffrage qualifications; instead, they desired simply to prohibit government abridgment of the right of citizens to vote on the basis of race, color, or previous condition of servitude. The initial failure of the Republicans to unite on a plan almost destroyed the chances of securing the two-thirds vote needed for congressional approval of a constitutional amendment, particularly since the Democratic minority opposed any federal guarantee of black suffrage and exploited the differences within the GOP. However, at the end of February 1869, after a two-month struggle that occupied nearly all of this lame-duck session, the Republicans settled for what could be passed, namely, an ambiguous commitment to the black franchise known as the Fifteenth Amendment.

While the final draft may have adhered to the canons of political realism, it proved inadequate as an instrument for protecting the southern Negro. The Fifteenth Amendment did not confer the suffrage on anybody, but merely stipulated that states could not invoke race as a ground for disfranchising people otherwise eligible to vote. The tender of protection in such negative form left the states free to evade the intent of the amendment as long as the barriers they devised against Negro suffrage were not overtly racial. In the North, whites came to accept black voting, but in the South, they resisted en-

forcement of the Fifteenth Amendment from the outset, as
their initial tactics were dependent on their fluctuating prospects of controlling their own affairs. Later, other variables affected the level of Negro voting in the South: Supreme Court
decisions, an erratically rising curve of northern apathy to the
welfare of blacks, and a corresponding drift into defeatism on
the part of the latter.

The most determined effort to protect Negro suffrage occurred immediately after the ratification of the Fifteenth
Amendment in 1870. Congress passed a series of statutes designed to punish those who interfered with the right to vote.
The Enforcement Acts of 1870–1871 prohibited state officials
from applying election laws in a racially biased manner, outlawed physical threats and economic intimidation against voters, and forbade individuals from conspiring to interfere with
a person's right to cast a ballot. To implement the act,
Congress authorized the appointment of supervisors to watch
for election irregularities, scrutinize enrollment procedures,
and certify election results. In addition, the president was
given the power to dispatch federal troops and marshals to
carry out court decrees.[7] From 1870 to 1877 the Justice Department prosecuted an average of over 700 cases annually,
but the proportion of successful convictions dropped from 74
percent in the initial year to 10 percent at the end of the
period.[8]

Several factors inhibited the Justice Department in its ability
to protect Negro voting rights. For one thing, southern authorities had increasingly harassed federal personnel who
tried to perform their duties. In the states not under radical
Republican control, marshals, supervisors of elections, and
soldiers were taken into state custody and charged with an assortment of crimes. Officially sanctioned intimidation pro-
voked a wave of private lawlessness throughout the South.
The Grant administration buckled under the pressure in 1874
and switched to the tactic of prosecuting only the most flagrant violations in the hope of producing "obedience to the
law and quiet among the people." [9]

Already hampered by massive resistance in Dixie, the federal government was dealt its most severe blow by the judiciary. In 1876, in *United States v. Cruikshank* and *United States v. Reese,* the Supreme Court greatly weakened the effectiveness of the Enforcement Acts. The justices declared that in order to secure convictions based on these statutes, federal attorneys had to prove that the accused operated under the color of state law and intended to discriminate for reasons of race.[10] Following the Supreme Court's rulings, the Justice Department's indictments fell sharply to less than 200 per year. Government lawyers had already experienced difficulty in persuading southern white juries to convict civil-rights offenders, and after the court opinions federal prosecutors found it nearly impossible to convince unsympathetic panels that a defendant interfered with an individual because he was a Negro who intended to vote.[11]

These debilitating decisions of the Supreme Court and the subsequent retreat of the Justice Department reflected a pattern of thought that emerged in the North during the 1870s. If W. R. Brock is correct, and the "concept of Negro equality demanded interference with the processes of local government on a scale never before contemplated in America or in any other nation," few northerners were willing to pay the price for drastically transforming the federal system.[12] After fifteen years of civil war and reconstruction, northerners were content to let white southerners manage racial affairs without much outside supervision. Some believed that southern blacks having received the ballot could protect themselves and did not require further assistance; others ceased caring, because they were disillusioned with the results of Radical Reconstruction. Appalled by the corruption of the period, they found a scapegoat in the Negro and came to regret having given the suffrage to the "uneducated" freedman in the first place. The protection of civil rights ceased to be an appealing issue for the Republican party, and a majority of its members turned their attention to development of the country's economic resources. Anxious to reunite the nation and to exploit industrial opportunities jointly with southern whites, the GOP agreed to the Compromise of 1877, which symbolically marked the end of Reconstruction. Coming on the heels of the disputed election the preceding November, it resulted in the seating of a Republican president and the removal of the remaining troops from the South. Deprived of military support, the Republican Justice Department brought a meager twenty-five franchise cases to trial the following year.[13]

As the sequel made clear, the Negro was sacrificed on the altar of sectional reconciliation. Left to their own devices, the redeeming governments of white southerners reduced the number of black electors by half within the next fifteen years.[14] South Carolina led the way in manufacturing legal obstructions to keep the Negro from the polls. In 1882 its lawmakers enacted a registration measure requiring individuals of voting age to enroll between May and June of that year or to risk permanent exclusion from the suffrage lists. Minors were to be enfranchised when they reached the age of twenty-one if a registrar found them qualified. In addition, citizens were compelled to register each time they moved, a stipulation designed to penalize migrating black sharecroppers and tenants. The 1882 statue also established eight categories of national, state, and local elections with separate ballot boxes for each. Illiterates would have made mistakes in any case, but the "Eight Box Law" permitted election officials to aid whites and to obstruct blacks who did not know what they were doing.[15]

A more subtle method of disfranchising illiterates was the adoption of the secret ballot. Before this innovation, political parties provided their adherents with specially prepared ballots on which the names of the preferred candidates were printed. With the introduction of procedures for secrecy, the easily identifiable party marker was replaced by a comprehensive listing of all nominees running for the various offices, requiring voters to pick out and select their choices from the several columns. In effect, this system turned the suffrage into a complicated matter for those unable to read, which meant that a significant proportion of adult blacks (and whites) stopped participating in the electoral process.[16]

Most of the ex-Confederate states preferred to discourage blacks through legal methods, but intimidation and fraud were employed without hesitation by local whites and proved to be an effective weapon. In certain areas, election campaigns resembled combat maneuvers with militia companies parading around town just before voting day to scare away blacks. Occasionally there were angry confrontations between the races. In 1882, black voters in Darlington County, South Carolina arrived at the usual polling place only to discover that the ballot boxes had been suddenly moved the night before to the courthouse. The Negroes rushed to the new location but were too tardy, as a mob of armed whites blocked the entrance to the building and forced the blacks to retreat. Sometimes threats of violence abruptly ended years of Negro political involvement. In Crittenden County, Arkansas, in the late 1880s, blacks held a few important offices until a group of influential whites proclaimed that they were tired of "Negro domination." Fortified with Winchester rifles, this band of vigilantes rounded up the elected black officials and compelled them at gunpoint to flee across the Mississippi River into Memphis, Tennessee. Incidents such as these confirmed that a white southerner was not exaggerating in boasting that only "the shotgun keeps Negroes from the polls." Yet whites had less terroristic tricks to prevent black votes from materializing. Negroes who chanced trying to cast ballots often found themselves delayed by the perfunctory challenges of devious officials, so that at closing time many blacks were still standing in line, shut out from voting.[17]

Despite such practices, the most resourceful southern blacks continued to exercise the franchise and to hold public office in the 1880s and 1890s. In Mississippi, seven Negroes sat in the state legislature as late as 1888, and during the last decade of the nineteenth century, Congress admitted black representatives from North Carolina, South Carolina, and Virginia.[18] Factional struggles slowed the disappearance of the Negro from southern politics. More often than not, he was an ally of conservative whites and helped them to thwart the recurrent bids of depressed farmers for political power. In return, the blacks received a share of the minor offices and variable protection of his voting rights.[19]

This biracial coalition was unstable for two reasons. In the first place, patrician whites refused to treat black politicians as equal partners. For example, although Wade Hampton, the aristocratic governor of South Carolina, appointed some Negroes to state offices in 1877, he did not accept black political involvement in anything but a subordinate role. In typical paternalistic fashion, Hampton supported Negroes in their right to the suffrage, less from a commitment to the principle than from a desire to avoid giving the federal government cause to revive Reconstruction days by vigorously guarding the franchise.[20] Secondly, while the white redeemers counted on a controlled black electorate to keep them in power, Negro leaders found it too difficult to deliver the votes of their own people for a party hitherto associated with the slave system. Moreover, during the 1880s many impoverished blacks chose to vote their economic interests and align with the agrarian insurgents against the wealthy conservatives. As the white rulers alarmingly observed the Negroes' display of political independence, they had two options—the upper-class leaders could either maintain dominance through the customary means of terror and deceit or could disfranchise blacks. In either case, the Negro was bound to lose.

By 1890 it was apparent to the Republican party that it would disappear completely in the South unless something were done to protect the Negro voter. So Congressman Henry Cabot Lodge of Massachusetts introduced legislation providing for federal supervision of national elections. The measure permitted a group of citizens to request the appointment of federal inspectors to monitor registration procedures, voting, and the counting of the returns. The agents would next submit their reports to the circuit courts for final judgment.[21] The Lodge "Force Bill" narrowly passed the House in 1890, but was stymied in the Senate, where northeastern Republicans interested in a high tariff and western Republicans favoring a silver-purchase act deserted party ranks in hope of attracting southern Democratic support for their pet measures.[22]

Although the Lodge bill did not become law, its introduction frightened many southerners. Congressman John Hemphill of South Carolina did not object to the black man receiving his full rights, but "he cannot have his rights and mine too, and the Lodge bill was intended to put him again in control of the government of the Southern States."[23] To forestall this possibility and check the movement for federal intervention, white suffrage "reformers" suggested cleaning up elections back home. They traced the problem of corruption to the presence of Negro voters in the electorate, and hence they suggested disfranchisement as a solution. According to their reasoning, taking the right to vote away from blacks would ensure honest elections, because competing white candidates would not be tempted to buy or steal Negro votes in order to win the contests. Henry Grady, the apostle of the "New South," explained the rationale behind disfranchisement:

> Let the whites divide, what happens? Here is this dangerous and alien influence that holds the balance of power. It cannot be won by argument, for it is without information, understanding, or traditions. It must be bought by race privileges granted as such, or by money paid outright.[24]

In sum, Negroes had to suffer for white sins. A white Republican from Virginia, an opponent of disfranchisement, noted sarcastically that Negroes had to lose their suffrage right "to prevent the Democratic election officials from stealing their votes."[25]

However, the disfranchisers were attempting to do more than wipe out corruption. By 1890 there were still enough black voters remaining to fuse with disgruntled whites, and the Populist uprisings throughout the last decade of the century posed a serious threat to the patrician rulers. Opposed to the economic policies of the conservative planters and businessmen, agrarian radicals at first mobilized the blacks as well as the poor whites to overthrow the Bourbon regimes. Although the Populists rejected the principle of racial integration and opposed the Lodge bill they nevertheless encouraged Negro voting, spoke out against disfranchisement measures, and allotted to blacks a few positions of leadership within their party. They were successful enough in achieving interracial political cooperation to frighten conservatives who retaliated by arousing dormant racial hatred. The transparent effort to divide the poor by raising the spectre of "nigger domination" succeeded. The obsession with white supremacy replaced the preoccupation with economic issues, persuading white radical leaders that the latter would never receive a fair hearing as long as the Negro voted. What started as a reform crusade against aristocratic planters and their middle-class allies ended in a union of rich and poor whites for the purpose of disfranchising blacks.[26]

The period of disfranchisement that erupted with the Populist insurgency completed the efforts to locate ways of confining blacks to the subordination they had known during slavery. Emancipation had not affected whites in their belief that blacks were inferior creatures who could not thrive without close supervision. Although some historians are certainly correct in labeling the years between 1877 and 1890, when Negroes still voted in sizable numbers, as "transitional," clearly the political status of blacks was very precarious and steadily deteriorating. Even before the Populists were defeated and state constitutional conventions met to eliminate what was left of Negro suffrage, most of Dixie's legislatures had already enacted some type of statute to reduce black voting. Neither the white apostles of paternalism nor the agrarian radicals believed in a biracial southern society based on equality. Both were willing to use blacks to promote their own political interests but were content to discard them under pressure. Whites accepted black participation as a means of maintaining racial domination and ensuring social control. In different ways, each side made token gestures toward preserving citizenship rights for Negroes so long as they obeyed white leaders and remained subject to their regulation. In the end when neither faction could totally manipulate black electors, a white consensus was forged to proclaim that disfranchisement would achieve Caucasian hegemony and keep politics immune from black contagion. The nearly total loss of the franchise during the 1890s coincided with the rigid imposition of Jim Crow laws. Both forms of discrimination marked the termination of any flexibility in race relations that previously existed, and completed the degradation of the Negro into a separate and unequal position within southern life.[27]

All southern states rewrote their constitutions between 1890 and 1910, but Mississippi took the lead in devising legal guidelines to end Negro suffrage and finish the process that had begun with statutory disfranchisement in the 1880s. As V. O. Key pointed out, the Magnolia formula was simple. It called for penalization of Negroes without any explicit reference to blacks as members of a racial group.[28] Residence requirements were aimed at transient black sharecroppers and tenant farmers, and the disqualification for conviction of crimes was created to take care of the race's alleged predisposition toward criminal behavior. But the really ingenious devices were found in the chapters on "literacy and understanding tests" and the poll tax. Under ordinary circumstances, a fair application of literacy tests would have prevented large segments of both races from qualifying for the suffrage. However, the understanding provision furnished uneducated whites with a possible escape clause. It allowed an illiterate to enroll if he could "understand any section of the state constitution read to him . . . or give a reasonable interpretation thereof." In this way, white registrars might exercise their discretion in evaluating the applicants' performance on the exams by passing whites but failing blacks.[29]

The Mississippi poll tax was meant to cut down the size of the electorate of both races so that the affluent could best manage the political contests. Advocated by conservatives from the Black Belt who vividly remembered the agrarian radicalism in the state during the 1880s, the tax handicapped economically distressed whites as well as blacks. As a further impediment to voting, the two-dollar duty had to be paid before February 1st of the election year. According to one commentator who later studied the operation of the poll tax, "this was like buying a ticket to a show nine months ahead of time, and before you know who is playing or really what the thing is all about. It is easy to forget to do." [30]

The Mississippi document received favorable reviews from the Supreme Court, and the majority of the southern states copied the Magnolia model. In 1898, the high tribunal in *Williams v. Mississippi* declared that the suffrage qualifications were not "on their face" discriminatory between the races, that the plaintiff failed to demonstrate that there had been a biased application of the requirements, and thus, the Mississippi franchise measures did not violate the federal constitution.[31] Following this opinion, from 1898 to 1910, Louisiana, North Carolina, Alabama, Virginia, Georgia, and Oklahoma wrote disfranchisement rules similar to Mississippi's into their organic laws. The constitutional framers frankly admitted that they were attempting to restrict Negro voting, in the guise of "racially neutral" qualifications. After the Alabama Convention of 1901, Governor William Dorsey Jelks expressed his belief that the registrars "would carry out the spirit of the Constitution, which looks to the registration of all [white] men not convicted of crime, and only a few negroes." [32] That same year, Carter Glass, a delegate to the Virginia Constitutional Convention and later United States senator, described what he expected the work of the convocation to be, "Discrimination . . . to discriminate to the very extremity of permissible action under the limitations of the Federal Constitution, with a view to the elimination of every Negro voter who can be gotten rid of legally, without materially impairing the numerical strength of the white electorate." [33]

A few years earlier, the Louisiana convention had "improved" on the Mississippi plan by ensuring that the literacy test would exclusively disqualify blacks. In 1898, the state adopted the Grandfather Clause, which suspended the educational requirements for those males eligible to vote in the

United States on or before January 1, 1867. Since few Negroes had been qualified to vote prior to that date, this exemption applied almost exclusively to whites. However, in order to take advantage of this provision, individuals had to enroll by September 1, 1898.[34]

The introduction of the direct primary in the South climaxed the movement for suffrage restriction and ensured white supremacy. Around the turn of the century, generally affluent reformers calling themselves progressives tried to restore order to an American society racked by the growing pains of industrialization. After the agrarian revolts of the 1890s, middle- and upper-class southern whites attempted to stabilize political affairs in order to prevent future insurgency. The suffrage requirements written into the state constitutions made fusion of the discontented virtually impossible, and the direct primary guaranteed that political disagreements would be confined within the Democratic party. Josephus Daniels, the progressive editor of the Raleigh (North Carolina) *News and Observer,* explained, "Without the legal primary the fear was expressed by several that the divisions among white men might result in bringing about a return to deplorable conditions when one faction of white men called upon the Negroes to help defeat another faction." [35] Whatever internecine struggles developed would not be complicated by the presence of the remaining black electors who were proscribed first by custom and then by law from participating in the party contests.[36] Barred from them, Negroes could only function as a rubber stamp and waste their votes at the general elections. Therefore, they really had little incentive to make an effort to enroll as electors, a procedure that the registrars continued to make difficult.

During the disfranchisement years, black spokesmen expressed attitudes that consoled the white supremacists. Led by Booker T. Washington, they believed that Negroes should concentrate on securing economic independence before they actively engaged in politics. Although Washington did not condone discriminatory registration practices, he accepted the idea of a restricted suffrage, for both races. The Alabama educator was essentially an elitist who did not believe that the majority of either race was intelligent enough to cast ballots. However, he opposed the constitutions as they were written by the bigoted state conventions. The founder of the Tuskegee Institute wrote in 1899:

> These disfranchisement measures . . . violate the spirit, if not the letter of the Federal Constitution. I am not saying a word against *all legitimate efforts to purge the ballot of ignorance, pauperism, and crime.* But few have pretended that the present movement . . . is for such purposes [emphasis added].[37]

According to Louis Harlan, Washington "lacked faith in the democratic process," and although he attacked the various ruses that singled out the Negro for disfranchisement, he did not believe that they would harm blacks in the long run. Indeed, Washington had faith that prominent blacks like himself who still had an opportunity to vote would "set the example for the less fortunate ones and at the same time, the educated class being small in numbers, can thus pave the way for the gradual introduction of a larger voting population as the years pass by."[38] While the Tuskegee president did contribute financially for challenges against violations of the Fourteenth and Fifteenth Amendments, he operated so secretly that whites erroneously confused his brand of gradualism with an admission that Negroes could never expect more than second-class citizenship.

In the meantime, the disfranchisers had achieved their aim. Their constitutions survived judicial scrutiny and their racist-inspired requirements, for all practical purposes, dealt the final blow to the short-lived experiment of Negro suffrage in the South. The statistics that we have, although quite fragmentary, indicate that black voting on a large scale in the South was mainly a thing of the past. Two years before Louisiana revised its constitution in 1898, some 130,000 Negroes were registered to vote; in 1900, only 5,000 blacks remained on the rolls.[39] In Virginia the effect of the constitutional provisions was to reduce the black electorate from 147,000 to

21,000.[40] Reliable figures for the other states in the period preceding the revised constitutions do not exist and make comparisons impossible. But the evidence available confirms low black registration immediately following ratification. In Mississippi, the pioneer of disfranchisement, after adopting the constitution, 8,615 Negroes out of an adult black population of 147,205 (ca. 6 percent) were enrolled to vote.[41] A similar result occurred in Alabama, where 2 percent of the black voting-age population were enrolled in 1906.[42] Furthermore, the gap in registration between the races had increased tremendously. In Mississippi, two-thirds of the adult whites were still on the lists, and in Alabama the percentage was an even higher eighty-three.[43]

The formal rules of disfranchisement were part of a larger process that kept Negroes from voting. The racist caste structure that hardened with the agreement on white supremacy during the 1890s contributed to the erosion of the Negro suffrage. Terror, intimidation, and reprisals reinforced the Negrophobe's command against black participation in politics. At the bottom of the economic system, dependent on white employers and creditors, and isolated in rural areas subject to the white-man's law, blacks hesitated to confront the system and learned to accept the notion that "politics is white folks' business." The lessons of a Jim Crow education taught them that "good" Negroes did not get involved in public life. As Gunnar Myrdal later explained, "Where white students are taught the Constitution and the structure of governments, Negroes are given courses in 'character building', by which is meant courtesy, humility, self-control, satisfaction with the poorer things of life. . . ." [44] That many blacks became apathetic should not be surprising. The historian of the Mississippi Negro, Vernon Wharton, elucidated this phenomenon:

> Altogether . . . rebuffed by unfriendly registrars, frowned on by the mass of the white population, and absolutely forbidden to support any candidates save those of a party based on white supremacy, the Negro voters found it, in the words of one of their

leaders, 'a mighty discouraging proposition'. More and more of them as time went on, simply abandoned the effort." [45]

As the twentieth century dawned, the prospects for black enfranchisement were bleak but not hopeless. The most encouraging factor was the emergence of black leaders who championed the cause of political emancipation. Inspired by W. E. B. Du Bois, a sociologist-historian graduated from Harvard University and a critic of Booker T. Washington, a "talented tenth" consisting of black professionals living mainly in the North argued that the ballot was a prerequisite for full citizenship. Although Du Bois knew that the right to vote would not instantly destroy racist institutions in the South, he was certain that ballot power was necessary for reform and was essential for workingmen and property owners to defend their rights. Voting would yield more than material gains. Du Bois vehemently attacked Washington's philosophy of political restraint because it suggested that blacks relinquish their self-respect. "Negroes must insist continually," he asserted in 1903, "that voting is necessary to modern manhood." [46] In 1905, when Du Bois and his followers founded the Niagara Movement to agitate for civil rights, one of their major demands was for universal suffrage. They deplored the fact that blacks did not share an equal opportunity with whites to vote in the South, and their platform urged Negro citizens to "protest emphatically and continually against the curtailment of their political rights." Plagued by financial problems and internal squabbles, this activist group was forced to disband in 1910.[47]

Meanwhile, Du Bois had come into contact with white liberals who were espousing ideas similar to his. As the legal status of the Negro deteriorated after 1890, the abolitionist spirit had revived to haunt the conscience of the North. Alarmed that the South was instituting a new form of slavery, the descendants of the Civil War radicals saw a need for establishing an organization to make emancipation a reality at long last. "This Union," William Lloyd Garrison, Jr., whose father had edited the fiery *Liberator,* declared in 1906, "can no more exist on the basis of the enfranchised whites and disfranchised blacks, than could a Union half slave and half free." [48] The "new abolitionists," like many of their forebears, also realized that prejudice was a national problem. Sharing their concerns were a number of settlement-house workers whose jobs exposed them to the agonizing plight of Negroes segregated in the northern ghettos.[49] The Springfield, Illinois race riot of 1908 mobilized some distinguished individuals, many from abolitionist and social-work backgrounds, to issue a call for a conference on civil rights.[50] In the abolitionist tradition, the meeting held in the spring of 1909 was attended by delegates from both races, and Du Bois and some of his colleagues from the Niagara Movement played important roles in the proceedings. At this gathering, the representatives planned for the creation of a permanent organization to promote the cause of racial equality and justice, and the following year the NAACP was founded to carry out this mandate.

The NAACP was committed to extending the franchise through litigation. Because the Supreme Court had validated suffrage requirements that were not inherently discriminatory, the association first attacked those qualifications obviously based on racial categories. The Grandfather Clause provided an excellent target. In 1910 Oklahoma amended its constitution to excuse from taking a literacy test those individuals who were entitled to vote on January 1, 1866 or "anyone who was a lineal descendant of such persons." Although the provision did not overtly single out blacks for unequal treatment, its intent was clearly to block members of their race from registering. Hence, Justice Department attorneys prosecuted several Oklahoma registrars, charging them with violating a section of the Enforcement Acts of 1870, which outlawed racial discrimination in congressional elections. A jury convicted, the circuit court of appeals affirmed the sentence, and in 1914, the Supreme Court heard the appeal. On behalf of the NAACP, its president Moorfield Storey filed an *amicus curiae* brief with the high tribunal. Neither he nor the Justice Department lawyers questioned the constitutionality of the literacy test, but they argued that the criterion for the exemption was cleverly worded to disfranchise Negroes. In 1915, the Court agreed. "The January 1, 1866 standard," Chief Justice Edward White ruled:

> had the purpose to disregard the prohibitions of the Fifteenth Amendment by creating a standard of voting which on its face was in substance but a revitalization of conditions which when they prevailed in the past had been destroyed by the self operative force of the Amendment.[51]

Oklahoma Negroes won the first round, but the fight continued. Although the Court had clearly declared the Grandfather Clause unconstitutional, the "Sooner State" devised a different technique for disfranchisement. In 1916 the legislature decreed "that all citizens qualified to vote in 1916 who failed to register between April 30 and May 11, 1916 should be perpetually disfranchised excepting those who voted in 1914." In practice, this measure automatically enabled whites who had been qualified to vote under the Grandfather Clause to retain their status as voters, but it required blacks, prevented from voting by the clause until 1915, to enroll within a short twelve-day period or forfeit their right to the suffrage.

For over twenty years the law went unchallenged, until Robert Lane, a Negro from Waggoner County who had not registered within the stipulated time limit, tried to enroll.[52] After his application was rejected by a registrar citing the 1916 statute, Lane convinced the NAACP to plead his case. An unfavorable opinion by the United States Court of Appeals in September 1938 sent the association to the Supreme Court for relief. In its brief, the NAACP asked the justices to recognize the disputed registration statute as "the same invalid law in a new disguise of words, having the same discriminatory and unconstitutional intent, operation, and effect and violative of the Fifteenth Amendment." [53] Denying this contention, the state claimed that the sole purpose of the 1916 law was to establish a permanent list of qualified electors, and because most whites already had their names on the 1914 suffrage rolls, there had been no need to make them reregister.[54] The Court was not fooled. Speaking for a six-man majority in 1939, Felix Frankfurter concluded:

> The [Fifteenth] Amendment nullifies sophisticated as well as simpleminded modes of discrimination. It hits onerous procedural requirements which effectively handicap exercise of the franchise by the colored race although the abstract right to vote may remain unrestricted as to face. The legislation of 1916 partakes too much of the infirmity of the grandfather clause to be able to survive.[55]

The elimination of the Grandfather Clause did not make much of an impact on Negro voting, because complex enrollment procedures remained intact. In Oklahoma, where Negroes counted for 7.2 percent of the total population in 1939, as well as in the Deep South states with a much heavier concentration of blacks, biased registrars were still able to keep nonwhites off the voter rolls. Furthermore, until 1944, black citizens had to observe the crucial Democratic primaries from outside the voting booths, and in eight states those who cared to vote in the general election had to surmount the poll-tax obstacle. Nevertheless, the NAACP's triumphs signaled the beginning of a new era. Prodded by the association, the judiciary was responding favorably to the arguments for enfranchisement.[56]

While the NAACP was pursuing its cause through the judiciary, Negroes barely maintained a tradition of voting in the South, and this use of the franchise was confined mostly to urban areas. In southern cities where Negroes were better educated and wealthier than their rural brothers, they were more likely to have developed an interest in politics. Although the Democratic primaries were closed to them and control of GOP organizations was falling into the hands of "lily whites," black urbanites still could participate in local nonpartisan elections and bond referenda. For example, in 1921 Atlanta Negroes holding a balance of power had helped defeat a school-bond proposal that did not allocate a fair share of the money raised for their children's learning. Later when black leaders were promised that a larger portion of the funds would go for the education of their race, Negro voters provided the winning margin for the measure.[57] Even if such opportunities to demonstrate black power were rare, they did allow Negroes to keep alive a spirit of civic consciousness for the future.

During the New Deal, rural blacks were given a small chance to participate in the political process. Starting in 1938 Franklin Roosevelt's agricultural program enabled cotton operators, tenants, and sharecroppers to vote in annual crop-restriction referenda. Writing in 1940, Ralph J. Bunche, who did an exhaustive study of Negro suffrage in this period, observed that "many thousands of black cotton farmers each year now go to the polls, stand in line with their white neighbors, and mark their ballots independently without protest or intimidation, in order to determine government policy toward cotton production control." Bunche concluded that this type of black involvement was important because it tended to "accustom a great many whites to the practice of Negro voting."[58] However, the significance of this exception to the southern norm should not be exaggerated. Whites readily accepted black voters as long as their involvement did not adversely affect the policy of crop regulation. Expected to play a submissive role, Negroes never got elected to administrative posts within the control program. Whites simply would not tolerate having blacks in positions of authority. "If we had," one white farmer bluntly explained, "it would mean a nigger'd be working on a white man's work sheet and he'd have to sit down with that nigger across the table."[59]

On balance, the New Deal aided the Negro cause. Although Roosevelt did not give civil rights a high priority on his legislative agenda, and although many of his relief programs implemented in the South discriminated against impoverished blacks, the president did make the black plight a concern of the federal government. He appointed Negroes to high positions in Washington from which they had been virtually excluded since the southern Democratic administration of Woodrow Wilson. For the first time in American history, blacks as well as whites received direct aid from Washington in time of economic crisis. That some of the people appointed by Roosevelt to head the recovery agencies were racially biased is beyond dispute, but he also selected liberal southern whites such as Aubrey Williams and Clark Foreman, who treated blacks fairly and compassionately.[60] Bernard Sternsher has placed the accomplishments during the Roosevelt years in the proper perspective, "Negro gains during the New Deal, 1933–1938, may appear slight from the standpoint of the 1960's, but they are more impressive when judged against the Negroes' situation in the 1920's."[61] Negro voters certainly agreed with this judgment, for by 1936, a majority of them, in recognition of the economic benefits that they had derived from the New Deal, had abandoned the party of Lincoln and joined the party of Roosevelt.

However, having attracted Negroes into the same party as white southerners, Roosevelt was pulled in opposite directions, making forward motion in the civil-rights field difficult. He had to pay attention to the demographic changes that had paved the way for blacks entering into the Democratic coalition. During World War I, as Negroes journeyed northward out of the South, they congregated in large urban states where their votes were pivotal in local and national elections. These black migrants exerted pressure on federal lawmakers to help their brethren left behind in Dixie. Yet Roosevelt also had to consider the mighty faction of southern Democrats, who wielded enormous influence within Congress and his party. Franklin D. Roosevelt, the power broker par excellence, acted on behalf of the Negro when he thought the delicate political balance in the country allowed him to. According to the president and his advisers, blacks did not need special treatment because their economic condition would improve as the New Deal programs brought recovery and relief in general. They postulated that as the Negro advanced materially, white racism would diminish.[62] This formulation meant that Roosevelt showed much more interest in pushing for social welfare measures than in securing particular civil-rights legislation such as antilynching and antipoll-tax bills. In so doing, he posed a perplexing question for succeeding white liberal administrations to answer, namely, whether Negro rights proposals should be sacrificed for the greater good that might result from the passage of socioeconomic legislation.

Despite the improvements, southern Negroes still had a long way to go before they achieved full citizenship rights. In 1944, Gunnar Myrdal, drawing upon Bunche's intensive research, estimated that less than 250,000 blacks, 5 percent of the adult Negro population, had voted in the southern states within the previous five years.[63] Of course with such limited voting strength, they had little chance of electing members of their race to public office. Most of the legal barriers in the path of the suffrage continued to stand tall, and the economic structure that reinforced white supremacy and perpetuated black apathy had not been improved materially after a decade of depression and reform.[64]

Yet, by the mid 1940s Negroes had several reasons to be encouraged about the future. Blacks strategically located in the North were becoming an influential voting bloc in national politics and were vocally demanding freedom for their southern brothers and sisters. The Supreme Court had begun using the Reconstruction amendments as instruments to tear down the solid edifice of racial bias. As the walls of discrimination started to crack, southern whites appeared more inclined to accept Negro voting than other forms of equality. In fact, the Myrdal survey concluded that political disfranchisement ranked near the bottom of the white southerners' list of prejudices.[65] These positive factors encouraged Negroes, led by the NAACP, to intensify the emancipation struggle. On the ballot front, Bunche pointed out in 1940, "the real test . . . remains in the Negro's ability to break through the white primary."[66] And the NAACP troops had begun to storm the barricades.

2

The Rise and Fall of the White Primary

THE ATTEMPT to demolish the white primary in the South set the pattern for the other phases of the franchise struggle. Blacks, assisted by white liberals, petitioned the federal government to redress their grievances. Civil-rights lawyers propounded ingenious theories that helped the judiciary enlarge the scope of the Fourteenth and Fifteenth Amendments. Often responsive to these arguments, the courts nevertheless proved to be cumbersome and slow instruments for ensuring the right to vote. As judges struck down one type of biased practice, southern racists developed other methods to perpetuate the discriminatory system. Frustrated by such dilatory tactics, the suffragists urged the president to use his administrative powers against those who kept blacks from casting ballots.

During the first two decades of the twentieth century, it was possible for Texas Negroes to vote in Democratic primaries. A 1905 law gave each county the option of conducting racially restricted primaries, but not all had chosen to do so. In most areas Negroes had already lost their suffrage through intimidation and the inability to pay a poll tax and pass a literacy test. Nevertheless, there were counties where blacks remained on the rolls and white candidates actively competed for their ballots. In San Antonio, Negroes displayed exceptional loyalty to the Democratic standard and were rewarded with improvements for their community, including paved streets, new schools, a library, and a public auditorium. However, such devotion to the Democracy was unusual, for the bulk of Negro voters were Republicans. Yet black ties to the GOP were growing very precarious in the face of the party's lily-white tendencies, and an increasing number of blacks bolted to the Democrats or lined up behind independents.[1]

A minor political dispute led to the extension of the white primary throughout the Lone Star State and virtually eliminated Negroes from political involvement. In 1918 D. A. McAskill and John Tobin battled each other for the position of district attorney of Bexar County. The black vote in San Antonio, the county's largest city, played an important role in electing Tobin. An embittered McAskill responded by calling upon the Texas legislature to enact a statute barring Negroes from voting in the Democratic primaries.[2] In this appeal he attracted support from the Texas Ku Klux Klan, a group powerful enough in 1922 to control the Democratic state convention and get one of its members elected to the United States Senate. One of the few places where Klan nominees did poorly in the early 1920s was San Antonio, and the robed bigots could be expected to rally around McAskill's plan.[3]

The forces of white supremacy found legal ammunition in a growing number of court decisions to support his personal vendetta. In a series of rulings since 1916, the Texas Supreme Court had decided that a political party was a private, voluntary association, that party officers were not government officials, and that a primary did not fall in the same category as a general election. In 1921 the United States Supreme Court also held that the act of nomination was not part of the electoral process. The high tribunal set aside the conviction of Truman Newberry, the victorious candidate over Henry Ford in the 1918 Michigan senatorial primary, for violating the Federal Corrupt Practices Act. It decreed that the congressional power to regulate elections did not cover party contests.[4]

The Texas lawmakers took their cue from the judiciary. In 1923, the Klan-dominated legislature resolved, "[I]n no event shall a negro be eligible to participate in a Democratic primary election held in the state of Texas, and should a negro vote in a Democratic primary election, such a ballot shall be void and election officials shall not count the same." On July 26, 1924, election officials faithfully executed this mandate to exclude Negroes from the Democratic congressional primaries.[5]

Disturbed by this move to reinforce second-class citizenship, Negroes turned to the NAACP for help. On August 2nd the president of the El Paso branch of the civil-rights group asked the national association to initiate a court case against the white primary.[6]

The interracial organization offered the best hope for fighting the court battle to a successful conclusion. Taking a case up to the Supreme Court required money and legal talent. Although not a wealthy group, the national association could raise money to contribute to the slender funds of its local branches. More importantly, the NAACP had attracted to its Legal Committee some of the nation's outstanding attorneys who furnished their services without fee. The group's president, Moorfield Storey, a Boston Brahmin and an eminent constitutional lawyer, had been an advocate of racial equality since he served as Charles Sumner's personal secretary during Radical Reconstruction.[7] He was assisted by Louis Marshall, who, as president of the American Jewish Committee, had discovered first hand that southern Jews, like Negroes, were the targets of vicious bigotry.[8] On behalf of the association in 1915, Storey and Marshall had joined in the successful litigation against the Oklahoma Grandfather Clause.

The association would enter a case when it concerned an important constitutional right and the chance of victory seemed good. The proposed Texas suit met the first criterion, and as NAACP Executive Secretary James Weldon Johnson explained, "Since the Democratic primary constitutes the entire machinery of election to office in most Southern states, this case involves the only effective way of striking a blow for the Negro's right to vote." [9] A confident Storey favored bringing litigation against the "absurd" white primary statute, which he concluded was "right in the teeth of the Fifteenth Amendment." [10]

L. A. Nixon, an El Paso physician agreed to become the plaintiff in the test case. As head of the local chapter of the NAACP, Dr. Nixon had closely watched the deliberations of the legislature in thwarting Negro suffrage, and discussed the situation with patients who came into his office. After Nixon was personally blocked from voting in the July 1924 Democratic primary, he sued C. C. Herndon, the election officer who refused to provide him with a ballot on account of his race.[11]

In devising a legal strategy, the NAACP lawyers hoped to convince the judiciary that a primary was an election within the meaning of the Fifteenth Amendment. Storey and Fred C. Knollenberg, a sympathetic white Texas lawyer who handled the case in the lower courts, contended that Texas law regulated the Democratic contest, thereby making it a public election subject to the immunity from racial discrimination guaranteed by the Fifteenth Amendment. According to this line of reasoning, the legislature violated the Constitution when it passed the law preventing Negroes from voting because of their color.[12]

These arguments were rejected by the federal district court in 1925, but Louis Marshall pressed these points again to the Supreme Court. In a carefully prepared brief he wrote that the Fifteenth Amendment protected the right to vote in any form. Disputing the Texas claim that a political party was a voluntary association and its selection of nominees a private action, he maintained that parties currently functioned as an essential part of the voting machinery, governed by state law. Marshall furnished election statistics demonstrating that the Democratic primary constituted the real election in the Lone Star State, because more voters cast their ballots in the pri-

mary than in the final election, and nearly all the party nominees later won. The NAACP counsel also suggested that the
act violated the equal-protection clause of the Fourteenth
Amendment by requiring an arbitrary classification based on
race.[13]

In its October 1926 term, the Supreme Court decided the
case. On January 4, 1927 the jurists listened to Arthur
Spingarn, the Chairman of the NAACP's Legal Committee, as
he delivered the argument. The second son of a prosperous
Jewish immigrant from Vienna, Spingarn had become interested in the association through his elder brother Joel, who
served as chairman of the board.[14] He based Nixon's appeal
on the guarantees of the Fifteenth Amendment. Although the
justices had recently decided in the *Newberry Case* that a party
primary was separate from the election process and consequently not included within the protection of the Constitution, they did not have to apply this precedent to the facts
before them. Instead, Chief Justice William Howard Taft
probed whether the Court could strike down the white primary law under the Fourteenth Amendment. When he asked
Spingarn for his opinion on this point, the NAACP attorney
did not hesitate to respond affirmatively. Justice Oliver Wendell Holmes remarked to Spingarn, "I cannot conceive how
any state could pass such legislation and expect it to be
upheld." [15]

On March 7, 1927, Justice Holmes, speaking for a unanimous Court, held that the Texas resolution violated the Fourteenth Amendment, but he considered it unnecessary to decide whether the controversial rule also upset the Fifteenth
Amendment. A state could do a good deal of classifying,
Holmes read from his opinion, but the legislature deprived
Negroes of the equal protection of the law when color was the
basis of discrimination.[16]

The NAACP had won the skirmish, but the war still raged.
The association's lawyers believed that the Fifteenth Amendment protected the right to vote in party contests. However,
the Court, by invoking the Fourteenth Amendment, left open

the question as to whether a primary was part of an election. Without such a ruling, a state might find other methods to exclude blacks from primaries and not offend either the Fourteenth or Fifteenth Amendments. Although the justices had chosen to ignore its principal contention, the NAACP had gained an important constitutional victory and had introduced legal theories on which to design future litigation that seemed certain to follow.[17]

On June 7, several months after *Nixon v. Herndon,* the Texas legislature responded to this decision by decreeing that:

> every political party in the State through its State Executive Committee shall have power to prescribe the qualifications of its own members and shall in its own way determine who shall be qualified to vote or otherwise participate in such political party.[18]

Subsequently, the Executive Committee of the Democratic party resolved to allow only white participation in its primaries. By shifting this power to the party executive committees, the state intended to remove itself as the source of racial discrimination. Texas officials reasoned that if the party rather than the legislature was biased, the Fourteenth and Fifteenth Amendments did not apply. These articles protected individuals only against "state action," and as long as the courts viewed political parties as private agencies, Texas politicians thought they could legally keep Negroes out of Democratic affairs.

Blacks rushed to persuade the judiciary to affirm their constitutional rights. Dr. Nixon sued James Condon, the election officer who had refused to give him a ballot in the 1928 Democratic primaries.[19] Although Louis Marshall believed that the new case fell under the Fifteenth Amendment, he realized that the failure of the Supreme Court to consider a primary as a feature of a public election left the NAACP with little chance but to concentrate on the Fourteenth Amendment.[20]

The lower federal court rejected Nixon's claim. On July 31, 1929 District Judge Charles A. Boynton of El Paso ruled that the members of the Democratic Executive Committee were not state officials, and thus were not prevented by either the Fourteenth or Fifteenth Amendment from depriving Negroes of their right to vote. Boynton insisted that the 1927 act did not confer additional authority over membership qualifications to the party committee, because "such inherent power remains and exists just as if said act had never been passed." [21] Frank Cameron, a local white attorney hired by the NAACP to argue the case, thought that the judge had made up his mind before hearing the suit. He complained to association headquarters, "In rather an active practice in the courtroom for many years, I never in my life felt such prejudice." [22]

Once again, Arthur Spingarn spoke for Nixon in the Supreme Court chambers. On January 7, 1932 he argued that since the 1927 law specifically delegated to the party executive committees the authority to banish Negroes, the conduct of the Democratic Committee represented state action. Spingarn reasoned that his client could properly sue the election officer who derived his power to exclude blacks from state law, and went on to assert that Texas, for a second time, had deprived Negroes of the equal protection of the law in abridgment of the Fourteenth Amendment. Both the statute and the party resolution, he asserted, sanctioned and worked an arbitrary classification based on color.[23] In addition, the NAACP legal chairman revitalized the arguments founded on the Fifteenth Amendment, previously developed by Louis Marshall in the first *Nixon* case. However, because the judiciary had previously avoided dealing directly with Marshall's points, they necessarily played a supporting role.[24]

Two prominent Negroes from Houston filed an *amicus curiae* on behalf of the association. J. Alston Atkins, an attorney, and Carter Wesley, editor of the Houston *Informer,* presented some original arguments. Assuming that the Fifteenth Amendment gave Nixon the legal right to vote in the statutory primary election, they insisted that the law was unconstitutional because the state tacitly adopted it as a method to disfranchise blacks. They claimed that state action existed, not solely, as the NAACP contended, in any delegation of power to the executive committee, but in the statute's recognition and enforcement of the power to exclude blacks from the primaries. The Houston lawyers warned that unless the Court declared that the plaintiff had a constitutional right to cast a ballot in the primary, political parties, acting as private clubs, would continue racial discrimination.[25]

The attorneys for Condon, the election judge, submitted a brief denying that the Democratic party's exclusion of Negroes from voting in the primary violated either the Fourteenth or Fifteenth Amendments. In their view, a political party, as a private association, had the "inherent right" to determine the qualifications of its own members. Answering the contention that mere legislative regulation made a political party a state agency, Condon's lawyers admonished that such a conclusion could prevent a church congregation or a social club from rejecting Negroes.[26]

In a rebuttal brief, Nixon's counselors replied to Condon's defense. Conceding that a political party might traditionally be considered a private organization, they maintained that Texas had legislated the primaries as part of the state electoral process. "When . . . political parties come to the polls," Spingarn reasoned, "when an organized effort is made to choose public officials through state machinery of elections, political parties have been subjected to the state's sovereign control and function as part of the electoral system." [27] The association rested its case after it showed how Texas laws controlled the principal functions of a political party.

Answering for the Court, Justice Benjamin Cardozo upheld the NAACP's main contention but left the path open for continued disfranchisement. He agreed that the 1927 statute had lodged the power to prescribe membership qualifications "in a committee, which excluded Nixon by virtue of his race, not by virtue of any authority delegated by the party, but by virtue of an authority originating in the mandate of the law." However, Cardozo admitted that in another set of circumstances the Democrats might legally bar blacks. In fact, he pointed out the way by stating, "Whatever inherent power a state political party has to determine the content of its membership resides in state convention." [28]

Justice James McReynolds, speaking for the four-man minority, found no such distinction between action by an executive committee and a party convention. Echoing the propositions presented by the defendants, the minority opinion held that political parties, like business, religious and social clubs, were "in no sense" governmental instrumentalities. The fact that the party itself paid for the expenses of conducting the primary election helped convince the dissenters that no state action existed. [29]

The five-to-four decision represented only a narrow victory. William Pickens, NAACP Field Secretary, observed that Negroes still had to face party officials who discriminated without state authorization. [30] Furthermore, Cardozo had hinted that state party conventions could use their inherent power to prevent blacks from voting. In effect, the question still remained whether the Texas Democratic party performed a public function in managing a primary whose winners usually triumphed in the general election. If so, did the Fifteenth Amendment protect the right to vote in the Democratic contest? The majority of the justices, by continuing to avoid this essential issue, allowed Texas again to circumvent their decision. [31]

On May 23, 1932, two weeks after the Court handed down its opinion in *Nixon v. Condon,* the Texas Democratic Executive Committee rescinded its resolution barring Negroes from voting in its primaries. A few days later, the party convention decreed that all qualified white citizens "shall be eligible to membership in the Democratic party and as such entitled to participate in its deliberations." In keeping with this order, election officials refused to distribute ballots to Dr. Nixon and all other blacks at the July party primary. [32]

As a result, on May 31, 1933 the persistent Nixon sued a third election official. Before a district judge in El Paso, his NAACP attorneys pointed out that since the Democratic Convention was established under Texas law, racial bias by the party constituted state action. "Even if there were no regulations of the State as to participants in primary elections," the lawyers postulated that the party convocation was a "quasi public body" that performed a "quasi governmental function." They also advanced the thesis that when election officials vested with state power deprived Negroes of their right to vote, they did so in violation of the Fifteenth Amendment. By accepting these arguments, the Court might prevent a state from enforcing racial bias practiced by a "private" agency.[33]

On February 7, 1934, District Judge Charles Boynton ruled in favor of Nixon. By strictly applying Cardozo's opinion in *Nixon v. Condon,* the judge refused to comment on the association's far-reaching arguments.[34] Consequently, this case had little effect on the behavior of officials in the Lone Star State. On the eve of the July Democratic primary, Texas Attorney General James V. Allred stubbornly advised Negroes that they could not participate. However, in order to avoid another civil suit, the election officer in El Paso's sixth precinct finally allowed Nixon to vote, but then marked "colored" on the back of his ballot.[35] Thus, after ten years of litigation and an expenditure of over $6,000, blacks still had not regained their right to vote in the most crucial contest in the South.[36]

The NAACP, weakened financially and disappointed by the lack of compliance with the court rulings, decided to try a different approach to open the ballot boxes to a larger number of Negroes. The association attempted to persuade the Department of Justice to institute criminal proceedings against recalcitrant election officials. Legal experts advised that the department could prosecute under Title 18, Sections 51 and 52 of the United States Criminal Code, punishing violations of constitutional rights by conspiracies of private individuals and by persons acting under color of state law.[37] "Negro Democratic voters," a black civil-rights advocate growled, "expect just as much attention from the Department of Justice in enforcing citizenship rights as in apprehending gangsters." [38]

However, after reviewing sworn affidavits alleging racial discrimination, Attorney General Homer Cummings chose not to seek indictments. He knew that the Supreme Court of Texas had upheld in 1934 the inherent right of a party, through its convention, to determine the qualifications for membership. Consequently, election supervisors, in prohibiting Negroes from voting, were acting in good faith. Under this circumstance, no jury would render a guilty verdict by finding the "wilful" criminal intent set forth in the Criminal Code.[39]

With little chance of winning criminal cases, the Justice Department was reluctant to anger the white South, so important to the fortunes of the Democratic party. On December 28, 1934 Assistant Attorney General Joseph Keenan told NAACP officials that suffrage prosecution was "loaded with political dynamite." While the white voters of Dixie had overwhelmingly supported Franklin Roosevelt in 1932, blacks throughout the nation stuck with the party of Abraham Lincoln. Thus, in 1934, despite the urging of Walter White, executive secretary of the NAACP, Democratic administration leaders refused to alienate the South by acting on behalf of a potential, but as yet uncommitted black voting bloc.[40] In addition, the president was relying on powerful southern congressmen for getting his New Deal, emergency legislative programs passed as quickly as possible. Also, civil rights was not on Dr. New Deal's prescription list to cure the depression. In the order of Justice Department priorities an interstate anticrime program came before equal suffrage. The FBI needed the cooperation of local law-enforcement agents, and for Attorney General Cummings to institute criminal proceedings against Texas Democratic party officials would have upset Texas authorities.[41]

Spurned by the federal government, the NAACP also found itself preempted from filing another civil suit. Richard Randolph Grovey, the plaintiff in a new case challenging the Texas white primary, was an astute political organizer in Houston. He had worked hard to unite all elements of black society—teachers, doctors, preachers, maids, and cooks—into the Third Ward Civic Club. Until the white primary was abolished, however, Grovey and his followers would have to delay testing their ability to influence Democratic affairs. In the meantime, Grovey intended "to use reason, the public press, and the courts to let the world see Texas democracy as it really is." [42]

During the 1920s and 1930s Houston was a center of civil-rights activity. Carter Wesley, the militant black editor of the Houston *Informer*, had lent both financial and journalistic support to court battles against disfranchisement. He had also collaborated with J. Alston Atkins, a prominent black lawyer, to submit an *amicus curiae* brief to the Supreme Court in *Nixon v. Condon*. While these Negroes considered the NAACP a valuable organization, they believed that it wanted to exclude other groups from handling important court battles. [43] Because the national association operated on the grass-roots level only through one of its branches, Wesley believed that it often bypassed independent black leadership outside of the formal group structure. Furthermore, the Houston faction consisted entirely of blacks, while the NAACP contained white members. Atkins bitterly criticized the association for hiring white lawyers to manage the primary cases when black attorneys such as himself were available. [44]

While the NAACP leaders were vainly attempting to persuade the Justice Department to act, the Texans were hatching plans for another court test. Prohibited from controlling the case and unwilling to risk wasting money on a suit it was not certain of winning, the association tried to dissuade its rivals from initiating litigation. However, the Houston group refused to budge, and after a county clerk declined to give Grovey a ballot for the July 28, 1934 Democratic primary, it took the case to court. [45]

Atkins and Wesley built upon the arguments offered by the NAACP in the previous white primary cases. Following the lead of Louis Marshall, they contended that the Democratic convention resolution barring Negroes from primary elections violated the Fifteenth Amendment. The lawyers still had to prove that a primary was an election within the meaning of that article. They maintained that the Democratic contest constituted such an election, because, "whenever in substantial relation to the selection of persons to fill offices of government, voting is going on under either the mandate or authority of the state, there the Fifteenth Amendment is present to strike down . . . any barriers of race and color." [46]

The primary, as the real election in Texas, fit their definition of having a "substantial relation" to the choice of government officers. Furthermore, they asserted that the Democratic Convention, governed by legislative statues, functioned as an agency of the state, and thus could not limit voting rights on the basis of race or color.[47] No matter how valid these points may have been, they did not convince the district court. Consequently, Grovey brought his appeal to the high tribunal.

He did not have any better luck there. On April Fool's Day, 1935 Justice Owen Roberts, speaking for a unanimous court, delivered a decision that saddened Negroes.[48] The justice noted each of Grovey's contentions, but rejected all of them. He conceded that the primary election was held under statutory compulsion but concluded that it was still a party matter, because the Democrats paid for the expenses. Roberts accepted the argument that the Democratic party was a private body, even though he recognized that state laws controlled the party convention. Furthermore, he set aside the claim that a Negro could not be denied a ballot at a primary merely because its outcome determined the result of the general election. To so reason, Roberts declared, was "to confuse privilege of membership in a party with the right to vote for one who is to hold public office." [49]

Nixon v. Condon guided the court. To define what constituted state action within the Fourteenth and Fifteenth Amendments, the justices had said that they would examine the statutory basis for the discrimination. In *Grovey v. Townsend* they did not discover any explicit mandate for racial exclusion, and the jurists accepted Cardozo's reasoning that the Democratic party convention was free to fix membership qualifications. The court failed to take into account, as was critically pointed out in one issue of the political journal, the *New Republic,* that the "primary and the election are mere separate aspects of an organic process of selection; the result depends as much upon the naming of the candidates as upon the final choice among them." [50]

The adverse ruling against Richard Grovey not only dealt a blow to the Houston Negroes but also to the NAACP. Justice Roberts rejected precisely those arguments that the association's lawyers had developed in the *Nixon* cases. Although the civil-rights group realized the tremendous setback suffered for enfranchisement, its leaders did not view the loss as a personal defeat for its strategy.[51] James Marshall, who had replaced his father Louis on the legal committee, confided to Walter White that the "case was badly mishandled. The points that we intended to raise were either omitted or not presented in clear form." [52] In light of Roberts's logic, perhaps the NAACP too harshly condemned the Houston lawyers. It is true that in their presentation, Atkins and Wesley produced scant evidence to prove that Townsend acted on behalf of the state. They thought that fact self-evident since he was a county clerk. Nevertheless, Roberts did not consider what Townsend's position was; he simply ignored the question.[53] One must conclude that had the association directed the case, the result would have been the same.

Determined to overturn this decision, the competing groups of blacks put aside their differences. They closed ranks behind the leadership of Charles Houston, special counsel to the NAACP. As Dean of Howard Law School in the late 1920s and early 1930s, Houston had established a close-working relationship with the NAACP by encouraging his faculty and students to confer with the association's attorneys about legal strategies for attacking racial discrimination. One of his brightest pupils was a young black from Baltimore, Thurgood Marshall. In law school, one of his colleagues later recalled, "Marshall did everything he was asked, from research on obscure legal opinions to foraging for coffee and sandwiches." A few years after this eager fellow graduated, his former teacher hired him as assistant counsel to the NAACP.[54]

The appointments of Houston and Marshall signaled the

growing emphasis on promoting black leadership within the interracial organization's hierarchy. Under Houston's expert direction, black attorneys increasingly took over the job of arguing court cases from whites like Storey, Louis Marshall, and Knollenberg.[55] Jack Atkins, who in the past had felt slighted by the NAACP, wrote Houston after the *Grovey* disaster, "I am more and more convinced that grave legal questions . . . need expert direction and leadership from Negro counsel occupying some such position as that which you now hold with the NAACP." [56] At the same time, in order to coopt the independent black leadership into the movement, the association created the Texas Conference of Branches of the NAACP. Significantly, C. F. Richardson, who edited the Houston *Informer* with Carter Wesley, was picked as conference president in 1938.[57]

Actually the NAACP had never intended to abandon the fight against the white primary. In May 1935 its house organ, the *Crisis,* editorialized, "While *Grovey v. Townsend* delivered a heavy blow at the Negro's status as a citizen in the South, it cannot long stand in the way of qualified Negroes securing the ballot." [58] Charles Houston labeled Owen Roberts' opinion "pure legalism," and he criticized the justice for refusing to recognize the "verities of the situation." The special counsel thought that litigation should be prepared attacking the "primary at every point where the state lends any of its officers or gives any sanction to primary machinery." [59] However, the NAACP did not start a new case immediately, because as Houston explained in the midst of the Depression, "we are somewhat pinched for funds." [60]

Over the five years following *Grovey,* the NAACP, in cooperation with Texas Negroes, worked hard to finance and prepare a suit. Not only did the state branches raise money, but they also gathered important information on which to base the court challenge. In 1938, Charles Houston had urged them to "compile a very factual examination of the operation of the primary that would disclose a comprehensive state control and supervision." With this analysis, he hoped to persuade the

Supreme Court "to look through the subterfuge of private party regulation and declare that in essence the primary is a public-state-controlled undertaking and therefore comes within the prohibitions of the Fourteenth and Fifteenth Amendments." [61]

It took the black Texans two years to finish the detailed research. By that time, Thurgood Marshall had replaced Charles Houston, who had resigned because of poor health, as special counsel. At the May 1940 meeting of the Conference of Branches at Corpus Christi, the new special counsel outlined a ten-year program to achieve full citizenship rights. Elimination of the white primary headed the list of goals. In order to wage the battle harmoniously, the Texas conference expanded its legal redress committee to include all black lawyers in the state.[62] This accomplished, the association represented Sidney Hasgett of Houston in his suit against an election judge who refused to provide him with a ballot in 1940 at the July 27th and August 24th, Democratic primaries. In *Hasgett v. Werner,* the NAACP hoped finally to prove that the Democratic primary in Texas was part of the election machinery of the state. Its lawyers furnished the results of the branch studies, which demonstrated that most public officials belonged to the Democratic party, and more people voted in the primary than did in the general election.[63] However, the *Grovey* decision continued to haunt black plaintiffs when on May 5, 1941 District Judge Thomas Kennerly of Houston used that precedent to deny Hasgett's claim.[64]

Before the NAACP could present its appeal, the Justice Department prosecuted a case that laid the foundation for getting the *Grovey* ruling overturned. Although *U.S. v. Classic* did not involve blacks or the white primary, it did concern the relationship of the primary to the election machinery of the state.[65] Voting irregularities were a regular feature of the turbulent political life in Louisiana, and Huey Long and his heirs had mastered most of the sordid techniques. In 1940, the Criminal Division of the Justice Department was investigating charges that the Longites threatened to fire, demote, or make work unpleasant for public servants who did not support them. Preparing to crack down on the Kingfish's disciples, the government lawyers unexpectedly discovered other political opportunists who in their quest to overthrow the Long machine had engaged in fraud. Patrick Classic, a New Orleans election official, was a member of an insurgent group fiercely opposed to the scandal-ridden Long Ring. Anxious to make certain that T. Hale Boggs won the Democratic nomination for congressman, on September 10, 1940, Classic and several other dissident election commissioners altered and falsely counted votes in his favor.[66]

The Civil Liberties Unit of the Justice Department supervised the case. Created in 1939 by Attorney General Frank Murphy, this section within the criminal division had the responsibility of prosecuting those who disobeyed federal civil-rights statutes. As a New Deal governor of Michigan in 1937, Murphy had been praised by civil libertarians for exercising considerable restraint in not using the state militia to evict sit-down strikers from the General Motors plant. When he became attorney general, Murphy demonstrated that the government could actively extend individual freedom, a notion contrary to traditional liberal philosophy. "For the first time in our history," the attorney general pledged, "the full weight of the Department will be thrown behind the effort to preserve in this country the blessings of liberty, the spirit of tolerance and the fundamental principles of democracy." [67]

Accordingly, Murphy sought to discover how much authority the federal government had to bring civil-rights criminals to trial. The Ku Klux Klan Enforcement Act, on the books since 1870, punished interference with "any right or privilege secured . . . by the Constitution or laws of the United States," and, "any rights, privileges, or immunities secured or protected by the Constitution and laws of the United States." [68] The vague wording of these sections had obliged the Supreme Court to interpret which rights the statutes protected. In 1884 the tribunal declared that the right of a qualified voter to participate in a federal election and have his ballot fairly tallied was guaranteed by the Constitution.[69] The Civil Liberties Unit tried to expand this coverage to primary elections. But first the Justice Department had to persuade the judiciary to reverse *Newberry v. United States,* which proclaimed that party contests were not part of the electoral process.

Francis Biddle, the solicitor general at the time, later recollected that he believed a victory in this nonracial case would pave the way for the extension of the right of Negroes to vote in the southern Democratic primaries.[70] Nevertheless, the government's brief, written in large part by Herbert Wechsler, a former law clerk to Justice Harlan Fiske Stone, did not specifically request the court to overrule *Grovey*. In fact, Wechsler distinguished *Classic* from the earlier white primary decision. To this end, he argued that Texas had not made the primary an integral part of the electoral system. His brief concluded, "[The] implicit premise of the *Grovey* decision is that the Negroes excluded from the Democratic primary were legally free to record their choice by joining an opposition party or by organizing themselves." [71] In Louisiana, however, the voters had expressed their preference only to have their ballots nullified. This distinction indicated that a victory by the Justice Department did not automatically guarantee the demise of the white primary.

On the other hand, approval by the Supreme Court of the government's main contentions and a rejection of the defendant's main points would reinforce the NAACP's future legal position. Wechsler reasoned that the Louisiana election was a two-step process, namely, the primary and the general election; therefore, constitutional safeguards applied to both stages. Furthermore, his brief supplied evidence to prove that as a matter of law and practice, the Democratic primary determined the victor at the general election.[72] The NAACP had expounded these principles as early as the first *Nixon* case. Contrary to the association's interests, lawyers for Classic requested the court to accept the *Grovey* precedent. If it did so, the high tribunal would have to reaffirm that political parties could hold their nomination elections as they pleased, and that exclusion from the primary did not mean a denial of suffrage rights.[73]

Fortunately for the cause of black enfranchisement, the Supreme Court upheld the reasoning of the Civil Liberties Unit. On behalf of a six-man majority, Justice Stone, who had joined in the *Grovey* ruling, said that the Constitution protected the right to vote not only in a general election but also in a primary "where the state law has made the primary an integral part of the procedure of choice, or where in fact the primary effectively controls the choice." [74] Although the court overruled *Newberry*, it remained silent as to the status of *Grovey*. As a matter of law, for *Classic* the court did not consider whether an individual could be denied party membership on the basis of race, but it merely ruled that registered Democrats could not be fraudulently deprived of their vote in a congressional primary. Yet only the myopic missed Stone's handwriting on the wall. The logic of his opinion vindicated the association's position in absentia. One lawyer jubilantly remarked that the "decision removes the blindfold from the eyes of Justice, and admits the true vision that in one party states the primary is not only an integral part of the election system but in fact tantamount to election." [75]

Armed with this new ammunition, the NAACP's Board of Directors voted to drop the pending *Hasgett v. Werner* and file new litigation directly based on the *Classic* doctrine. Meeting on November 10, 1941, the board members agreed that a favorable opinion from the judiciary would prompt the Justice Department to use the invigorated criminal statutes to prosecute voting offenses. Such a procedure would relieve black citizens of the heavy financial burden of litigation.[76] As long as *Grovey* technically remained in force, the Justice Department had not bothered to seek indictments against biased party officials. Only a direct reversal of this precedent could provide a clear basis for criminal prosecution.

With Thurgood Marshall in command, the NAACP substituted *Smith v. Allwright* for *Hasgett v. Werner*. Lonnie Smith, a Houston dentist and NAACP member, sued a Texas election official for $5,000 for refusing to give him a ballot in the 1940 Democratic congressional primaries. Joining Marshall in arguing the case was W. J. Durham, a distinguished black lawyer from Texas. They were rebuffed in the lower courts, which ruled that *Grovey* was still controlling in the Lone Star State. Both the District Court and the Circuit Court of Appeals dismissed Smith's complaint, holding that *Classic* was a criminal case in Louisiana and did not involve Texas statutes. On June 7, 1943 the Supreme Court granted *certiorari*.[77]

In arguing its case before the high bench, the NAACP did not have the direct assistance of the federal government. President Roosevelt heard "a good deal of howl" from the national association and the American Civil Liberties Union (ACLU), one of the liberal, white organizations that participated as a "friend of the court," because the Justice Department did not file an *amicus* brief.[78] Justice lawyers recognized that a victory in the *Smith* case would require a substantial step beyond the Louisiana fraud decision since the former dealt with a person excluded from party membership by the organization itself, while the latter concerned the right of an admittedly qualified voter to cast a ballot and have it tabulated. Yet the new Solicitor General Charles Fahy admonished Attorney General Biddle that:

> although the legal questions have difficulties, whether or not to participate is essentially a policy question. We have already assisted the negroes by winning the *Classic* case which gives them their principal ammunition. Should we go further in their behalf and make a gesture which cannot fail to offend many others, in Texas and the South generally, in a case in which we are not a party? I think not.[79]

Afraid of overextending himself especially when he needed southern congressional support for his World War II measures, Roosevelt went along with Fahy's recommendation.

Yet the newly named Civil Rights Section (the former Civil Liberties Unit) expressed sympathy with the NAACP grievance. However, the most it could do, given the administration's political decision was to permit one of its staff, Fred G. Folsom, to write an article for the *Columbia Law Review* endorsing the association's viewpoint. In the winter of 1943, just as the NAACP attorneys were getting ready to go before the Supreme Court, Folsom's commentary appeared. In it he concluded that *Classic* had indeed modified *Grovey* by posing the important question as to whether the "primary election laws operate to restrict seriously the choice of candidates at the general election." In Folsom's opinion, Texas law incorporated this dual-phase electoral system.[80]

In total agreement with Folsom's analysis, Thurgood Marshall and William Hastie, the successor of Charles Houston as Dean of Howard Law School, petitioned the Supreme Court to strike down the white primary on the basis of *Classic*. In their oral presentation before the justices on November 12, 1943 they provided evidence demonstrating that Texas had made the primary an integral portion of the procedure of choice, and that this contest effectively determined the selection of candidates for governmental office.[81] The counselors reminded the judges that the election official who refused to allow Lonnie Smith to vote derived his power solely from state statute. Consequently, as long as such functionaries acted "under color of state law," they contravened the Fourteenth and Fifteenth Amendments. Furthermore, the lawyers disputed the conclusion of *Grovey*. After reexamining the structure of the Democratic party in Texas, they had determined that it operated not as a voluntary political association, but as a "loose-jointed organization" with no identifiable membership. Marshall and Hastie claimed that the state election laws provided the only rules that governed the party and its elections. Thus, the two black attorneys implored the bench to discard *Grovey*, which was perpetuating the disfranchisement of over 540,000 adult Negroes in Texas.[82]

The failure of W. J. Durham to participate in the oral argument of the case confused many black Texans who did not know about the rule limiting debate before the justices. Although Durham had journeyed to Washington, he did not get the opportunity to address the tribunal because court regulations allowed only two lawyers from each side to speak. After attorneys for the state of Texas requested a reargument in January 1944, Marshall allayed bruised feelings by bringing Durham back to Washington to help him prepare the rebuttal to the Texas Attorney General's brief. Marshall lamented that after fighting this most important case for three years, "there has to be a lot of running off at the mouth. We can always stick together when we are losing, but tend to find means of breaking up when we are winning. One of the best ways to lose a case is to create dissension." [83] Despite this short burst of tempers, the special counsel was still confident of victory.

Having listened to the final arguments on January 12th, the justices retired to their conference room to discuss the case. Of the group, only Stone and Roberts had participated in the *Grovey* decision. The "constitutional revolution" of 1937 had brought to the court seven new faces who seemed inclined to overturn that precedent. Nevertheless, some questions remained. Justices Hugo Black and Robert Jackson originally voted against Smith. Jackson expressed concern over what he perceived might be a threat to the right of individuals to form private associations, and both he and Wiley Rutledge did not like the thought of the judiciary supervising state elections. Chief Justice Stone won over his doubting brethren by reminding them that the case under review involved "not all primaries but this primary." [84]

Choosing a spokesman became a delicate chore. Originally the chief justice had assigned Felix Frankfurter, but he reconsidered after Jackson cautioned that the decision would be weakened "if the voice that utters it is one that may grate on Southern sensibilities." Like the executive branch, the judiciary carefully weighed the feelings of the white South. Felix Frankfurter, a Jew from an Ivy League law school in abolitionist Massachusetts, would not be the ideal person to announce the death of the white primary. Instead, Jackson recommended that a Democrat, preferably a southerner, undertake the assignment. Stone then tapped Stanley Reed, a conservative Kentucky Democrat who had served as Franklin Roosevelt's solicitor general.[85]

For the first time, the Supreme Court interpreted the Fifteenth Amendment as a shield for the right to vote at primary elections. But overruling a nine-year-old precedent required an explanation. Reed had to elucidate why the court, looking at identical facts, discovered state action in 1944, when it could not find any nine years earlier. He located the answer in the Louisiana election case. According to Reed:

> the *Classic* case bears upon *Grovey v. Townsend* not because exclusion of Negroes from primaries is any more or less state action by reason of the unitary character of the electoral process, but because the recognition of the place of the primary in the electoral scheme makes clear that state delegation to a party of power to fix the qualifications of primary elections is delegation of a state function that may make the party's action the action of the state.[86]

On April 3, 1944 the court ruled that Texas had designated the primary as an integral feature of its election machinery by excluding from running in the general election unsuccessful primary candidates and by requiring officials to withhold ballots from those not qualified under convention rules. In allowing the Democratic party to adopt regulations to prohibit black voting, Texas also had joined in this disfranchisement. Reed warned those who might try to design a new version of the white primary that the right to vote for public officials could not be "nullified by a state through casting its electoral process in a form which permits a private organization to practice racial discrimination in the election."[87]

This outright reversal of *Grovey* angered Justice Roberts, the author of that controversial decision. In a dissenting opinion marked by personal pique, Roberts criticized his brethren for placing court rulings in the same class as a "restricted railroad ticket, good for this day and train only." In contrast with Stone, who had departed from his *Grovey* opinion, the minority jurist did not believe that the *Classic* dictum had eroded his earlier words.[88]

Blacks rejoiced over the majority opinion. Remembering the outcome of one pre–Civil War judicial precedent, Dr. Lonnie Smith enthusiastically predicted that his victory would have a greater effect on the political history of the nation and the future of Negroes than any decision since Dred Scott.[89] Thurgood Marshall wrote interested correspondents that the Texas Primary case "is so clear and free of ambiguity," and had settled "once and for all the question of the right of Negroes to participate in primary elections similar to those in Texas." [90] He expected most of the states affected to follow this pronouncement. William Hastie guessed that future historians might write that the "Supreme Court released and galvanized democratic forces which in turn gave the South the momentum it needed toward ultimate leadership in American liberalism." [91]

Most observers, black and white, North and South, responded to the decision more cautiously than did the triumphant participants. The Chicago *Defender* hailed the triumph as a "milestone in the battle to fully integrate Negroes into the mainstream of American life. But we cannot expect its full effect to be immediately felt." The liberal *New Republic* doubted that the opinion was such a "sweeping victory for human rights" or a great blow to white supremacy as long as requirements like the poll tax remained a qualification for voting.[92] In the South, the response appeared remarkably calm. In the upper region, observers tended to accept the outcome more readily than did their southern neighbors; however, even in the heart of Dixie many newspapers were resigned to accepting the ruling. Although the Dallas *Times-Herald* deplored the Supreme Court decision, it beseeched Texans to refrain from acting in contempt of "that august body." Likewise, the Atlanta *Constitution* called *Smith v. Allwright* "a shock and poorly timed but [it] cannot be ignored." [93] On the ominous side, however, southern senators as diverse as Claude Pepper, a liberal New Dealer from Florida, and "Cotton Ed" Smith, a South Carolina Negrophobe, both condemned the court's pronouncement and vowed to maintain white supremacy.[94]

Having won the civil suit, the association resolved to take the next step and solicit the Justice Department to enforce the criminal codes. With this in mind, Thurgood Marshall informed Attorney General Biddle that the NAACP had invested $11,000 to prove that constitutional protection of the suffrage extended to primaries. Now he demanded vigorous prosecution of individuals who blocked Negroes from voting. Marshall surmised that any "failure of the Department of Justice to act will be for political rather than legal reasons." [95] The civil rights lawyer had hit the mark. Jonathan Daniels, the president's adviser on race relations and a North Carolinian whose father was Roosevelt's boss at the Navy Department during the Wilson administration, heard that the Justice Department planned to institute criminal prosecutions in connection with the denial of the right of Negroes to vote in the 1944 Alabama Democratic primary. Consequently he informed Roosevelt that after talking with Alabama Senator Lister Hill:

> I strongly share his sentiments that any such action by the Federal government at this time might be the fact which would translate impotent rumblings against the New Deal into actual revolt at the polls. . . . Any such action . . . would be a very dangerous mistake.[96]

Attorney General Biddle retreated for several reasons. He believed that legal technicalities rendered the government's chances of winning criminal prosecutions unlikely. In order to obtain a conviction under the appropriate statutes, Justice Department lawyers had to prove that a state election official had "wilfully" deprived a Negro of his suffrage rights. Local juries, which often shared the racial prejudices of the accused, might acquit on the ground that the defendant was merely following Democratic party orders. Furthermore, with the administration concerned about the political risks of offending southern white lawmakers, it did not seem worth the effort of going into court with so little chance of winning. Such reasoning presumed that blacks could rely on the good will of white officials in Dixie to guarantee equal voting rights. The Justice

Department placed its faith in conciliation rather than coercion, for as Attorney General Biddle told the National Urban League Conference in 1944, "Successful enforcement of the *Smith v. Allwright* decision will . . . depend on public opinion." [97]

Not satisfied to wait that long, Thurgood Marshall pressed the Justice Department to bring voting offenders immediately to trial. The NAACP leaders tried to discourage sundry groups from filing additional suits until the attorney general had a reasonable time to move. Otherwise, Marshall feared that this would give Biddle an excuse to postpone seeking criminal indictments while civil litigation was pending. Furthermore, the association perceived its role as a clearinghouse for collecting authentic complaints by disfranchised blacks and sending them to Washington. Through this method, the NAACP sought to avoid the kind of hasty action that it believed Houston Negroes had started in *Grovey*. [98]

The situation in Georgia provided the initial test for this policy. In July 1944 the State Democratic Executive Committee resolved that the recent Texas Primary Decision did not apply to Georgia. By order of the committee, county election judges barred Negroes from voting in the following month's primary. In response, a citizens group of blacks from Columbus prepared to file a suit financed by the local branch of the NAACP. At the same time, in Atlanta, the Fulton County Chapter of the NAACP and the Citizens Democratic Club, led by C. A. Scott, the black publisher of the Atlanta *World*, were planning litigation. But after consulting Thurgood Marshall, the Atlanta organizations agreed to delay court action until the attorney general had the opportunity to investigate. Convinced, however, that their attempt would not hamper a federal probe, in the fall of 1944, the Columbus blacks initiated *King v. Chapman*. [99]

In the meantime, Biddle had been in touch with Marshall and Hastie, but he would not give them a commitment until after the November general elections. In December, the prospects of federal intervention did not look good. The attorney general informed C. A. Scott that the Justice Department would have difficulty in prosecuting suffrage violators because of the necessity of fixing responsibility upon persons whom the law considered wilful offenders.[100] Still unhappy, the Atlanta faction asked Marshall and Hastie to confront Biddle about his intentions. Consequently, on April 14, 1945, during a lull in the funeral services for President Roosevelt, Biddle bluntly told the NAACP duo that he had "decided not to proceed with criminal prosecutions at this time." [101] Thus, the following month, Marshall gave the green light to his Atlanta allies to initiate a civil case.

Although the association prepared a new suit, the District Court decided the Columbus case first. On October 12, 1945 Judge T. Hoyt Davis of Americus, Georgia, applied the reasoning of *Smith v. Allwright* to end Georgia's white primary. When the state appealed, the NAACP filed an *amicus* brief, and on March 6, 1946 the Court of Appeals affirmed Davis's opinion. Although Georgia law did not require that primary elections be held, the three-judge panel found state action because the statutes regulated the contest once the party had initiated it.[102] However, this victory did not produce the long-delayed emancipation. Georgia lawmakers devised a new scheme to keep blacks from the polls. In February 1947 the legislature nullified the practical effect of the *King* decision by repealing its primary laws.[103]

This came as no surprise to Negroes long accustomed to having favorable court rulings circumvented. After *Smith v. Allwright,* legal scholars guessed that some states might attempt to get around this decision by erasing all the primary election statutes from the books, thus ostensibly making the party contest a private affair divorced from governmental supervision.[104] Even before Georgia acted, South Carolina had fulfilled this expectation. On April 20, 1944 its General Assembly passed 150 acts removing all laws relating to primaries. Eschewing use of the index, extra-careful government officials "turned the statute books page by page, . . . to find out if anything was there that wasn't properly indexed." [105] Few could doubt the assembly's motives since Governor Olin Johnson, in summoning the special session implored the representatives to repeal the measures and maintain white supremacy. As for the consequences, he declared, "let the chips fall where they may." [106]

The NAACP accepted the challenge to wipe out this latest subterfuge. Throughout 1946 the Justice Department had declined to institute criminal proceedings because the legislature had separated the primary from the state election process; as a result, a new test case provided the only alternative for the association.[107] In January 1947 Thurgood Marshall and his staff, aided by a seminar of Columbia University Law School students, completed a brief to meet this novel form of disfranchisement. In this document they contended that according to *Classic*, Article I, Sections 3 and 4 of the United States Constitution protected the right of citizens to vote in congressional primaries against improper interference by both the state and private individuals. They argued that *Classic* offered two tests to judge whether Article I applied to party contests, "where the state law has made the primary an integral part of the procedure of choice or where in fact the primary effectively controls the choice." The brief furnished statistics to indicate that the South Carolina Democratic party primary satisfied the latter criterion by consistently producing the winner of the general election.[108] Furthermore, Marshall and the student lawyers accused the state of abridging the Fourteenth and Fifteenth Amendments. They submitted that in reality the South Carolina scheme allowed the Democratic party to perform a state function in conducting state and federal elections.

Before advancing these arguments in the courts, Marshall had informally asked Fred Folsom for his comments. The Civil Rights Section attorney offered a few minor suggestions, but "on the whole [he] liked the . . . brief." [109] This interchange suggested that the Department of Justice would provide advice in preparing civil suits when it did not want to risk criminal proceedings.

Fortunately for the NAACP, District Court Judge J. Waties

Waring, who first heard *Elmore v. Rice,* stood ready to brave the enmity of white South Carolina. A native of that state and a prominent Democrat, Judge Waring nevertheless believed that the Fourteenth Amendment bestowed on all people equal opportunity and prevented discrimination based on race. Waring was ready to take a bold stand because he sincerely "felt that [his] state was backward, that it had been blind to decency and right, and that somebody had at last to face the issue." [110] Despite threats of physical harm to his family if he so decided, the courageous jurist struck down his state's "private" primary. As long as the Democratic primary constituted "the only material and realistic election," Waring pronounced on July 12, 1947 that Negroes were entitled to vote in it. In words which did not endear him to many of his neighbors, Waring admonished South Carolina, "[R]ejoin the Union. It is time to fall in step with the other states and to adopt the American way of conducting elections." [111]

On December 30, the Fourth Circuit Court of Appeals affirmed Waring's decision. Ironically, the judge who delivered the opinion, John J. Parker of North Carolina, had failed to receive the Senate's consent for a Supreme Court post in 1930 largely because of NAACP opposition. The organization had found him objectionable for making racist remarks as a candidate for governor of his state in 1920.[112] However, Parker did not hold any grudges, and he solemnly warned the South, "[N]o election machinery can be upheld if its purpose or effect is to deny to the Negro . . . any effective voice in the government." [113] When the Supreme Court refused to hear this case in 1948, these sweeping rulings reigned as the law of the land.[114]

After learning of Waring's decision, William Hastie, sitting in the governor's mansion in the Virgin Islands as a result of an appointment by Harry Truman, jubilantly concluded that it "nailed the lid down on the coffin of the white primary." He congratulated his colleague Thurgood Marshall, with whom he had won some notable court battles, on what he thought was his greatest legal triumph. "When we realize that *Grovey v.*

Townsend was law as recently as 1944, it is hard to believe that so complete a victory has been won in our most vital fight and against such tremendous opposition," he wrote the special counsel in July 1947.[115] The NAACP had already recognized Marshall's talents and the significance of his accomplishments. In 1946, the association had awarded its top lawyer the coveted Spingarn Medal, in large measure for successfully arguing the Texas Primary Decision, which might "have a more far reaching influence than any other act in the ending of disfranchisement based upon race or color." [116]

Blacks everywhere could take pride in these gains. Mainly through the pressure of the NAACP and independent black organizations, the Supreme Court gradually had formed opinions that eradicated the legal foundation of the white primary. During the twenty-year struggle, the interracial association came to rely less on white attorneys like Louis Marshall and more on blacks like Thurgood Marshall. Yet sympathetic whites did make a significant contribution to this cause of enfranchisement. The ACLU and other liberal organizations rendered aid as friends of the court and fundraisers; Judge Waring intrepidly reprimanded South Carolina politicians only to be snubbed and threatened by his Charleston neighbors; and counsellors like Moorfield Storey and Louis Marshall developed the original arguments upon which their black successors based their persuasive briefs.

Despite constant badgering, the Justice Department only indirectly had furnished assistance. The Roosevelt administration had presided over a "constitutional revolution" in federalism by expanding national supervision of the economy, and the creation of the Civil Liberties Unit pointed toward an increased commitment for federal action to extend equal rights. However, by the end of World War II, officials in Washington hesitated to force the southern states to protect Negro suffrage. Men like Attorney General Biddle, while personally favoring the cause of black freedom, put their faith in mediation rather than coercion to improve race relations in the South. Biddle insisted that given the opportunity, enlightened leaders in the local communities could direct public opinion against civil-rights offenders and could sooth racial tempers from flaring. Furthermore, the Roosevelt strategists checked whatever inclination they might have had to confront directly southern racial discrimination for fear of alienating the whites politically and of provoking retaliatory violence. Thus, the Justice Department limited the kinds of aid offered to Negroes in the South. The attorney general issued statements condemning lawlessness against blacks and the Civil Rights Section gave counsel in the preparation of private litigation, but violators usually escaped criminal sanctions. In reality, white southern politicians failed to demonstrate the necessary compliance, proving instead that only federal intervention could modify their bigoted behavior and secure constitutional safeguards for Negroes. Even criminal prosecutions, however unsuccessful, might have served as a deterrent. In the meantime, the civil rights groups carried a heavy burden.[117]

Since the white primary had erected a solid fortress keeping blacks out of the polling booths, its demolition opened the iron clad doors to the most important election in southern politics. The decision arrived at a time when the majority of blacks had recently abandoned their historic attachment to the GOP for the party of Franklin Roosevelt. For Negro Republicans in the South, the one-party system was a mighty cross to bear in addition to the poll tax and literacy tests. The opening of the Democratic primary coming as most blacks were joining the New Deal coalition presented opportunities for participation in electoral politics missing since the 1890s. In 1940 Ralph Bunche guessed that 250,000 Negroes were registered to vote in the southern states; by 1947, the estimated number had jumped to 775,000. Especially in Texas and Georgia, where the judiciary had toppled the white primary, did Negroes take advantage of their newly acquired freedom.[118]

After *Rice v. Elmore,* thousands of blacks also showed their determination to vote for the first time in the South Carolina Democratic party contests. They paid scant attention to the vicious pranks of Ku Klux Klansmen who drove a motorcade around the South Carolina state capitol and later burned crosses in front of black churches.[119] At the August 1948 Democratic primaries, 35,000 Negroes shrugged off these threats and appeared at the ballot boxes. Thurgood Marshall derived a great deal of satisfaction as he "personally watched Negro and white citizens of South Carolina, in Charleston and Columbia, voting together." [120]

Amidst the exhilaration of having won the opening battle, the NAACP was nonetheless realistic enough to know that the war was far from over. Blacks still had to hurdle the obstacles placed by the poll tax, biased registrars, apathy, and intimidation. The civil-rights organization might well have remembered the statement of William Andrews, a former field secretary, made during the struggle to overturn the white primary, "Legal victories are not of themselves open sesame to political suffrage." [121]

3

The Poll Tax Must Go

AFTER *Smith v. Allwright* the poll tax remained as an obstacle to hinder Negro suffrage, and it provided a visible target for critics of southern antidemocratic procedures. Along with literacy tests and registration requirements, the tax had dramatically sliced voter turnout and discouraged the organization of political-party opposition. The removal of this financial burden was unlikely to produce spectacular results, at least not immediately, because blacks had long been conditioned to stay away from the polls and because other important legal and extralegal barriers would still stand. Yet reformers harbored great expectations as to the benefits of an assault on the poll tax for impoverished members of both races. According to the Chicago *Defender*, a leading black weekly newspaper, an unencumbered franchise would:

> hasten the advent of certain white progressive elements to power. With a clear perception of the mandates of a functioning democracy, liberal white Southerners would so implement state laws as to usher in a new era of justice and equality to a mass of inarticulate whites and Negroes.[1]

The economic climate created by the Great Depression likewise encouraged the emancipationists, multiplying the numbers of the discontented who sought relief through the ballot box. For indigent southerners of this persuasion, the poll tax loomed as a roadblock to fulfillment of their economic aspirations. The ones lucky enough to work brought home an average of $5.60 per week in 1939, leaving them with little inclination to pay for the privilege of voting. Furthermore, Alabama, Georgia, Mississippi, and Virginia compounded the difficulty of meeting the assessment by totaling the successive amounts owed. An annual rate of $1.50 in Alabama might accumulate after twenty-four years to $36, while in Virginia a similar rate would accrue to a maximum of $4.50 after a three-year period. Even if the father of a family could scrape up enough money to satisfy the requirement, he probably could not afford to also pay for his wife. Therefore, those hardest hit by the Depression found it most difficult to pay back poll taxes, or if up-to-date, faced the possibility of running up a sizable debt for the future.[2]

The attempts of the New Deal to restore economic health promoted a desire to remove the head tax. Programs like the National Labor Relations Board (NLRB), Agricultural Adjustment Administration, and Farm Security Administration pulled the disfranchised poor into the political process. Participation in the NLRB plant elections and crop-control referenda aroused the interest of workers and farmers in regaining a complete franchise. Organized labor, enjoying an unaccustomed growth under the encouragement of Democratic legislation, viewed the capitation tax as an obstacle to greater unionization in the South. H. L. Mitchell of the Southern Tenant Farmers Union blamed the levy for preventing workers on the cotton plantations from securing justice. "They cannot vote, and public officials who are not elected by votes of this group have little or no responsibility in seeing that their rights are respected."[3] At the nation's capital, union leaders complained that unsympathetic poll-tax congressmen dominated the committees that handled labor's bills. Morever, as the federal government necessarily intruded into the lives of more Americans, Senator Elbert Thomas, a Democratic stalwart from Utah, argued that it became more important for "the submerged third to have a voice in selecting those who represent him so that through the democratic process the greatest opportunity and security should be retained by him." [4]

During 1938, Franklin Roosevelt took a swipe at the poll tax. In late March, after criticizing the economic system of the South as "feudal," the president wrote the Alabama-born Aubrey Williams, director of the National Youth Administration: "I think the South agrees with you and me. One difficulty is that three-quarters of the whites in the South cannot vote—poll tax etc. [*sic*]." [5] Three months later, Roosevelt launched his campaign to construct a more liberal party, and "Polltaxia" provided a choice place to purge the Democracy of its more conservative members. As part of his political crusade, the president gave covert aid to the foes of the franchise tax in Arkansas. Writing to the Little Rock repeal advocate, Brooks Hays, on August 31st he privately expressed delight with the removal effort because this suffrage restriction is "inevitably contrary to fundamental democracy and its representative form of government in which we believe." [6] At his news conference a little more than a week later, Roosevelt publicly assailed the tax as "a remnant of the Revolutionary Period" that the country has been getting away from. [7]

When the Democratic voters of Georgia and South Carolina rejected Roosevelt's primary candidates, they severely damaged the prospects for electoral reform. Stung by these defeats, the president withdrew from his clear advocacy of repeal and tried to soothe the feelings of southern politicians distressed by his foray into Dixie. After Mississippi's Senator Pat Harrison rebuked·him for supporting the Arkansas reformers, the president explained that "at no time and in no manner did I even suggest federal legislation of any kind to deprive states of their rights directly or indirectly to impose the poll tax." [8] The following year when Tennessee insurgents requested that the chief executive telegraph their governor in support of abolishing the tax, he refused to intervene "in campaigns of state issues." Resorting to a half-truth, his press secretary Stephen Early contended that Roosevelt "has followed this course ever since he has been in the White House with exception of certain issues in his New York State." [9] Chastened by the painful outcome of the previous fall, the president decided not to do anything further to antagonize the conservative forces in the South. Nevertheless, for a short time he had thrust the poll-tax issue into the national limelight.

Meanwhile, pressure for repeal was being generated by blacks who were mindful of the fact that the poll tax hampered some four million of them from participating in elections.[10] Roy Wilkins, assistant secretary of the NAACP, was in the forefront of the drive for repeal that would ostensibly give the Negro some influence over the conditions under which he lived. Granted a voice in the election of municipal and state officials, Wilkins asserted, blacks could mitigate racial bias and persuade whites to extend equal rights to them.[11]

Poll-tax repeal attracted supporters from throughout the country; a Gallup survey taken in 1942 disclosed that 63 percent favored abolition. A majority easily assented to this reform, because it carried on the tradition in the United States of expanding the right to vote through eradication of property and other financial requirements. To one champion of repeal the duty seemed "un-American" because it subverted the democratic creed to "right your wrongs by the vote." [12] Some white reformers in the South also viewed representative government as the main issue and separated it from the Negro-identified fights against lynching and job discrimination. Southern moderates like Virginius Dabney, editor of the Richmond *Times-Dispatch,* Ellis Arnall, Governor of Georgia, and congressman Brooks Hays supported state prohibition of the valuation, chiefly to topple entrenched political machines by expanding the white electorate.[13] The Gallup poll estimated that 35 percent of the adults residing in the poll-tax states supported repeal, compared with 51 percent in those southern states that had already removed the burden.[14] With a concerted campaign abolition seemed a good bet.

The assault on the poll tax as a voting restriction earnestly began in the South with the formation of the Southern Conference for Human Welfare (SCHW) in November 1938. The conference met to discuss the civil rights of workers and Negroes, as well as the severely depressed economic conditions in the South. While still optimistic about the chances of reorganizing the Democratic Party, President Roosevelt had urged Joseph Gelders, a former physicist at the University of Alabama and a convert to Marxism, "to undertake a crusade to abolish the poll tax as a requirement for voting in the Southern states, in the interest of democratic government." [15] Armed with a presidential endorsement, Gelders and other conference leaders took steps to release this economic brake on southern progress.

To this end, Gelders joined by Mrs. Virginia Foster Durr founded the Civil Rights Committee within the conference. Unlike Gelders, a Jewish radical who had once received a brutal beating for his protest activities, Mrs. Durr epitomized the polite southern lady from a respected family. The daughter of a Presbyterian minister and the wife of a brilliant young lawyer working for the Reconstruction Finance Corporation, this sister-in-law of Justice Hugo Black became concerned with suffrage expansion as a member of the Women's Division of the Democratic Party. Like the president, she considered the poll tax a hindrance to the extension of the New Deal throughout the impoverished South. Her husband Clifford had teamed up with other liberal southerners working for the Roosevelt administration in Washington to write a report on poverty in Dixie, and with him Virginia concluded that repeal of the poll tax was one important way of ending minority rule in the South and rescuing it from economic bondage. [16]

The SCHW's Civil Rights Committee emphasized that the southern poll tax was a matter of national concern. It did so largely for tactical reasons. While Florida, North Carolina, and Louisiana had removed the qualification, the prospect for further state action appeared dim. Gelders lamented that "the total vote in Arkansas, Mississippi, and South Carolina is so small as to constitute rule by an oligarchy; an oligarchy unwilling to vote itself out of power." [17] Furthermore, embedded within the various state constitutions, the restriction required a cumbersome and time-consuming procedure for its repeal. Consequently, national action, through Congress or the federal courts, seemed to provide the best hope for reform. In a shrewd appeal to northern political self-interest, Gelders and Durr reminded their neighbors above the Mason-Dixon line that "while a Southerner used to represent three-fifths of a slave, now by the fact of the poll tax, each Southern vote represents twenty times what a Northern vote would." [18] Thus, the call went out to northerners and southerners, white and black, to unite for the emancipation of the disfranchised southern poor and for the advancement of New Deal liberalism throughout the nation.

Like the foes of the white primary, the opponents of the poll tax initially turned to the courts for relief. In September, 1939, the SCHW represented Henry Pirtle, a white challenger of the Tennessee poll tax. Despite the fact that a unanimous Supreme Court in *Breedlove v. Suttles* only two years earlier had upheld a similar Georgia qualification for voting, the repealers pressed the new case.[19] They attempted to distinguish the facts in their suit from those in the previous one by pointing out that the appellant in *Pirtle v. Brown* sought the right to vote only in federal elections and not in state elections as Breedlove had done. Emphasizing this contention, counsel concluded that any state tax imposed on the federal franchise would impair the national government's sovereignty and deprive a citizen of a privilege protected against state abridgment by the Fourteenth Amendment.[20] In March 1941 the Sixth Circuit Court of Appeals rejected this argument. Judge Xenophon Hicks ruled that because the states conferred the suffrage, Tennessee had not infringed upon any voting privilege arising out of national citizenship. Although the court was following tradition by interpreting the "privileges and immunities" clause of the Fourteenth Amendment very narrowly, nevertheless, Hicks' opinion deviated from a long line of precedents which declared that a person derived his right to vote in federal elections from the United States Constitution and not the states.[21] Shortly thereafter, all hope for the reformers disappeared when the Supreme Court refused to grant a writ of *certiorari* in *Pirtle v. Brown.*

In the meantime, the progressive forces had advanced on Washington. Having failed to persuade a southern congressman to introduce a repeal measure, Gelders tapped Lee Geyer as the SCHW's spokesman. Geyer, a Representative from Los Angeles, had ardently supported social-welfare legislation; furthermore, a common isolationist outlook drew the two men together.[22] In late 1939 the California congressman introduced a bill that sought to prevent the "pernicious political activity" of paying an elector's poll tax in return for his support. Aware that the Supreme Court had sanctioned the poll-tax qualification, Geyer did not attack its constitutionality but justified congressional repeal as a means to ensure honesty in federal elections. The measure's sponsor argued that experience had proven that corrupt politicians bought and peddled poll-tax receipts, and Congress could best check such frauds by eliminating the restriction completely.[23]

To further his cause, Geyer began to conceive of forming a National Committee to Abolish the Poll Tax (NCAPT) as the need for a new organization had become obvious.[24] While the Civil Rights Committee had concentrated on repeal, it was still responsible for other matters involving Negro rights, and the Southern Conference, although soliciting nationwide support, had a regional orientation. By creating a national, single-issue lobby, repealers hoped to avoid confusing their movement with the related struggle for Negro voting rights. In an attempt to check Negrophobic appeals, some reformers wanted to play down the effect that eradication of the capitation tax would bring on black suffrage. One sympathizer admonished, "Bring in Negroes, saying that they are in the fight too, but know that removing the poll tax alone will still leave them a long way from their goal." [25] After all, he might have remembered, North Carolina, Louisiana, and Florida had rescinded the requirement without any marked increase in Negro voting. As long as a committee devoted itself solely to removing the poll tax, it could attract organizations disagreeing on various policies to contribute financially to a special, limited campaign. When it officially came into existence, the NCAPT gathered together the AFL, CIO, NAACP, National Negro Congress, National Urban League, YWCA, United Jewish Youth, ACLU, National Lawyers Guild, and League of Women Shoppers, groups that had already cooperated informally to challenge the poll tax in the judiciary and Congress.[26]

At first Gelders resisted channeling the repeal efforts away from the South into a national mobilization, but he soon reversed himself as the poll-tax issue attracted increased congressional attention.[27] Drumming up support for remedial legislation demanded greater funds and publicity than he could manage by lobbying out of Congressman Geyer's office on "a financial shoestring." Moreover, Geyer's untimely death in 1941 forced the antipoll-taxers to look for a more permanent base of operation. Consequently, Gelders and Virginia Durr decided to officially incorporate the reform coalition into a national committee. By August 1941 the NCAPT had received a charter, and the SCHW dissolved its Civil Rights Committee.[28] Still, an informal relationship between the Southern Conference and the NCAPT continued to exist in the interlocking directorship of its officials.[29]

The NCAPT mainly directed its energies toward lobbying and political education. The committee functioned as a federation of autonomous organizations, supplementing its own small staff by utilizing the Washington delegates of its sponsoring groups to influence Capitol Hill legislators. Its personnel consisted of a chairman, vice chairman, executive secretary, and researchers. Throughout most of its existence, Jennings Perry, editor of the Nashville *Tennessean* and leader of his state's repeal forces, served as its chairman, while Virginia Durr held the post of vice chairman. The latter and the various executive secretaries carried on the organization's daily operations, while Perry reigned as a figurehead.[30] Serving in the army during World War II, Joe Gelders did not hold any office. The group published a newsletter, *The Poll Tax Repealer,* and distributed handbooks, fact sheets, posters, and buttons exhorting the public to rise up against the head tax.

All of this time, Durr continued to search for a southerner to lead the fight in the Senate. In her efforts she received the aid of Eleanor Roosevelt, the darling of both white liberals and civil-rights organizers. The First Lady believed that the "minimum that anyone can do is to vote, and you cannot be a democracy and deny the vote to any individual." Supported by the president's wife, Mrs. Durr persuaded Florida Senator Claude Pepper to marshal the Senate forces.[31] A New Dealer "sound" on the race issue, he seemed a good choice. In 1937, the "Sunshine State" had abolished the one-dollar poll tax, and Pepper reflected that its repeal "contributed to my very large majority in 1938 in the first primary." Once in the Senate the following year, however, the liberal Floridian had established credit with his more conservative southern brethren. Joining them in the filibuster against the antilynching bill, Pepper had also spoken out against Negro voting as a threat to white supremacy. "Neither the Constitution nor federal troops," he warned, "would enable the black man to cast his ballot in the Southland." [32]

The bill introduced by Pepper in 1941 differed from the House version. Although both pieces of legislation proposed wiping out the voting requirement for national elections, only the Senate draft covered primary contests. Tacking his bill on as an amendment to the Hatch Act, Geyer had justified his action as a means of combating the purchase of blocks of poll-tax receipts by boss-controlled machines. Senator Pepper took a more direct course. He drew on the insights of two of Roosevelt's brain trusters, Ben Cohen and Abe Fortas, contending that the state tax was not a "reasonable" voting qualification, and that it improperly interfered with federal elections.[33]

Unfortunately, the *Breedlove* case discouraged legislative action, although the reformers insisted that the justices, in ruling that the Constitution did not prohibit the poll-tax qualifi-

cation for voting, had left unanswered the question of
whether Congress could enter the field to protect federal elections. To bolster this contention, they cited the *Classic* decision,
which affirmed a constitutional right to vote in national elections, and which appeared to suggest that the Congress held
the power to legislate against state encroachments.[34] In fact,
Justice Stone, who had joined in the 1937 decision, confided
to a friend:

> I had not studied the history of the suffrage clauses of the Consti-
> tution at the time of the *Breedlove* Case. When the *Classic* Case
> came to us, I made a thorough study of the clauses dealing with
> federal elections and came to the conclusion that the purpose was
> to give the Federal Government power over the whole electoral
> process.[35]

Most jurists, however, continued to interpret Article One,
Section One of the Constitution as a roadblock to repeal. This
clause stipulated that the qualifications for voters in federal
elections must be the same as those for electors choosing officials for the most numerous branch of the state legislature.
Apparently, one could not eliminate a requirement for voting
in national elections while retaining it for state contests. Admitting that the states possessed the initiative in determining
voting standards, one modern-day suffragette contended that
Congress did not have to accept all conditions which a state
imposed. Eleanor Bontecou, a volunteer NCAPT researcher
and a Bryn Mawr dean, defined "qualification" as the "standard of fitness of an elector," and rejected the capitation tax as
having a reasonable relationship to one's ability to cast a ballot.[36] Once congressmen accepted such reasoning, they could
deal with this unfair burden as part of their power over the
"manner" of holding elections.[37]

On the other hand, poll taxers rejected these arguments as
pure sophistry. They summoned evidence to show that the
Founding Fathers had considered poll taxes within the meaning of the word "qualification" and contended that the constitutional framers had given Congress a supervisory role over

the "manner" of conducting elections to prevent state legislatures from refusing to provide machinery for congressional elections. Defenders of suffrage limitation tried to refute the claim that the ruling in *United States v. Classic* had modified the Supreme Court's previous decision on the poll tax. They agreed that the right to vote for federal officials stemmed from the Constitution but added that the fundamental law left the states to decide the actual suffrage regulations. According to this interpretation, the court had affirmed the constitutional protection of the suffrage only for those who were already enfranchised under state statute. In any event, opponents of repeal contended that in denying a writ of *certiorari* in *Pirtle v. Brown,* the court had chosen not to apply its *Classic* opinion to the poll-tax controversy.[38]

The outbreak of World War II armed the antipoll-tax forces with powerful ideological weapons. Blacks launched a "Double V" campaign—victory for democracy at home and abroad. At Los Angeles, the first NAACP wartime convention resolved that in "a war to prevent the destruction of democracy, national morale will be stronger in proportion as democracy which we defend is made real."[39] Hence, the group pledged vigorously to fight segregation in the armed forces, discrimination in employment and education, and the denial of the franchise in the South. White advocates claimed that the war made elimination of the tax an urgent measure. Fighting against both Hitlerism and the southern oligarchs occupied the forces of democracy, and repealers compared the death of free elections in fascist Europe with the disfranchising effects of the poll tax in the South. The CIO, frustrated by antilabor poll-tax congressmen, warned that the denial of full political participation undermined workers' morale. Once Nazi troops invaded Russia, the American Communist Party vigorously attacked the levy as an "unpatriotic detriment to the war effort."[40]

The war actually stimulated Congress to take positive action against the tax. The necessity of allowing soldiers to cast ballots away from their homes opened the path for partial repeal.

On July 20, 1942, when Representative Robert Ramsay of West Virginia offered a bill that would establish machinery to furnish absentee ballots to qualified servicemen seeking to vote in federal elections, Estes Kefauver rose on the House floor to propose an amendment forbidding any poll-tax requirement that might apply to these GI's. The Democratic congressman from Tennessee voiced his concern that some soldiers risking their lives for the United States could not vote because they had failed to pay the fee. With most of its members absent, the House passed the bill but turned down the Kefauver rider.[41] When the bill reached the Senate floor, Senators Brooks of Illinois and Pepper of Florida revived the antipoll-tax amendment and extended its coverage to party contests. With repeal advocated as a war measure, the Senate voted to remove the qualification for those serving in the armed forces. Southerners had not bothered to filibuster because they found it difficult to justify the deprivation of the right to vote to men fighting for their country. Furthermore, there was little risk in allowing a vote upon the proposal. By the time the House had accepted the Senate version and the president signed the Soldier Vote Act on September 16th, the southern states had already held their congressional primaries in the customary fashion.[42]

This legislative action foreshadowed the bitter debate on wiping out the poll tax for civilians. Repealers hoped to apply this precedent to enfranchise a greater number of citizens. Senator George Norris applauded the passage of the Soldier Vote Act for giving "assurance that Congress will vote to wipe out the poll tax entirely" as a requirement for voting in federal elections.[43] However, opponents of the bill grew more determined to prevent the complete abolition of the tax. Virginia Durr's father, an "unreconstructed Southerner," wrote his daughter that after the passage of the absentee ballot act "all white people in Alabama are buying pistols and other ammunition in preparation for the race war which is coming." One worried southerner wrote Senator Burnet Maybank of South Carolina that enactment of the antipoll-tax resolution "will invite more trouble, leading to bloodshed, race riots, fighting at the polls, corruption at the polls, buying up negro and illiterate votes." [44] In October, after a discharge petition forced the reluctant House Judiciary Committee to release the Geyer bill, the stage was set for the antagonistic forces to collide.

Behind the clash loomed the spectre of the race issue. Representatives from constituencies with a significant black electorate announced their intention of supporting the bill in order to give disfranchised southern Negroes the vote. Arthur Mitchell, the black congressman from Chicago's south side, forecast that "this poll tax bill, if enacted into law, will eventually aid in wiping out the disfranchisement of Negroes . . . in the Southern states." Congressman John Robsion of Barbourville, Kentucky, where Negroes voted without trouble, supported the repeal bill, and candidly asked Walter White if he "would bring this matter to the attention of the colored voters of my district." Emanuel Celler of Brooklyn, New York, categorized the tax as "a deliberate disfranchisement of Negro voters." [45]

Southern congressmen vigorously opposed repeal because they saw it as the first step toward expanding black suffrage. Representative William Colmer of Mississippi suspected that "the direct object of this movement is to enfranchise the Negro in the South. If Congress can remove poll tax requirements it can also remove educational requirements and registration itself." Sam Hobbs, speaking for the whites of Selma, Alabama, ostensibly opposed federal legislation on constitutional grounds. However, he privately applauded Alabama's monetary qualification with its cumulative provisions for ensuring "rule by those who are fit to rule." Lest there be any mistake as to whom he meant, Hobbs, congratulated one of his state's constitutional framers for not relying exclusively on the Grandfather Clause.[46] Lawmakers from the southern states that had already repealed the levy joined their neighbors in condemning the bill, indicating that the real issue was the possibility of future action by Congress to extend Negro voting rights.[47]

However, southern congressional supporters of federal abolition proposals did not advocate Negro enfranchisement. In 1942, Luther Patrick, representing industrial Birmingham, spoke out for the Geyer Bill, a measure that he hoped would emancipate poor whites "from the reactionary political and economic interests [that] would like to keep the South in a semifeudal condition." Patrick assured his southern colleagues, "[We] are well able to handle any race proposition that may arise, and it is not wholesome to work a hardship . . . on good white people, using the colored people as an excuse." [48] Estes Kefauver, joined by five members of his state's delegation from eastern and middle Tennessee, supported abolition, primarily as a way to topple the political machine of Boss Ed Crump in Memphis. These reformers believed that one of the keys to Crump's power lay in his corrupt purchasing of poll-tax receipts. [49]

When the showdown came in the House, the poll-tax foes won a smashing victory. On October 13, 254 congressmen overwhelmed eighty-four members to approve for the first time ever a repeal measure. Although the vote broke down along sectional lines, nine southerners supported abolition, whereas eleven northerners lined up against it.

Meanwhile, the Senate quietly considered its version of repeal. Since June, 1941, its judiciary committee had heard voluminous testimony on the merits and constitutionality of Claude Pepper's bill. In October, 1942, the five-man subcommittee that conducted the hearing recommended withholding it from the Senate floor. With Tom Connally of Texas, a poll-tax state, as spokesman, the group concluded that Congress could not alter the qualifications of electors and counseled that the "only way to 'modernize' the Constitution is to amend it." However, the full committee led by George Norris rejected this advice. [50]

Throughout his long political career, Norris had fought to make rulers more responsive to the will of the people. Consequently, he had advocated direct primaries so that citizens could have a greater voice in choosing candidates. As a congressman in 1910 he had led the successful attack that took some of the enormous powers out of the hands of the speaker and returned them to the representatives. During the 1920s he had supported the attempt to allow Congress to overrule by a two-thirds vote unpopular decisions rendered by an appointed Supreme Court. And, as author of the Twentieth Amendment, Norris checked lame-duck officials from prolonging their influence.

The Nebraskan's opposition to the economic restriction on the ballot signaled his final effort to democratize the political process. He reported to his colleagues that:

> When the Congress of the United States has had brought to its attention these poll tax laws by which millions of our citizens are in effect deprive of their right to vote, it is the duty of Congress itself to pass the necessary legislation to nullify such unconstitutional laws.

Dealing directly with the race issue, Norris contended that the tax served illegally as an "artificial qualification" to prevent Negroes from voting.[51]

The Geyer-Pepper Bill, having survived the journey through congressional hearings, discharge petitions, and debates, finally collided with the stone wall of the filibuster. To shut off the talk marathon, the bill's supporters required the assent of two-thirds of the senators present and voting. This antimajoritarian cloture rule most recently had thwarted passage of bills to punish lynchers. From the moment Senate Majority Leader Alben Barkley of Kentucky brought the measure to the floor, on November 14, the poll-tax defenders displayed their parliamentary wizardry. Relentlessly calling for quorums, demanding the complete reading of the *Journal* and appealing the decisions of the Chair, southerners prevented the Senate from formally taking up the proposal at all that day. But Barkley showed that he would not retreat easily. To muster a quorum, he secured authority to have the Sergeant-At-Arms issue arrest warrants for the return to the Capitol of seven southern senators still in Washington. With their feelings ruffled, the southerners earnestly began the filibuster.[52]

The majority leader tolerated delay for eight days. During this time the discussion centered around constitutional questions. Yet the vituperative Negrophobe, Theodore Bilbo from Mississippi, revealed what plagued his more restrained colleague's minds, "If the poll tax bill passes, the next step will be an effort to remove the registration qualification, the educational qualification of the negroes. If that is done we will have no way of preventing negroes from voting." [53] Debate finally reached an end when Barkley agreed to an offer made by Tom Connally to permit a vote on cloture and then to withdraw the bill if the attempt failed. Subsequently, by a vote of thirty-seven to forty-one, the Senate rejected the cloture petition. Providing the margin of victory to help the South were ten northern Democrats mostly from the Rocky Mountain region and seven Republicans from the Northeast and Far West. Coming mainly from sparsely populated states with few Negroes, they valued the protective principle of unlimited debate more than the cause of equal opportunity.

President Roosevelt must assume some of the blame for failing to push harder for passage of the repealer. He had left his supporters dangling on a limb. Barkley had angered many of his colleagues by commandeering a quorum, Pepper had risked his constituency's anger by appearing on the "wrong" side of the race issue, and Norris had helped to overturn his subcommittee's unfavorable report. Ironically, in return for their boldness, the NCAPT accused them of taking part in an "unconscionable deal" to table the bill.[54] However, the president's silence on the matter had given them little choice but to retreat. At a news conference during the debate, Roosevelt claimed no knowledge of a poll-tax filibuster, and declined to comment as to whether he favored passage of the measure.[55]

At the same time, the chief executive's hesitancy created doubt about his dedication to poll-tax repeal. He was flirting with the idea of having Attorney General Biddle institute a suit against Mississippi to challenge its poll-tax restriction. But when the Senate thwarted the appropriate legislation, the president did not turn to the courts.[56] In all fairness to Roosevelt, he did not have time on his side. Practicing as "Dr. Win-the-War," the chief executive needed southern support for his vital wartime legislation. Although he might give initial encouragement, Roosevelt quickly backed down to avoid angering Dixie's senators.

Rather than disintegrating, the abolitionist coalition vigorously followed up the attack. With Geyer dead, the NCAPT searched for another House sponsor for its proposal. Desiring the widest possible support, the committee selected a bipartisan group to steer the legislation through the lower chamber. Democrats Warren Magnuson of Washington and Joseph Gavagan of New York joined Republicans George Bender of Ohio and Joseph Clark Baldwin of New York to introduce bills identical to the one approved by the Senate Judiciary Committee in 1942. On March 9 and 10, 1943 at a strategy meeting in Washington, D.C., the NCAPT laid plans to concentrate its efforts on Baldwin's resolution.[57] However, before the committee supporters could follow through on this design, they had to deal with the presence of Vito Marcantonio: the American Labor Party congressman from New York City who represented a primarily Italian district with few Negroes. Known as an ally of both blacks and impoverished whites, his support was nonetheless, a liability. Not only did he antagonize southern lawmakers for his stubborn defense of civil rights and the extension of social-welfare measures, but his name also symbolized the threat of communism for many Americans. At the beginning of 1943 after a bitter fight, southern Democrats had succeeded in blocking the radical New Yorker's appointment to the influential House Judiciary Committee. Furthermore, a noninterventionist until 1940, Marcantonio, with his sudden approval for the Allies after Nazi Germany had invaded the Soviet Union, became implicated with Stalinism. Thus, the NAACP and CIO, identified with the anticommunist left, expressed doubt about the wisdom of supporting H.R. 7, a copy of the Pepper bill introduced by Marcantonio.[58]

Nevertheless, the NCAPT's bipartisan coalition agreed to adopt H.R. 7. It had little choice. Led by Virginia Durr, the committee had sent a delegation to persuade Marcantonio to move aside. However, having been the first to lodge a discharge petition, the congressman refused to step back. He told Mrs. Durr flatly that he would not budge. To maintain a united front, the committee backed down. In a way, this presented a good political solution, because many Democrats preferred not to fall in behind the bill with the Republican Baldwin's name as sponsor. As for the communist issue, the steering committee reached a gentlemen's agreement that it would not refer to H.R. 7 as the Marcantonio bill and that "if any substantial difficulty is encountered with the present procedure, then some other bill will be substituted therefore." [59] Furthermore, northern liberal Democrats like Warren Magnuson "thought nothing of Marcantonio's politics, because he is practically unknown out in [my] part of the country." Representing a district in the State of Washington with few Negroes, Magnuson served as the bill's floor manager to avoid the charge of capitulating to black pressure groups. [60] This strategy succeeded in bringing the bill to the House floor. On May 24th, 268 congressmen voted to consider H.R. 7.

During the ensuing debate, race again dominated the discussions. Each side split as to whether the repealer would enfranchise Negroes. On the one hand Representative William Whittington claimed that the poll tax did not discriminate against blacks, while his Mississippi colleague Jamie Whitten growled that its repeal would create political equality. In the opposite corner, while George Bender suggested that H.R. 7 did not guarantee that Negroes would vote, Emanuel Celler predicted that the bill would open up the franchise to blacks. [61]

As noted earlier, the war provided the reformers with a potent argument. The *Poll Tax Repealer* cautioned that "our country today is engaged in a war between a free and a slave world. A war in which the prerequisite for a victory is that we move forward now to full freedom for the common man." [62] Evan Owen Jones, a twenty-one-year-old white sailor seated in the public gallery of the House, added the only excitement during the one-day perfunctory debate. He startled the representatives by rising to his feet and shouting, "Why should a man be taxed to vote when he can fight without paying? I am a man in the service. I speak for thousands who cannot be here. I would like to ask you why a man has to pay tribute for the right to vote." [63] Apparently the majority of the House agreed with the young seaman, for H.R. 7 was easily approved by a vote of 265 to 110.

As expected, the Senate slowed down the repeal juggernaut. Joseph O'Mahoney, who had previously chaired the Senate Judiciary Subcommittee's hearing on the Pepper resolution, opposed the legislation. Skeptical of the constitutionality of such a statute, the Wyoming Democrat had recommended repeal by amendment.[64] After the House passed H.R. 7, the Senate Judiciary Committee decided to gather additional evidence on the constitutionality of the bill. The repeal forces accused the committee of stalling because it had already listened to voluminous testimony on the question. From October 25 to November 2, 1943, the full committee heard a parade of witnesses representing Negro pressure groups and organized labor attest to Congress' power to pass the measure. In rebuttal, the foes of the plan invited the eminent constitutional historian Charles Warren to testify that the legislative branch did not have the authority to prohibit by simple statute the payment of a poll tax. Finally, on November 12, the reformers jumped the initial hurdle when the Judiciary Committee voted to report out the proposal, and rejected the O'Mahoney resolution for a constitutional amendment.[65]

Before the provision reached the Senate floor, the poll-tax struggle assumed an even greater significance. When the Supreme Court struck down the white primary in April 1944 the financial requirement remained as a legitimate way to keep the ballot box closed. It became increasingly important for southerners to retain firm control over their electoral machinery. The chairman of the Alabama Democratic Executive Committee, Gessner T. McCorvey, advised his state's legislators, "I think that the poll tax, with its cumulative feature, should be maintained in full force and effect. It is a lawful . . . method of getting rid of a large number of people who would not cast an intelligent ballot even if they were given the right to vote." [66] Senator Maybank expressed his concern that the Supreme Court "could not have picked a worse time" to render its Texas decision and thus "stir up the subject." [67]

This new development diminished whatever slight possibility for favorable Senate action there was. At the beginning of the year, the Chicago *Defender* had reported ugly rumors of an agreement to take a cloture vote early in the filibuster and then discard the bill if the result proved unsuccessful. [68] Wary of this possibility, the NCAPT stressed the position that the vote for cloture provided the test for the lawmakers' commitment to repeal. "If a Senator will not vote for cloture he is opposed to the legislation," it declared. [69] Furthermore, the abolitionists viewed with alarm the conservatives' emasculation of a stronger Soldier Vote Act in January 1944. Although unable to reinstate the poll-tax requirement for absentee servicemen, the Dixie bloc led by James Eastland, Kenneth McKellar, and John McClellan succeeded in assigning ballot distribution to the states that retained control over qualifications. After examining the law, Senator John Overton of Louisiana rejoiced that the South could maintain white supremacy. [70]

True to form, the Senate acted out the script. With Claude Pepper preoccupied with a tough primary battle in Florida, the NCAPT had to tap Judiciary Committee Chairman Pat McCarran as its bill's manager. When the Nevada Democrat exhibited little enthusiasm for the measure, the national committee secured the assistance of James Mead, a New York Democrat. Originally hoping to bring up the issue by mid March, the repealers failed to secure a commitment for the Senate to consider the proposal until after the Easter adjournment. On May 9, almost one month after Congress had returned, McCarran finally moved to discuss the measure. Following a brief two-day debate, the leadership capitulated to the filibusterers and called for a cloture vote. To no avail, the

NCAPT issued an "Open Statement To The Senate" welcoming a "vote for cloture as a vote for the antipoll-tax bill." [71] The thirty-six-to-forty-four vote fell far short of achieving the necessary two-thirds approval, and Senator Barkley successfully moved to make a veterans' bill the order of business. As was the case two years earlier, a coalition of northern Republicans and Democrats collaborated with the southerners to defeat cloture.

Without the staunch backing of the president, the administration forces in Congress had failed to mount a sustained attack. Writing in the Washington *Post,* columnist Marquis Childs reported that the poll-tax fight in the Senate had "all the violence and fervor of a game of ping pong in an old ladies home." According to the journalist, with a little pressure inside both parties a cloture vote would have succeeded.[72] But President Roosevelt did not encourage the legislation because he thought it would cause harm to the liberalization of the Democratic party in the South and damage the chances for reelection of Claude Pepper, one of his most enthusiastic supporters. The bitter controversy over the Soldier Vote Act had already frightened conservative white southerners who believed that the administration had tried to pass it as a first step toward federalizing elections and enfranchising Negroes. Hearing the political rumbles echoing from the South, presidential adviser James F. Byrnes of South Carolina had warned Roosevelt against entering the poll-tax fray in order to stop the momentum of dissidents in Texas, Mississippi, and South Carolina who were working to pledge their states' committeemen to the Democratic National Convention against the incumbent. Roosevelt's passive policy reinforced his followers in Dixie, who beat back the anti–New Deal insurgency.[73]

The president refused to follow the poll-tax strategy he had outlined the previous year. During the fall of 1943 he suggested putting "all emphasis on cloture as the real test of a member's attitude toward the bill, and hold back the vote on it until there can be no excuse for a demand for further debate." [74] In this way the Democratic chieftain thought reluctant Republicans might be goaded during an election year to support cloture. However, Roosevelt discarded this plan, and Senate leaders pursued the opposite course without seeking a second vote. To his credit, the president publicly restated that he had always believed the poll' tax undemocratic and privately counseled that he would not object if administration spokesmen introduced a repeal measure. Yet, by June, 1944 the chief executive, through his wife, was informing Virginia Durr that he favored a constitutional amendment as the only practical way to eliminate the assessment.[75] Apparently, Roosevelt was walking a delicate tightrope, struggling to balance his concern for equal suffrage with his desire to keep his allies in control of the Democratic party in the South. His adviser on race relations, Jonathan Daniels, was "impressed with the similarity of our situation to that of the last century when the extreme abolitionists and the violent secessionists almost collaborated to leave sensible people helpless in the middle." [76]

For their part, the Republican leaders also failed to encourage an end to the filibusters. In fact, Minority Leaders Charles McNary and Wallace White opposed cloture and had moved against it. Furthermore, Thomas E. Dewey, the 1944 Republican presidential nominee, refused to endorse H.R. 7. He blandly commented, "I have always fought against the poll tax and every other device to deprive free people of their votes." [77] In fact, the GOP gave up on congressional repeal by advocating in its platform the elimination of the poll tax by constitutional amendment.[78]

The repealers would never accept the amendment strategy. The NCAPT executive secretary Katherine Shryver warned that such a procedure would furnish the "perfect face-saving gesture" for many senators. Leslie Perry, legislative representative of the NAACP's Washington Bureau, called the Republican suggestion an "idle gesture. Instead of fighting the poll tax on one front—Congress, we would have to spread ourselves thin over forty-eight state fronts." [79] Perhaps most important, the abolitionists feared that adoption of an amendment would establish a precedent thwarting future action to extend the suffrage by congressional legislation.

The attitude of the poll taxers fueled the reformers' skepticism about the possibility of repeal by amendment. Although arguing that the amendment route provided the only constitutional method, many southern legislators hinted that they opposed such a plan. Senator Maybank viewed the ratification of an amendment as a "danger . . . which might interfere with the ability of the states to regulate their elections in other ways." The leader of the House forces against abolition, Sam Hobbs, claimed that "it was a question strictly for state determination, and that the Federal Government had *no authority whatever* . . . to intrude into this exclusive province of the states" [emphasis added].[80] South Carolina, Alabama, Mississippi, and Virginia turned down initial attempts at state repeal, while only Georgia eliminated the tax during the 1940s. Nevertheless, in a brief departure motivated by wartime democratic feelings, most of the poll-tax states passed special legislation that temporarily abolished the restriction for their soldiers. This did not prevent the Dixie politicians from cleverly wording the statues to prevent Negro GI's from profiting.[81]

Before the abolitionists could exert new pressure on Congress, President Roosevelt died. His successor, Harry S. Truman, seemed likely to work for repeal. As a member of the Senate from Missouri, Truman had voted for cloture to choke off the filibuster against H.R. 7, and he also had supported the Soldier Vote Act with the antipoll-tax rider.[82] Like his predecessor, however, Truman had little intention of forcing a showdown in Congress. On April 6, 1946 Truman informed a gathering of high-school journalists in Chicago that he did not see any immediate solution to the poll-tax question in the South. The chief executive concluded that the states would have to work out the problem for themselves.[83] For this gloomy analysis the president came under immediate attack from the advocates of national legislation. To clarify his view, a few days later Truman publicly elaborated, "There is no contradiction between Federal and state action on this matter. It may be that the possibility of Federal action has stimulated state action. Federal and state action should supplement one another wherever possible."[84] Privately, however, the president wrote Alabama Senator John Bankhead, who had cheered his Chicago remarks, "There never was a law that could be enforced if the people didn't want it enforced." [85]

Not surprisingly, when the moment of truth came for the legislation, the Truman administration saw no point in making a strong fight. In February 1946 Majority Leader Barkley advised the NCAPT that H.R. 7, which had routinely been adopted by the House for the third time, "can't get over the hurdle of a filibuster." Stung by the Senate's talking to death of the recent FEPC bill, Truman griped, "I am not looking for another filibuster." [86] Resigned to defeat, late in the July 29th session, the administration forces introduced a cloture petition to cut off debate even before it had actually commenced. When the Senate could not raise the necessary votes to curb discussion, the bipartisan repeal coalition retracted the bill.

Truman did take one important step to break the legislative stalemate. Prodded by influential Negro leaders protesting the upsurge of violence against blacks after World War II, in December 1946 he issued an executive order that established a Presidential Committee on Civil Rights. The decree authorized this group to report on the condition of political rights in the United States. As part of its study, the committee investigated the effects of the poll tax in the South. The president hoped to use the advisory agency's suggestions to form the basis of his legislative civil rights program.[87]

Subcommittee Number One, charged with the responsibility of investigating the poll-tax issue, had four choices.[88] It considered endorsing the elimination of the restriction by either a national act, state statute, federal court decision, or a combination of these. When the group agreed to the first proposal, its members then discussed the possibility that such a plan might violate the Constitution. In fact, the subcommittee talked about offering a generally worded election law rather than a specific antipoll-tax act, but it still wanted to attack the fee directly. After months of deliberation the panel advised "that the recommendation be so couched as to recognize the possibility that a constitutional amendment rather than a statute may be necessary." In accepting this judgment, the full committee called upon either the states or Congress to initiate repeal of the poll tax as a suffrage qualification.[89]

On February 2, 1948 the president followed up his committee's report, *To Secure These Rights,* by requesting that Congress pass an act outlawing the poll tax. Although he welcomed state abolition, Truman recognized the need for federal leadership. In this crucial election year, the Democratic incumbent had decided on this course, which would appeal to northern liberals, labor, and Negroes, all vital elements of the New Deal coalition. He thought that such a position could be taken without irreparably alienating important southern Democratic voters.[90] As William S. White reported in the *New York Times,* the antipoll-tax bill "is relatively the least objectionable to Southerners among the four main civil rights proposals of Truman." [91]

With the Republicans in control of the Eightieth Congress, some reformers predicted the end to the long, bitter struggle. House of Representatives 7 had given way to H.R. 29 sponsored by George Bender, a Cleveland Republican, and the House had passed the bill by the greatest majority to date during the 1947 session. As a result, the NCAPT predicted that the "Republican majority in the Senate is strong enough—with the aid of those Democrats who have staunchly fought for an untaxed vote for years—to break any filibuster." [92]

However, a realistic analysis of the three cloture votes indicates that this hope was illusory, because a coalition of nonsouthern Democrats and Republicans had blocked the bill's consideration in the past. In 1942, while twenty-one Democrats and sixteen Republicans had supported cloture, twelve nonsouthern Democrats and ten Republicans had joined twenty southerners to defeat the petition. A change of fifteen votes would have ended debate. Two years later seventeen Democrats and eighteen Republicans voted for cloture, but thirteen nonsouthern Democrats and thirteen Republicans added their approval to the eighteen southerners in opposition. The repealers fell eighteen votes short of victory. In

1946 the abolitionists came closest to achieving success. Twenty-four Democrats and fifteen Republicans approved an end to debate, while seven nonsouthern Democrats and seven Republicans tallied their votes with the nineteen southern Democratic negative votes. A switch of nine votes would have changed the outcome. Thus, although a bipartisan coalition of nonsouthern Democrats and Republicans had approved cloture, a combination of votes from them had defeated the petitions. Furthermore, a slightly higher percentage of the total Republican votes than the nonsouthern Democratic votes cast had prevented approval of an end to discussion. Consequently, even with a Republican-dominated Senate the repeal prospects should have appeared dim.

Before the Bender bill came up to the Senate floor during the July special session convened by the president, the Republican leadership had a difficult decision to make. The GOP could stick with a simple bill, or it could substitute a resolution for a constitutional amendment as the party's 1944 platform had pledged. Quickly, the Republicans had their hands forced by the opposition. Democratic Senator Carl Hayden of Arizona offered a bargain to strike out the wording of the House bill and exchange a provision for a constitutional amendment. If the Senate adopted such an approach, Hayden guessed that the states would ratify the article in a shorter time than they had the women's suffrage amendment.[93] Richard Russell of Georgia, the southern bloc's leader, responded that his allies would not filibuster against the amendment resolution if they "can have clear and definite assurance that the Senate would stand fast to its position in proposing this matter to the people . . . and against any effort to deal with it by statute."[94] However, on July 29th, Republican party spokesmen Robert Taft of Ohio and Kenneth Wherry of Nebraska flatly rejected the offer. With the presidential election approaching in November, Republicans hoped to recapture many of the votes of the northern Negroes who had defected to the Democrats during the New Deal. In fact, the GOP's position appealed to NAACP Executive Secretary Walter White, who doubted "whether ratification can be obtained since specious states' rights arguments will be made against the constitutional amendment in the state legislatures." [95]

Having selected this course, the Republicans did not press very hard to check the filibuster. For three days after July 29th, when H.R. 29 had become the order of business, southerners prolonged debate on the motion to consider the measure and not on the bill itself. On August 2nd, a bipartisan group presented a cloture petition to close discussion, but Senator Russell appealed to the chair that they could only use this procedure against a pending measure. Presiding over the Upper Chamber as its president pro tempore, Michigan Republican Arthur Vandenberg, although favoring H.R. 29, sustained Russell's point of order. In so doing, Vandenberg admonished his colleagues that the cloture rule had to be altered before they could pass such legislation. With so dim a prospect, the Republicans gave up the fight. When Wherry presented a motion that had the effect of displacing the poll-tax bill, forty-eight Republicans joined twenty-one primarily southern Democrats to discard the repeal measure; sixteen nonsouthern Democrats alone objected.[96]

The following year, when the Senate returned to Democratic control, the Republicans showed that they did not seriously intend to curb filibusters so that an antipoll-tax bill could pass. On March 11th, Truman's newly elected Vice President Alben Barkley, the presiding officer, set aside Vandenberg's previous ruling on the proper procedure for filing a cloture petition. When Senator Russell challenged Barkley's interpretation, twenty-three Republicans led by the Michigan senator joined the southern Democrats to override the vice president. Five days later, William Knowland, a conservative California Republican, proposed a cloture rule change requiring a two-thirds vote of the entire Senate rather than of those present to shut off debate. Enough Republicans joined southern Democrats to adopt this resolution, which made it more difficult than ever before to stifle filibusters.[97]

The failure to secure a liberalized cloture rule ended the

possibility of enacting a congressional statute to remove the poll-tax qualification for voting. Although the Truman administration continued to expend energy, it was not enough. In 1949 the Justice Department wrote a slightly revised antipoll-tax bill, and for the first time an attorney general testified in its favor. While the House overwhelmingly passed it, the Senate, wary of the increased difficulty in ending the filibuster, declined to call up the measure.[98] During the next decade, Congress only actively considered resolutions for constitutional amendments. It passed such a proposal in 1962 and by August 1964 enough states ratified the Twenty-fourth Amendment, which banned poll-tax payments as a prerequisite for voting in national elections.

The NCAPT fizzled along with the chance for congressional repeal. Finances were hard to obtain as a postwar conservative reaction set in, and liberal organizations felt the pinch. Customary friends like the SCHW and the CIO could not afford to provide economic aid, and in the summer of 1948, the bankrupt NCAPT permanently closed its doors.[99] Moreover, after the introduction of Truman's omnibus civil-rights program, key sponsoring groups decided to channel their funds into securing the comprehensive bill. Thus, Roger Baldwin, Director of the ACLU, rejected a plea for money to keep alive the committee's attempt to lobby for an antipoll-tax bill, since "so many organizations are interested in pushing it with the rest of the program we feel efforts should be concentrated on the job to push it as a whole." [100]

The hysteria over the communist menace also helped to break up the cooperation on the suffrage issue and to destroy the NCAPT. As Congress investigated the influence of foreign subversion and President Truman established procedures to ensure loyalty in the federal government, liberal groups attempted to clean out their own houses. During 1946–1950, the ACLU, CIO, and NAACP tried to purge suspected Communists from their ranks. In disassociating themselves from the radical left, the anticommunist liberals also abandoned the "red" tainted NCAPT. This organization, as well as its prime mover the SCHW, had been condemned as communist fronts by various governmental agencies. As early as 1940, one foe of the tax had admonished against associating with Joe Gelders, because there "is certainly a widespread belief that his sympathies are strongly aligned with the Communist Party, even though he may not be a member." [101] Likewise, the intimate connection of Vito Marcantonio, portrayed to the public as a Russian sympathizer, with poll-tax abolition alienated the liberals from the NCAPT.

The association of the poll tax with other civil-rights issues further hurt the chances of abolition. Although the NAACP figured prominently in the repeal movement, the NCAPT strove to keep its struggle separate from acrimonious controversies like the passage of an FEPC bill. Its Executive Secretary Katherine Shryver lamented that the question of racial discrimination in employment "tends to swamp us emotionally. We are valiantly striving . . . to keep the issue a franchise issue." [102] Nevertheless, the close alliance of the suffrage movement with the causes of the Negro heightened southern trepidations.

In focusing attention on obtaining a congressional statute, the NCAPT hardened the opposition's will to resist. As pointed out earlier, many roadblocks stood along the constitutional amendment path, but at least Dixie legislators assented that taking such a route was proper. Even those southerners whose states had abolished the tax shared their colleagues' fear that by ending the qualification Congress "could with the same propriety advocate repeal of the literacy test" and other educational requirements. With the white primary destroyed, such legislative action would endanger the remaining barriers limiting Negro voting. By insisting on a simple act rather than an amendment, the repealers worried the Dixie bloc about creating a precedent for establishing federal sanctions against racial segregation.[103]

Ultimately, the NCAPT could not overcome the institutional obstacles present in the Senate together with the unwillingness of both political parties to assign poll-tax removal as a high-priority measure. Unless the filibuster collapsed, nothing could be done. The conservative coalition consisting of southern Democrats, northern Democrats mainly from western states with few Negroes, and most Republicans thwarted the imposition of cloture. Each party paid lip service to poll-tax abolition but failed to mount a sustained attack to choke off dilatory debate. Although the black electorate in the North was becoming a subject of increased partisan consideration during the 1940s, northern politicians did not want to risk losing legislative support from powerful southern lawmakers in control of important committees.

Yet despite its numerous legislative setbacks, the NCAPT helped educate the southern people against the voting restriction. *The Public Opinion Quarterly* estimated that in April 1949, 53 percent of the South favored abolition; this represented a 10 percent rise from eight years before. Although this new backing did not translate into more favorable southern votes in Congress, it did materialize as reform agitation within *Polltaxia*. In 1944 Virginia Durr had speculated that no state would succeed in removing the levy "without constant pressure from the national Congress. The pressure will be kept up without a doubt as the progressive forces of the country are united on this measure." [104] Fulfilling this prophecy, by the mid 1950s South Carolina and Tennessee had repealed the tax, while Alabama had reduced its cumulative payment.

Although the NCAPT did not survive, the struggle to eliminate the poll tax had forged an interracial, liberal coalition. Predominantly white labor unions, religious groups, and civil-liberties organizations joined the NAACP and other Negro associations to coordinate lobbying activities in Washington. While this cooperative movement had been organized to confer the franchise on all, it was a suitable vehicle for pressing forward Negro equality. The NCAPT foreshadowed the creation of the Leadership Conference on Civil Rights, which mobilized an assault by both races on discriminatory practices in employment, education, housing, and voting.

The poll tax had been an important issue for blacks, not

because its destruction would yield mass enfranchisement but rather because its repeal would put the white South on notice that ample legislative power existed for the removal of other racist-inspired restrictions. With the poll tax gone as a qualification for suffrage, the spotlight would shine on the biased registration procedures that kept a majority of southern Negroes from casting ballots. The defeat of antipoll-tax measures, however, did not mean that the franchise movement was dead. Civil-rights advocates continued the fight in the states, the judiciary, and Washington until circumstances changed and legislative action to extend voting rights became possible.

4

The South Fights Back: Boswellianism and Bilboism

THERE WAS A STORY sarcastically told by southern Negroes during this century. It concerned a black man who went down to the courthouse intending to sign up to vote. He was confronted by a white registrar who quizzed him about the meaning of *habeas corpus*. After pondering the question for a few moments, the applicant solemnly replied, *"Habeas Corpus*—that means that this black man ain't gonna register today." His answer was quite correct, but it was not the one the registrar was looking for, and no response would have been satisfactory.[1]

This anecdote might be a folktale, but it sadly captured the reality of black disfranchisement in the South. With the Democratic primary pried open and the poll tax under siege, restrictive voter registration systems offered southern whites the best way of curtailing the size of the Negro electorate. Determining the eligibility of the would-be voter was a two-step process. Legislators set the general standards that had to be met, and enrollment officers then decided whether an individual possessed these qualifications. By administering the tests so that they disqualified blacks, southern registrars could preserve white supremacy.

To this end, all of the former Confederate states except Texas and Arkansas had written into their constitutions literacy tests for suffrage. Since blacks suffered most from a lack of schooling, they bore the heaviest burden of proving that they could read and write. As late as 1950, 44.6 percent of black Alabamians over the age of twenty-five had received less than four years of formal education. Even those who persevered after the fifth grade faced the handicap of a separate and unequal education. Especially in the rural, black-belt counties where Negroes outnumbered whites, Jim Crow had produced poorly trained teachers, dilapidated school buildings, and a shortage of supplies.[2] Therefore, any literacy test, however impartially applied, would effectively stifle mass Negro suffrage.

For registrars to have administered the educational examinations fairly would have led to the exclusion of illiterate whites. A sizable number would have been involved. As late as 1950, 13.4 percent of Caucasians over twenty-five years of age in Alabama had never progressed beyond the fourth grade. Then and earlier, however, registrars had applied a double standard in administering tests that allowed most illiterate whites to enroll. In so doing, the southern states differed from eleven of their northern neighbors that used literacy exams as a means of examining potential voters regardless of race.[3]

In the South, county boards entrusted with such responsibilities were a law unto themselves. They implemented the rules as they saw fit and functioned independently of each other—a system that ensured considerable diversity within a state. The lack of centralized direction enabled the clerks to use their imagination in restricting Negro suffrage and many proved to be quite resourceful. Although most of the southern states technically accepted reading or writing parts of their constitutions as proof of eligibility, clerks ignored the law and disqualified blacks for insufficient knowledge of governmental procedures. In Birmingham, Alabama, Negroes experienced difficulty in answering, "What is the Constitution made of?" and "How does the government of the United States operate?"

Even when black college students and teachers could respond, boards failed them on minor points. One educator did not pass the inquiry because she supposedly omitted the word "more" in reciting the preamble of the Constitution from memory. White applicants did not go through this procedure.[4]

Clerks were able to discourage enrollment even without administering any examinations. Working at a snail's pace, they kept Negroes standing in long lines. Some boards effected a slowdown by refusing to provide any assistance in filling out the necessary application blanks. Then at the closing hour, the registrars called it a day, no matter how many people still waited. Performing in this way, they acted within the law; however, some officials deliberately deceived blacks by falsely claiming that they had run out of registration cards or that the board did not have a quorum present to conduct business.[5]

In Alabama, boards employed a voucher system which hampered Negro citizens. In some instances, they demanded that black petitioners get two white men to identify them. This requirement delayed registration until a Negro could convince witnesses to spend half a day and personally appear at a usually busy courthouse. The voucher law should have applied equally to both races, but frustrated Negroes complained that the officials strictly enforced the law for them while permitting white acquaintances to register without the necessary testimony.[6]

Little recourse existed for the disappointed applicant. Although he had thirty days to appeal for relief to the county circuit court, local boards often nullified this option by waiting more than a month to notify a person that he did not meet the qualifications. On occasion, to forestall judicial action the clerks might agree to register the complaining party. In this way, they could keep out of federal court and prevent possible injunctions against their discriminatory methods. Thus, a few persistent blacks could pass, but the larger group remained without the ballot.[7]

Even if a Negro citizen managed to enroll, he might subsequently find his name removed. A legitimate practice to strike from the rolls those who had died or moved away, purging furnished some southern officials with an opportunity to eliminate black registrants. In Dublin, Georgia, before the 1946 primaries the board found 75 percent of the Negroes ineligible to vote. The clerks sent out notices to the purged to appear for a hearing, and those who failed to come lost their right to the franchise. On the other hand, those whites summoned who did not show up at the courthouse remained on the books. In this manner, approximately 20,000 Negroes throughout the state suddenly lost their suffrage.[8]

As in most of the states of the Deep South, Alabama had deliberately designed its registration system to block Negro voting. From the beginning of the twentieth century, the state had employed a literacy examination that discriminated against blacks. Going beyond legal requirements, registrars made Negroes explain esoteric portions of the state and federal constitutions. Furthermore, dipping into their bag of tricks, the boards used the voucher system, slowdowns, and deception to disqualify educated blacks while they registered illiterate whites. In the face of these subterfuges and the white primary, the number of black electors drastically declined after 1900 to 3,700 from over 100,000 just before the turn of the century.[9]

Throughout the next four decades, the fear of mass Negro suffrage had perpetuated Alabama's passion to disfranchise its black citizenry. Although not a majority of the state's population in 1940, Negroes outnumbered whites in eighteen of sixty-seven counties. With 75 percent of this total concentrated in the black belt, white planters took the hardest line against an unbiased franchise. In one such county, Macon, the home of Tuskegee, a probate judge warned, "If we had an open registration, every Negro at the Institute and everyone who works at the Veterans Hospital would come down here."[10] Yet even in the cities of Birmingham and Mobile, Negro suffrage lagged behind the major urban areas of the South.

Until 1944, the white primary had proven an effective

means of curtailing Negro voting in the only meaningful election. Following *Smith v. Allwright,* the Department of Justice considered prosecuting officials who continued to practice racial discrimination at the polls. To forestall federal action, the State Democratic Executive Committee eliminated the restrictive qualification for participating in its party contests. Thus, on the surface, this change opened the way for an expanded Negro electorate. Observing this compliance with the Supreme Court's mandate, the NAACP optimistically commented, "the New Day may not be here as yet, but it is definitely on its way." [11]

However, some Alabama Democratic leaders had no intention of easing the way for black suffrage. Rather, they resolved to exchange the toppled primary for a more prohibitive registration law. In addition to the clause requiring a prospective voter to read and write satisfactorily any article of the Constitution, restrictionists proposed to add an amendment further that the applicant also understand the prescribed section. This would legalize the practice that many registrars already followed. "A smart parrot could be taught to recite a section of our Constitution," remarked the chairman of the Democratic Executive Committee, Gessner T. McCorvey, a vociferous advocate of white supremacy, and he elaborated on the rewards of revision, "This of course, would give certain discretion to the Board of Registrars and enable them to prevent from registering those elements in our community which have not yet fitted themselves for self government." [12] Furthermore, by discarding the $300 property requirement that previously qualified a person to vote, the framers hoped to prevent "the average Negro who owned a car . . . from gaining an unrestrictive ballot." Consequently, to take Alabama "out from under the effect" of the Texas decision, E. C. Boswell, representing the black-belt county of Geneva, initiated the measure in the legislature. In May 1945 his colleagues overwhelmingly agreed, and the plan went to the electorate for ratification in the next year's November elections. [13]

As might be expected, the NAACP and black voter leagues

opposed the Boswell amendment, and a number of whites aided them. After the white primary decision, the SCHW's Committee for Alabama had participated with the NAACP in organizing Negro voter registration drives and publicizing unfair franchise practices. The Committee's chairman, Aubrey Williams, as Roosevelt's National Youth Administrator, had advocated economic assistance to the South's poor irrespective of race. Williams interpreted the Boswell amendment as a scheme to deny the suffrage to qualified Negroes. These groups were joined by the interracial CIO, which was embarking on a postwar operation to unionize workers in Dixie. The CIO found it "unthinkable that a foreigner comes to Alabama and after a few years can vote while hundreds of Negroes who are substantial and well-respected citizens are denied the franchise." This coalition received political direction from the 1946 gubernatorial candidate James E. Folsom. A self-styled Jacksonian Democrat with unbounded faith in majority rule and a practitioner of Aubrey Williams's brand of New Dealism, "Big Jim" decried the malicious denial of the Negroes' right to vote.[14]

In contrast, some white critics of the Boswell proposal were not known as sympathetic to Negro rights. Richard T. Rives, a Montgomery lawyer, had defended a board of registrars against a Negro's charge of discrimination. Although favoring a "gradual registration of qualified Negroes," he recommended a more stringent literary test, impartially administered to prevent mass black voting. While Senator Lister Hill, a loyal New Dealer and friend of the working man, spoke out against the Boswell plan, he had initially castigated the Supreme Court for freeing the Democratic primary from racial restrictions.[15]

Progressive politics linked these dissenters. Inheritors of the populist-progressive tradition and firm proponents of the New Deal, they did battle with the wing of the Democratic Party representing the big planters and "big mule," Birmingham industrialists. The white liberals feared that the Boswell amendment might disfranchise "those whom the Big

Mules do not approve." Richard Rives suspected the sincerity of those trumpeting ratification as a means of preserving white supremacy, since under the old system Negroes could enroll less than 1 percent of the total registrants. Instead, most of the reformers worried that registrars serving the conservative political machine would use their arbitrary power to discriminate against working people and poor farmers. The CIO's Political Action Committee vigorously campaigned for Folsom, and the predominantly white Alabama Farmers Union spoke out against Boswellianism.[16]

The amendment's supporters cast the issue as a racial struggle. Mostly leaders of the state Democratic organization, they were becoming increasingly alienated from the national party. These ardent foes of racial equality were deeply suspicious that the Roosevelt-Truman liberals had grown too cozy with Negroes and labor unions. Given this perception, the Boswellians believed that strong measures were necessary to perpetuate Alabama Democracy as the last bastion of white supremacy and economic privilege.[17] The Macon *Times-Standard* recognized the amendment as a "legal ruse," but considered it "the only means short of intimidation and violence by which the people of the Black-Belt can preserve the political and social conditions which have enabled the white man and the Negro to work and live in peace." Reconstruction days were conjured up by the party organ *Alabama Democrat,* which admonished that blacks would "TAKE OVER IF THE AMENDMENT LOSES. VOTE WHITE, VOTE RIGHT—VOTE FOR THE AMENDMENT." Making no excuses for his compulsion to maintain racial inequality. Horace C. Wilkinson, a former president of the Alabama Bar Association, urged the amendment's adoption because "no Negro is good enough, and no Negro will ever be good enough to participate in making the laws under which the white people in Alabama have to live." [18]

Unlike the Democratic solons that had given the Boswell plan nearly unanimous approval, the voters narrowly ratified it. On November 5, 1946, 53.7 percent of those going to the polls subscribed to franchise limits. The margin of victory pri-

marily came from the counties with a heavy concentration of
Negro population and the wealthier portions of Birmingham.
In opposition, Negroes, farmers from areas with fewer blacks,
and urban workers disapproved of the scheme. However, the
campaign appeals to white supremacy had brought results,
since nineteen counties with no real chance of Negro domination supported the amendment, as did many of the rank-and-
file of the labor unions.[19]

Some boards wasted little time taking advantage of their
newly legitimized power. Since most Negroes long ago had
ceased voting in the black belt, the cities provided the main
arena for suffrage restriction. The Jefferson County Board of
Registrars further whittled down the potential black electorate
in Birmingham by asking such questions as, "What is meant by
the veto power of the UN?," "How are members of the Cabinet elected?," "What is meant by the pocket veto?," and "How
many Associate Justices are on the Supreme Court?" These
enrollment officers, none of whom had completed high
school, alone determined the correct explanations; consequently, they succeeded in failing Negro college graduates
and decorated war veterans eager to register. When the Board
did turn away whites, it reflected an antilabor bias. One survey
showed that "men in overalls and working clothes have been
more extensively questioned by the Board than were those
whose appearance indicated they were professionals and businessmen." [20]

Once the Boswell amendment went into effect, Negro
groups took the lead in its overthrow. For several years the
NAACP had been planning to initiate legal action against registrars in Birmingham and Mobile for unfairly administering
literacy tests. With the amendment sheltering the clerk's customary abuses under state law, the association had clearer
grounds to invoke the protection of the Fifteenth Amendment. Consequently, its Alabama Conference of Branches
sponsored "Operation Suffrage" to raise funds for a test case.
However, in their efforts, Negroes missed the full cooperation
of organized labor. The usually sympathetic CIO refrained

from participating in this litigation, perhaps in recognition of the bitter divisions that the race issue produced among its members.[21]

In November 1946, immediately following ratification, the NAACP's lawyers formulated their plans for a judicial attack. To check the possibility of other states' copying Alabama's amendment, they concentrated on proving the statute inherently unconstitutional. The attorneys had to convince the courts that independent of any clerical maladministration, the vague standards established by such a law should invalidate it under the Fourteenth and Fifteenth Amendments. In developing this point, chief counsel Thurgood Marshall had to persuade the judiciary to answer negatively, "Can a state delegate to individuals the right to pass upon the right to vote without placing in the statute itself understandable limitations?" After studying the problem for more than a year, the association decided to broaden the assault on Boswellianism. In April 1948 its counsel challenged not only the statute's absence of definite standards but also the clerk's discriminatory application of the explanation clause to Negroes.[22]

While the NAACP prepared the case in conjunction with Arthur Shores, a lawyer for its Birmingham branch, an independent Negro group in Mobile had filed suit in March. The Voters and Veterans Association (VVA) functioned as an agency to encourage Negro registration and to make endorsements of approved candidates. It undertook a separate challenge, in part, because of conflict with the local NAACP chapter. Reminiscent of the controversy surrounding the handling of the Texas white primary cases, this dispute revolved around a struggle for leadership in the Negro community. The VVA, which included individual members of the NAACP, wanted Mobileans to rally under its banner. However, the NAACP branch could not lend any financial assistance, because it had to support the national office's case in Birmingham. The VVA's president, J. J. Thomas, did not fully appreciate this obligation, and he reminded officials of the rival organization that they should contribute to his group's suit, "because you've got to live in Mobile." [23] In contrast, the local NAACP leaders doubted the ability of the VVA to win its case. John LeFlore, Secretary of the Mobile branch, remembering the disastrous outcome in *Grovey v. Townsend,* decried the "reckless abandon of 'so-called' independent groups assuming the responsibility of an organization like the NAACP which, with its trained staffs and recognized legal leadership in the field of constitutional law, has done a good job." [24]

Although the two local organizations remained at odds, their attorneys cooperated in pleading the case. The VVA's lawyer, George Leighton, an ACLU attorney from Chicago, welcomed the help of the national association. He recognized the expertise and greater resources at its disposal and accepted the arguments put forth by Thurgood Marshall's staff. For its part, the NAACP continued to pursue the Birmingham case but shared with Leighton the product of its thorough research.[25] As it turned out, the NAACP's unselfishness proved wise, since the federal district court hearing both cases considered the Mobile action first.

The Mobile County Board of Registrars had a history of hindering the Negro franchise. Led by its chairman, Milton Schnell, the clerks used their discretionary power to curb an expanded black electorate. In 1944 the board had disqualified an influential Negro from acting as a voucher because he had previously testified for a large number of his black neighbors. Two years later Schnell charged that a Negro postal worker was engaged in political activity that violated federal regulations. Alarmed by an increasing black registration, the chairman assailed John LeFlore, the NAACP official, for his efforts in promoting suffrage.[26] Thus, the crafty Schnell provided a prime target for the challengers.

During December 1948 the three-man federal district court heard testimony against Alabama's registration procedures, especially as carried out by the Schnell Board. Perhaps the most damaging evidence of racial discrimination came from an unexpected source. One of the Mobile registrars, E. J. Gonzales, frankly admitted that he and his colleagues had treated the two races unequally. He indicated that they had purposely questioned black applicants, but made no similar attempt to discover the level of white understanding. Other witnesses testified that the registrars turned down Negro veterans who could not "satisfactorily" explain constitutional provisions, while at the same time, passed white applicants without having them submit to such a detailed interrogation.[27]

The District Court judges Clarence Mullins, Leon McCord, and John McDuffie did not have to rely solely on this evidence to reach a verdict favorable to the Negro plaintiff. As residents of Alabama, they had first-hand knowledge of the racial motives behind the enactment of the Boswell amendment. Speaking for the trio in *Davis v. Schnell,* Judge Mullins recounted how the State Democratic Committee had led the fight for ratification "to make the Democratic Party in Alabama the White Man's Party." Looking at the history of the plan, the court correctly viewed its creation as a means of avoiding the decision in the Texas white primary case. The judges struck down the law for delegating an arbitrary power to the registrars to pass on the qualification of electors. Mullins reasoned that:

> the words "understand and explain" do not provide a reasonable standard. A simple test may be given one applicant; a long, tedious, complex one to another; one applicant may be examined on one article of the Constitution; another may be called upon to "understand and explain" every article and provision of the entire instrument.[28]

Consequently, the court found, that in violation of the Fifteenth Amendment, the Boswell amendment allowed the Mobile clerks to disfranchise Negroes by applying unequal standards.

At the same time, the court made it clear that it would approve a "uniform, objective, standardized test with proper questions or guides." Such a literacy test framed in this way could give the judiciary "something definite to act upon in ascertaining whether an applicant had been rightfully or arbitrarily and unjustly denied the right of suffrage." In furnishing this gratuitous suggestion, the justices did not sound the "death knell for those who would rely on strict formalism in the law," as one reviewer wrote; instead, they left the way clear for a new attempt to block Negro registration.[29]

This judicial "triumph" turned into a Pyrrhic victory as white supremacists carefully read the court's opinion and invented new measures to thwart enrollment. By 1952 they had succeeded in obtaining ratification of a Voter Qualification Amendment. Designed by J. Miller Bonner, representing the black belt county of Wilcox where no Negroes voted, the new law followed the reasoning of *Davis v. Schnell* and provided for a standardized, written literacy test.[30] Even if administered impartially the questionnaire, prepared by the state's supreme court justices, would prove complex enough to confound the less educated. Although overt racial discrimination continued in some areas, county boards could operate without bias and still keep the black electorate small. Clearly any solution to the problem would have to entail stimulating a desire on the part of Negroes to cast a ballot and educating them as to how to meet the standards.[31]

Had Negroes not faced these formal registration barriers, they still would have found it difficult to vote. Because of their economic subservience, blacks encountered the danger of intimidation, particularly in rural counties. In these areas, as sharecroppers they were dependent on white landlords; as small shopkeepers they owed money to white bankers; and as schoolteachers they acquired and lost employment from white schoolboards.[32] To stifle signs of militancy, leaders of the white community might remind Negroes about the source of their economic well being. In Greenwood, Mississippi, a white insurance agent hinted to his Negro client that unless he refrained from trying to vote, the policy on his automobile would expire unrenewed.[33] For those not convinced in this subtle way, brutal beatings and murders furnished a more potent lesson. However, white supremacists did not always have to resort to actual threats or deeds. Passed on through generations, the pervasive fear of the possible reprisals often sufficed to disfranchise the bulk of black citizens.

While Alabama maneuvered to disqualify Negroes, Mississippi instructed its Dixie neighbors how to combine effectively the discriminatory management of voter-registration procedures with intimidation to maintain white control. As the state containing the highest proportion of blacks, Mississippi had worked long and hard to perfect methods that would keep the Negro submerged. Most whites agreed on the race question. Both the wealthy delta planters and the poor hill farmers, while at odds over economic issues, fought to keep the franchise lily white. Following withdrawal of federal troops in 1877, for two decades the redeemers raised the specter of Negro supremacy in order to crush farmer insurgency, and if that didn't work, they used fraud and violence to block opposition at the polls. Worse still, at the turn of the century, when the rednecks successfully revolted, they had outdone their rivals in shouting "nigger." The career of James K. Vardaman was a case in point. This demagogic showman warned Negroes to shun politics and accept second-class citizenship. He expressed his attitude about the possibility of helping the Negro: "Why squander money on his education when the only effect is to spoil a good field hand and make an insolent cook?" [34] Up against the literacy test, white primary, poll tax, and intimidation, blacks had little alternative to accepting their lot.

Theodore G. Bilbo had also carried the redneck flag through the first four decades of the twentieth century. Whether serving as state legislator, lieutenant governor, governor, or United States senator, "The Man" championed Mississippi's poverty-striken whites. As a progressive, he worked to increase aid to education, build hospitals, and limit lobbying by large corporations. In Washington as a New Dealer, Bilbo supported farm tenancy legislation, old-age pensions, and relief. A Democratic loyalist, he helped halt a Delta-inspired move to commit his state's 1944 presidential electors against Roosevelt. [35]

Haranguing his way to the top, "The Man" directed his reform energies for whites only. Much of his success in surviving the rough and tumble of Magnolia politics came from his exploitation of the race issue. Not the first to join demagoguery with populist appeals, Bilbo had few peers to match the virulence of his anti-Negro tirades. He was an outspoken bigot whose storehouse of invectives was plentiful enough to insult Italians, Catholics, and Jews. Hodding Carter, the Pulitzer Prize editor of the Greenville *Delta-Democrat,* observed:

> There was nothing in the Constitution or its Bill of Rights which reserved the blessings of America for 100 percent Anglo Saxon Protestants. Apparently Senator Bilbo, like other disciples of the cult of the master race, finds this irritating. It must take a great deal of courage to rampage against Italians and Catholics who in this State are in such a small minority, or against Jews whose members here are infinitely small or against Negroes who don't vote or talk back.[36]

Bilbo saw little place in American society for Negroes and indicated that they could never attain equal rights. On the campaign stump in 1940 he affirmed to his fellow Democrats that he would always fight for white supremacy, and objected that:

> These unconscionable maligners have tried to represent to the people that I favor the repeal of the poll tax making it possible for Negroes to participate in governmental affairs. This is the biggest lie that has been uttered against me in this campaign. I want to make it absolutely impossible for the Negro to vote . . . and thus guarantee white supremacy.[37]

To those Bilbo called "negro-lovers" who wanted to destroy the color line by eliminating the tax, he raved, "Go Straight to Hell."[38] Bilbo warned that the ultimate solution to the racial problem required the repatriation of blacks to Africa, for "America cannot be saved from the fate of mongrelism except by the physical separation of the races."[39]

This Mississippi Negrophobe became a vivid symbol of political repression in the South. In a country having recently fought a victorious war against fascism, Bilboism represented for many the "malevolent forces which . . . seek to enthrone Adolf Hitler's lies in this nation at the expense of Thomas Jefferson's great truths, written into the Declaration of Independence." [40] More specifically, this backwoods legislator epitomized a way of life that sanctioned minority rule. Not only blacks kept fearful by a tradition of terrorism but also a majority of apathetic whites acquiesced in exclusion from politics. On the average, a smaller percentage of Mississippians over twenty-one years of age cast their ballots in senatorial elections than did the citizens of any state except Alabama. [41] "The Man" also carried his oligarchic ideas outside of Dixie. In the Senate as chairman of the Committee on the District of Columbia and "Mayor of Washington," Bilbo obstructed attempts to grant the suffrage to the residents, most of them black, of the nation's capital.

In 1946, during his campaign for renomination to the Senate, "The Man" gave a classic lesson on how Bilboism operated. He brazenly counseled the county registrars to use their discretionary powers to prevent Negroes from qualifying to vote. The senator bluntly suggested that if "there is a single man or women serving . . . who cannot think up questions enough to disqualify undesirables then write Bilbo or any good lawyer, and there are a hundred good questions which can be furnished." [42] Lest the registrars feared court action against this type of discriminatory behavior, he confidently asked, "How many registrars do you think can be convicted here in the State of Mississippi?" Getting the message, his listeners would thunder, "None!" As the shouts died down, Bilbo delivered the clincher. Lowering his voice, he hissed, "But you know and I know what's the best way to keep the nigger from voting. You do it the night before the election. I don't have to tell you any more than that. Red-blooded men know what I mean." [43] And with a final wink, Bilbo left his audience cheering.

Apparently the circuit clerks got the message. Serving as registrars in the Magnolia State, they confronted Negro applicants with insurmountable obstacles, some of them illegal. If an individual could not read or write, according to the Mississippi Constitution, he had the alternative of proving that he understood portions of that document when read to him. Yet many registrars disregarded this optional provision and demanded that blacks demonstrate their literacy by answering difficult questions. Some clerks frustrated Negro enrollment by functioning slowly and closing the polling books early; others took a more direct approach by threatening those stubbornly striving to exercise their rights.[44]

Bilbo seemed personally to profit from the electoral chicanery in the primary. The results indicated that the senator's brand of inflammatory remarks had worked to his advantage. In a five-man field, he received a bare 4,000 vote majority, enough to avoid a runoff. Out of 350,000 Mississippi Negroes eligible for registration, 2,500 actually signed up. An impartial enrollment would have enabled black voters to cause another contest. Moreover, the vicious campaign oratory had frightened some Negroes from making an attempt to vote.[45]

However, this time Bilboism did not go unchallenged. The idea that "politics is white folks' business," reinforced by over forty years of black disfranchisement, appeared to be on the decline. Two years before the heated primary, Negroes behind the "Magnolia Curtain" began to develop plans to secure their rights. Designed by the small, urban, middle class, a vehicle for protest emerged within the state. In 1944 T. B. Wilson, the secretary of the Jackson branch of the NAACP, had organized the local chapter of the National Progressive Voters League. Dedicated to interesting black voters in the franchise, this organization had first faced the task of liberating the closed party elections.[46]

While Mississippi politicians refused to accept the ruling in *Smith v. Allwright* as applying to their state, Negroes treated the decision as a second emancipation. By prohibiting the white primary, the court opinion encouraged the Voters League to set up suffrage drives. Wilson explained that prior to the 1946 elections, Negroes "were indifferent, disinterested, but when we worked up this case of registering them and voting them because the Supreme Court decision gave us to understand that we could vote, then they began to go to register." [47]

Perhaps an even greater boost to the demand for full citizenship arose during the aftermath of World War II. The message of the Progressive Voters League appealed to the returning black GI who expected to find a new order. He had fought against "villains [who] talked of master races, of force, of the insignificance of the individual, of the might and power of the state, of the necessity of conquest and slavery," Roy Wilkins pointed out. As the assistant secretary of the NAACP remarked, "These were things . . . that American Negroes, even though 'educated' in Mississippi could understand easily." For the black soldiers who had dodged enemy fire in Europe "bullets or threats of bullets, are not likely to cause them to bow and scrape once they are home." [48]

Although they had served in segregated armed forces, Negroes had whetted their appetite for freedom. Many black soldiers had listened carefully as their chaplains advised them to make use of their suffrage privilege when they became civilians. Moreover, those who went abroad received a first-hand education from newly liberated countries "which did not require poll taxes or registration forms." Returning to the South, these veterans wanted the United States "to give us the same rights." [49]

Once home, the veterans placed a strong emphasis on using the franchise to obtain justice. They reasoned that so long as Negroes could not determine who governed them, they would continue to suffer from unequal treatment.[50] Disfranchisement meant that elected officials could discriminate without having to answer directly to the black community. One discharged soldier from Georgia expressed the sentiment of many Negroes including those going back to Mississippi:

> Now that the war has been won, the most difficult job ahead of us is to win the Peace here at home. "Peace is not the absence of war, but the presence of justice" which may be obtained, first, by your becoming a citizen and registered voter. If you will become a registered voter we may be able to win the Peace.[51]

Inadvertently, Mississippi itself stimulated the desire of black GI's to cast their ballots. Probably not realizing the full impact of its action, the state legislature in 1946 exempted the homewardbound soldiers from having to pay their poll taxes for the previous two years. Of course this also applied to Negro veterans, but the politicos expected the literacy test and the white primary, which the state still considered legal, to deter black enrollment. With this in mind, Bilbo informed his opponents that Negroes had no right to register to vote for the Democratic party primaries and "should not be permitted to do so." Nevertheless, hundreds of black servicemen, with discharge papers in hand, went down to the courthouses to obtain certificates freeing them from liability for the poll-tax assessment. For the Negro it signified the first step over the political threshold.[52]

During the spring and early summer of 1946, Bilboism pushed down the rising aggressiveness of the black veterans. In the eastern Mississippi town of Decatur, Medgar Evers, armed with his service release, looked forward to voting against Bilbo. Since he had managed to register, he listened with interest to the senator's advice to keep Negroes from voting by visiting them the night before. In fact, on election eve a group of whites came to his house and warned Evers's father to restrain his son from voting. Despite the visit from this nocturnal committee, the next day Medgar and four other young veterans showed up at the polling place. However, they never did vote, as some white men brandishing pistols turned them away.[53] Episodes like this repeated throughout the state taught the former GI's that combating their domestic enemy might bring as much danger as they had risked overseas.

Reports about the plight of Mississippi Negroes alarmed civil-rights groups in the North. Already deeply involved with destroying the last vestiges of the white primary, the NAACP realized that Bilboistic tactics could subvert its legal victories. The forces of intimidation had spread to Georgia, where Eugene Talmadge, seeking the gubernatorial nomination, took a page from the Bilbo handbook and warned that "wise Negroes will stay away from the white man's ballot boxes."[54]

As long as this climate of fear prevailed unchecked, few blacks would dare to exercise their franchise privileges. Thus, during the Bilbo campaign the national association carefully collected evidence of racial discrimination.

The NAACP planned to arouse national interest against disfranchisement ruses in the Deep South. To this end, its officials called for a public Senate investigation of Bilbo's campaign with the hope that the upper chamber would reject the Mississippian. Even if the Senate hesitated to take this drastic action, the nation would still have obtained a glimpse at the systematic exclusion of Negroes from southern political life. Consequently, Charles Houston, a member of the group's National Legal Committee, drafted a $75,000 budget to conduct an intensive nationwide public relations campaign, which would show "The Man's" Negrophobia and expose the "basic danger to American democracy if Bilbo is seated." The appropriation proved too steep for the NAACP to allocate, but the organization continued to work quietly through its Jackson office to acquire affidavits documenting the senator-elect's harassing demagoguery.[55]

Bilboism had also attracted the ire of some predominantly white groups in the country. As a senator, the Mississippian had included in his attacks labor unions, radical southerners, and suspected communist "fellow travelers." For instance, he had labeled the "so-called" SCHW "the most insidious and damnable of all these racketeering, communistic organizations."[56] Joined by the CIO, for which he had no less harsh words, the SCHW petitioned for a halt to the violation of constitutional rights in Mississippi.[57] The Civil Rights Congress, tainted as a communist front, took a leading role in rallying leftist opposition against Bilbo. After the 1946 election, one of its attorneys, Emanuel Bloch, who later would defend accused atom spies Julius and Ethel Rosenberg, traveled to Mississippi, where he elicited from Negroes sworn statements attesting to their fear of personal violence if they had voted. In addition, the Civil Rights Congress sponsored a National Committee to Oust Bilbo, chaired by the noted authors Quentin Reynolds and Vincent Sheean, to raise funds and generate publicity for this cause.[58]

Protests by these groups, no matter how well meaning, presented obstacles for a united strategy against unseating Bilbo. The NAACP refused to cooperate with the left-wing Civil Rights Congress. The association believed that the presence of such leadership would gain for the senator sympathy from even those who disapproved of his methods. To prevent this from occurring, Walter White argued that "it is imperative that this [campaign] be done under non-Communist auspices lest there be support for Bilbo as a victim of the 'Reds'." [59]

On the other hand, both organizations, with their national headquarters in New York City, wanted to avoid the charge that outsiders had inspired "contented" Negroes to revolt. Thus, they depended on Mississippi blacks to build up the case. The Civil Rights Congress assisted Percy Greene, editor of the Jackson *Advocate,* in his efforts to persuade Negroes to supply testimony. The black journalist accepted this task because he considered the right to vote his race's most important weapon for full citizenship. The NAACP intended to lessen xenophobic Mississippi criticism by supporting the labors of its Jackson representative, T. B. Wilson. This participation by Greene and Wilson, both leaders of the Mississippi Progressive Voters League, helped soften the impact of the conflict between the two national groups.[60]

Bilbo's foes petitioned the Senate to hear their complaints. Shortly before the July 2nd primary, "The Man's" antagonists had carried their charges to the capital, where Glen Taylor received them. The Idaho Democrat, a New Dealer and a champion of Negro rights, placed these accusations before the Committee on Privileges and Elections. Chaired by Rhode Island Democrat Theodore F. Green, "an all right guy" according to an NAACP official, the committee directed the matter for further investigation to a Special Committee on Campaign Expenditures.[61]

Unfortunately, the membership of this probing body foreshadowed a whitewash of Bilbo. The Democratic majority of this five-man committee came from states that had discriminated against Negro voting rights. Chairman Allen Ellender of Louisiana and Burnet Maybank of South Carolina represented areas that still conducted white primaries despite the Supreme Court's ruling and used arbitrary literacy tests. Ellender, an avowed adherent of white supremacy, claimed that Mississippi could also keep its party contests restricted until the high bench declared otherwise.[62] The court only recently had forced Elmer Thomas's Oklahoma to abandon the Grandfather Clause.[63] There was a distinct possibility that these three senators might exonerate their fellow Democrat and save their party from embarrassment. In contrast, Republicans Styles Bridges of New Hampshire and Bourke Hickenlooper of Iowa came from states with few Negroes and had no stake in black disfranchisement; moreover, they might attract Negroes to the national GOP by publicizing the atrocities committed against their race by the Democrats in the South.[64]

Even a completely neutral inquest faced a difficult problem in evaluating Bilbo's culpability. Negroes alleged that the senator discouraged them from voting, and as a consequence of his harangues, obliging whites had perpetrated violence against qualified blacks. The NAACP acknowledged the handicap of having to connect Bilbo directly with the incidents that had occurred in Mississippi.[65] Proving this link would be more difficult since the other candidates had preached, although not quite as vociferously, against an unbiased suffrage. For example, during the campaign Bilbo's nearest rival, Tom Q. Ellis, had opposed Negro voting because the black man "has not advanced far enough for an intelligent participation in the government of this country." [66] To establish Bilbo's wrongdoing, the committee would have to distinguish between the senator's personal guilt and the system that nurtured him. As a result, field investigators dispatched by the special committee easily substantiated that Bilbo had delivered the inflammatory speeches, but they had trouble measuring the actual effects of his rhetoric, because this was the first effort of the Negro in Mississippi to vote in a primary and hence precedents used in a relative or comparative sense are practically precluded, making it difficult to draw even an approximate line of demarcation between hereditary and traditional fear and what may be termed Bilbo fear.[67]

In November, after sifting through the preliminary reports provided by its staff researchers, the committee agreed to schedule public hearings in Mississippi for early December. Although Ellender could find no confirmation that Bilbo had personally prevented Negroes from voting, he did not block Hickenlooper's motion that the senators travel to Jackson. However, the chairman adopted strict ground rules designed to benefit "The Man." The Louisiana Democrat turned down an NAACP request to serve as counsel for the witnesses, declined to subpoena Negroes to testify, and refused to summon newspaper reporters to verify their stories describing Bilbo's campaign oratory.[68]

Negroes did not allow a belligerent Ellender to deter them, and they voluntarily packed the courtroom to testify before a gallery of friends, enemies, and the national press. With veterans in the lead, they braved the danger of possible retaliation from angry whites resentful of opening their society to the scrutiny of the outside world. Thus, a sympathetic committee investigator had compared the witnesses' plight to that of "a pedestrian in any typical American city or community, attempting to cross the street with a green light and the law in his favor but who, nevertheless is seriously injured or killed in the process." [69] On December 2nd Negroes came from all over the state to shatter the myth of black satisfaction with the system.

For three days black veterans spotlighted their frustrated attempts to either enroll or vote. Proudly wearing his Army Good Conduct Medal, Etoy Fletcher claimed that a group of white men assaulted him after he had tried to register. According to the former soldier, on June 12th he had gone to the office of the Rankin County Circuit Clerk in Brandon, where the official responsible for veterans' affairs cautioned him that "Negroes are not allowed to vote in Rankin County, and if you don't want to get into serious trouble get out of this building and don't mention voting any more." Fletcher took the hint, left the courthouse, and went to wait for a bus. On his way, two carloads of whites pulled alongside, forced him to enter one, and drove him to a wooded area where they took turns flogging him across his legs. Afterward they returned the Negro to town and warned their victim never to try to register again.[70]

Throughout this testimony, Ellender took Bilbo's side as "The Man" hurriedly jotted down questions on slips of paper for the chairman to ask. In this way, the Louisiana senator drew from Fletcher the admission that he had no scars to show for his ordeal, nor could the accuser identify his assailants or the doctor who treated him. Ellender dramatically brought in the attending physician, a chiropodist, who disputed the witness' account by revealing that Fletcher had told him that he was beaten up by Negroes. Exchanging winks, Bilbo smugly watched Ellender assail the ex-GI's credibility.[71]

Another former soldier described how a law-enforcement officer had brutally discouraged him from casting a ballot. Convinced that a veteran's certificate guaranteed his registration, Richard Daniel brought this document to the Gulfport courthouse in order to vote. However, the clerk told Daniel that he was not properly registered, and the Negro left the building. Outside a policeman arrested him and brought the veteran to jail, where he assaulted the prisoner. Later, a judge fined Daniel ten dollars for disorderly conduct and drunkenness.[72]

Again playing the role of defense attorney, Ellender called upon the Gulfport police officer to challenge Daniel's assertions. The sheriff remembered arresting Daniel for drinking and cursing outside the polling station. As for the beating, the policeman admitted "[hitting] him in the mouth a few times," but only after the accused attempted to escape from custody.[73] Nevertheless, despite these contradictory recollections, nobody denied that Fletcher and Daniel had been deprived of the right to register and vote.

More potent but less spectacular Negro testimony detailed racial discrimination by the circuit clerks. The witnesses demonstrated that the misuse of the literacy exam constituted an effective way to ensure disfranchisement. Some registrars asked only Negroes to interpret complicated provisions of the Mississippi Constitution. Leon Dowdy recalled that after he and a few others had answered pages of questions, the clerk for Greenville candidly informed them that "he didn't care which way we answered those questions, it wouldn't come up to his satisfaction . . . that we could quote the Constitution backward, it wouldn't come up to his satisfaction." When asked by Dowdy if everybody had to submit to this test, the official had replied, "No, only the Negro veterans." Managing to pass the examination did not guarantee registration. In Pike County, according to Napoleon Lewis, he successfully named the president's cabinet, described how the chief executive and the governor of Mississippi were elected, and knew who served as county sheriff. But the clerk rejected him for presenting a photocopy of his discharge papers, instead of the original, in order to qualify for the poll-tax exemption. Apparently the official fabricated this rule on the spot.[74]

Perhaps the registrars themselves supplied the most damaging evidence of Bilboism in operation. Emmett Reynolds, the Louisville Circuit Clerk, admitted that he had advised a group of Negroes, "in a nice friendly manner," not to vote in the primary. From Pike County, Sheriff William Moore explained that he had exhorted blacks not to cast their ballots, because "in the Southern states it has always been a white primary, and I just couldn't conceive of the idea of this darkey going up there to vote." The Pike clerk who had rejected Napoleon Lewis's application acknowledged that by asking Negroes additional questions, he did so without legal authority. Wendell Holmes justified his action, since "the registrar is the sole judge as to whether they are qualified or not." Clifford Field of Natchez confirmed that this was not an isolated incident.

The clerk asserted that he employed a double standard for the races; only Negroes had to read and understand the state Constitution.[75] Shocked by the candor of these admissions, Senator Bridges interrupted the testimony to express dismay at the unequal application of the law. As he observed the proceedings for the NAACP, Charles Houston commented that these public servants "were . . . so dumb and vicious they proved the charges rather than refuted them. Sometimes I think Jesus Christ must be ill at ease in Mississippi." [76]

Although these revelations obviously portrayed the injustice of the Mississippi system, Ellender tried to divorce Bilbo from direct responsibility. The Louisianan prodded the registrars into conceding that they would have acted in the same manner without having heard "The Man's" speeches. In fact, a few of the clerks claimed that they were political opponents of the incumbent. Furthermore, the chairman badgered most of the Negro witnesses into agreeing that white people customarily had "resorted to every means necessary" to bar blacks from the franchise and would have done so in 1946 regardless of whether Bilbo had run. However, some complainants steadfastly maintained that the senator's threats had dissuaded them from voting.[77]

The hearings were not complete until Bilbo testified. Throughout the three days, "The Man," apparently confident, frequently jumped out of his seat and exited into the corridors to chat and shake hands with admirers. However, not even he could avoid the strain, and on December 5, when he took the stand the "slight, wizened [Bilbo] looked old and ill." [78] Reading from a prepared statement, he denied all of the charges against him, and attempted to clarify his campaign oratory by now suggesting that he had advocated only "lawful" means to keep Negroes from the polls. He added that blacks had no right to participate in the white, Democratic primary, and anyone explaining this to them on election eve did his duty to avert bloodshed the next day.[79]

Despite this rationalization, Hickenlooper and Bridges still wanted to ascertain whether Bilbo had advocated intimidation.

They placed into the record a transcript of an August "Meet the Press" program, in which a panelist had asked the senator if his advice to see blacks the night before was meant "to intimidate any Negroes who might have differed with your interpretation of the law and to keep them from the polls." At that time, Bilbo had carefully replied, "You call it what you may." Under Hickenlooper's cross-examination, the senator admitted that he had made the statements, but reiterated that he believed that Negroes could not legally participate in the closed primary. However, the final witness refuted Bilbo's interpretation of the law. George Butler, a member of the State Democratic Committee, declared that *Smith v. Allwright* gave Negroes a constitutional right to vote in the Mississippi Democratic primary. This testimony implied that anyone who fostered black exclusion acted illegally.[80]

Once the hearings adjourned, the committee had to decide whether the evidence warranted its recommendation to keep Bilbo out of the Senate. The panel could heed the NAACP's arguments that the senator's speeches "taint[ed] his credentials with fraud and corruption, and disqualified him." The association contended in its brief submitted to the Ellender committee that the upper chamber could invalidate the election, since the candidate had acted in a manner "contrary to sound public policy, harmful to the dignity and honor of the Senate, and dangerous to the perpetuity of free government." The Washington *Post* concurred that "whether it is the system or the Senator himself that kept Negroes from the polls is not of primary importance. Bilbo's guilt in either case is inescapable."[81] Or, the legislators could follow their chairman who found "The Man's" conduct firmly rooted within the white southern tradition.

As expected, Burnet Maybank and Elmer Thomas joined with Ellender in exonerating Bilbo. A defender of white supremacy, the South Carolinian had little trouble supporting the Mississippi senator's right to take his seat. However, the decision for the Oklahoma Democrat was more complicated. Twice he had supported cloture on the antipoll-tax bill, which would have boosted black voting. Thomas received a great amount of pressure from the NAACP, which bragged that Oklahoma's 40,000 Negro electors had furnished the margin of victory in his last election. Nevertheless, the senator signed his name to the majority report. In so doing he placed the blame for the lack of Negro voting mainly on the absence of a Republican organization to channel black discontent. Apparently Thomas failed to recognize that Bilboistic exhortations to white supremacy perpetuated the one-party system, but perhaps this thinking enabled the Oklahoman to remain loyal to his party's senator from Mississippi.[82]

The majority report completely absolved Bilbo from any illegal activity. It attributed the causes of Negro disfranchisement to the white-primary tradition and lethargy. Agreeing with Bilbo that the Texas decision had not invalidated Mississippi's electoral statutes, the senators did not condemn him for upholding what he believed was the law, nor did they find evidence that "The Man's" words had moved the registrars to discriminate against Negroes. The report observed that the senator had only dispensed "friendly advice" and called "slips of the tongue" his occasional failure to use the term "lawful means." Finally, this document shifted the blame for the vituperative campaign from Bilbo to "the unwarranted interference with the internal affairs of the State of Mississippi by outside agitators, seeking not to benefit the Negroes, but merely to further their own selfish political ends." [83]

The Republican committee members drew the opposite conclusions from the testimony. Bridges and Hickenlooper accused Bilbo of deterring Negro voters by having recommended the use of "artifice, deception, fraud and outright refusal," to the registration clerks as "plainly as the English language is able to convey ideas from one person to another." The two Republicans were aware of the white-primary tradition in the South; however, they resolved that "the ordinary type of Southern campaign oratory does not include the impertinent, illegal, and indiscreet" type of speech consistently employed by Senator Bilbo.[84]

This partisan lineup of the investigatory group generally previewed the division in the Senate. The Republicans intended to stop Bilbo at the door and then have sworn in the newly elected members who would give them a majority in the Eightieth Congress. After organizing the chamber, they would fix a date to discuss the senator-elect's permanent exclusion. Not only did the Republicans find the Mississippi senator's behavior reprehensible, but by identifying the GOP with banishing Bilbo they could play up the racist influence within the Democratic party and invite Negroes to rejoin their ranks. This approach obviously did not please Alben Barkley, the Democratic leader, who insisted on seating "The Man" immediately and considering his case later. Bilbo's fate hinged on which procedure was adopted. The Republicans pointed out that the Senate could reject his credentials by a majority vote at the beginning of the session, but once he took the oath the Constitution required the more difficult two-thirds vote for expulsion.[85]

The tense drama unfolded on January 3, 1947. Glen Taylor, who had first brought the Senate's attention to the Bilbo matter, introduced a resolution that blocked the Mississippian from taking his seat until the Committee on Rules and Administration conducted further hearings on the dispute. John Overton of Louisiana countered this proporsal by moving to seat Bilbo without delay. Ten Democrats, mostly from the East and far West, rejected party regularity and lined up behind the Republican forces managed by Robert Taft to table these motions. Before another motion against Bilbo could be offered, the southerners led by Ellender launched a filibuster that threatened to leave the Senate unorganized.[86]

After a day and a half of delay, the Senate found a way out of the stalemate. Frantically working behind the scenes, Barkley arranged with Bilbo to step aside voluntarily. "The Man" nccdcd an operation for cancer of the jaw, and his credentials would lie on the table until he recovered his health. At the time this solution appeared inconclusive. The managing editor of the Pittsburgh *Courier* lamented the "sacrifice of moralism on the altar of political procedure. I saw them take the 'easy way' out . . . when the weight of the entire nation demanded positive action." In the end, however, the remedy proved permanent; on August 21st, unable to bear the burden of his fight against the malignancy, "The Man's" heart stopped beating.[87]

Although Bilbo had departed, the system remained intact. The senator's congressional colleague William Colmer aptly pointed this out in a eulogy to his friend, "Even though Senator Bilbo is dead, the principle of the Southern way of life, of which he was a most vocal and persistent advocate, lives on." The Pittsburgh *Courier* recognized that "Bilbo is a symbol of a rotten system of disfranchisement and political terror . . . [and] unless Congress takes steps to end the one party political dictatorship in the South other Bilbos will follow." The selection of John Stennis to replace Bilbo meant that only the inflammatory rhetoric and not the policy had changed. The *Courier* was soon castigating Stennis for defending the tradition of "handling the Negroes of the South in typically Southern fashion." Within their state, Mississippi Negroes continued to meet difficulties in trying to vote. The State Democratic Committee in 1947 required those seeking to vote in the primaries to swear opposition to the proposed federal legislation abolishing the poll tax, punishing lynching, and establishing a fair employment practice commission—something that few black citizens would do in good conscience.[88]

Nevertheless, Negroes benefited from having stood up to Bilboism. The hearings demonstrated the awakening political consciousness, especially of younger blacks. Despite the new obstacles placed in their path by the Mississippi Democrats, nearly 20,000 Negroes had their names entered into the registration books by 1950. The courage of the veterans helped mobilize blacks throughout the South to gain access to the suffrage. Southern white politicians might still justify their racial policy on the basis that Negroes were content with their lot, but the blacks who braved their white neighbors' animosity to appear in Jackson visibly discredited that explanation. In fact, white Mississippians vaguely perceived that their rhetoric was hollow. Anxious about black restlessness and convinced that the nation north of the Potomac frowned on their racial practices, "Magnolia State" officials began to install what James W. Silver has dubbed "the closed society" of repression; otherwise, why shut the curtain across Mississippi if black citizens were happy? [89]

No matter how hard Mississippi tried, however, it could never totally divorce itself from outside influence and exterminate the forces of change from within. Medgar Evers and his comrades persevered despite the brutality, waiting for the day when politics and principle combined in Congress to produce legislation protecting the franchise. Sadly for the blacks who expected political freedom after the white-primary decision, they found instead the familiar surroundings of second-class citizenship. The events since *Smith v. Allwright* in Mississippi, Alabama, and South Carolina demonstrated that, left to their own devices, many southern politicians would go to great lengths to defy the Constitution in order to preserve white supremacy. With this situation in mind, civil-rights advocates realistically argued that Washington alone had the necessary power to enforce the guarantees of the Fourteenth and Fifteenth Amendments. As one discouraged black journalist perceptively wrote shortly after Alabama ratified the Boswell amendment, "Each time the United States Supreme Court outlaws one of these 'Negro stoppers' a new one is invented. It is clear, therefore, that sooner or later the Federal Government will have to step in." [90] In the meantime, President Truman was agonizing over how much effort to devote toward assisting southern blacks to gain their right to vote.

5

The Suffrage Crusade
in the South:
The Early Phase

MAKING THE RIGHT TO VOTE a reality called for innovative techniques. Civil-rights groups expected the federal government to enforce the laws against those who continued to resist an unbiased suffrage, because the legal victories gained by Negroes meant little without a willingness by vigilant officials in Washington to take action against lingering, discriminatory practices. At the same time, suffragists directed their energies toward voter education. They faced the problem of destroying the state of mind, perpetuated by white supremacy, that Negroes should avoid politics. Thus, in the decade after *Smith v. Allwright* reformers called for a dual attack on disfranchisement—political and psychological.

The Department of Justice had the authority to combat interference with the use of the ballot. Title 18, Section 51 of the *United States Code* provided government lawyers with the power to seek indictments against conspiracies by individuals to hinder the exercise of civil rights, while Section 52 allowed the attorneys to bring charges against public officials who wilfully deprived a person of his constitutional privileges. The judiciary had determined which liberties these provisions shielded. In 1884 the Supreme Court had decided that the statutes protected the right of a qualified voter to participate in federal elections and have his ballot fairly counted, free from racial discrimination. Sixty years later, the opinion in *Smith v. Allwright* carried these guarantees to party primaries for both federal and state officials.[1]

Federal prosecutors, however, found difficulty obtaining convictions under these laws because grand juries responsive to local prejudices against minorities often refused to return indictments. Even if a case did go to trial, there was slim chance of getting a verdict against those who interfered with would-be black voters. Federal lawyers were required to demonstrate that the defendant's motive was racial, but even the presentation of conclusive evidence did not guarantee victory. A case in point occurred in 1942 when the Justice Department convinced a South Carolina panel to indict three members of the State Election Board for declining to register a qualified Negro to vote in a presidential election. The jury routinely acquitted the trio, causing one prosecuting attorney to remark:

> The . . . verdict of not guilty . . . under the circumstances [prejudice against the Negro victims] and considering the locale, is not surprising. This case is a perfect example of a situation where the Government succeeds in proving all the allegations of the indictment but in spite of this a jury returns a verdict of not guilty.[2]

Three years later in *Screws v. United States,* the Supreme Court seemed to diminish even further the possibility of gaining favorable results in most civil-rights cases. The case involved the shocking incident of a Georgia sheriff who, abetted by a policeman and a deputy, brutally beat to death a prisoner in his custody. The Justice Department brought Sheriff Claude Screws and his accomplices to trial for violating Section 52 by acting "under color of any law . . . willfully" to deprive an individual of his rights secured by the Constitution. A Baker County jury found the lawmen guilty, and the judge punished each of them with a $1,000 fine and a three-year prison sentence. After the lower federal courts affirmed the convictions, the high tribunal heard the case. Speaking for a five-man majority, Justice William O. Douglas upheld the constitutionality of the statute but severely limited its operation. Known as a staunch defender of civil liberties, Douglas placed great value in the procedural safeguards in the Bill of Rights for those accused of perpetrating crimes. He believed that criminal statutes must clearly spell out standards for determining guilt, and so he interpreted willful action to mean depriving a person of a right "made specific either by express terms of the Constitution or laws of the United States or by decisions interpreting them." Because the trial judge had failed to charge the jury properly concerning the definition of willfulness, the court ordered a new trial. This time the twelve-man panel did not find that the defendants' action met the strict criterion, and the accused went free.[3]

The Justice Department found this Supreme Court ruling a great hindrance in its ability to prosecute suffrage infractions. Turner Smith, Chief of the Civil Rights Section, spoke for the bulk of his colleagues when he observed, "The burden that the Government now has under the general theme of the Screws case in proving the necessary willful intent in such cases is going to continue to build up very high hills to climb."[4] But some legal experts questioned this cautious analysis. Since the high bench had recently determined that voting without racial discrimination in primary elections was definitely a constitutional privilege, the *Screws* decision did not necessarily present an added hardship for enforcement of the criminal statutes.[5] Robert Carr, a Dartmouth College political scientist who studied first-hand the operation of the Civil Rights Section during the 1940s, concluded that "In the final analysis it seems fair to say that the CRS has been unduly cautious in prosecuting election cases, and that a more vigorous policy in this respect would have a wholesome effect in safeguarding the right of suffrage."[6]

Part of the hesitation in undertaking criminal procceedings

stemmed from an ambivalent attitude toward enfranchisement by the leading Civil Rights Section official, Turner Smith, who was responsible for bringing to trial those who blocked Negroes from voting. A long-time resident of Albany, Georgia, Smith apparently had some reservations about extending the Negroes complete access to the ballot box. While he disapproved of ruses to avoid the white primary decision, the CRS chief suggested that there were other methods to thwart a rush to the polls by blacks. Smith predicted that the Supreme Court would declare unconstitutional the repeal by South Carolina of its primary election codes, and he wrote the Selma, Alabama congressman Sam Hobbs, "As reluctant as any of us might be to reach a conclusion like this, I am convinced that this is the way it is and that we ought to face it now and put strong registration laws on the books rather than repeal all of these statutes." [7]

Held back by a policy of restraint, the Department of Justice generally failed to prosecute those who obstructed Negro suffrage. From April 1944 through January 1947 the attorney general received numerous complaints from the NAACP charging intimidation by Mississippi officials to keep Negroes from registering, but the Civil Rights Section did not proceed against the individuals responsible for the coercion. One association staff member bitterly remarked that the department's attitude "does not evidence an over-zealous desire to prosecute persons who violate the right of Negroes to vote throughout the South." [8] Other complaints from Florida and Georgia, revealing assaults on Negroes, the sending of threatening notices by the Ku Klux Klan, and the ordering of blacks away from the polls by armed election officials, did not result in federal action beyond preliminary investigations. [9]

While the Department of Justice was viewing its role narrowly, President Truman contemplated greater involvement for the central government. In June 1946 he had wired the annual NAACP convention his greetings, in which he acknowledged that the "ballot is both a right and a privilege," and pledged that the "right to use it must be protected and its use by everyone must be encouraged." [10] As the black delegates listened to these encouraging words, events in the South dramatically highlighted the need to follow up the president's rhetoric with force. Reports of Bilboistic-inspired terrorism were filtering northward through the Magnolia Curtain, at the same time as white brutality against Negroes mounted in Georgia, Tennessee, and South Carolina. Prodded by a group of black leaders protesting this wave of violence, Truman, who was deeply disturbed by this lawlessness, created a President's Committee on Civil Rights (whose investigation of the poll tax is discussed in chapter 3).

In addition to Truman's humanitarian reasons for setting up the committee, the disastrous defeat of the Democrats at the polls in November made the pro-Negro gesture good political sense for the future. As southern blacks migrated to large urban centers in the North, where the ballot was not restricted, they could affect the outcome of close elections by voting as a bloc. Appealing to this black electorate might be risky because conservative elements of the Democratic party in the South were becoming increasingly disenchanted with their national leaders over racial policy. But the rank-and-file southern Democrats were considered safe bets to remain within the New Deal–Fair Deal coalition. With such calculations added to Truman's genuine concern for the safety of blacks, on December 5th, the day the Bilbo hearings terminated, the president promulgated Executive Order 9808, decried the breakdown of law and order, and promised the participation of the federal government to protect civil liberties. [11]

Lawyers in the Civil Rights Section wanted new laws to battle disfranchisement. On February 27, 1947 Maceo Hubbard, the section's only black attorney, suggested that the committee propose legislation curtailing the arbitrary powers of local registrars. He advocated enactment of a statute nullifying any state regulation "which requires that any act designated as a prerequisite or qualification for voting shall be performed to the satisfaction" of the enrollment officer. [12] Such a ban would eliminate the practices that the Bilbo hearings had exposed and would wipe out subterfuges such as the Boswell amendment. The Civil Rights Section also requested authorization to seek injunctions to check harassments before they occurred and not have to wait to step in until after the crime had taken place and the election was over.[13] This approach appealed to Justice Department officials who found criminal prosecutions frustrating and who welcomed civil remedies as an alternative to dealing with southern juries.[14]

Taking the civil route required a reorganization of the Civil Rights Section. Since its inception in 1939 the section had operated as a unit within the Criminal Division, using the penal codes to punish voting-rights violators. With the shift in orientation, the Civil Rights Section would have to handle an added load of civil cases, a difficult chore for the section, which in 1947 employed only seven lawyers and largely depended on the expertise of the division's criminal-trial attorneys. Under the existing arrangement the Civil Rights Section had a subordinate position within the Department, and it was difficult for its attorneys to wield influence for an all-out enforcement of civil-rights laws. According to Robert Carr, who had been appointed the committee's executive secretary, "Specific recognition of the Civil Rights Section . . . would help a great deal, for that would give the agency and its program a sense of permanence which they now lack." Responsive to this line of thought, the president's committee called for the upgrading of the section into a division.[15]

The committee also urged that the Justice Department utilize civil measures to challenge discrimination. By obtaining an injunction against the biased practices of a recalcitrant registrar before an election, the government could ensure that qualified Negroes cast their ballots. The report, *To Secure These Rights,* stated that "civil remedies should be used wherever possible to test the legality of threatened interferences with the suffrage before voting rights have been lost." If a clerk still managed to keep an individual away from the polls, the presidential panel proposed that the Civil Rights Division respond by filing suit for damages. It was reasoned that a jury would be more likely to award the plaintiff monetary compensation than reach a verdict sending the guilty person to federal prison.[16]

The committeee members placed themselves squarely on the side of those who argued that the federal government was an ally and not an oppressor of civil rights. Libertarians had only recently abandoned their traditional view that the authoritarian state was the main threat to personal freedom. As Jerold Auerbach has described, the La Follette Committee's investigations of unionization during the 1930s showed that the gravest dangers of repression came from localities and private corporations, and had recommended that the national government wield a countervailing power to uphold the Bill of Rights. Moreover, in 1939 Attorney General Frank Murphy had responded to this suggestion by forming within his department a Civil Liberties Unit to prosecute transgressions against the broad range of civil rights.[17] Eight years later, the presidential board welcomed added national assistance, stating, "While it may be impossible to overcome prejudice by law, many of the evil discriminatory practices which are the visible manifestations of prejudice can be brought to an end through proper government controls."[18]

The appeal for federal protection was influenced by foreign-policy considerations. The cold war with the Soviet Union focused attention on race relations inside the United States and spurred anticommunist reformers to remind the nation about living up to its egalitarian preachings. The NAACP's *Crisis* admonished that "only if our system distributes . . . the rewards of democracy to all citizens regardless of race, will it prevent Russia from dominating certain European states and prevent sneers and snickers to our righteous words."[19] During the hearings, Channing Tobias, a black member of the committee and a former YMCA director, observed that President Truman had deplored the absence of free elections in Poland. Pointing out how southern states were trying to circumvent the white primary ruling, Tobias insisted:

We are assuming a great deal if we assume the people of Eastern Europe who are under question now about free elections don't know about South Carolina and Georgia. There was a time or two when Molotoff [*sic*] shocked Mr. Byrnes by referring to those specific instances.[20]

Thus, in its final report the committee pointed out, "An American diplomat cannot argue for free elections in foreign lands without meeting the challenge that in sections of America qualified voters do not have free access to the polls."[21]

President Truman shared the views of his appointees. While the committee was preparing its report, the chief executive vowed earnestly to defend civil rights. On June 29, 1947, addressing NAACP convention delegates from the steps of the Lincoln Memorial, Truman proclaimed, "The National government must take the lead in safeguarding civil rights. We cannot afford to delay action until the most backward community has learned to prize civil liberty and has taken adequate steps to protect the rights of all its citizens." He recognized that such a commitment would strengthen the nation's case for democracy throughout the world. "Putting our house in order," the president calculated, would gain the "support of disparate populations of battle ravaged countries who must be won for the free way of life."[22]

After the release of the report, the Truman administration began fashioning legislation to implement the proposals. For the 1948–1949 legislative sessions, the Justice Department included in its civil rights package a measure allowing the attorney general to seek injunctions against interference with the right to vote and a provision creating a Civil Rights Division supervised by an assistant attorney general. This revitalized agency was expected to take the offense and uncover civil-rights infractions, something that the Civil Rights Section had never done.[23] By 1950, the Senate had buried these measures, and not for six years did legislation embodying Truman's recommendations reach the congressional floor.

Legal sanctions alone were not a sufficient remedy. An eminent black historian, Luther P. Jackson, noted in 1948, "It is not always the barriers to voting which disqualify the colored people, but sometimes the absence of a voting consciousness among them." [24] Southern Negroes first had to break the mental bonds shackled upon them by the racist caste system. "Traditional people everywhere," sociologists have explained, "are characterized by a reverence for the past, a passive acceptance of the present, and a fatalism about the future." [25] Thus, before Negroes could be expected to register and vote in large numbers in the rural and small-town South, it was necessary to convince them that exercising the franchise would improve their lives.

This would not be an easy task, because southern society had robbed Negroes of the crucial will to vote. In an exhaustive study of the Negro and southern politics, Donald R. Matthews and James W. Prothro correctly attributed much of black apathy to the effects of a hostile white environment:

> Their [Negroes] political activity has been discouraged for generations; the benefits they have derived from government have been few. To maintain a personal sense of civic competence would seem difficult when attempts to influence government are doomed to failure.[26]

A black resident of Walton County, Georgia, the scene of several unsolved lynchings after World War II, voiced such a feeling of political helplessness, "There is no need to vote, it won't amount to anything anyway. White folks are running things and will keep on doing so." [27]

Suffrage expansionists had to break this habit of nonvoting by stimulating registration and getting out the electorate to the polling booths. They started voter-education drives to provide citizenship training for those unfamiliar with the political process. These campaigns emphasized the rewards gained from political power and furnished Negroes with the necessary information to pass successfully through the enrollment procedure.[28]

The NAACP, while concentrating its efforts in the courts,

nevertheless spent much time promoting the use of the ballot. After the victory in *Smith v. Allwright,* the association spread the news to Negroes that they could legally participate in the vital southern primaries, and many of its branches established citizenship schools to teach their black pupils how to fill out the registration forms and to answer typical questions that the clerks posed. The national office presented inducements to take up this work. In 1947, the association awarded its Monroe, Louisiana, chapter a $50 prize for conducting a drive that stimulated over 600 Negroes to register in one year.[29] Assistant Secretary Roy Wilkins expressed the importance to blacks in creating these classes, "The issue of civil rights is politics. If we are to win the fight for civil rights we must use our political strength." [30]

As part of its voter project, the NAACP encouraged payment of the poll tax in those states that imposed the duty as an effective barrier to voting. In Virginia, Arkansas, Texas, and Tennessee, where the tax rather than literacy tests effectively operated to disfranchise blacks, the civil-rights organization instructed black citizens how to meet the qualification. In May 1947 the Richmond *Times-Dispatch* reported:

> A Negro man wearing an NAACP badge on his coat lapel was supervising the poll tax payments and registrations of Negroes yesterday. He patrolled the first floor of the City Hall and directed Negroes to the line. As soon as each Negro paid his poll tax, he told him, "Now go to the fourth floor . . . that's where you register." Meanwhile a truck equipped with loud speakers continued to make rounds of all Jackson wards and other Negro residential areas urging them to pay their poll taxes and register.[31]

Negroes formed voter leagues to reach an audience outside of the NAACP's membership. These groups had several advantages over the more established association. They solicited support from various organizations—civic, fraternal, and religious—in the black community, and therefore recruited many individuals beyond the national association's sphere of influence. In 1946 an Atlanta All Citizens Registration Committee was formed, because "previously NAACP registration drives had failed to reach the masses." [32] Within four months, this committee helped bring out 18,000 Negroes to sign up to vote. After touring through the South, a correspondent for a Negro newspaper wrote that in "union halls, church basement rooms, private homes, business establishments, farm groups, and small county associations, men and women are pooling their strength for a new and increasingly important role in the changing political scene of the South." [33] The churches likewise provided a platform from which to broadcast the message of political participation. From the pulpits ministers exhorted their flocks to "go to the polls and vote—or else!" An AME bishop pointed out to a Charleston, South Carolina, congregation that the ballot was the most potent weapon for race advancement, and during the Atlanta registration drives, Reverend Martin Luther King, Sr. preached for the cause of enfranchisement through his sermons. [34]

Although in the past the NAACP had found local black groups to be a nuisance in formulating legal strategy, its branch leaders welcomed the assistance of these independent leagues and helped to create them. The Virginia chapter president, J. M. Tinsley, joined Professor Luther Jackson to coordinate the activities of the state voters league. Alabama attorney Arthur Shores, active in the NAACP's challenge of the Boswell amendment, followed Tinsley's example by organizing the Jefferson County Progressive Democratic Council in Birmingham. At Tuskegee, the civic association's leaders, Dr. Charles Gomillion and William P. Mitchell, formulated registration plans from the NAACP's offices. A member of the National Legal Committee, Austin T. Walden, became known as a top "Negro vote getter" for the Georgia Association of Citizens Democratic Clubs. Harry T. Moore, the national association's coordinator of Florida branches, wore another hat as chairman of the Progressive Voters League. [35]

These franchise organizations served a dual purpose: (a) advancing enrollment and (b) endorsing candidates whom they considered sympathetic to the interests of the black community. Because the NAACP adhered to a strict policy of nonpartisanship (a position that explains the NAACP's ready cooperation with the leagues), many Negroes joined the voter groups, hoping to influence the outcome of political contests. Following the lesson of other ethnic groups, the leagues shaped voting blocs, which provided a balance of power in tight elections. In 1946, black electors of the Fifth Congressional District in Atlanta furnished the margin of victory for Helen Douglas Mankin, a supporter of the liberal, Ellis Arnall. That same year in Augusta, Roy V. Harris, Speaker of the Georgia House of Representatives and an outspoken critic of the white-primary decision, blamed his defeat on the votes given his opponent by newly enfranchised Negroes.[36]

In addition to the black voter leagues, unions attempted to influence the size and direction of the black vote so that registered Negroes would become the political allies of white workingmen. American Federation of Labor and CIO affiliates launched campaigns to get the disfranchised of both races to pay their poll taxes where required, and occasionally, eager labor organizers extended loans to union members to meet the assessment.[37] The unions also made available their facilities to hold citizenship classes. In the two years after *Smith v. Allwright,* leaders of CIO Local 22 at Winston-Salem's R. J. Reynolds Tobacco Company aided 3,000 Negroes to get their names on the polling lists. In 1947, these black North Carolinians helped elect to the Board of Aldermen Kenneth Williams, the first Negro to hold this position since Reconstruction.[38] During the 1948 Texas Democratic primary, the son of A. Willis Robertson, a segregationist Virginia congressman, unhappily reported to his father that he had attended a precinct meeting where "Negroes outnumbering whites almost 3–1 were led by local CIO and AF of L leaders," and this mutual cooperation forced the retreat of the Dixiecrats present.[39]

Racial bias, however, limited the effectiveness of the worker–Negro coalition. While labor officials tried to forge an interracial partnership, the union's rank-and-file often failed to cooperate. A knowledgeable observer of Negro voting in the South, Margaret Price, concluded: "Aside from shedding some of their prejudices, labor union members do not want to turn a single line of employer and community resistance into two lines of resistance, with the second developing because of an alliance with Negro voters." [40] When the CIO decided not to participate in the NAACP's litigation against the Boswell amendment in 1948, Emory Jackson, editor of the black Birmingham *World* and secretary of his city's NAACP chapter, blasted local union leaders for doing "much less than their ability to do on the whole question of Negro registration. The Alabama CIO is giving lip service rather than living action to the question of Negro suffrage." [41] Overt racism emerged in 1950 when a bigoted Alabama local of the International Woodworkers of America elected to terminate its affiliation with the CIO, because the parent body subscribed to a non-segregation policy. [42]

The groups striving to expand the Negro electorate assumed that exercising the franchise would crack the racial caste system. While the Florida Progressive Voters League worried that a "Voteless Citizen is a Voiceless Citizen," the Pittsburgh *Courier* explained, "it is well understood that once Negroes start voting in large numbers . . . the jim crow laws will be endangered and the whole elaborate pattern of segregation threatened and finally destroyed." [43] By 1954 over one million southern blacks, double the number in 1946, had succeeded in registering, and sometimes this recently acquired political power brought the forecasted benefits. Commentators noted during this period more humane behavior by police and the hiring of black patrolmen; the increased construction of health, educational, and recreational facilities; and the paving of streets in the ghettoes. The greater turnout at the polls also had encouraged Negroes to seek political office and resulted in the election of nearly a dozen black candidates to posts as aldermen, county supervisors, and city councilmen. [44] Witnessing this progress, the Arkansas *Gazette* proclaimed:

> The Negro has arrived as a factor in Southern politics . . . aware of the new status he has acquired in a single decade. Nobody can

doubt that it has happened and no politician can seriously believe that the South will ever return to a system of legal and extralegal disfranchisement under which a fourth of its people were denied an effective voice in government.[45]

Nevertheless, the cause for jubilation seemed premature. Other evidence indicated that by 1954 Negroes still had a long way to go before becoming a potent force in southern politics. A survey by the interracial Southern Regional Council (SRC) reported, "For the whole region, registration among Negro citizens of voting age is only about one-half as widespread as among white citizens." [46] Very few of the black office-seekers won, and most of these victories occurred in a few cities of the upper South. Moreover, a surge in black voting produced a white backlash. In 1950, Senate liberals Frank Graham of North Carolina and Claude Pepper of Florida lost in the Democratic primaries to opponents who shouted about the danger to white supremacy posed by heightened black political activity.[47]

Despite the gains made since the demolition of the white primary, Negroes fell short of reaching their registration potential. Although the number of enrolled Negroes quadrupled from 1940 to 1954, some 75–80 percent of black adults still had not qualified for the franchise. In 1952 Walter White had set a goal of two million black registrants for the presidential election of that year; however, the disappointed NAACP secretary counted only one million Negroes eligible to cast their ballots for Eisenhower or Stevenson.[48] The SRC called the five-year upswing in black enrollment before 1952 "particularly disappointing when we consider that the 1947 registration was the fruit of a few months' intensive effort following court decisions. The slight advance made since, under much more favorable conditions, appears puny by contrast." [49]

The voter leagues had skimmed the cream off the top and succeeded with those most receptive to their message. Negroes located in the urban areas of the upper South and the larger cities in the heart of Dixie made up the largest proportion of the augmented black vote. They possessed to a greater extent than did their rural brothers the characteristics necessary to arouse political consciousness, namely, wealth and education. The irrepressible poll-tax foe Virginia Durr commented:

> So far this crusade to get out the vote is confined to the small, upper group of Negroes in the South; that is its weakness. The overwhelming mass of Southern Negroes simply do not have the time, the money, or the knowledge to become voters; but above all they do not see the importance of voting.[50]

Enfranchisement moved at its slowest pace in counties where Negroes outnumbered whites. The higher the percentage of blacks living in a southern community, the more whites feared Negro voting and tried to resist it. In one black-belt county where Negroes constituted 84 percent of the population, a horrified white cotton ginner anticipated the consequences of an unbiased suffrage:

> The niggers would take over the county if they could vote in full numbers. They'd stick together and vote blacks into every office in the county. Why you'd have a nigger judge, nigger sheriff, a nigger tax assessor—think what the black SOB's would do to you![51]

Such sentiments made an impact, for as Mathews and Prothro discovered, "Negro commitment to voting declines as white disapproval of Negro voting increases. Not only are fewer Negroes registered where white attitudes are less permissive, but fewer Negroes express a desire to vote."[52] White hostility had erected a stone wall against Negro registration in twenty-four black-belt counties spread throughout Alabama, Georgia, South Carolina, Louisiana, and Mississippi, where no Negroes were enrolled at the end of 1952.[53]

The socioeconomic structure of most of the South worked against black political participation. Interest in casting a ballot was directly related to education and income, and black-belt Negroes, with little schooling and money, demonstrated the least desire to vote; furthermore, in these rural areas they could not develop leadership because even the tiny group of professionals remained tied to white purse strings. School boards threatened to fire black teachers who exhibited signs of militancy. Aware of these drawbacks, the SRC suggested that the "main problems today must be solved in the community rather than the courts. As more and more Negroes emerge from dependency to self sufficiency, from farm tenancy to economic independence, from poverty to basic well-being, obstacles to the ballot prove less formidable." [54]

But an economic revolution in the South would not completely end disfranchisement, for legal and extralegal barriers remained to retard black registration. In 1951, reviewing the situation in post–Bilbo Mississippi, *Ebony* called the voting outlook "grim," where poll taxes, antagonistic sheriffs, and "understanding" clauses deprived blacks of their vote. [55] The picture was bleak elsewhere. After touring the South a few years later, the Pittsburgh *Courier*'s top political analyst concluded, "What keeps the Negro out of the voting booths are complicated literacy tests required to qualify in registering, the type of officials who give these tests, and the arbitrary power they have to approve applicants who are wanted, and reject those not wanted." [56] Subsequent quantitative studies confirmed these impressions. Matthews and Prothro, keeping other variables constant, found that in states that combined the poll tax with the literacy exams, the actual level of black registration dropped 6.3–14.3 percentage points below the predicted figure. [57]

In some instances, the use of intimidation buttressed these politicoeconomic causes of nonvoting. Having journeyed through the South during 1948–1950, a French newspaperman, Daniel Guerin, communicated back to his countrymen that the "most effective means of prevention of the Negro vote remain threats and terror." On the eve of an election in March 1948 the columnist had witnessed Ku Klux Klan members parading through Wrightsville, Georgia, where the Grand Dragon warned that "blood would flow" if Negroes exercised their voting rights and the next day most of the black registrants stayed away from the polls. [58] On September 8th of that year, two white brothers cautioned Isaac Nixon, a black veteran, not to cast his ballot in a forthcoming Georgia election. The former GI disregarded this advice, voted shortly after dawn, and was murdered before sunset. As he lay dying, Nixon had revealed the names of his assailants to D. V. Carter, the president of the local NAACP branch and a leader in organizing registration campaigns. A few days later a band of whites attacked Carter at his home, fractured his wrist, and forced him to flee to Atlanta for safety. In November, an all-white jury acquitted the two white men charged with Nixon's homicide.[59]

Negroes who actively worked for an expanded black electorate risked serious danger. In June 1950 Alvin Jones, a black college instructor educated in the North, tried to aid a group of Louisiana Negroes to register. At St. Landry Parish Jones was informed by the clerk that "Niggers can't register here," and when the educator declined to accept this explanation, a group of whites brutally beat him and his companions inside the courthouse. Jones later succumbed to his injuries.[60] A Florida black activist met a similar fate. After the white primary decision, Harry T. Moore, the president of the state's Conference of NAACP branches, had formed the Florida Progressive Voters League. This group had contributed greatly in nearly tripling the number of registered Negroes by 1950. In November 1951 the league had secured the appointment of a black deputy sheriff in Brevard County, where Moore lived.[61] The next month, on Christmas Eve, a bomb exploded in Moore's house, killing him and his wife. After an investigation of the tragedy, Walter White revealed that before the assassination three persons had "expressed alarm over the growth of Negro voting strength in Florida. They thought too many Negroes were getting 'funny ideas' like Harry T. Moore." [62] The killers were never brought to trial.

The Supreme Court's landmark *Brown v. Board of Education* decision further applied the brakes to decelerate the pace of Negro registration. The school-desegregation case, according to Donald Strong, a noted political scientist, "has made many Southern whites more sensitive to any action which they regard as Negro assertiveness. The desire to vote in areas where Negroes have not voted before is interpreted as such assertiveness, and some whites may be even more determinedly resistant than before." [63] In his study of the Negro and Florida politics, Hugh Price agreed that the "increasing tension over the segregation issue . . . is strengthening the remaining opposition to Negro registration and voting, especially in rural areas." [64] A student of Justice Department operations, John T. Elliff, has asserted that the Civil Rights Section "did not meet formidable resistance to Negro voting until after" the 1954 opinion.[65]

The rate of black enrollment, however, did not suddenly plummet with the announcement of the ruling by the high bench. In many areas, Negro registration had slowed down after 1947. Where statistics are available, they indicate that in the two years before 1954, the decline continued. Calculations based on the data in Table 1 show that in five of ten southern states the greatest percentage increase in registration took place during 1940–1947, particularly after *Smith v. Allwright*. In Alabama, Florida, Louisiana, Mississippi, and Arkansas the proportion of Negroes qualifying to vote did show a greater rise from 1947 to 1954 than in the previous seven-year period.[66] Yet even in Florida the percentage gains remained about the same in the crucial two years immediately preceding and following the desegregation ruling; in Mississippi the number of registrants remained constant between 1952 and 1956; while in Arkansas, Louisiana, and Virginia Negro enrollment grew more sharply in the two years after 1954 than it had in the period prior to the Court decision.[67] Thus, in the two years after the *Brown* case, many Negroes actually enrolled but progress was very slow.

The rate of enfranchisement was dropping before the *Brown* opinion, in part, because white resistance to black militancy had grown in response to the Supreme Court's authorization of desegregation in state-supported universities. Aware of the court's gradual dismantling of the "separate but equal" doctrine, southern politicians had prepared for the final blow

TABLE 1.   ESTIMATED NUMBER OF NEGROES REGISTERED TO VOTE IN
THE SOUTH, 1940–1956

State	1940	1947	1950	1952	1954	1956
Alabama	2,000	6,000		25,596	49,377	53,366
Arkansas	21,888	37,155		61,413	67,851	75,431
Florida	18,000	49,000	116,145	120,919	128,329	137,535
Georgia	20,000	125,000		144,835		163,389
Louisiana	2,000	10,000		120,000	118,183	152,378
Mississippi	2,000	5,000		20,000	19,367	20,000
North Carolina	35,000	75,000		100,000		135,000
South Carolina	3,000	50,000		80,000		99,890
Tennessee	20,000	80,000		85,000		90,000
Texas	30,000	100,000		181,916		214,000
Virginia	15,000	48,000	65,286	69,326	71,632	82,603
Total	168,888	585,155	181,431	1,009,005	454,729	1,223,592

Sources: Margaret Price, *The Negro and the Ballot in the South* (Atlanta: Southern Regional Council, 1959); T. Cothran and W. Philips, "Expansion of Negro Suffrage in Arkansas," *Journal of Negro Education* XXVI (Summer 1957), 291; Joseph Matt Britain, "Negro Suffrage and Politics in Alabama Since 1870" (unpublished Ph.D. dissertation, Indiana University, 1958); Allan P. Sindler, *Huey Long's Louisiana, State Politics, 1920–1952* (Baltimore: Johns Hopkins University Press, 1956), pp. 256–257; H. D. Price, *The Negro and Southern Politics, A Chapter in Florida History,* p. 33; *Congressional Record,* 85th Congress, 1st Session, p. 8603; *Report of the Estimated Number of Voters in Virginia, State Board of Elections, 1948–1956.*

to white supremacy. Governors James Byrnes of South Carolina, Herman Talmadge of Georgia, and Fielding Wright of Mississippi, all seeing the judicial handwriting on the wall as early as 1950, had vowed that their states would not permit the intermingling of the races in the public schools.[68]

Nevertheless, when the *Brown* timebomb exploded it produced a devastating shockwave throughout the South. The growth of the White Citizens' Councils demonstrated the relationship between hostility toward integration and abridgment of the right to vote. Formed in Sunflower County, Mississippi in July 1954, the councils struggled to thwart desegregation. Their leaders reasoned that discouraging black registration would help impede integration, because not having to make appeals for black ballots, legislators would be free to jump on the white-supremacist bandwagon. Roy Harris, a president of the Citizens' Councils of America, had learned the hard way how Negro voting power could discipline racist politicos. In 1946 Negroes in Augusta, Georgia, balloting for the first time had contributed to Harris' defeat for election to the State House. Years later Harris still raged, "Some people think the nigger is beneath their dignity. They talk Constitution but they look at the nigger question. They talk states rights but they mean nigger. This never will be a dead issue. Some issues never die." [69] Executive secretary of the Mississippi Council, Robert Patterson, sarcastically complained about the results that black enfranchisement would bring, "Why it'd be like giving the vote to these children of mine, you give the vote to my children and you know who they'd elect for President? Elvis Presley!" [70] Behind this exaggeration lurked a fear not of rock idols but of moderates who might gain office with black support.

The councils mobilized the economic resources of whites to curtail black registration. In 1954 the chief architect of this strategy, Mississippi judge Tom Brady, had pointed out the financial risks awaiting Negroes demanding their rights, "Over 95 per cent of the negroes of the South are employed by white men or corporations controlled by white men. A great many negro employees will be discharged and a deplorable situation will arise for the negro." [71] A Mississippi registrar described a variation of this retaliatory plan:

> The Council obtains names of Negroes registered from the circuit court clerks. If those who are working for someone sympathetic to the Councils' views are found objectionable, their employer tells them to take a vacation. Then if the names are purged from the registration books they are told that the vacation is over and they can return to work.[72]

Professionals also suffered. After Dr. Clinton Battle tried to vote in Indianola, Mississippi, white plantation owners warned their sharecroppers against going to the physician. Deprived of patients, Battle was forced to abandon his practice and leave the state.[73]

The Louisiana council took advantage of registration statutes to disfranchise Negroes. Under state law, any two enrolled voters could challenge the qualifications of another registrant. *The Citizens' Council* advised its readers that when a clerk certified "unqualified persons as voters, the Councils in the parish should be informed and should by proper resolutions and delegations call the matter to the attention of the registrar."[74] Consequently, council adherents in thirteen parishes pored over the books and had blacks purged from the rolls for incorrectly filling out the application forms. Many Negroes found themselves disqualified, because they had incorrectly computed their ages in years, months, and days or had erroneously interpreted a section of the state constitution. In Ouachita Parish, 4,000 Negroes had registered by September 1956, but due to segregationist challenges over 3,000 blacks lost their right to vote within the month.[75]

While the councils prided themselves on having attracted a respectable membership, differing from the white-sheeted followers of the Klan, they created an atmosphere that fostered both threats and violence. Black Mississippians who tried to vote faced great peril from white reprisals. In 1953 George Lee, a Baptist minister from Belzoni, and Gus Courts, a shopkeeper from the same town, had become unpopular when they complained to the Justice Department that Humphreys County Sheriff Ike Shelton refused to accept poll-tax payments from Negroes. To avoid a federal indictment, Shelton agreed to collect the tax without bias. However, the forces of disfranchisement reappeared two years later. In March 1955 a delegation of Citizens' Councilors attempted to persuade Courts to strike his name from the registration lists. He refused, and Courts' landlord terminated his lease, which closed down the Negro's grocery store. The following month, in the midst of efforts to sign up black voters, Lee was fatally shot by unidentified assassins.[76] Courts carried on the slain minister's suffrage activities and received a bullet wound for his trouble. The black activist presented bitter testimony about the forms of white intimidation:

> Not only are they killing the colored people who want to vote and be citizens, but they are squeezing them out of business, foreclosing their mortgages, refusing them credit from banks to operate their farms. They either won't vote or leave town.[77]

In the decade after *Smith v. Allwright,* the federal government had partially responded to the pleas of southern blacks seeking the suffrage. Harry Truman had given the cause of enfranchisement a big push, and on this issue he set the pattern that future presidents followed. For the first time in the twentieth century, a chief executive identified the Negroes' battle for equal citizenship rights as a matter for active national concern. His civil rights committee's program—a multifaceted one that challenged both disfranchisement and segregation—would serve as the legislative agenda during the next three administrations. In choosing to fight racism, Truman was swayed by a combination of principle and politics. The violence and degradation that blacks were forced to endure in the South moved him deeply. At the same time, Negroes who had migrated northward during and after World War II were becoming a potent political force. As a conservative reaction set in after the end of the war, it was necessary for Truman to strengthen the crumbling liberal New Deal coalition in order to lead the Democrats to victory in 1948. Thus, the northern Negro vote concentrated in urban centers played a central role in the president's reelection strategy. Furthermore, his foreign policy was connected with freedom at home. In vigorously pursuing the cold war against the Soviet Union and fostering an anticommunist national consensus, the chief executive maintained that racism within the United States provided the Russians with potent propaganda. A favorable civil-rights policy would go a long way toward bolstering our image abroad.

Yet Truman was not without his faults. The president's

rhetoric had a way of outdistancing his firm commitment to action. For example, his statements on the poll tax were contradictory and left his supporters confused. Whether by temperament or design, he often staked out a bold position and quickly retreated. Like Franklin Roosevelt after 1938, Truman usually faced a hostile Congress dominated by a coalition of southern Democrats and conservative Republicans intent on destroying reform legislation. Congressional rules on debate, particularly in the Senate, and seniority in committee assignments strengthened these forces of obstruction. Confronted by the conservative bloc, the chief executive, who had neither the political skill nor popularity of FDR, often walked too careful a line. Although civil rights legislation was important to him, it was not his top priority. Instead, plans to erect cold war defenses and to expand New Deal social welfare programs drew most of his attention. Therefore, to win congressional approval for these measures from the southern wing of his party, Truman sacrificed his civil-rights proposals. In the end, however, this strategy yielded only minimal gains. Congress gave Truman the weapons to fight the cold war, not so much because of the president's deftness as a legislative taskmaster, but because of what it viewed as Soviet aggression in Eastern Europe and the Balkans. And while the increases in social security, minimum wages, and public housing that Congress passed were modest, the president's cherished Fair Deal recommendations on federal aid to education and health insurance went down to defeat.

Because Truman had done more than any of his recent predecessors to respond to Negro demands, he had also lifted black expectations to unprecedented heights. The president's path-breaking executive orders, the volatile international situation, and the strategic location of the northern Negro voter improved the prospects that the United States could be pressed to live up to its promises of racial equality. For blacks there was no turning back, and they would not be satisfied with tokenism. Liberal lawmakers who were sympathetic to black aspirations would have to deliver concrete results or expect little thanks. Charles Houston, the astute former counsel for the NAACP, expressed this tough attitude in February 1946, "The President may do this and he may do that as leader, but if he cannot produce, well, there is no such thing as gratitude in politics." [78]

Voting rights provided a test case of whether the liberals could fulfill black desires. Although the gap between promises and results was closing, there still was a long way to go. Between the two landmark decisions outlawing the white primary in 1944 and school segregation in 1954, the percentage of registered blacks in the South leaped from 5 to 20, from 250,000 to over one million. Nevertheless, for 80 percent of adult southern Negroes submerged under the rigid racial caste system, politics continued to be viewed as "white folks' business," and the future did not appear brighter. In fact, in the months following December 1955 southern extremism grew. As blacks became bolder and launched bus boycotts in Montgomery, Alabama, and Tallahassee, Florida, and Autherine Lucy presented herself for matriculation at the University of Alabama, frantic white southerners sounded the alarm against these challenges to the racial status quo.

By 1955, civil-rights groups had done all that they could to add to the number of registered Negroes. The intensified wave of discrimination in the wake of the Supreme Court's desegregation decision halted substantial access to the polls by blacks. Voter-registration drives could not successfully continue in this hostile climate without federal supervision. The Civil Rights Section, still a stepchild within the Department of Justice, did not have the power to move in advance to enjoin interference with the franchise. Yet during this period, the Truman civil-rights proposals to authorize federal intervention on behalf of black citizens lay on the legislative table.

6

Politics and the Origins of the Civil Rights Act of 1957

FROM 1941 through 1952, the executive and judicial branches had expanded Negro rights. Presidential orders had challenged employment discrimination, dismantled segregation in the armed forces, and established an investigatory committee, while Supreme Court rulings had attacked inequality in voting, housing, and education. In contrast, Congress had thwarted black aims. House-passed antipoll-tax and FEPC bills were interred in the Senate graveyard, a victim of the stranglehold of the filibuster applied by the southerners and their conservative allies. There was no reason to believe that matters would improve when the GOP recaptured the White House in 1952.

The victorious candidate, Dwight D. Eisenhower, had been lukewarm if not hostile to Negro aspirations. As General of the Army he had cautioned against total integration of the military. Indeed, in 1948 he had advised the Senate Armed Services Committee:

The Negro is less well educated than his brother that is white, and if you make a complete amalgamation, what you are going to have is in every company the Negro is going to be relegated to the minor jobs, and he is never going to get his promotion . . . because the competition is too tough.[1]

Originally from Texas and susceptible to the opinions of southern-born field commanders, Eisenhower never grew out of his fondness for the South.[2] "Many of my dearest friends are in that region," he said, "I spent a not inconsiderable part of my life in the South or in border states, and moreover, this question of assuring civil rights of all citizens does not apply exclusively to the Southern states."[3] He was certain that gradualism was the best approach for overcoming bigotry. As he asserted to the Senate Armed Services Committee, "The problem will disappear through education, through mutual respect, and so on. But I do believe that if we attempt to force someone to like someone else, we are just going to get in trouble."[4] Although Eisenhower expressed compassion toward the plight of the Negro, his words sometimes sounded patronizing. The general insisted "that a Negro can improve his social standing and his respect for certain of the standards that we whites observe, as well as we can . . . and I believe he is entitled to the chance to show his own wares."[5]

As a candidate for the presidency in 1952, Eisenhower had scarcely thought about the special problems of the Negro. During his campaign, he had taunted the Democrats over "Communism, Korea, and Corruption," relegating civil rights to a minor issue. In his few speeches on the subject, he expressed hostility to a compulsory, federal FEPC, causing a black Republican to lament, "There is a feeling of complete frustration and indignation [among black party workers] because of apparent lack of interest on the part of the county and state committees in the Negro vote."[6] This assessment proved accurate, and on election day, Negroes in a losing effort delivered 73 percent of their ballots to the Democratic contestant, Adlai Stevenson.[7]

After his landslide victory, Eisenhower did not immediately tap any member of his staff to deal full-time with minority groups, but as various problems arose, Maxwell Rabb eventually began functioning as race advisor. A former assistant to Henry Cabot Lodge, Jr. and an organizer of the "Draft Ike" movement in Massachusetts, he handled racial affairs in addition to his official duties as secretary of the cabinet. This Boston lawyer had no experience in the area of civil rights, but it made no difference to Eisenhower, because, as Rabb recollected, the president

> did not think that there should be a special minorities man as such, designated for that purpose, bearing that title . . . that this was running down other people . . . to feel that they needed special treatment when in effect their ethnic origins were such that they could make a vital contribution to the country and should not be singled out with a caretaker in charge of them.[8]

Eisenhower did appoint a Negro to the White House staff. After serving as Advisor on Business Affairs in the Department of Commerce for two years, in 1955 E. Frederic Morrow, a former executive at the Public Affairs Department of the Columbia Broadcasting Network, was named as White House Counselor for Special Projects. In this capacity he eventually did become involved with civil-rights matters.[9]

Forces outside the White House quickly turned the administration's attention to civil rights. On June 4, 1953 Adam Clayton Powell, the flamboyant Harlem Congressman, publicly charged that Negroes encountered segregation in a number of hospitals, schools, and Navy yards run by the federal government. An inquiry substantiated Powell's allegation, and Sherman Adams, Eisenhower's chief of staff, delegated Maxwell Rabb to inform Secretary of the Navy Robert Anderson of the situation. The president was persuaded to remedy this particular situation and to order the desegregation of installations at Norfolk, Virginia, and Charleston, South Carolina.[10]

The chief executive was sensitive to racial discrimination in the nation's capital. Both the Republican platform and the candidate's pronouncements had explicitly pledged "appropriate action to end segregation in the District of Columbia."[11] As president, Eisenhower conferred with the heads of the major film studios, convincing them to bring pressure on the local theater managers to end Jim Crow seating in Washington movie houses. At the persuasion of the White House, lily-white hotels began accepting black guests and the fire department and other municipal agencies abandoned segregation. The recently reorganized President's Committee on Government Contract Compliance, with Vice-President Richard Nixon in command, prevailed upon the Capitol Transit Company to hire black bus drivers and streetcar operators. The committee also coaxed the Chesapeake and Potomac Telephone Company, serving the District of Columbia, to integrate its business offices.[12]

By the end of 1954 Eisenhower had received recognition for his behind-the-scenes efforts against bigotry. The once critical Adam Powell exuded with all the zeal of a recent convert, "In less than two years in the White House, President Eisenhower, without political trumpeting, has quietly started a revolution which, I firmly believe, means an era of greater promise for Negro citizens."[13] Roy Wilkins praised Eisenhower's "personal leadership where the executive can act."[14] Dismayed southerners, acutely perceptive to even the most minute changes in racial patterns, also attested to the president's accomplishments. An alarmed Senator Burnet Maybank wrote back home to a constituent in South Carolina, "President Eisenhower is doing everything in his power . . . to do away with segregation in all of the Government agencies and in all of the Government housing projects."[15]

Despite these exertions on behalf of the Washington Negro, the president demonstrated an ambivalent approach toward civil rights. Loyal to the principle of state's rights, he acted swiftly only if the national government had clear-cut jurisdiction. Before the *Brown v. Board of Education* decision, Eisenhower issued a decree to integrate schools at southern military bases. After the landmark court opinion, the president encouraged the District of Columbia's Board of Supervisors to make Washington a model for desegregation, but he steadfastly declined to force compliance in the South.[16] "The federal government," Eisenhower explained, "should act only when the states show their inability or their refusal to grapple with the question." [17]

Furthermore, Eisenhower doubted whether legislation could produce equality. "As I have always believed," he remarked in 1956, "we have got to make certain reforms by education. No matter how much law we have, we have a job in education, in getting people to understand what are the issues involved." [18] For him prejudice was a moral problem that had to be solved primarily in the home or in church rather than in the halls of Congress. On one occasion he told the daughter of Booker T. Washington, "I like to feel that where we have to change the hearts of men, we cannot do it by cold lawmaking, but must make these changes by appealing to reason, by prayer, and by constantly working at it through our own efforts." [19] Apparently he did not consider that laws could at least provide immediate relief from discriminatory behavior even if white racial attitudes did not instantly change.[20]

Yet Eisenhower did not strictly apply his own reasoning with respect to the suffrage. Whereas he considered enforcement of school integration in the states beyond his sphere of influence, Eisenhower had indicated that enfranchisement was a proper concern. On September 9, 1952, during a campaign stop at Wheeling, West Virginia, he declared, "We must work for the abolition of restrictions remaining anywhere on the basic American right to vote." Over a month later, the Republican candidate denounced the poll tax as a "blemish upon our American ideal of political equality." [21] In typical campaign fashion he did not elaborate, but it was noteworthy that Eisenhower mentioned the ballot as a proper subject for reform.

The president required constant goading to act on his basically cautious instincts. This task was taken up by the Leadership Conference on Civil Rights (LCCR). Emerging out of the unsuccessful civil-rights mobilization in support of a federal FEPC in the early 1950s, the LCCR coordinated strategy for over fifty national organizations favoring the elimination of discrimination and segregation. In reality, the delegates of a few groups—NAACP, Americans for Democratic Action (ADA), United Automobile Workers (UAW), B'nai B'rith Anti-Defamation League—shouldered the burden of the work. Although their respective constituencies pushed other special issues, conference leaders asserted:

> The fact that more than 50 national organizations of diverse interest and viewpoints were united in a demand for civil rights was in itself of inestimable value in impressing upon legislators and the public generally that the expansion of civil rights was the concern not only of minority groups but of the community at large.[22]

The LCCR carried on the interracial approach utilized by the National Committee to Abolish the Poll Tax, but departed from its spiritual ancestor in several ways. Like the NCAPT, the leadership conference sheltered under its umbrella autonomous associations interested in fighting injustice. However, where the national committee had concentrated exclusively on the poll tax, the LCCR did not give "top priority" to its elimination. Arnold Aronson, secretary of the conference, affirmed, "We all recognize that the poll tax is no longer the major impediment to Negro voting and that the barriers imposed by literacy tests, intimidation . . . are far more significant."[23] Although many former members of the NCAPT joined the new coalition, one of the most prominent remained excluded. To preserve its anticommunist reputation against McCarthyite-inspired charges, the LCCR barred its doors to the Southern Conference Education Fund, a descendant of the "red tainted" SCHW, thereby exiling the core of southern radicals who had provided the leadership against the poll tax.[24]

Yet the LCCR perpetuated the struggle for enfranchisement. Originally its leaders believed that strengthening the Department of Justice would effectively secure the right to vote. At the direction of the conference's steering committee, Will Maslow of the American Jewish Congress prepared a memorandum calling for an overhaul of the federal agency's civil-rights machinery. He suggested tripling the size of the seven-man Civil Rights Section staff and elevating the section into a division supervised by an assistant attorney general. On May 1, 1953 a delegation from the LCCR led by its chairman, Roy Wilkins, discussed Maslow's proposals with Attorney General Herbert Brownell, his Deputy William Rogers, A. B. Caldwell, Chief of the Civil Rights Section, and Maxwell Rabb. In reviving only this recommendation of Truman's Presidential Committee, the civil-rights groups realized that neither the administration nor Congress at the time was receptive to ideas for sweeping legislation.[25]

Over the next year and a half, the liberals learned that executive action would not be enough to achieve political equality. The attorney general did not take any steps to reorganize the puny Civil Rights Section, and the Justice Department often retreated from vigorously enforcing the criminal statutes prohibiting disfranchisement. Since the Civil Rights Section found grand juries uncooperative, the government declined to seek indictments against registrars who thwarted black enrollment. Instead, the United States attorneys worked through local community leaders to induce clerks to end discrimination voluntarily. In a few Louisiana and North Carolina counties this subtle persuasion worked, but elsewhere white resistance proved adamant. In Forrest County, Mississippi, where some officials asked black applicants such questions as, "how many bubbles are in a bar of soap?" the U.S. attorney failed in his attempt to enlist the aid of the Bar Association in convincing the registrars to cease these practices.[26]

During the same period, the Republican-dominated Congress did not offer the reformers much comfort. Only one measure to establish a Commission on Civil Rights received more than fleeting notice. When the Senate convened in January 1953 Republican Everett Dirksen of Illinois introduced a bill to create an investigation committee with the intention of removing "this very knotty problem from constant controversy," and ensuring that "credit [goes] to the Republican Party."[27] Dirksen hoped to shift the spotlight away from Hubert Humphrey, a liberal Democrat from Minnesota who had dropped a similar bill into the hopper. Having played a leading role in strengthening the civil-rights plank in his party's 1948 platform, Humphrey sought to shove "civil rights legislation off dead center and proceed then on a systematic, methodical, informed basis, moving step by step to fulfill what is necessary to build a solid bulwark of civil rights law." [28] In January, 1954, when a Senate Judiciary Subcommittee held hearings on the proposal, protest groups showed little enthusiasm, and the proposal was shelved. Clarence Mitchell, legislative representative for the NAACP, summed up the disappointment with a bill that contained no enforcement powers, "The colored people of the United States are tired of being studied." [29]

By March 1955 the LCCR had begun to reevaluate its program. The conference decided to intensify pressure "on the entire civil rights front . . . and press for enactment of all measures comprising the so-called civil rights package." [30] Thus, the LCCR lined up behind the various Truman-inspired bills reintroduced early in 1955. When legislative leaders refused to convene extensive hearings that year, the chagrined liberals concluded that the Democrats, once again in control of Congress,

> have subordinated the need for civil rights to the pressures of party harmony, while Republicans, seemingly content with the record of executive actions in civil rights taken by the Administration, have shown no inclination to jeopardize their coalition with the Southern Democrats on economic issues.[31]

The liberals assigned the highest priority to the bills designed to protect the suffrage. Civil-rights advocates had consistently appraised the ballot as "the indispensable weapon in the . . . fight for full citizenship." Henry Lee Moon, publicity director for the NAACP, in his provocative book *Balance of Power,* described the vote as "a tool to be used in the ultimate demolition of the whole outmoded structure of Jim Crow." [32] His organization officially maintained that with "federal protection of the right to vote, Negro and white citizens of the

South could handle many of their problems at local and state levels." [33] John Gunther, Washington lobbyist for the ADA, concurred with the statement that he "heard Roy Wilkins make several times, that the real problem in the South is the inability of the Southern Negro to do anything for himself." [34]

The 1954 school-desegregation decision produced the side-effect of making franchise legislation a good focal point. While southerners defended their reluctance to abandon a long and hitherto legal racial custom, they had difficulty justifying disfranchisement, which defied both American tradition and law. Of course the suffrage was regarded as a local matter, and extension of Negro voting rights had already produced white resistance. But as Edward Hollander, ADA national director, discerned, the southern apologists were faced with a dilemma:

> What is at stake here is an acknowledged Constitutional right, which almost all Americans agree to in principle, and which involves none of the subtleties inherent in the argument that segregation is discriminatory. Denial of the franchise to Negroes is clearly discriminatory, and the southern states are supplying abundant evidence of it. [35]

Few politicians sworn to uphold the Constitution could justify a hands-off policy toward the suffrage with the same reasoning offered by Eisenhower when he admonished integrationists:

> Let's never forget . . .[that] from 1896–1954 the school pattern of the South was built up in what they thought was absolute accordance with the law, with the Constitution of the United States, because that's what the decision was, equal but separate thing [sic]. [36]

The bloodshed in Mississippi throughout 1955 underscored the need for federal intervention to secure equal access to the polls. The murders of George Lee and Lamar Smith for their suffrage activities and the verdict acquitting two white men of the slaying of fourteen-year-old Emmett Till proved to the biracial coalition the immediate necessity of safeguarding the suffrage. The UAW Executive Board declared that the trial of the Till case before an all-white jury in "a county where, because of ruthless intimidation and threats of reprisals, not a single Negro vote was cast in the August 1955 . . . primary election—constitutes flagrant violations of the democratic concept." [37] It seemed to Gunther that the "recent violence in Mississippi, along with the elections in that State . . . set the stage for a real drive on civil rights by those of us in the Leadership Conference." [38]

Meetings between civil-rights lobbyists and congressmen confirmed the judgment of rallying around the issue of suffrage expansion. Late in the fall of 1955 Clarence Mitchell discussed proposals for the coming legislative session with sympathetic House members of both parties. Richard Bolling, Democratic Representative from Kansas City and a respected House liberal, suggested that the Negroes must first achieve political power in order to solve their problems. Bolling believed, moreover, that voting legislation "was far less susceptible than school desegregation to inflammatory opposition by racists." [39] Mitchell accepted this argument and urged the NAACP to work for a measure "which would meet the current need to protect the right to vote and to protect individuals against violence." [40] Fearful that the mounting wave of lawlessness in the South endangered black suffrage, the NAACP placed enfranchisement on top of its 1956 legislative list. [41] In turn, Democrats Bolling and James Roosevelt of California, their black party colleagues Adam Powell and Charles Diggs of Michigan, and Hugh Scott, a Pennsylvania Republican, promised to solicit the cooperation of their respective House leaders in support of a voting bill. [42]

Unknown to the civil-rights proponents, inside and outside Congress, the Justice Department was already drafting remedial legislation. After the killings of George Lee and Emmett Till, in November 1955 Attorney General Herbert Brownell had requested a report on the tumultuous situation in Mississippi. Prepared by Maceo Hubbard, the black Civil Rights Section career lawyer who had helped draft Truman's civil-rights proposals, and submitted by Warren Olney III, head of the Criminal Division, the memorandum revealed that the Mississippi Citizens Council was plotting to thwart black registration by using economic and physical threats. To counter such tactics, Brownell, sometime before the Christmas holidays, sent word to the Civil Rights Section to draw up a bill.[43]

Brownell's desire for new civil-rights laws had emerged slowly. He undoubtedly thought that introducing measures to shield the suffrage was the moral thing to do, as the strife in Mississippi appalled him. Nevertheless, during the three years of Republican control of the White House and two years of Congress, the attorney general had displayed a lack of enthusiasm for additional legislation. As late as September 2, 1955, he told the black National Bar Association that the passage of statutes was not enough, because "in the long run education and persuasion rather than compulsion are the most effective weapons in dealing with this problem at the national level." [44]

Brownell's conversion that winter to a legislative solution resulted as much from his horror at the shocking conditions in Mississippi as from his evaluation of the Republican party's political future. According to Sherman Adams, the chief executive "had more confidence in Brownell's political advice than he had in anyone else's." [45] Eisenhower's serious heart attack in September, 1955, had prompted the attorney general to reappraise the fortunes of the GOP in the next year's elections. Although the president won in 1952 without the support of Negroes, another candidate who was not a popular hero might find it difficult to do so. Brownell, as did most of the president's aides, concluded, "Among Republicans only Eisenhower was sure of victory in November." [46] E. Frederic Morrow, the first black appointee to the White House staff, gravely commented on November 6th, "Now we are faced with the startling fact that he [Eisenhower] may not be a candidate and that any other Republican nominee will have rough going." [47]

In a close contest, the black vote would be crucial. During the preceding three decades over two and a half million Negroes had migrated from the South to settle principally in seven states that cast 197 electoral ballots. Outside of the South the percentage of blacks in the population had leaped, ranging from an increase of 52 percent in the West North Central states to 97 percent along the Pacific Coast. Negroes relocated selectively. They constituted more than 5 percent of the residents in seventy-two of 315 congressional districts outside Dixie. In sixty-one of these areas they held a balance of power in the 1954 races, electing thirty-two Democrats and twenty-nine Republicans. Fourteen of these constituencies sent Democrats to the House with less than a 55 percent share of the vote, while twenty-five picked Republicans by an equally slim margin. To win control of the House in 1956, the GOP had to gain fifteen seats, and a shift of the black vote in the Democratic marginal districts would nearly achieve that majority. Needing a net increase of two seats for Senate domination, the Republicans also looked forward to replacing the Democrats in Missouri and New York, where Negroes wielded a balance of power.[48]

Brownell characteristically attempted to build up support within the potent northern Negro bloc. The attorney general, a familiar figure in New York politics, had come to appreciate the importance of appealing to the black electorate. As chairman of the Republican National Committee in 1948, Brownell had watched Dewey go down to defeat by running poorly in the nonwhite districts of the large northern cities.[49] The attorney general was too shrewd not to learn the lesson of this experience, for as *Time* remarked, "Few would question the fact that as a national political planner and organizer, he [Brownell] is the top man in his party."[50] This mastermind of Eisenhower's first nomination once had boasted, "For me politics is winning elections . . . ," and in 1956, race relations and politics had become intertwined.[51]

With the president convalescing, Brownell had to persuade the decisionmaking cabinet to give the go-ahead on civil rights. Although Eisenhower's predominantly conservative advisors were hesitant, the attorney general found an ally in

Maxwell Rabb. Distressed by a recent Gallup Poll that showed Negroes still identifying with the Democrats, the cabinet secretary feared that many administration counselors would write off the black vote. Rabb guessed that the failure to convert the Negro despite the president's executive actions resulted because "we have been . . tender in soft pedalling our accomplishments. Perhaps it is time to give some serious thought to our problem." [52] In late November he had grown increasingly disturbed when Fred Morrow warned of an impending "dangerous racial conflagration in the South," and confided that northern Negroes with their kinfolk below the Mason-Dixon Line expected a White House statement indicating "the Administration is aware and condemns with vigor any kind of racist activity in the United States." [53] On Decmber 2nd Rabb heard Brownell tell the Cabinet that there were "moves organized to prevent Negro voting and to bring economic pressures." [54] He responded to the attorney general's account by convincing the president to touch upon civil rights in his upcoming State of the Union address.[55]

Eisenhower based his message on the information he received from his race advisor. On January 5, 1956 he communicated to Congress "that in some localities allegations persist that Negro citizens are being deprived of their right to vote and are likewise being subjected to unwarranted economic pressure." Consequently, the chief executive recommended that Congress establish a bipartisan commission to examine the substance of these charges "so that it may arrive at findings which can receive early consideration." He catalogued the progress that his administration had made toward assuring racial equality and promised: "We must expand this effort on every front." [56] Thus, the president heralded the shift from the executive to the legislative arena.

In the meantime, the attorney general and his staff were composing a civil-rights program beyond the president's request. The same day Congress heard Eisenhower's suggestion, Brownell consulted with William Rogers, his Executive Assistant John V. Lindsay, the Solicitor General J. Lee Rankin,

Warren Olney, and Civil Rights Section Chief A. B. Caldwell. The Civil Rights Section official thought "that the heart of the whole problem of racial discrimination lies in determined efforts to prevent the Southern Negroes from participating in local government through the use of the vote." Caldwell wanted to combat disfranchisement by securing legislation allowing the attorney general to bring civil suits for preventive relief. He also recommended that the federal district courts take jurisdiction in such cases regardless of whether an individual had "exhausted any administrative or other remedies that may be provided by law." [57]

During the next two months the Justice Department carefully refined its plan. On March 5, Brownell approved a draft that created a Civil Rights Commission (Title I), elevated the Civil Rights Section into a division presided over by an assistant attorney general (Title II), and authorized the attorney general to seek injunctions against violations of civil rights in general (Title III) and voting rights in particular (Title IV).

To obtain White House consent, Brownell stressed the temperate nature of the injunction features. In a memo circulated within the cabinet the attorney general explained the reasonableness of relying on civil procedures. He wrote that the department intended to resort to preventive instead of punitive remedies because:

> criminal prosecutions for civil rights violations when they involve state and local officials as they often do, stir up an immense amount of ill feeling in the community and inevitably tend to cause very bad relations between state and local officials on the one hand and the federal officials responsible for the investigation and prosecution on the other.[58]

Nevertheless, Brownell's attempts at conciliation did not bring over some presidential advisors to his line of thinking. On March 9th he formally presented his four-part program to the cabinet. However, FBI Director J. Edgar Hoover, accompanying the attorney general, delivered a half-hour speech that undermined his superior's cautious analysis. Hoover noted that racial tensions in the South had mounted since the desegregation ruling, blamed much of the strife on communist agitators, and recommended "education, calmness, and understanding" to deal with the complex problem. Several of those in attendance opposed immediate action, their doubts reinforced by the FBI Director's solemn comments. Secretary of Agriculture Ezra Benson suggested "waiting for a Republican Congress to submit the program"; Georgia-born Marion Folsom only accepted the provision for a fact-finding commission, observing that school integration endangered Department of Health, Education, and Welfare (HEW) projects; and disarmament advisor Harold Stassen, who did not believe that Congress would pass the bills, called for the appointment of a special White House assistant for integration.[59]

Despite these criticisms, Brownell's omnibus bill remained intact. At the end of the meeting, Eisenhower:

> approved the Attorney General's sending to the Congress a statement embodying the four-point program subject to (a) a final review by the President and interested members of the cabinet on the language of the proposed statement . . . [and] (b) consultation with the White House Staff with respect to editing, timing, and mode of presentation to the Congress.[60]

Carrying out this directive, representatives of the Justice Department conferred with several presidential aides, and on March 19th Brownell submitted a slightly revised bill to the cabinet for "final review."[61]

The attorney general's design, however, continued to attract objections. On March 20th Republican congressional chiefs counseled the president to limit the administration's offering. Senator William Knowland of California, the Minority Leader, believed "that with the exception of the Assistant Secretary proposal [*sic*] and possibly the exception of the Commission, there is little prospect of securing Civil Rights legislation this session."[62] Moreover, Eisenhower had announced his intention of running for a second term and thus removed the urgency of building a strong civil-rights record on which a possible GOP successor could appeal. When Brownell returned to the Cabinet on March 23rd, his plan received a mixed reception. Worried that the legislation might heighten racial friction, Secretary of Defense Charles Wilson, Secretary of State John Foster Dulles, HEW Secretary Folsom, and Secretary Benson warned against introducing it. In contrast, Director of the Office of Defense Mobilization Arthur Flemming, Secretary of Labor James Mitchell, and United Nations Ambassador Henry Cabot Lodge agreed with Brownell's contention that the president owed Negroes a strong civil-rights program.[63] Unsure, the chief executive asked the attorney general to delay transmitting the measures to Congress.

Within two weeks Eisenhower finally arrived at a decision. As he had told the cabinet, he concluded "that as a result of recent tensions, some of the hard-won advances in recent years toward better relations [in the South] had actually been lost." [64] Consequently, he sought to avoid aggravating the situation by reducing the civil-rights program to the least controversial features—creation of a commission and a Civil Rights Division. The president expected the commission "to provide for helpful discussion and clear understanding of problems." [65] In taking these minimal steps, Eisenhower gave some recognition to the cause of civil rights without angering the white South.

When Brownell turned to Congress, however, he deftly revived his original package. On April 9th he conveyed to Vice President Nixon and House Speaker Sam Rayburn drafts of the White House approved proposals, together with a statement that the legislators also consider empowering the attorney general to pursue preventive relief in civil- and voting-rights cases (Titles III and IV). The next day Brownell positively exceeded the president's orders. Appearing before the House Judiciary Committee, he reiterated the demand for passage of the bills to set up the commission and the division, and added that he personally believed the other two items should be enacted immediately. The sharply attuned Democratic chairman of the committee, Emanuel Celler, interjected,

"You said 'personally.' You speak for the Administration do you not?" Brownell's response made it appear that Eisenhower sponsored all four parts:

> Yes, I think I am authorized to say as the letter in fact points out that these are submitted for the consideration of Congress. If Congress doesn't pass them this session, we certainly want them considered by a Commission.[66]

The attorney general then completed his legislative coup by sending copies of the two withheld sections to New York Representative Kenneth Keating and Senator Everett Dirksen, who introduced them in Congress.[67]

Over the next several months, Eisenhower refrained from endorsing Brownell's total plan. In May, while the attorney general defended the entire omnibus bill before the Senate Judiciary Committee, the president was listing as "necessary for this session" only those parts covering the Civil Rights Commission and Justice Department Division.[68] When Congressman Charles Diggs called the chief executive inquiring what happened "to the important phases of the package," White House assistants Bryce Harlow, in charge of congressional relations, and Maxwell Rabb recommended to the president unequivocal support for all of the measures. Yet on June 7th Eisenhower reiterated that he had sent down the two bills and "the other two I said I thought they [Congressmen] should instantly study and see whether they wanted to put them in legislative form. And I think we are just following the same pattern." [69]

Although the president hesitated in his support of the strong omnibus legislation, other Republicans, with an eye toward the northern black electorate, clamored for its passage. In 1954 Philadelphia Congressman Hugh Scott came to the House by winning 50.6 percent of the vote. This slender victory highlighted the importance for his future of maintaining the backing of the Negroes, who made up 4 percent of his district's population. With this in mind, in January 1956 Scott had written presidential confidant Sherman Adams, "I think I ought to have the opportunity to introduce some key Civil Rights Bills. This seems desirable in the interest of the Administration and for my own Congressional District where I have 22,000 Negro voters." [70] Responding to this plea, the White House permitted him "to take a leading part in handling such legislation." Similarly, Maxwell Rabb saw "the need to get some operating depth into the Administration's Civil Rights program . . . in order to strengthen our political position vis-a-vis the coming election." [71]

At the same time, the civil-rights advocates among the Democrats fretted that the Negroes' allegiance to their party was diminishing. They correctly regarded the southern Democrats as the main liability in retaining the nonwhite vote. Dixie senators had blocked legislation by using or threatening to employ the filibuster, and furthermore, in early 1956, Mississippi racist James Eastland had assumed the chairmanship of the Judiciary Committee, where he bottled up all civil-rights proposals. For good reason Eastland was a prime target of Negroes. Years earlier, as chairman of the Judiciary Subcommittee on Civil Rights, he had boasted how he illegally kept civil-rights legislation from reaching the Senate floor. "You know," he declared, "the law says the committee has got to meet once a week. Why, for three years I was chairman, that committee didn't hold a meeting. I had special pockets put in my pants, and for years I carried those bills around in my pockets everywhere I went and every one of them was defeated." [72] As a result, the pro-Democratic Chicago *Defender* editorialized that a "major realignment of the so-called Negro vote, which in a large measure represents the balance of power, is almost certain, unless the Democrats can free themselves of their Dixiecrat leaders." [73] Charles Diggs estimated that "support among the Negro population for the Democratic party has reached its lowest ebb since before the time of F.D.R." [74] This predicted trend, Richard Bolling recalled, upset Democratic politicians, who were disturbed that the loss of black votes would diminish their party's fortunes. In fact, to counteract the negative effect of the Dixie Democrats on northern black voters, Emanuel Celler counseled a worried Democrat who was running an uphill race for election to the Senate from New York, "[Y]ou could . . . state that I, as Chairman of the House Judiciary Committee, can neutralize anything detrimental to civil rights that Eastland might try to do." [75]

Efforts to get the omnibus bill onto the House floor evidenced the election year jockeying between the parties. With the approaching political contests in mind, Bolling helped delay its course along the committee route. A member of the Rules Committee, he was concerned that when the House recommendations arrived in the Senate, they "would be cut to pieces by a Southern filibuster, and the Democrats would suffer at the polls." He hoped to preclude this possibility and still give liberal congressmen a chance to go on record for civil rights. Bolling convinced the leadership to slow down the movement of the bill so that the House passed it, but the Senate would probably not have sufficient time to deliberate on the measure and thereby expose the rift in the Democratic party. Consequently, the Judiciary Committee did not release H.R. 627—the Brownell package—until May 21st. [76] Complications developed when Rules Committee Chairman Howard Smith of Virginia stalled the program, threatening to prevent any roll call that session. To report the bill out, the committee's five northern Democrats needed the aid of the three Republicans. The White House "spiked the anticipated Democratic defense that the civil rights bill was blocked with [GOP] support" by exerting enough pressure to forge the alliance, and on June 27th the committee granted a rule for H.R. 627. [77]

On July 16th, as the House began formal consideration of the bill, representatives were given the opportunity to offer their views for home consumption. Not more than thirty congressmen stayed on the floor to hear the debate; yet those interested in making more than prepared speeches for the *Record* did discuss the major issues. Martin Dies of Texas confronted Kenneth Keating on the question of whether the president approved all four sections of H.R. 627 or only the two that Brownell had suggested on April 9th. The New Yorker cooly assured his adversary, "President Eisenhower and his Administration favor this bill . . . before us today." [78] The opposition also charged that Title III permitted the attorney general to initiate school-integration suits, an interpretation that Celler and Keating accepted.[79] Furthermore, William Colmer of Mississippi pointed out that the civil-litigation process described in the bill did not entitle an individual in contempt of court to a jury trial. Admitting this allegation, James Roosevelt, a liberal Democrat from California, explained the reformers' rationale, "Criminal proceedings in the field of civil rights have been highly ineffectual. Local sentiment had made jury convictions almost impossible." [80]

Throughout the week, the advocates portrayed the bill as a mild one related mainly to voting rights, while their rivals interpreted the measure as harsh and a threat to individual liberty. Charles Vanik, an Ohio Democrat, summarized the suffragists' argument, "This bill merely establishes Federal protection of the right to vote. The recommendations of the Judiciary Committee are only a moderate step forward. Vast areas of civil rights untouched remain the work of a future Congress." Adam Clayton Powell lamented that the legislation was "too weak. This is not a omnibus civil rights bill, this is a right to vote bill." [81] But most southerners disagreed. They echoed the sentiments delivered in a manifesto signed by eighty-three representatives on July 13th that a "politically minded attorney general could subject the governments of states, counties, towns and localities and the officials and the citizens of same to insults, intimidation, and terror against which there would be no redress" or trial by jury.[82]

The House confrontation produced one significant alteration in the bill and changed one opinion. Martin Dies, who had run the House Committeee on Un-American Activities (HUAC) without much regard for the rights of those investigated, moved to amend the suggested Civil Rights Commission's procedures to include additional safeguards for witnesses. To encumber commission hearings, he introduced the

rules that Emanuel Celler had originally offered for the conduct of HUAC, and the House of Representatives incorporated the Dies amendment without a roll-call vote.[83] Before
the final ballot on July 23rd, William Miller, a conservative upstate New York Republican who had been an original sponsor
of the plan, defected to the opposition because he feared the
bill was a hazard to states' rights. A shocked Minority Leader
Joseph Martin warned other Republicans: "If they follow the
Southern Democracy in the defeat of this bill, they will
seriously regret it," intimating electoral defeat.[84] Martin had
little to worry about as 168 Republicans joined 111 Democrats
to pass H.R. 627, while only twenty-four GOP congressmen
joined 102 Democrats against it.

With a few days left in the session, the House bill died in the
Senate before sectional strife could tear the Democrats apart.
On July 23rd, Lister Hill of Alabama, the temporary presiding
officer, quickly referred H.R. 627 to the Judiciary Committee
where Eastland did not intend to act on it. In fact, the committee had already held up since April a civil rights omnibus bill
reported by Thomas Hennings' Subcommittee on Constitutional Rights.[85] Paul Douglas of Illinois, Herbert Lehman of
New York, and Hennings of Missouri attempted to file a discharge petition in order to free the recently captured H.R.
627, but they ran afoul of the Senate rules allowing such a motion only on a new legislative day. Since July 13th, the Senate
had been recessing rather than adjourning, and Majority
Leader Lyndon Johnson would not change this procedure.[86]
The Texas senator objected to a last-minute debate on civil
rights, because it would block passage of foreign aid and social-security legislation as well as expose the North-South
Democratic party split in an election year.[87] On July 24th
Johnson's colleagues overwhelmingly backed him up, seventy-
six to six, rejecting a motion to adjourn for five minutes so
that Douglas could present the petition.[88]

Once Congress concluded its business on July 26th, the parties directed their attention to the presidential election. No
matter which candidates triumphed, Negroes could expect ef-

forts to guarantee the franchise. The Democratic convention promised its party support for "full rights to vote," and the GOP platform pledged Republicans to work for enactment of the omnibus bill approved by the House.[89] On October 15th the Democratic nominee, Adlai Stevenson, asserted that the job could be done by a resourceful president even without additional legislation. In the waning days of the contest, Eisenhower, who had been reluctant to give the nod to all of Brownell's program, belatedly recommended passage of the four sections.[90]

In 1956, the black vote appeared up for grabs. Increasingly disquieted about civil rights, Negroes had grown restless with the South's grip on the Democratic party. "Up here," Roy Wilkins stated from the offices of the NAACP in New York City,

> Senator Eastland's name is not on the ballot. We did not make him chairman of the Senate Judiciary Committee, where he has life-and-death power over civil rights bills. But up here we can have something to say about the party that made Eastland chairman of a Committee which can choke up. Up here we can strike a blow in defense of our brothers in the South, if necessary by swapping the known devil for the suspected witch.[91]

One black Philadelphian asserted to *The Reporter*, "Negroes won't be going for or against Republicans or Democrats. They'll be voting against the South, against segregation, against the handling of the Till case, and the rest of it." [92] A *Newsweek* survey confirmed that for the first time since 1936, "there is widespread dissatisfaction with the Democratic party among Negroes." [93] Vivid proof for such evaluations came on October 12th, when Adam Powell switched to Eisenhower.[94]

The Republicans did respond indirectly to the grumblings of black dissatisfaction with the Democrats. In the midst of the campaign, the Justice Department designed a strategy to gain for the administration maximum publicity with minimum action. The Civil Rights Section had suggested filing a suit against registration officials in Ouachita Parish, Louisiana, to test whether the attorney general already possessed civil remedies to protect suffrage rights without any new statutory authority. Brownell rejected this quiet approach, which probably would not have made much of an impression on the electorate.[95] Instead, on October 10th Warren Olney reaffirmed the need for the omnibus bill. He informed the Senate Subcommittee on Privileges and Elections that registrars in ten Louisiana parishes were cooperating with the White Citizens' Council to purge the names of qualified blacks from the registration books.[96] This revelation served as good campaign ammunition. Picking up the story, the pro-Eisenhower Pittsburgh *Courier* headlined: "Dixie Democrats Kill Negro Vote," and emphasized that the Eastland Committee detained legislation that could enfranchise blacks in Louisiana.[97]

The election returns indicated that the Republicans had run up some political mileage from the civil-rights issue. Eisenhower did not get a majority of the black ballots, but compared with his showing in 1952, the president increased his vote among Negroes throughout the country. In thirty-five pivotal northern districts where Negroes formed more than 10 percent of the population, the incumbent's share of the vote rose 5 percent over the four years, about double his total point increase nationally. The Republican candidate received a majority of the black vote in ten northern cities, including three he had lost in 1952, namely, Baltimore, Atlantic City, and Columbus. In the South, where the Democratic party clearly represented white supremacy, this GOP upswing was sharper than in the rest of the nation. Eisenhower did particularly well among urban blacks. In a striking reversal from 1952, the majority of black electors in twelve southern cities—Atlanta, Nashville, New Orleans, and Richmond among them—moved their support from the Democratic to the Republican presidential column.[98]

These results brightened the outlook for Negro rights legislation in 1957. The GOP still needed to become identified with an attractive policy to capture the majority of black voters, who had remained faithful to the Democrats. *New York Times* columnist Arthur Krock observed:

The Republican high command was persuaded that the party needed an aggressive position on an issue popular in the country at large to defeat the Democrats in 1958 and 1960. The drive for civil rights legislation was an obvious choice, since the Democrats were split.[99]

Political analyst Samuel Lubell agreed. "Republican leaders will probably choose to appeal to the Negro rather than the South," he wrote shortly after the election.[100] Eisenhower was pleased at his party's growing appeal among black voters. "I enlarged the sizeable vote I had received four years earlier among Negroes of the North and throughout the South," the president later noted.[101] Many northern Democrats hoped to reverse this trend. According to *Time,* the Negro defections convinced them that their party had to "pay more than lip service to civil rights."[102] In this vein, Paul Douglas, who was deeply upset about the strong influence southern politicos had within the Democratic party in Congress, suggested that northern Democrats should emphatically work for a positive civil-rights program. The Illinois senator advocated this strategy, "because equal opportunity is right and just. And the Democratic party . . . must work for this with heart and soul for the good of the country and for its own good."[103]

Compared with Harry Truman, Dwight Eisenhower spoke with a muted voice on civil rights. The Republican president consistently refused to endorse the Supreme Court's desegregation opinion, and he spoke the same language as the southern Democrats when he admonished against federal interference with states' rights and preached gradualism in solving racial problems. Nevertheless, within this framework of restraint, Eisenhower found room to act for the expansion of southern black voting rights. He had no difficulty supporting enfranchisement, because the suffrage was specifically guaranteed in the federal Constitution. Moreover, the president believed that, as Negroes gained access to the polls, they could peacefully relieve some of the racial ills that bothered them. The attainment of their goals would come slowly, but it would give the white South time to accept the demise of its cherished racial customs. These considerations had no appeal for the civil-rights advocates who wanted the administration to assault discrimination along a broad front. Although the liberals never stopped demanding items concerning school integration and equal job opportunity, they wisely concentrated on the voting area endorsed by Eisenhower. In this way, the suffragists might gain an important victory, for when it came to managing legislation President Eisenhower had resources not available to Truman—an enormous personal popularity and influence with conservative Republicans.

7

Politics and the Passage of the Civil Rights Act of 1957

A VARIETY OF FORCES focused the concerns about civil rights onto legislation to protect voting rights. The nature of the statute that emerged was influenced by President Eisenhower's belief that suffrage, rather than school integration, was the legitimate subject for federal lawmaking. The chief executive's philosophy suited a number of key Democratic politicians anxious to preserve party unity. They needed a bill that could pass through southern congressional roadblocks and still meet demands for combating racial bias. A reluctant South might give up a little and for the moment gain a lot; the civil-rights groups would temporarily lose a few key points but would achieve some important goals; only those in the middle would come away completely satisfied, having sacrificed no major principles. Suffrage legislation provided the forum for a classic political compromise.

From the outset of 1957, Eisenhower left no doubt that the administration sanctioned all of the features of the omnibus bill. Meeting with Republican congressional leaders on New Year's Eve, the president urged them to push for the legislation creating the commission and the Civil Rights Division, and enabling the attorney general to secure injunctions against those hindering civil and voting rights. He displayed this new determination a week later in his State of the Union Address. Unlike his message the year before, the chief executive specifically requested that Congress enact these measures.[1]

Eisenhower's goal of enfranchisement particularly pleased the liberals. Roy Wilkins proclaimed, "Protection of the right to vote is the Number One item on the list for Congressional action." [2] Speaking for his fellow civil-rights advocates in the Senate, Hubert Humphrey promised, "We are going to keep battling . . . this year until we succeed. I am convinced we can pass the right to vote bill, which in my mind is the most important piece of civil rights legislation that we have ever proposed or considered." [3] This emphasis on the suffrage coincided with administration thinking. Assistant Attorney General Warren Olney III declared that the "key civil right is the right to vote. Wholesale discrimination against substantial groups in a community cannot exist under our democratic system unless those groups are also deprived of an effective voice at the polls." [4]

Senate proponents tried to open the way for passage of civil-rights legislation by revising Rule XXII dealing with cloture. Section 3 of that Rule posed a severe problem for the reformers, for it stipulated unlimited debate on a motion to change the procedure governing cloture. The liberals hoped to surmount this obstacle by convincing their colleagues that the Senate, not tied to the rules of the past, could write different ones when each new Congress convened. They argued that deliberation on all bills, resolutions, and treaties received a fresh start in each new Congress, at which time the Senate was organized and new committees were formed. According to this reasoning, a simple majority of the upper chamber possessed the authority to adopt a procedure making it easier to shut off debate. However, the Senate traditionally viewed itself as a continuing body, and since two-thirds of its members held over from one Congress to the next, its rules also carried over to subsequent sessions. At any rate, in 1953 the Senate had rejected the reformers' argument.[5]

Once again, the foes of Rule XXII met defeat. On January 8, 1957 Clinton Anderson, a Democrat from New Mexico, offered a motion that the Senate proceed to consider a new set of rules. Majority Leader Lyndon Johnson quickly moved to table it, and the following day, by a vote of fifty-five to thirty-eight, the Senate shelved the Anderson proposal. Twenty-eight Republicans and twenty-seven Democrats lined up behind Johnson, while seventeen Republicans and twenty-one Democrats supported Anderson.[6]

Nevertheless, the rules fight generated optimism regarding the future of civil-rights legislation. The reformers had picked up seventeen allies since 1953, including eleven eastern Republicans who had reversed their earlier positions. Many of them came over after Vice-President Nixon, in his role as presiding officer, advised that new regulations could be selected "under whatever procedures the majority of the Senate approves." [7] At least some alteration in Rule XXII seemed a good possibility. Although Minority Leader William Knowland did not approve of the Anderson motion, he promised to lend his assistance for a cloture revision at a later date.[8]

The increased strength for reform signaled danger warnings for the Dixie obstructionists. The defeated liberals elicited a pledge from Lyndon Johnson that he would call for round-the-clock sessions to break any filibuster on civil rights.[9] At the same time, the astute majority leader warned his southern brethren that once their dilatory tactics failed, the Senate would enact harsher measures than those for safeguarding the ballot.[10] Persuaded that the use of the filibuster presented great risks, the southerners modified their customary strategy. Rather than talk the omnibus bill to death, they intended to weaken it by deleting some sections and attaching crippling amendments to others. They would portray the proposals as going beyond their stated aim and depriving individuals of time-honored liberties.

The opponents utilized the congressional commitees as a forum for their allegations. During open hearings conducted by a House Judiciary Subcommittee in February, several southern witnesses argued that the attorney general had written Title III not to protect civil rights in general, but particularly to force integration of the public schools. Representative Ed Willis of Louisiana was ostensibly shocked that the attorney general would "set up a Federal judiciary to try to run our schools when it is utterly impossible for a Federal Court to run the schools of this country." If Congress granted the Justice Department the authority to obtain injunctions, a former president of the Arkansas Bar Association brooded, "We think the Federal government will destroy the rights of the various States to run their school districts." [11]

The southerners also expressed concern over the treatment an accused civil-rights offender would receive. They claimed that an individual who disobeyed an injunction secured by the government could go to jail without the benefit of a jury trial, because in such cases, a magistrate handled contempt proceedings alone. Alabama Circuit Court Judge George C. Wallace, who would be elected governor in 1960, summarized the complaint:

> In civil rights cases these bills would abolish the most fundamental of civil rights, that of trial by jury in these cases and substituting therefore, the most drastic writs, that of injunctive process. The bills are aimed at Southern juries, that you don't trust them [*sic*].[12]

This latter contention upset the committee. In marking up the bill, one southern member offered an amendment providing for jury trials in criminal contempt cases. Chairman Celler and Kenneth Keating, the ranking Republican, barely beat back this challenge by a seventeen-to-fifteen vote. On April 1st the committee reported H.R. 6127 incorporating the White House proposals.[13]

In the meantime, the administration's companion S. 83 faced tough going in the Senate Judiciary Committee. The southerners used the hearings to demonstrate the "evils" that they suspected were hidden in the Eisenhower program. Sam Ervin, recently appointed by Eastland to the Hennings Subcommittee on Constitutional Rights, sounded the alarm. The North Carolinian, a graduate of Harvard Law School and a respected former judge on his state's Superior Court, preferred that others do the delicate work of political maneuvering, savoring for himself what might be considered the dull explication of constitutional technicalities. Combining a sharp lawyer's mind with the demeanor of a country boy, he interlaced a prodigious recall of judicial precedents with cracker-barrel wit. On February 14th Ervin clashed with Brownell over the motives of the bills' framers. In addition to raising the jury trial issue as those opponents in the House had already done, the senator doggedly questioned Brownell as to whether the bill permitted the president to dispatch troops in order to enforce federal court decrees obtained by the attorney general. Ervin maintained that it did, because the bill was part of an amendment to the Enforcement Acts of 1870 empowering the chief executive to mobilize the armed forces to implement school desegregation in defense of the civil rights protected by the statute.[14]

Ervin's interrogation flustered Brownell. The angry attorney general labeled the senator's claims "irresponsible." "No one has had in mind," he asserted, "any use of the militia in this situation and I don't think that there should be any implication that they do." Furthermore, he insisted that the Justice Department's plan "is a moderate approach, that it only applies in . . . one area, a well-tested and fair legal procedure for the purpose of ensuring the voting rights of the citizens." But Brownell did reveal that with the new remedies he could file suits for injunctions against individuals "seeking to interfere with the school authorities in their attempt to comply with the ruling of the Supreme Court."[15] In drawing out this last admission, Ervin had cleverly laid the basis for later attacks on the purpose and scope of the program.

When the hearings drew to a close on April 5th the southerners delayed the bill in the full committee. Chairman Eastland, up to his usual tricks, prohibited any deliberation until the printer furnished the final transcript of the investigation. After the committee formally took up the bill two weeks later, Eastland intentionally recognized one southerner after another, bypassing Thomas Hennings, who desired to specify an early date for reporting out S. 83. The chairman perpetuated the slowdown by convening meetings only once a week for a few hours at a time and confining discussions to amendments of the bill. The Mississippian claimed he was following "normal legislative procedure, giving civil rights no special treatment." [16] Frustrated by these successful maneuvers Hennings lamented, "Sledding in the Judiciary Committee on civil rights is rough. In fact we are making little or no progress." [17] When the committee did move, it did not help the liberal cause. On June 3rd the group tacked on to the bill a jury-trial amendment offered by Ervin.

Meanwhile in the House, the Rules Committee had trapped H.R. 6127. On April 8th Richard Bolling proposed that the group immediately hold hearings for rapid clearance of the bill, but his motion failed to carry when Republicans Leo Allen of Illinois and Clarence Brown of Ohio joined the four southern Democrats to defeat it, by six to four. The two senior GOP congressmen explained that they had made this decision because of their opposition to placing restrictions on the chairman's power to fix the agenda. Consequently, Howard Smith seized the opportunity to conduct unusually long hearings on the legislation. From May 2nd the committee spent nine working days listening to twenty-four congressmen give their views on H.R. 6127.[18]

As the witnesses paraded before the rules panel, the White House was pressed to help release the bill. Michigan's liberal Democratic Representative John Dingell questioned the president about rumors "circulating that Republicans on the Rules Committee . . . made a deal with opponents of civil rights legislation to kill progress of the bill." [19] An aide conveyed to Dingell the chief executive's doubts concerning the gossip, and on May 15th Eisenhower publicly stood behind his proposal as "a very moderate thing . . . to move in strict accordance with the Supreme Court's decision, and no faster and no further." [20] Unsatisfied with this explanation, the Detroit congressman called upon the president to push "members of his own Party on the House Rules Committee to have them report out the bill." [21] On May 21st, nearly three weeks after the hearings had begun, the administration was relieved when Allen and Brown provided the crucial votes to adopt a rule for H.R. 6127.

The jury-trial issue aired before the various committees threatened enactment of the sections granting the attorney general civil powers. The complicated dispute concerned whether trial by jury extended to persons perpetrating criminal acts in violation of court orders. The emotional attachment to this long-cherished right clouded the legal facts. Prior to 1957, defendants guilty of contempt were not entitled to a jury trial in civil cases originated by the United States. This applied even where a contemptuous act was likewise outlawed by state or federal penal statutes. Therefore, if the entire civil rights package were enacted, an individual who disobeyed a government-obtained court injunction against interference with the suffrage could be sentenced summarily by a judge to jail. It made no difference that under existing civil-rights statutes such an offender committed a crime for which he was entitled to a trial by jury had the Justice Department prosecuted.[22]

Most liberals opposed jury trials in contempt cases, and they viewed the South's belated defense of civil liberties as a means of reducing the effectiveness of the bill's enforcement procedures. Roy Wilkins warned:

> Adding a jury trial provision to the bill would encourage . . . state officials or lawless elements to defy a court's order, because they would count on a jury that would share the community's prejudice against Negro constitutional rights to nullify the court's order by voting to acquit regardless of the clear evidence of guilt.[23]

A number of prominent lawyers backed up Wilkins's analysis. Deans of the Columbia, Yale, Fordham, and Pennsylvania University Law Schools declared:

> While we support trial by jury in its proper sphere, we fear that its unnecessary injection into the legislation will only hamper and

delay the Department of Justice and the Courts in carrying out their constitutional duty to protect voting and other rights of citizens.[24]

The liberals thought that Negroes had a better chance of getting their voting rights protected by federal district judges than by juries in the South. It was true that most of the federal jurists in Dixie were born, raised, and educated at law schools in that region. They shared the segregationist values of the community in which they presided, and as Jack Peltason has pointed out, the judge "must eventually leave his chambers and when he does he attends a Rotary lunch or stops off at the club to drink with men outraged by what they consider judicial tyranny." [25] Yet there were counterpressures operating on the judge which lessened his inclination to read personal biases into the law. He had a duty to follow the opinions of the appellate courts, which ultimately meant the reformist Supreme Court, and his professional reputation was based on how well he performed without having his rulings continually reversed.[26] Thus, the liberals were resigned to resting the fate of their suffrage program on these district judges. Paul Douglas recalled how he had weighed the matter:

> [In] the South, [the judges] were not as prejudicial against Negroes as were the main mass of the population and of jury members. And yet, as a class, the judges were overwhelmingly Southern-born and trained, and were not prejudicial against their fellow white Southerners. A closer, although still imperfect approach to justice would be obtained without—rather than with—a jury trial.[27]

The administration took the same line as the liberals. In April, Assistant Attorney General Olney characterized the jury proposal "as a clever device to nullify the . . . civil rights legislation. If enacted with this amendment the new law would be no more effective than present laws in protecting the constitutional right to vote." [28] At a June 5th news conference, Eisenhower criticized the Senate Judiciary Committee for adding a jury trial amendment to S. 83. The president asserted,

"One thing I have been struck by was Chief Justice Taft's comments on a similar effort; and he stated that if we tried to put a jury trial between a court order and the enforcement of that order, that we are really welcoming anarchy." [29] In similar language Brownell admonished Congress that passage of the amendment would "undermine the authority of the federal courts by seriously weakening their power to enforce their lawful orders." [30]

On June 5th, H.R. 6127 came up for debate in the House, and supporters of a jury trial provision pounced on the bill. They charged that the government was deliberately attempting to destroy a precious liberty. Representative Willis claimed the measure deprived "everyone of the right to trial by jury in civil rights cases by the simple and cynical and ugly device of making the Attorney General the guardian of all personal rights of the people." According to Carl Albert, a Democrat from Oklahoma, "The bill before us is substantially a criminal statute . . . and men will be jailed for the same offenses not upon verdict of a jury, but within the discretion of a federal judge." [31]

These critics were partially correct. The government favored civil remedies, not to eliminate jury trials, but certainly to evade them. This much the liberals admitted. "Juries in at least five states will be composed exclusively of those who are qualified to vote," Emanuel Celler averred, "while those individuals or groups who are denied the vote or who fail to qualify, perhaps by the very action of the defendants, will be denied the right to be on a jury list." Speaking bluntly, Representative Dingell conceded, "Southern juries will not convict a man charged with contempt of court in cases contemplated by this particular piece of legislation. That is the reason we seek to avoid the jury trial here." [32] Nevertheless, the administration professed it was guided by the best of intentions. Brownell insisted that the legislation removed a registrar from the risk of criminal prosecution by giving him the opportunity to comply with a court order issued before an election. [33]

While Congress listened to the discussion of these issues, Negroes were preparing to exert direct pressure for the legislation. In February the Reverend Martin Luther King, Jr., one of the dynamic leaders of the Montgomery Bus Boycott, had presided over a conference of southern black leaders who proposed a "Pilgrimage of Prayer" to Washington, D.C. In preparing for this spiritual demonstration, Dr. King received the assistance of Roy Wilkins and A. Philip Randolph, the organizer of the March on Washington Movement in 1941. They called for "all believers in the God-given concept of the brotherhood of man and in the ideal of equality, to assemble, review the national scene, give thanks for progress to-date, and pray for wiping out the evils that still beset us." [34]

These three men brought somewhat different approaches and backgrounds to the civil-rights struggle. Randolph, the elder statesman at sixty-eight, was a Florida-born socialist who had journeyed up north to organize the Brotherhood of Sleeping Car Porters during the 1920s. Convinced that non-violent civil disobedience furnished the most effective method of mobilizing the black masses and of awakening white Americans to the cruelty of the Jim Crow system, in 1941 he had planned a march on Washington that prompted President Roosevelt to create the Fair Employment Practices Committee (FEPC). Seven years later he threatened to counsel Negro youths to resist the draft, successfully pushing Truman to order the desegregation of the armed forces. Randolph's tactics were termed "militant," but he personally was a gentle man who avidly read the works of Shakespeare. Although Roy Wilkins condoned the Randolph style of confrontation on certain occasions, he still preferred to seek equality mainly through the judiciary, congressional lobbying, and educational campaigns. This fifty-six-year-old head of the NAACP, born in St. Louis and raised in St. Paul, had received a degree in journalism from the University of Minnesota. When Wilkins's NAACP worked for first-class citizenship, it chose a quiet, methodical campaign, not "the kind that picks a fight with the sheriff and gets somebody's head beaten . . . then marches

down to the mayor's office in a protest demonstration."
Through a variety of methods, Wilkins and the NAACP had
breathed new life into the constitutional guarantees provided
in the Fourteenth and Fifteenth Amendments. Absorbing lessons in leadership from both Randolph and Wilkins, Martin
Luther King, Jr. rounded out the trio as its youngest member
and the only one currently living in the South. Born and educated in Atlanta, he had ventured northward to earn a Ph.D.
in theology from Boston University, but he soon returned to
Dixie. In 1955, as the minister of the Dexter Avenue Baptist
Church in Montgomery, Alabama, King had helped coordinate the boycott against the city's segregated bus system.
When it was successfully concluded, the young pastor moved
to Atlanta, where he founded the Southern Christian Leadership Conference (SCLC) to continue the battle against Jim
Crow along several fronts. Like Randolph, Dr. King advocated
passive resistance as the ultimate weapon in combating racial
discrimination, but he also recognized the value of traditional
techniques, including voter-registration drives and litigation.
In this way, Reverend King bridged the gap between the older
reformers and the younger militants who were growing impa-
tient with the traditional ways of challenging racism.[35]

On May 17, 1957, the third anniversary of the Supreme
Court's desegregation decision, approximately 27,000 people
congregated in front of the Lincoln Memorial, where they
heard three hours of speeches decrying violence against Negroes in the South and supporting the pending civil-rights bill.
The importance of the right to vote emerged as the day's key-
note theme. In his best rhetorical style, King thundered the
message:

> Give us the ballot and we will no longer have to worry the Federal
> government about our basic rights.

> Give us the ballot and we will by the power of our vote write the
> law on the . . . statute books of the Southern states and bring
> to an end the dastardly acts of the hooded perpetrators of vio-
> lence.

> Give us the ballot and we will fill our legislative halls with men of goodwill.

> Give us the ballot and we will place judges on the benches of the South who will do justly and have mercy.[36]

After addressing himself to the crowd, King made this appeal directly to the administration. On June 13th the clergyman conferred privately with Vice President Nixon and mapped out a plan for a massive voter-registration campaign. After the meeting, King told reporters, "Across the South we now intend to extend the voting clinics to help Negroes overcome the continued and artificial obstacles to their registration and voting." [37] As the initial step toward this goal, King received Nixon's assurance that the White House would not retreat from its commitment to the civil-rights bill.

On June 18th the House passed H.R. 6127 without a jury-trial requirement, after beating back attempts to insert one. The margin of victory was comfortable and reflected the close cooperation of Democratic liberals and most northern Republicans. On the final tally, the legislators, including ten from the upper South, overwhelmingly approved H.R. 6127.[38]

In the middle of June, the equality legislation looked in good shape, and the administration's statements and actions so far on behalf of the bill pleased the reformers. "Things seem to be popping out all over," an optimistic Roy Wilkins remarked:

> the Heir conferring with the Montgomery Man; the Boss characterizing jury trials in certain cases as likely to produce 'anarchy' that is quoting with his endorsement good safe conservative William Howard Taft (no New Dealer he); the civil rights bill over the jury trial hurdle in the House; strange talk of attempting to by-pass Ole Marse Eastland's Senate Judiciary Committee.[39]

The "strange talk" that Wilkins heard accurately described the liberals' daring plan for delivering the omnibus package onto the Senate floor. Since S. 83 still remained in the clutches of the southern obstructionists on the Judiciary Committee, the Senate civil-rights advocates decided to use a novel procedure to place H.R. 6127 directly on the calendar for consideration. By invoking Rule XIV they could prevent referral of the House bill to the Eastland group if after the second reading a senator objected to sending it to committee. Therefore, the reformers vigilantly guarded the entrance to the Senate chamber, planning to prevent the bill from slipping by them and winding up in the hostile committee.[40]

The liberal strategy succeeded by breaking the southern Democratic–conservative Republican alliance. Minority Leader William Knowland, a spokesman for the GOP right wing, supported the effort to bypass the Judiciary Committee. The California senator often could be counted on to criticize Eisenhower's programs, particularly in foreign affairs, but he was quite willing to rally around the president's civil-rights measures. Backing him up was Vice President Richard Nixon, the presiding officer of the Senate. Both men had been closely identified with the anticommunist crusade rather than the cause of racial equality; however, Knowland intended to run for governor of California in 1958, Nixon eyed the presidency in 1960, and they probably realized that the support of the Negro bloc could help fulfill their ambitions.[41] On June 20th, when H.R. 6127 came up for a second reading, Knowland lodged an objection based on Rule XIV. Richard Russell of Georgia, leader of the southern opposition, raised the point of order that under Rule XXV all bills must go to committee. The vice president disagreed, giving the opinion that Rule XXV merely defined a committee's jurisdiction, but did not mandate a procedure for referral. To be sure, Nixon submitted Russell's point of order, and the Senate rejected it by forty-nine to thirty-six, putting H.R. 6127 on the calendar. The thirty-seven Republicans furnishing the bulk of the support included most of the conservatives who had helped the southerners block civil-rights proposals in the past. Eight Democrats from the far West and a few easterners, agreeing with their majority leader to follow the regular procedure, temporarily replaced the GOP conservatives in the coalition with Dixie.[42]

Having aired the issue of trial by jury, southern senators found another. Although the attorney general and civil-rights proponents had admitted on several occasions that Title III authorized the government to intervene in desegregation suits, Richard Russell "revealed" that the administration had covered up its true intention. Until that moment, the White House had portrayed the bill as a measure intended mainly to protect the franchise. On June 19th, however, the Georgia senator rose on the floor and admonished his unsuspecting colleagues:

> Those who talk about voting are hiding behind a smokescreen in an effort to give the Attorney General vast powers to bring about a certain condition in the Southland. The purpose is to enable the Attorney General of the United States to invade the South and deal with the question of enforcement of the Supreme Court's decision in the school cases.[43]

On July 2nd Russell repeated this accusation and further declared, "I doubt very much whether the full implications of this bill have ever been explained to President Eisenhower."[44]

The chief executive's reaction reinforced Russell's claims. The president reiterated that the objective of his program "was to prevent anybody illegally from interfering with any individual's right to vote, if that individual were qualified under proper laws of his state." Since the Georgia senator had charged that the suffrage legislation concealed "a cunning device to enforce integration of the races in the South," *New York Times* columnist James Reston asked at a July 3rd news conference, "Would the President agree to have the bill rewritten so that it dealt only with the right to vote?" Eisenhower's reply left his audience wondering whether he fully understood the proposal:

> I was reading part of that bill this morning and there were certain phrases I didn't completely understand. So, before I make any more remarks on that, I would want to talk to the Attorney General and see exactly what they do mean.[45]

During the next week, the southerners took advantage of Eisenhower's apparent confusion to depict the dire consequences that would result from passage of the bill. If Congress enacted H.R. 6127, Sam Ervin shrieked that it "would reduce the status of . . . officials in the southern States to a point inferior to that enjoyed by murderers, thieves, counterfeiters, dope peddlers, parties to the Communist conspiracy, and all other persons charged with a crime." [46] Conjuring up memories of a South controlled by federal bayonets, James Eastland grumbled that Title III empowered the chief executive "or his subordinate to move the troops into a locality to enforce" government-secured court orders.[47] Olin Johnston of South Carolina, predicting a violent reaction to the new law, introduced "A Proposal to Provide for Homeward Shipment of Deceased Members and Employees of the President's Civil Rights Commission at Federal Expense." [48]

Disturbed by these harsh comments, Eisenhower attempted to clear up the southerners' misunderstanding of his program. On July 10th the president met with Russell at the White House and vowed that the administration would not use the legislation to punish the South. Although he was shocked by Johnston's admonition that bloodshed would result from passage of the act, the chief executive did not withdraw from the commitment he had made to protect the suffrage. "This was the overriding provision of the bill I wanted set down in law," he informed Russell. "With his right to vote assured, the Negro could use it to help secure his other rights." [49]

The administration's main goal was to guarantee Negro voting rights, and Eisenhower believed that Title IV would achieve that aim. To keep this highly valued provision safely intact, he sacrificed Title III. This was not a difficult choice, because the president typically distinguished between legislation protecting the ballot and enforcing the integration of schools. With respect to carrying out desegregation, Eisenhower maintained as late as June 21, 1957, "I don't believe you can change the hearts of men with laws or decisions." [50]

In contrast, Eisenhower believed that the denial of the franchise clearly violated America's democratic principles, and he desired to safeguard the "right of Negroes to vote on the same basis as all others and to protect them in doing so." Not usually known as an astute politician, in this instance the president realistically gauged the mood of Congress. He was aware that the southern lawmakers could live with a suffrage statute, because many of them told him "privately . . . that in the matter of voting rights they agreed on the justice and need for [his] stand." [51]

President Eisenhower found approval for his policy of stressing the franchise. The *New York Times* editorialized on July 11, "It would in no way prejudice the inexorable forward march of school desegregation in the South to make it clear that this bill deals exclusively with voting rights." [52] That same day, nationally syndicated columnist Walter Lippmann agreed, "It is the duty of the Federal Government to use its legal powers to secure and protect the right to vote. But to promote integration it is its duty to use persuasion in order to win consent. The two objectives—voting and integration—ought not to be lumped together." [53] Even the South understood the logic of the president's decision. "If Part III is stricken," the Tampa *Tribune* declared, "the South can live with the bill. Conversely, what remains in the measure will help protect the Negro's vote right which is what sensible northerners are seeking." The Raleigh (North Carolina) *News and Observer* agreed that the "right to vote unlike the right to attend certain schools is spelled out in the Constitution in so many words and does not depend upon interpretation of the word 'discrimination'." [54] Richard Russell confessed "that the American people generally are opposed to any denial of the right of ballot to any qualified citizen. It is easy to array them in support of a bill represented as confined to this purpose." [55]

The Senate prepared to reach a compromise based on this reasoning. Albert Gore, a Tennessee Democrat, announced he favored "a plan which gave full protection to voting rights, but withheld Federal power to force school integration." [56] After the chamber voted to consider H.R. 6127 on July 16, Clinton Anderson and George Aiken, a Vermont Republican, cosponsored an amendment to delete Title III. This atmosphere of moderation prevailed a few days later, when the Senate unanimously repealed the Reconstruction statute that authorized the president to call out the troops "to aid in the execution of the judicial process." [57]

Eisenhower's deep reservations about legislation encouraging desegregation eventually surfaced into the open. Informed that the Senate had agreed to take up the omnibus bill, the president on July 16th routinely restated his commitment to the four points.[58] However, the following morning at a news conference the chief executive shied away from bestowing an unqualified endorsement on Title III. Rowland Evans, Jr. of the New York *Herald Tribune* asked him, "Are you concerned that it would be a wise expansion of Federal power at this stage to permit the Attorney General to bring suits on his own motion to enforce school integration in the South?" Eisenhower replied:

> Well, no; I have—as a matter of fact, as you state it that way, on his own motion, without any request from local authorities.
>
> I believe we have got to have laws that go along with education and understanding, and I believe if you go beyond that at any one time, you cause trouble rather than benefit.[59]

The distressed civil-rights advocates attempted to show that the president's statement did not mean disapproval of Title III. Senator Jacob Javits, a liberal New York Republican with a strong social conscience out of the mold of Fiorello La Guardia, reinterpreted Eisenhower's comment to signify, "he is not going to have the Attorney General rush in with a pocketful of subpoenas and complaints . . . that he hopes very much that with the backing of affirmative law and force of education and conciliation and desire to comply with the law . . . it will be possible to meet this issue." [60] Attorney General Brownell seconded this opinion in a televised interview with Congressman Keating on July 21, "The Supreme Court decision in the school case left responsibility on local school boards to start the implementation of the decision. There is no thought of changing that at all." [61]

Such last-minute appeals came too late. On July 24th the Senate voted by fifty-two to thirty-eight to remove Title III from the bill. With Eisenhower lukewarm toward the controversial section, eighteen Republicans deserted Minority Leader Knowland and joined the thirty-four Democrats for the Anderson-Aiken Amendment. All GOP senators from throughout the country were divided, and a breakdown of their votes does not show any clear regional pattern. In fact, Republican delegations from New Jersey, Maryland, Nebraska, North Dakota, Iowa, and Utah split their votes. On the opposite side of the aisle, the southern Democrats were aided by lawmakers mainly from the far West.[62]

The president's behavior during the senatorial debates worried the White House advisers on race relations. Negro staff member E. Frederic Morrow complained, "In the last few days the talk of the Administration capitulation to the South has resulted in a complete turnabout in the feeling and attitude by Negro leadership." [63] Maxwell Rabb sadly noted, "Unfortunately, we are being overwhelmed with mail from persons troubled about a lack of firmness in the Administration's position." [64] Distressed by the weakening of the legislation, Val Washington, Director of Minorities for the Republican National Committee, reminded the chief executive, "[Negroes] knew that in you we had a leader who would, when given the opportunity, rectify the flagrant injustices and inequities by which we have been penalized." [65]

Those anxious could relax, because Eisenhower intended to stand firmly behind the remainder of his program. While he had hesitated to foster integration, the president showed enthusiasm for assisting enfranchisement. At the July 17th news conference the chief executive made his thoughts very clear:

I think the voting right is something that should be emphasized. Certainly I have emphasized it from the beginning. If in every locality every person . . . qualified under laws of the State . . . is permitted to vote . . . he has got a means of getting what he wants in democratic government and that is the one on which I place the greatest emphasis.[66]

Title IV, protecting the ballot, was the core of his program, and he would not tolerate any tampering with it.

The president required the cooperation of Majority Leader Lyndon Johnson, and there were indications that a suffrage bill fit in with the senator's plans. The Texas Democrat had been a contender for his party's vice-presidential nomination, and perhaps he aspired to the top spot in 1960. To this end, Johnson had to break out of the provincial southern position if he expected to make an appeal to a nationwide electorate. Neither a congressional advocate of Negro rights—he had voted against antipoll tax and FEPC bills—nor a Negrophobe, Johnson had come to favor the passage of a civil-rights bill. "The senior senator from Texas," Washington columnist Roscoe Drummond noted, "is at one stroke removing from his path the single barrier which . . . has made it impracticable for the Democratic Party to select a Southerner for its presidential nominee—the barrier of opposition to civil rights legislation." [67] By mediating between the southern and northern liberal wings of the party, he placed himself closer to the Democratic center and preserved harmony.

As Majority Leader, Johnson could balance the competing concerns of the factions within his party. George Reedy, Johnson's press secretary and confidant, explained his boss's reasoning:

> In the past, it was possible to kill off all legislation simply because the Republicans were willing to cooperate. That is no longer true. The Republicans have made a calculated decision to build their party by appealing to the minority vote. The South is now completely without allies.[68]

Thus, by negotiating the enactment of a moderate bill, Johnson hoped to convince Dixie lawmakers that his version would be far better than the GOP's, which spelled "disaster for the

South." At the same time, according to Reedy, the majority leader would be satisfying the need of northerners to "take some of the edge off the Negro groups—who are the only ones with a direct interest." [69] Hence, the crafty Johnson persuaded Russell not to use the filibuster, and he set out to soften the allegedly harsh features of the proposal so that the South would only muster token resistance and the northerners would get a bill passed. After first lining up enough votes to eliminate Title III, he then maneuvered to fasten a jury-trial amendment onto Title IV. [70]

Johnson recruited some liberals in support of his plan, by taking advantage of their traditional hostility toward injunctions. In 1932, the passage of the Norris–La Guardia Act had given organized labor and its sympathizers a hard-fought victory against the use of arbitrary court injunctions. During the New Deal they had won another triumph in the National Labor Relations Act, which spurred union growth by sanctioning collective bargaining. As an ardent congressional ally of Roosevelt in the late 1930s, Johnson had acquired the friendship of New Deal policymakers—presidential aide Ben Cohen and Abe Fortas, then in the Interior Department. Twenty years later, he utilized their legal skills and reform credentials on the jury-trial issue. [71]

Cohen had been impressed by an article that the University of Wisconsin law professor Carl Auerbach wrote for the April 29th *New Leader*. Auerbach knew that jury trials in most southern communities "invite[d] popular nullification of the law." However, he did believe that there could be jury trials in certain instances without sacrificing Negro voting rights. Auerbach contrasted the remedial purpose of civil contempt with the punitive aim of criminal contempt. In the former case, a defendant freed himself of fine or imprisonment by complying with the judge's decree (he held the key to the cell door in his own hands), while the offender in the latter circumstance served a definite sentence for willfully disobeying the court order by allowing the registration period and election to pass without enrolling the Negro. Auerbach recommended limiting jury trials to criminal contempt adjudications, and contended that a judge using civil proceedings could effectively safeguard the suffrage in several ways. For example, a jurist rendering summary judgment might keep a recalcitrant clerk in jail until he consented to register qualified black citizens, or he might make an official post a bond to be forfeited if the order were disobeyed.[72]

Cohen sought to make direct use of Auerbach's reasoning. He first suggested to Joe Rauh, Chairman of the ADA, that the Leadership Conference on Civil Rights draw up an amendment based on Auerbach's idea. When Rauh turned him down, Cohen approached his old friend Lyndon Johnson, who readily supported such a compromise. During the spring, together with Fortas and another New Deal associate Dean Acheson, Cohen sketched a plan that authorized a jury trial for criminal contempt cases only.[73] In mid July Joseph O'Mahoney of Wyoming and his Democratic colleague Estes Kefauver of Tennessee cosponsored this version of an amendment in the Senate.

Both legislators had liberal credentials. The Wyoming senator had supported labor's efforts to curb injunctions, but he had taken positions unfavorable to Negro rights. O'Mahoney had voted against the antipoll-tax bills, reform of the cloture regulation, placement of H.R. 6127 directly on the calendar, and retention of Title III. He did not find much difficulty in choosing between curtailing injunctions and unconditional extension of the franchise. The senator did not oppose giving the Justice Department additional powers to protect the right to vote, but in this instance he was upset because the injunctive remedy would allow the government to bring civil suits against persons who had committed a crime and to try them without a jury on the basis of the United States being a party to the litigation. "Those who sought power for the Attorney General to institute civil action," according to O'Mahoney, "had as their sole purpose the avoidance of a basic Bill of Rights civil right . . . that criminal offenses shall be subject to jury trials." [74] Furthermore, O'Mahoney thought that his suggestion would give the civil-rights bill a wider appeal. He hoped that the amendment would "bring about a compromise" and persuade his "brothers of the South to help grant complete voting rights to Negroes." [75]

Estes Kefauver's attitude toward the administration's measure blended principle with politics. A long-standing advocate of suffrage expansion, he endorsed H.R. 6127 because "it is in fact pretty much of a middle of the road bill. The whole bill is designed to secure the right to vote." [76] Like Auerbach and Cohen, he believed that contempt proceedings would adequately safeguard the suffrage. "How many officials," he asked, "will prevent qualified voters from exercising their rights with even one day in jail" awaiting them? [77] Although he came from an area that had remained loyal to the Union during the Civil War, Kefauver represented a state that often sympathized with southern racial practices. The Tennessee senator, a man of genuinely liberal ideas, delicately balanced his votes on manners affecting blacks, lest he risk the ire of the white voters back home. He had supported the antipoll-tax bills and a change in Rule XXII but cast ballots against the FEPC, bypassing the Judiciary Committee to consider the omnibus bill and preserving Title III. As the debate on H.R. 6127 was to begin, one of his faithful supporters in Tennessee reminded the senator:

> Your personal views are so much more liberal than those of the majority of your constituents that, if you follow them on every occasion that arises, you will afront your constituents to the point that they will repudiate you and you will lose the opportunity to furnish the useful progressive leadership that is badly needed and which you are well equipped to provide.[78]

The liberals understood Kefauver's dilemma. "We know your difficulties," confided Paul Douglas, "and do not want you to commit suicide." [79] Consequently, by introducing the jury-trial amendment, Kefauver might mend political fences back home. The previously hostile Hamilton County *Herald* admitted that the senator's policy "strikes a responsive chord in our states' rights heart." [80]

The jury-trial amendment caused much soul-searching among the liberals, particularly Paul Douglas, a fervent defender of both unions and Negroes. Known for his keen mind, his intense preparation, and his quixotic forays against the windmills of economic privilege and racial discrimination, the erudite Douglas was usually outside the center of Senate decisionmaking. Many of his colleagues viewed him as a visionary, in contrast to Lyndon Johnson, who could get things done. On the present issue, the Illinois lawmaker was caught in a bind as he explained, "For half a century, labor had regarded the injunction as the most evil of legal instruments. I myself had written and spoken on its use in avoiding jury trials." Now southerners taunted him and other northern liberals who insisted on retaining jury trials in labor cases but not in those involving civil rights. After spending "several sleepless nights trying to reconcile these points," Douglas decided to oppose any amendment because he thought that "no white southern jury would ever convict a white Southern official of interfering with the voting rights of Negroes." [81]

As the major organization devoted to both civil rights and individual freedom, the ACLU was torn by such controversy. Having canvassed its affiliates during the first few months of 1957, the ACLU discovered that opinion on the jury trial amendment was almost evenly divided. Though the Indiana branch admitted that Negroes would never be able to obtain their rights so long as juries failed to convict racist offenders, it nevertheless considered that the "right to trial by jury is indispensable to the basic Anglo-Saxon system of justice, not only as a protection against the courts themselves, but as a protection against all-powerful Government that would send a citizen to jail under circumstances where twelve of his neighbors would not." The Indiana chapter and some other civil libertarians were not willing to "trade one basic right to secure another" and recommended approval of the jury trial amendment.[82] However, the parent group did not agree. The ACLU had supported the Norris-La Guardia Act's jury-trial provision because it protected individuals against oppressive government. But that situation did not exist in the South, where a jury trial protected tyrannical white officials rather than downtrodden blacks. "While there is always need to guard vigilantly against the misuse of government power," the ACLU declared in opposition to the amendment, "[t]he right of equal treatment under law is fatally undermined when community sentiment blocks the enforcement of law." [83]

Most of the liberal lawmakers concurred with this opinion and did not find the amendment based on Auerbach's arguments reassuring. Clifford Case, a New Jersey Republican, suggested that most contempt offenses under the act would be criminal and thus subject to jury trials. He explained that an official who defied an injunction to enroll a qualified Negro would be guilty of civil contempt. However, once the registration period expired and the election was held, according to Auerbach's plan, if the defendant had not complied he would be tried for criminal contempt by a jury. Paul Douglas agreed with Case "that there would be deliberate contempt and failure to remove it for the purpose of gaining a jury trial and a 'not guilty' verdict." Case expressed the liberals' lack of faith in southern justice by quoting the opinion of James Coleman, governor of Mississippi, "If the bill does pass it will call for jury trial. Then it especially would be a fairly harmless proposition." [84]

Nevertheless, the civil-rights advocates insisted that the measure, even without a jury-trial provision, was mild. Douglas doubted that local officials would fare poorly before district court judges in Dixie. "These men cannot be regarded as prejudiced against the white traditions of the South," he asserted, "on the contrary, the presumption may well be that they have some prejudices in favor of their native area and its prevailing traditions." [85] This last point did not seem to bother the liberals. The LCCR concurred that the "judges who would try those defying court decrees which guarantee voting rights to presently disfranchised Negroes are men drawn from the Bar of their local communities, appointed by the President, with the advice and consent of the Senate." [86] For good measure, Javits placed into the *Record* biographical sketches of the federal judges in the South, emphasizing their southern backgrounds.[87] Thus, in their desire to make the best argument against jury trials, the suffragists stressed how sympathetic white judges would be to the accused. Prejudiced juries had so long perverted justice that the reformers considered the judges as the lesser of the two evils.

The O'Mahoney-Kefauver amendment underwent one final modification intended to reduce the impact of some criticism made by the northern liberal bloc. Joseph Clark, a Pennsylvania Democrat, Richard Neuberger, an Oregon Democrat, and Paul Douglas belittled the notion of a fair trial in the South where lily-white juries invariably acquitted civil-rights violators. Since many states prepared their jury lists from the names on the registration rolls, they had prevented voteless Negroes from serving on the panels.[88] To strengthen the appeal of the amendment, freshman Democrat Frank Church of Idaho added a clause that gave any United States citizen over twenty-one years of age the right to serve on federal juries.[89]

Church exemplified the aid given by the West to soften the omnibus bill. He was sympathetic to the cause of racial equality, but he was more concerned with the extension of public power. This had been the dominant issue on which he had waged his successful Senate campaign in 1956. With his regional colleagues he sought passage of an act authorizing the federal government to construct and maintain a dam at Hell's Canyon between Oregon and Idaho. The westerners required the assistance of the southern Democrats who, in 1956, had collaborated with the conservative Republicans to defeat the proposal. By following Majority Leader Johnson on civil rights, they prodded the Dixie senators, more hostile to black equality than to public power, into reevaluating their position.[90]

Johnson developed his strategy around the nascent West-

South coalition. C. Vann Woodward, who was observing the controversy closely, remarked, "The history of every major sectional adjustment over Negro rights since 1866 has been studded with under-the-table bargains on tariff, monetary, and railroad bills." [91] The framing of the 1957 law perhaps added public power to the bartering list. On June 21st the majority leader had gathered the votes of five southerners—Sam Ervin, Richard Russell, James Eastland, Russell Long, and George Smathers—to help pass the Hell's Canyon bill, by forty-five to thirty-eight. The backing of these senators, who reversed themselves from the previous year, presented some circumstantial evidence that the West gained by voting for amendments to weaken the omnibus bill. Paul Douglas, a longtime advocate of public power and a supporter of the Hell's Canyon project, believed that the southern senators were rewarding the western liberals for supporting the jury-trial provision. If this were the case, however, the West only benefitted momentarily. At the conclusion of the Hell's Canyon vote, Douglas turned to Church and remarked, "Frank, I am afraid you Hell's Canyon folks have been given some counterfeit money." The Illinois senator predicted that the private-power interests would help kill the measure in the House, and he was proven correct.[92] The likelihood of even a tacit understanding between the two regions left the usually poised Eisenhower, a foe of the projected Dam, still fuming years later, "Just as a number of liberals . . . joined the conservative Southerners to oppose civil rights legislation, so now a number of well known conservatives joined the liberal forces to put over a one-half billion dollar incursion into the federal treasury." [93]

The capital buzzed with speculation about the possible bargain. Thomas L. Stokes, a nationally syndicated Washington correspondant, wrote that on the jury-trial issue the southerners were calling in the "mortgages they hold for this or that past favor." He listed as "most potent" the support they gave "to put over the Hell's Canyon high dam so dear to the Northwestern Democrats." [94] Linking the jury-trial provision with the dam, Ray Tucker reported in his "National Whirligig" column, "The public power advocates have not won a major victory on Capitol Hill in several years. They are now fighting what has been called a 'Custer's Last Stand' battle and it appears that Cowboy Johnson has ridden to their rescue."[95] Some leading newspapers in the Northwest picked up this theme. Opponents of both public power and the jury-trial amendment, they lambasted any deal. Typical was the Idaho *Statesman*, which did "not hesitate to suggest that what has been happening in the United States Senate . . . involved a number of trades. Senator Church has done a good turn for Senator Eastland, and Senator Eastland has done a good turn for Senator Church."[96]

These charges did not distract Senator Johnson, who was busy luring votes by gaining some influential labor support for the O'Mahoney-Kefauver-Church amendment. He discovered an ally in John L. Lewis, president of the United Mine Workers (UMW). Once heavily fined by a United States judge for disregarding an injunction, Lewis welcomed the proposal governing jury trials in contempt proceedings. On July 30th the majority leader read into the *Record* a telegram he received from the UMW chieftain admonishing that the "strong and harsh power of injunction [that] has been in the past so often abused . . . even for worthy purposes, must carry with it reasonable protection to all citizens who may be charged with violation and thereafter cited for contempt."[97] Lewis's endorsement exerted a good deal of pressure on Chapman Revercomb, a Republican senator from the coal-mining state of West Virginia. Revercomb, who had followed the GOP leadership on all the other civil-rights votes including Title III, suddenly wavered on the jury-trial issue.

The unions belonging to the Leadership Conference rushed to repair the possible damage caused by Lewis's statement. The UAW blasted the majority leader's "divide and conquer" tactic of wooing labor with the "jury trials it should have anyway on condition that it help to impose jury trials where they will mean continuing denial of the right to vote." Likewise, the

AFL, refusing to be sidetracked by the extraneous issue, rejected the amendment weakening H.R. 6127.[98]

At this juncture, several civil-rights advocates counseled moderation. Mark De Wolfe Howe, a legal scholar at Harvard University, advised his state's Democratic senator, John F. Kennedy, "I feel you should support the O'Mahoney Amendment. The issue has aroused more legal fuss than it deserves, and is certainly not a question which permits of stubbornness." Howe's colleague at the Cambridge law school, Paul Freund, agreed "that to accept the jury trial for criminal contempt would not in my view constitute a betrayal of principle." [99] Both law professors believed that the provision contained some merit because it would encourage compliance with the statute in the South, especially since the Dixie lawmakers favored the amendment. The Washington *Post,* which had originally editorialized against the amendment, changed its view during the course of debate. "The problem," the newspaper asserted, "is to bring about more general respect for voting rights without the sort of pyrrhic victory that would encourage political bitterness and divisions and stimulate a search for new evasions." [100] This reasoning received approval from moderate southerners. The Raleigh *News and Observer* declared that the bill was stronger with the amendment because it "would be more easily enforced and would meet with more voluntary compliance." Ralph McGill, editor of the Atlanta *Constitution,* echoed this sentiment, "Being for the right to vote and that of trial by jury is as axiomatic as being against sin." [101]

However, Eisenhower stood firmly against the compromise forces. The president repeated his desire to guard the suffrage unimpeded by jury trials. To one distinguished southern politician, James F. Byrnes, he wrote:

> It seems to me that the public interest in protection of voting rights is at least as great as public interest in maintenance of minimum wages, etc. In these instances . . . the Attorney General is authorized to enjoin violations of law . . . and violations of such injunctions are tried without jury.[102]

On July 31st, a few days before the crucial Senate showdown, the president gave journalists the "last word on the civil rights bill":

> I believe the United States must make certain that every citizen who is entitled to vote under the Constitution is actually given that right. I do not believe in any amendment to section four of the bill. I believe that we should preserve the traditional method to the Federal judges for enforcing their orders, and I am told that it is thirty-six different laws where these contempt cases do not demand trial by jury [sic].[103]

With both sides elbowing for last minute room, the outcome appeared too close to call. Thirty-eight senators, twenty-five Republicans, and thirteen Democrats had voted to bypass the Judiciary Committee and to retain Title III, while thirty-four of their colleagues had taken the opposition positions. The balance of power appeared to rest with the twenty-one "peripatetic" legislators, fifteen Republicans and six Democrats, most of whom had voted to place H.R. 6127 directly on the calendar but not to keep Part III in the bill. Since the result seemed to be a toss-up, the civil-rights proponents gathered together all of their adherents. On August 1st, they brought in for the balloting Tom Hennings, still recovering from surgery, and Frederick Payne, a Maine Republican recuperating from a serious heart attack.[104]

The fifty-one-to-forty-two tally for the amendment indicated that Eisenhower's firmness could not quite match Johnson's manipulation of the jury-trial question. Thirty-nine Democrats, including ten from the far West, one from the mid West, four from the Northeast, and twenty-four from the South, joined twelve Republicans to pass the amendment. On the losing side were nine Democrats and thirty-three Republicans.[105] A switch of five votes would have defeated it. Of the "peripatetic" senators, ten Republicans and one Democrat voted for the president's position.[106] Although the Democrats had provided most of the votes for the amendment, a closer analysis shows that the previous civil-rights supporters in both parties were to blame for the failure to kill the measure. If those who supported the administration on the controversial Title III had continued to do so, they would have helped keep the suffrage section intact. The margin of victory came from five Democrats and three Republicans who had supported the White House on Title III but defected on the O'Mahoney-Kefauver-Church amendment.

Johnson had fashioned the proposal in a manner that these lawmakers could favor and still go on record as upholding civil rights.[107] Democrats John Pastore of Rhode Island, John Kennedy of Massachusetts, and Frank Lausche of Ohio jumped over after the provision was revised to incorporate the distinction between civil and criminal contempts, and the state of Washington's Henry Jackson and Warren Magnuson deserted when Church offered his plan to make jury selection unbiased. The GOP's Chapman Revercomb bolted after John L. Lewis boarded the Johnson bandwagon.[108] As with the Hell's Canyon vote, it was difficult to pinpoint the specific influences affecting the alignment on the jury-trial issue. In a thoughtful analysis after the vote, James Reston elucidated the various forces in operation:

> . . . it has been clear from the start that this jury-trial question clearly disturbed many men in the Senate—Senator O'Mahoney is a vivid case in point—who are suspicious by experience of adding any new injunctive powers to the arsenal of the Federal Government. This plus the conviction that powerful minorities cannot be easily coerced to abide by procedures that are hateful to whole regions of the country, were undoubtedly the main reasons for the Senate's decision to try one step at a time. In any decision that finds the Senate so evenly divided, however, it is also true that personal and regional political considerations combine to influence votes. And while everybody in the Senate will, of course, explain his vote on the grounds of personal conviction, these other political factors undoubtedly had some effect. On many practical matters, the South and West tend to collaborate, even though this coalition brings together men of vastly different political philosophies.[109]

The Eisenhower administration hoped to overturn the verdict on Title IV. After the August 1st decision, Vice-President Nixon groaned, "This was one of the saddest days in the history of the Senate, because this was a vote against the right to vote." [110] The president interpreted the Senate action as a severe political defeat but trusted that representatives of both chambers in conference would delete the objectionable clause. Otherwise, if the obnoxious amendment became part of the statute, the chief executive warned, "it will . . . make largely ineffective the basic purpose of the bill—that of protecting promptly and effectively every American in his right to vote." [111]

Some Republicans wanted Eisenhower to veto the crippled bill, which easily passed in the Senate on August 7th. [112] Dissatisfied with the upper chamber's performance, Minority Leader Joseph Martin cautioned that there could be no compromise over the jury-trial amendment in the House, and that the legislation was "dead" for the present session. Since the Democrats supplied most of the votes weakening H.R. 6127, Martin reasoned, they would have the burden of explaining their record to the electorate in 1958. [113] Nixon also suggested that the president let the bill die and wait until next year to secure a stronger measure. [114] Frederic Morrow also believed that "an emasculated civil rights bill is worse than none at all" and worked with Maxwell Rabb to solicit telegrams from prominent Negroes informing Eisenhower of their opposition to the Senate version. [115]

In contrast, the liberal coalition actively threw its weight on the side of the compromise. The Democratic reformers did not desire the issue to be carried over to the next session when it could split their party in the 1958 congressional elections. Hubert Humphrey asserted that the bill would be killed "if the Republicans now show they are more interested in stirring up a partisan issue than in getting some constructive action." [116] The civil-rights lobbyists argued that the Senate's "half-loaf" proposal was better than nothing at all. Roy Wilkins defended this viewpoint that "If you are digging a ditch with a teaspoon, and a man comes along and offers you a spade, there is something wrong with your head if you don't take it because he didn't offer you a bulldozer." Furthermore, the NAACP executive concluded that with the presidential election coming up in 1960, the two parties would feel increased pressure to enact new legislation if the 1957 act failed to guarantee Negroes the promised right to vote.[117] The LCCR shared this opinion, and on August 7th it urged the House to accept the Senate's modifications of the bill.[118]

Blacks were disappointed over the attenuated H.R. 6127, and they divided over whether the president should endorse it. The Pittsburgh *Courier* did not accept the compromise "as the FULL ORDER for civil rights. It is a civil rights MINUS bill. But it is unquestionably a step in the RIGHT DIRECTION." [119] The *Afro-American* recognized that Congress had badly crippled the bill, but it had concluded that "A half-loaf is better than no bread at all." [120] The Atlanta *Daily World* grudgingly declared that if the jury-trial amendment could not be eliminated then "let the bill become law." [121] Both the *Amsterdam News* and the Norfolk *Journal and Guide* believed that the Senate had damaged the measure beyond repair, but did not make any suggestions for congressional and presidential action. The loudest dissent came from the Chicago *Defender,* which decried the "half-loaf" philosophy as a "hobo psychology" and labeled those who justified it as "Appeasers." [122]

In the meantime, the House Rules Committee was considering two motions dealing with the Senate legislation, namely, send it to conference or agree to the modifications. Since most liberals supported conciliation, the Democratic leaders approved the second alternative. Until Eisenhower reached a decision, however, the Republicans on the committee joined the southern Democrats to keep H.R. 6127 off the House floor. This deadlock pleased Howard Smith, who acknowledged, "I am inclined to follow the course most likely to result in no bill at all." [123]

Eisenhower made up his mind that the bill should pass, but

he sought to restore some strength to Title IV. The White House had the Justice Department draft a plan that removed jury trials in certain criminal contempt cases. On August 16th Deputy Attorney General Rogers suggested "that where the penalty to be imposed is imprisonment for not in excess of 90 days or a fine not in excess of $300," the judge would conduct the trial summarily.[124] At his news conference on August 21st, the chief executive announced that his congressional leaders would offer this revision of the jury-trial amendment. Eisenhower believed the latest compromise gave the bill sufficient effectiveness and "quieted any justifiable alarm that others might have to excessive punishment of any kind." [125] Three days later, Knowland and Martin met with Johnson and Rayburn. After some discussion, they settled upon a slightly different proposal which eliminated a jury trial where the punishments were jail terms of not more than forty-five days and a fine of up to $300.[126]

With the last stumbling block cleared on August 26th, the Rules Committee reported the bill with the Eisenhower amendment. The next day the House voted 279 to ninety-seven in favor of adopting the revised H.R. 6127. The moderate legislation received the blessing of some southerners who could support a measure limited to the franchise when the trial-by-jury principle was affirmed. For the first time during the two-year struggle, members of the Texas and Florida delegations, joining some of their border-state colleagues, went on record for civil rights. Speaker Sam Rayburn explained the "yea" votes of twelve fellow congressmen from the Lone Star State, "It is simply a right to vote bill." [127]

In the Senate, the southerners decided not to filibuster because they feared that the Senate might impose cloture and pass a stronger measure. Although no Congress had ever voted to close debate on a civil-rights bill, there were signs of change in 1957. The Republicans had deserted their southern Democratic allies and were firmly committed to passage of a suffrage measure. Furthermore, some of the Dixie lawmakers could not be relied on to actively take part in a filibuster be-

cause they too favored a franchise plan. Senator Olin Johnston explained the political facts of life to his constituents, "In
today's Senate, the size of our Southern group is decreasing.
We cannot count on the support of Senators from Tennessee,
Texas, Oklahoma, one from Kentucky, and one from
Florida." [128] Richard Russell had come to the conclusion after
taking "several careful canvasses," that without complete Dixie
backing and the assistance from conservative Republicans, his
side "did not have as many as 32 Senators who would stand
firmly against application of cloture." [129] Once the discussion
was terminated, the Georgia senator guessed, the South would
face the "disaster" of having Title III revived and possibly
passed by an embittered northern majority.[130] Even if the Senate did not take this radical step and end debate, the southerners worried that a filibuster would prompt their outraged
colleagues to at least revise Rule XXII. The suffrage antagonists recalled that the attempt to change the rules in January
had attracted additional support from among the northerners,
particularly Republicans. In demonstrating that a small minority could frustrate a popular civil-rights measure, the southerners would give the reformers a powerful argument for
modification of Senate procedures.

Moreover, the Dixie politicos accepted a roll call on H.R.
6127 because they had successfully narrowed its contents to
the suffrage. In fact, some southerners openly professed that
a republican form of government could not tolerate racial
disfranchisement. "Under no conditions," George Smathers of
Florida declared, "would I defend any public officials who
sought to deprive any citizen, regardless of race or color or
creed, of his right to vote. Voting belongs to all qualified
Americans." [131] Appearing on the nationwide television show,
"Face the Nation," Richard Russell disclosed, "I would very
readily support a right to vote bill universal in its application." [132] Russell Long of Louisiana told his colleagues, "Everyone recognizes the importance of the colored man voting if
he is to receive his share of the benefits which a government is
capable of bestowing upon its citizens." [133] These attitudes

were reflected in the confession one southern leader made to James Reston, "I am not going to kill myself arguing for anti-Negro voting procedures I don't approve and I don't think most of the South approves." [134]

On August 29, 1957, for the first time in the twentieth century, the Senate voted directly on a civil-rights bill. The southerners contented themselves with having "confined the Federal activities to the field of voting and [kept] the withering hand of the Federal Government out of the schools and social order." [135] Therefore, they refused to assist South Carolina's maverick Strom Thurmond when he blustered for over twenty-four hours against the legislation. This mini-talkathon concluded, the Senate concurred with the House version of H.R. 6127, by sixty to fifteen, as the mild bill gained the approval of three southerners—Johnson and Yarborough of Texas and Estes Kefauver of Tennessee. On September 9, Dwight Eisenhower placed his signature on the Civil Rights Act of 1957.

A number of presidential ambitions were boosted by the passage of the 1957 act. Lyndon Johnson, maneuvering the bill around a southern filibuster and then voting for the legislation, placed himself closer to the center of the Democratic party. The Houston *Post* praised him for his skillful strategy in avoiding a filibuster and the subsequent danger of "a deeper schism in the Democratic party," and Ray Tucker dubbed the Texan as a "modern Henry Clay who saved his party . . . from splitting on the rock of civil rights." [136] While denying that he aspired to higher office, the majority leader nevertheless increased his availability. In the opposite way, northern moderate John F. Kennedy raised his stock in the South. Although the young Massachusetts senator had displeased the liberals by supporting the jury-trial amendment, he enhanced his image with the Dixie Democrats, some of whom had shown interest in Kennedy for the party's vice-presidential nomination in 1956.[137] It appeared that perhaps the biggest winner was Richard Nixon, who emerged as a solid advocate of civil rights. The pro-Democratic Chicago *Defender* commented, "By virtue of his untrammeled position on integration and civil rights, Mr. Nixon's prestige has risen considerably. He has passed the litmus test." [138] *Time* awarded the decision in the civil-rights fight to Nixon "by a knockout." [139] The liberal *Nation*, a harsh critic of the vice president, suggested that if Nixon won in 1960, "the analysts will need to look no further than to the hot summer sessions of the 1957 Senate for the public disillusion which tipped the balance against the Democratic candidate." [140] Already, the editor of the black Birmingham *World*, Emory O. Jackson, who had never voted for a Republican, was giving serious thought about breaking this habit. "I feel certain," he wrote to Senator Douglas, "that the actions of the Western Democrats and Northern Democrats will weigh heavily in a reappraisal of members of the Negro group of the Democratic party which now by its Senate record shows that it is the party . . . deliberately opposed to the rights of Negroes to vote in the South." [141]

Against the forces of Lyndon Johnson and the administration, the liberals had proven no match. The most enthusiastic advocates of civil-rights measures among the Democrats—Paul Douglas, Richard Neuberger, Thomas Hennings, Joseph Clark, and Hubert Humphrey—generally worked outside of the Senate establishment and could not compete with the power of the institution's leaders. Likewise, ardent GOP reformers such as Jacob Javits, Clifford Case, and Thomas Kuchel of California were isolated from the mainstream of congressional, conservative Republicanism. The members of this bipartisan liberal coalition were considered extremists who did not know how to sacrifice for the good of a cause. It was relatively easy for Majority Leader Johnson to manipulate the resources at his disposal—patronage, campaign funds, the legislative agenda—to divide the supporters of civil-rights legislation. The Texan had a further advantage because whatever compromises northerners made on particular civil-rights provisions they could still go on record in favor of the final version of the law. In fact, the jury-trial amendment was a masterful stroke, giving moderate northern lawmakers the opportunity to compromise and still vote for the "civil right" of a trial by jury. Senator Douglas realized that there were only a handful of senators who would hold out for the most advanced programs fostering black equality. "While most of our people care about civil rights," he lamented, "they don't care deeply; whereas those who are opposed are very intense in their feeling." [142] His southern foes, with their control over vital committees and their knowledge of parliamentary rules, exerted greater weight on congressional chiefs than did the reformers. Although Douglas decried the dominant southern Democratic command over "the official position of the Democratic party in the Senate," there was little that the liberals could do about it.[143] They simply did not have the votes or leadership positions to refashion a truly progressive party. Yet they had performed a valuable service in raising the civil-rights issue and keeping it before Congress. The camaraderie they developed during the struggle would hold them together for future battles. "We few, we happy few," Douglas captured this spirit in a quote from Shakespeare, "we band of brothers. For he today that sheds his blood with me shall be my brother." [144]

Nevertheless, when the civil-rights advocates had a chance to calmly evaluate Congress's achievement, many of them concluded that the statute represented a victory for enfranchisement. One legal scholar writing in the *Howard University Law Journal* thought that capably "administered Part IV should go a long way toward making the right to vote meaningful." [145] Carl Auerbach, the inspiration behind the jury-trial amendment, declared, "The sanctions available to a resourceful Federal judge in a civil contempt proceeding are just as effective to ensure that Negroes will vote as are maximum penalties [with a jury trial] of a $1,000 fine and 6 months in prison." [146] A member of the San Francisco Civil Liberties Union elaborated on this point, "If [registrars] fail to comply with [injunctions] . . . the Courts may, and doubtless will, put them in jail or under other duress or disability until they grant such Negroes their voting rights." [147] A southern jurist, James Reston explained, "could insist that the injunction order hold not only for this election but the next one as well and not only for the particular registrar but for successors as well." [148] Such decrees would presumably take care of situations where an official resigned rather than complied with an injunction. Although the liberals had lost the battles over Title III and the jury-trial issue, Joseph Rauh asserted that "The new law is a substantial contribution to the right to vote. Conscientious federal judges will find ways . . . to protect the Negroes' right to vote." [149]

Furthermore, by enacting the legislation, the federal government made political equality the official program of the "second Reconstruction." According to C. Vann Woodward, "There is at least the opportunity to see if the policy can . . . work." [150] "With a bill in force," Roy Wilkins assured NAACP members," "it will be possible to assemble facts, rather than estimates. If the bill does not accomplish what it was supposed to do . . . this will become apparent after one or two registration periods." [151] Implementation of the 1957 act would demonstrate whether the model for enfranchisement required adjustments. To this end, Maxwell Rabb vowed: "The experience gained in using the new remedies and the findings that may be expected from the newly established Civil Rights Commission, can well be determinative of the form that additional needed legislation in this field should take." [152]

8

Justice Delayed . . . Justice Denied

THE EFFECTIVENESS of the Civil Rights Act would depend largely on the Department of Justice. It conferred on the attorney general the authority to sue for injunctions and a division to help carry out this purpose. The situation seemed promising. Yet within three years the federal government reluctantly admitted that it was not equipped to do the job only after the Civil Rights Commission had exposed the manifold instances of disenfranchisement that the Justice Department failed to eradicate. Prodded into action by the commission and its liberal allies, the chief executive proposed legislation that reflected his faith in the ability of the federal courts to expand the suffrage. While the reformers disagreed with Eisenhower's prescription, they lacked the power to change it. Thus in 1960 the civil-rights coalition in Congress was asked to accept another palliative measure, namely, a law testifying to lofty ideological intentions but flawed by the politics of expediency.

Meanwhile the president took his time in setting up the machinery to enforce the 1957 statute. Indeed, three months elapsed before he appointed a head to the Civil Rights Division. On December 9, 1957, with Congress adjourned, he named W. Wilson White for the post. A graduate of Harvard and the University of Pennsylvania Law School, White had served as a United States attorney and since 1956, as assistant attorney general in charge of the Legal Counsel Office. Although his credentials were impeccable, the Senate Judiciary Committee added to the delay in organizing the division, by holding up White's confirmation for eight months. In the meantime, the nominee ran the division as its acting assistant attorney general.

The appointment of White was closely connected to the Little Rock crisis that had boiled and exploded in September 1957, contributing to the protracted situation. During the summer debate on the Civil Rights bill, Eisenhower had assured the South that he could not foresee any circumstances that would prompt him to deploy troops into Dixie. Shortly thereafter, events in Arkansas tarnished the president's reputation as a prophet. On September 2nd, Governor Orville Faubus sent the state militia to block the federally decreed integration of Central High School. After a personal meeting between the governor and chief executive failed to produce compliance with the court orders, Eisenhower dispatched paratroopers to make sure that the mob violence by whites did not prevent nine black students from attending classes. As acting assistant attorney general in charge of the Office of Legal Counsel, White had supervised the drafting of the decree authorizing the chief executive to dispatch troops to surround Central High School.

The decision that brought the 101st airborne to Little Rock rallied southerners in opposition to the nomination of Wilson White. Although White merely had followed through on a decision made by Eisenhower and Brownell, the Dixie bloc singled him out as a convenient target for its animosity toward the administration's action. Using his Judiciary Committee as a forum, James Eastland, joined by fellow southerners Olin Johnston and Sam Ervin, sharply questioned White about the government's justification for involving the armed forces in school-desegregation cases. They particularly wondered why the president had mobilized soldiers in battle dress rather than the less menacing United States marshals.[1]

White carefully tried to defend the administration's position without further upsetting his antagonists. He stated that the chief executive called out troops because it was the only way to enforce federal court decrees under the pressure of mob violence. However, the acting assistant refrained from advocating such a course in the future. When asked by Johnston, "If you have the same circumstances arising again, will you call in the Armed Forces?" he prudently replied, "I don't think the same circumstances can arise, because in the future we will not be caught in that kind of situation." [2] As long as White offered these cautious remarks, Eastland could only postpone the confirmation, not bury it. On August 18, 1958 the Senate finally confirmed White by a vote of fifty-six to twenty.

With the nomination controversy settled, Justice Department officials gave southern critics little cause for worry. The men responsible for determining policy on civil rights viewed their role narrowly. Attorney General William Rogers, who had moved up from Deputy after Brownell resigned, and Wilson White with his assistant Joseph Ryan, agreed that the federal government should pay close attention to southern sentiment. "Sometimes progress can be made a lot faster without litigation," Rogers argued. "I think that you have to gear your law enforcement pretty thoroughly in with the development of public opinion." [3] To this end the Justice Department would prosecute only the most flagrant violations, first giving southerners a chance to obey the law without having to use force. The expectation was that once the government won a few landmark cases, most southerners would recognize the right of Negroes to vote. [4]

The department's overdeveloped self-control discouraged Negroes from looking to Washington for assistance. From 1958 to 1960, the Civil Rights Division received a meager twenty-three complaints alleging racial disfranchisement in the South. The assistant attorney general did not fully understand the reasons for black hesitancy. White attributed the poor showing to the fact that "in these communities where the Negroes have not been able to register, they have become discouraged to the point where they do not feel it is worth while to complain to anybody." According to White's assistant, Joseph Ryan, the civil-rights groups carried no weight in departmental decisions, nor should they expect government officials to launch a suffrage drive on their behalf.[5] He failed to comprehend that black fear could not be eased unless the Civil Rights Division became a forceful advocate. When the Civil Rights Division did not get so involved, the NAACP, which initially had submitted accusations of disfranchisement to the division, became disheartened and addressed its protests elsewhere.

The Civil Rights Division also moved slowly because it did not want to risk losing cases. Since each suit initiated would result in a challenge to the constitutionality of the 1957 act, the attorney general thought it "desirable to select cases where the evidence seemed clear."[6] The division spent most of its time gathering statistics on the number of blacks and whites registered and compiling the laws of the states where racial disfranchisement occurred. "The real accomplishment," Ryan testified in 1959, "is being prepared to get into this field." Thus, after exhaustive studies during 1957 and 1958, the Civil Rights Division had chosen three cases "because of the optimum factual vehicle that [they] presented."[7]

Terrell County, Georgia, furnished the Justice Department with the kind of setting it was looking for. Located in the southwest corner of the state, "Terrible Terrell," as civil-rights workers would later call it, had only forty-eight registered blacks in 1958. Whereas 1.7 percent of the county's 8,500 Negroes were enrolled to vote, 64.4 percent of its 4,700 whites could cast a ballot. In this black-belt area, white officials openly practiced discrimination and intimidation to maintain the rigid, racial caste system. In the county seat of Dawson, one registrar openly admitted that he had declined to pass five blacks on the literacy test, although he knew that some of them were college graduates. His colleague, J. G. Raines, a Harvard Law School graduate, declared that he had disqualified some black applicants because they "pronounced 'equity' as 'eequity' and slurred the word 'original.'" Furthermore, when a black schoolteacher with a master's degree from New York University complained to the Justice Department about this type of disfranchisement, the county board of education refused to renew her contract.[8]

Faithful to its policy, the Civil Rights Division prepared a strong, factual brief before going into court. On September 1, 1958 Wilson White reported to Attorney General Rogers, "I have not up to now recommended suit on any of these complaints, considering the evidence insufficient. Now we have completed preparation of a case which I believe fully justifies action." [9] Investigators for the division discovered that the registrars: (a) kept race-differentiated records, with differently colored cards for white and black applicants, (b) did not handle the applications of Negroes while they did so of whites during a period from October 1956 to February 1958, and (c) required Negroes to read and write a lengthier and more difficult paragraph of the national or state constitutions than they demanded of whites. Moreover, the enrollment officers expected the blacks to transcribe the sections from dictation, but they allowed the whites to write by copying directly.[10] To combat this blatant disfranchisement, on September 4th government attorneys filed a complaint in federal district court under the Civil Rights Act of 1957.

Despite the carefully documented evidence that the Justice Department had accumulated, on April 16, 1959 the lower court declared the act unconstitutional. Rather than examine the substance of the charges brought against the registrars, Judge T. Hoyt Davis considered whether the legislation allowing the attorney general to institute proceedings for preventive relief was appropriate within the meaning of the Fifteenth Amendment. The court would not decide "whether this particular fish is properly within the net, but whether the net is so large as to catch many fish not properly within it." In order to meet constitutional standards, state representatives had to perpetrate the racial discrimination. Judge Davis ruled that the 1957 statute did not satisfy this criterion because it permitted the attorney general to bring action against "any person" depriving another of the right to vote. "The fact that the instant case is a suit against state officials," Davis reasoned, "cannot alter the scope of the statute." [11]

Dismayed by the District Court's decision, the Justice Department petitioned the Supreme Court to reverse it. On January 12, 1960 William Rogers underscored the importance of the case to the administration by becoming the first attorney general in thirteen years to present an argument before the high tribunal.[12] The federal government contended that the Civil Rights Act was "admittedly constitutional as applied to the facts of the case, and the question of the constitutionality of [its] application in other hypothetical circumstances should not have been considered by the Court below." Rogers pointed out that the statute legitimately prohibited both private and official bias. He maintained that the attorney general's power under the act came from two distinct constitutional provisions: (a) Article I, Section 2 and (b) the Fifteenth Amendment. The first applied to both private and state action but was limited to federal elections, and the latter pertained to federal and state contests but was restricted to acts of discrimination under color of state law.[13] This argument was countered by the Georgia registrars' lawyers, who denied that the attorney general could properly seek an injunction "where the alleged deprivation is that of a private citizen acting as a private citizen." [14]

On February 29th the Supreme Court accepted the Justice Department's contentions. Delivering the unanimous opinion, Justice William Brennan asserted that the court followed certain rules in passing on the constitutionality of legislation. It would not allow "one to whom application of a statute is constitutional [to] be heard to attack the statute on the ground that it might also be taken as applying to other persons or other situations in which its application might be unconstitutional." Thus, confined to the information in this particular case, the bench ruled that:

> the conduct charged—discrimination by state officials, within the course of their official duties, against the voting rights of U.S.

citizens, on grounds of race or color—is certainly "state action" and the clearest form of it, subject to the law of the [Fifteenth] Amendment, and that legislation designed to deal with such discrimination is "appropriate legislation" under it.[15]

While the *Raines* case was rising through the judicial hierarchy, the Department of Justice targeted Macon County Alabama for a second suit. It was an excellent choice, because the Negroes living there possessed a high degree of political consciousness. Employed either at the Tuskegee Institute or the Veterans Administration Hospital, many blacks earned a decent income independent of local white purse strings. Macon ranked first among Alabama counties in the proportion of its adult Negroes who had at least a high-school education and in the percentage of those who held college degrees. Given these factors, a middle-class leadership had emerged. From the early 1940s, the Tuskegee Civic Association (TCA) had served in close cooperation with the NAACP to challenge registration abuses in the courts and urge citizens to enroll as voters.[16]

Despite their high qualification for suffrage, Macon County Negroes still shared with most southern blacks the common experience of disfranchisement. According to the 1950 census, 84 percent of Macon's 30,561 people were black, but in 1958, 3,102 whites had qualified to vote, compared with 1,218 blacks. White officials had resorted to an assortment of tricks to keep Negroes off the voting list. For various periods of time the Board of Registrars ceased publicly functioning; when in session it confined Negroes to a small segregated room in the courthouse and accepted only two black applications at a time; it required Negroes to read and copy long articles of the U.S. Constitution, and it permitted a Negro voter to vouch for only two applicants per year. Consequently, from 1951 through 1958, while Negroes made 1,585 formal requests to enroll, the board issued certificates to 510 or 32 percent.[17] Fearful that even this number represented too many black voters, the Alabama legislature in 1957 gerrymandered the boundaries of Tuskegee to exclude all but ten of 420 Negroes who had participated in city elections.[18]

For several years Tuskegee Negroes had been petitioning the federal government for redress of their grievances. In 1953 the Civic Association asked the Civil Rights Section to bring criminal action against the recalcitrant registrars, and in April 1958 the organization presented the Civil Rights Division with twenty affidavits complaining of disfranchisement in Macon County. During the debate over the 1957 act, a delegation led by William P. Mitchell, chairman of the TCA's Voter Franchise Committee, had advised a group of liberal senators in Washington that the bill could remedy some of the shocking abuses. Mitchell turned over to the Justice Department carefully documented records that he had compiled, showing the board's policy of bias. Almost a year and a half after passage of the statute, the attorney general finally brought a suit to enjoin the Macon County registrars from practicing racial discrimination.[19]

Once again a federal district judge suspended implementation of the Civil Rights Act. This time, however, the jurist did not declare the law unconstitutional, but ruled that it did not apply to the particular situation. Before the Justice Department instituted proceedings, two of the three men on the board of registrars had resigned to take other positions, and the third had died. Faced with no enrollment officers to sue, the government instead acted against the State of Alabama. Judge Frank M. Johnson held that Congress had not intended the attorney general to authorize preventive relief against the states but had restricted such litigation to "persons." Because the board members had resigned "in good faith," Johnson found, the attorney general had no one to enjoin from behaving prejudicially. Nevertheless, if the national legislature desired to include the states as proper defendants, Johnson voiced the optimistic opinion, "there is no doubt that such authority would be appropriate—and even in certain circumstances necessary—if Congress intended to give full and complete authority to the Attorney General to enforce constitutional rights here involved."[20]

Although the Justice Department challenged Johnson's decision before the Supreme Court, Congress rendered the appeal moot. A section of the Civil Rights Act of 1960 passed in May, to be discussed later, specifically empowered the attorney general to enter into litigation against the states.[21] Instructed to rehear the suit, Judge Johnson promptly issued an injunction for the plaintiffs, ordered those already discriminated against to be registered, and planned to watch closely the future operation of the Board.[22]

The final case designed by the Civil Rights Division to thwart discriminatory registration tactics resulted from the Louisiana purges (see discussion in chapter 5). Since 1956 the Justice Department had observed representatives of the Louisiana Citizens' Council in various parishes challenge the credentials of Negroes already enrolled. Government investigators had noted that registrars allowed council members to examine the applications of the black voters while ignoring those of the whites. After these officially sanctioned forays into the files, the race supremacists had demanded that many black electors be disqualified for having filled out the registration forms incorrectly. In Washington Parish, 1,517 Negroes were eligible to vote on November 30, 1958, but after the purges on June 30, 1959 the names of only 236 remained on the books. The Civil Rights Division reported that at least 50 percent of the registration cards of the enrolled whites contained the same technical defects as those of the disfranchised blacks.[23] The department charged that the parish registrar understood and approved of the council's racially motivated inquiries, and it asked the federal court to enjoin further raids and to order the purged blacks returned to the registration lists.

The Federal District Court delivered a severe blow to the council's schemes. First, Judge Skelly Wright upheld the constitutionality of the remedies provided in the Civil Rights Act. He dismissed the defendants' contention that the statute was void because it might also be interpreted as covering the discriminatory behavior of private persons. In sharp contrast to Judge Davis's opinion in the *Raines* case, Wright declared,

"This court has no right to consider these imaginary persons in the hypothetical situation conjured up by the defendants before this Court. The duty of this Court is to strain, if necessary, to save the Act, not destroy it." He ruled that the registrar and the Council members used Louisiana's purging provision to deprive black citizens of their suffrage rights. Subsequently, Wright issued the injunction requested by the United States attorneys, and he also ordered the names of 1,377 Negroes placed back on the rolls. On appeal, the same day it handed down the decision in the Georgia case, the Supreme Court affirmed Wright's judgment.[24]

After functioning for over two years, however, the Civil Rights Division had added few Negroes as registered voters. In Georgia and Alabama a small number of Negroes managed to enroll for the first time while in Louisiana over one thousand blacks, previously signed up, became eligible to vote again. The government could partially attribute these disappointing results to the barriers raised by the judicial system. Adjudicating cases before southern federal judges slowed down enforcement of the 1957 act. Reporter Anthony Lewis explained the devastating effects of Judge Johnson's initial decision in Alabama: "It seems certain to make Negroes in the Deep South, who were already hesitant about trying to vote, all the more skeptical about the ability of the Federal Government to help them out." [25] Still, the Civil Rights Division had to accept some blame for the limited accomplishments. Its policy of devoting so much time to research and of initiating a few symbolic cases eventually determined the constitutionality of the law but did not succeed in producing massive black enfranchisement. "We do not question the wisdom of the Justice Department's general position that federal power should be invoked with restraint lest it stir up more resistance," *The New York Times* editorialized. "But even given these factors the Civil Rights Division has surely done less than it should. It has been plodding when it should have been imaginative, timid instead of courageous, sluggish when swift action was needed." [26]

Comparing the performances of the Civil Rights Division and the Commission on Civil Rights (CCR) highlights the Justice Department's shortcomings. The commission functioned with some of the same handicaps as did the Civil Rights Division but nevertheless blazed new paths. An organization mainly interested in the suffrage problem, the CCR was not intimidated by southern intransigence and recommended proposals more far-reaching than those offered by either the civil-rights groups or the administration. In three years, the commission grew from a strictly impartial observer of the civil-rights scene to an advocate for equality.

The composition of the commission seemed designed to soothe racial tensions. In the aftermath of the Little Rock storm, Eisenhower eagerly sought to recommend to the commission the men who could quiet the passions aroused by that turbulence. The president made clear the kind of people he wanted to serve on the CCR:

> They ought to be men of national reputation, so that their opinions, convictions, their findings of fact will be respected by America. I think that we should, so far as possible, have represented on the Commission all types of thinking. There must be men who represent opinions of those who believe more in law . . . and whose reputation is that of being of a judicial turn of mind. In other words, I want to get the spectrum of American opinion on this matter.[27]

With this purpose in mind, Eisenhower carefully assembled a group that balanced both sectional and political loyalties. From the North he chose two university presidents, Michigan State's John Hannah, a Republican, and Father Theodore Hesburgh, an Independent from Notre Dame. The lone black member was Assistant Secretary of Labor J. Ernest Wilkens. Although sympathizing with the goal of racial equality, none of these appointees had been actively associated with the civil-rights movement. From the other side, the president picked two Democrats with typical white southern viewpoints. Former Governors John Battle of Virginia and Doyle Carlton of

Florida believed that segregation was too firmly entrenched in the South to be uprooted; yet, they cringed at the breakdown of law and order fomented by the rabid racists. Slightly more favorably disposed toward civil rights than were his colleagues, Robert Storey, Dean of the Southern Methodist University Law School, completed the Dixie trio. As a past president of the American Bar Association, he also fit the judicial mold desired by the chief executive.[28]

These nominations did not arouse great expectations as to the benefits the commission would bring for Negroes. The *Nation* commented that since the members were "chosen for their devotion to the cause of moderation, the Commission is not likely to break many lances crusading for civil rights." Antagonists in the civil-rights struggle, by praising the membership of the agency, affirmed the opinion that the commission would not move off dead center. Roy Wilkins's evaluation that the CCR "seems to be one which can do a good job" was seconded by Virginia's white supremacist Senator A. Willis Robertson, who called the group "a very splendid Commission."[29] However, White House assistant Fred Morrow provided a different appraisal as he lamented in his diary, "Things like this that vitally involve the Negro race are decided by men who have had little or no experience or contact with Negroes, and who must base their decisions almost entirely upon their own meager knowledge—or often upon the suggestions given them by social or political friends who may be equally uninformed."[30]

Like the Civil Rights Division, the commission got off to a slow start. The president took his time gathering those who might achieve the delicate balance which he desired. On November 7th Eisenhower finally announced his nominees, but the Judiciary Committee's Chairman James Eastland postponed hearings until February 1958. The Mississippi racist was a nuisance as usual; however, he could not deliver a fatal blow. After a favorable committee report on March 4th the Senate voted to confirm. Eastland further halted the inauguration of the commission's operation by refusing to schedule prompt hearings for the crucial post of staff director. Finally on May 14th, over stiff southern opposition, the Senate approved the appointment of Gordon Tiffany, a former New Hampshire attorney general and a political ally of Sherman Adams.[31]

In order to proceed, the commission needed formal complaints. At first the civil-rights groups funneled their allegations of disfranchisement to the Justice Department. Despite Roy Wilkins's initial optimism concerning the functioning of the CCR, the NAACP apparently "took the position that [the Commissioners] were a hopeless bunch and that it wasn't worth wasting time and postage or risking lives sending a complaint."[32] However, when the attorney general hesitated in initiating civil action, blacks petitioned the commission to investigate their grievances. Beginning with the summer of 1958 and ending a year later, the federal agency received 922 sworn affidavits, 310 of which concerned voting. Black citizens of Alabama, Louisiana, and Mississippi furnished the bulk of these written accusations.[33]

Once the CCR processed the complaints, it acted swiftly. While the Department of Justice, which had long known of the disfranchisement in Macon County, was painstakingly cautious in working up a suit, the commission decided to begin an investigation in Alabama soon after becoming aware of the matter.[34] The commissioners immediately faced a test that would demonstrate that they would not tolerate defiance of their duty to survey the suffrage scene. Preliminary to the hearing that they scheduled for Montgomery in December 1958, they sent their agents to subpoena the voting records of various Alabama counties. State attorney general John Patterson advised the registrars not to cooperate because Alabama considered them judicial officers who could not be investigated by an executive branch of the government. To forestall the federal examination, Alabama Circuit Judge George Wallace impounded the registration files of Bullock and Barbour Counties and warned, "If any agent of the Civil Rights Commission comes down here to get them, they will be locked up."[35] Confronted by this opposition, the federal representatives resolved to obtain the information through public exposure and litigation.

On December 8th the commissioners convened an open hearing in Montgomery to obtain the facts about disfranchisement in Alabama. Not since the Bilbo investigation in 1946 had evidence of voting discrimination been so clearly uncovered. This time, however, rather than reading about the proceedings, many Americans observed the testimony directly from their homes. Television, which had brought the country an armchair view of demagogues and mobsters, now exposed a number of vicious registrars before the cameras. With klieg lights glaring and cameras whirring, tight-lipped officials publicly revealed their hostility. In contrast, the video audience saw a group of dignified blacks recount the humiliations that they had suffered.

The superb quality of the black witnesses, most of them from Macon County, underscored the blatant racism practiced by the registrars. Of thirty-three Negroes, ten were college graduates, six held doctorates, while only seven had not finished high school. Most owned property and paid taxes. Several were veterans, and two had received Bronze Stars. Having intelligence, good character, and decent incomes, these citizens maintained that because of their race they had been prevented from becoming voters. No one could attribute their failure in registering to apathy. A woman with a B.S. degree, married to the chairman of Tuskegee Institute's Biology Department, explained her interest in voting: "It is the duty of citizens, and I have four children to whom I would like to be an example in performing that duty, and I want them to feel that they are growing up in a democracy where they will have the same rights and privileges as other American citizens." A Korean War veteran bitterly remarked, "I have dodged bombs and almost gotten killed, and then came back and being denied to vote—I don't like it." [36]

Most of them had found it impossible to hurdle the arbitrary barriers erected by the registrars. A retired procurement officer at the Veterans Administration Hospital described the delaying tactics used against black applicants:

> The colored people have to either wait in a small outerroom or fill up the hall waiting to get in to register. They take two in at a time. I have seen two or three different changes in the board of registrars, and each one changes the thing to suit them—whatever they want to do.

According to his eyewitness account, whites did not face the same conditions, "They meet in the grand jury room where there's a big table, where twelve or fifteen can sit around that table, and I never have seen any loafing in the hall." [37]

Getting in to see the registrars, however, did not guarantee success. A Tuskegee Institute graduate who finally came before the board related that she had been asked to copy Article II of the United States Constitution. Although she spent an hour meticulously writing out eight pages in longhand, she never heard from the board. Consequently, like so many others who had tried, the young woman could not file an appeal within the required thirty days because she did not know exactly when her application was rejected.[38]

The enrollment officers did nothing to refute these shocking charges. At the advice of the state attorney general, the Macon County registrars declined to take the oath in order to testify. Moreover, the commission could not get from them, or several of their colleagues in other counties, the subpoenaed registration files. Rebuffed, the commission called to the stand several probate judges in whose offices the files were normally kept. However, they too were not enlightening and in fact displayed a great deal of ignorance. Questioned by the commissioners, all of the judges denied that they knew anything about registration procedures.[39]

While these officials presented no tangible evidence of wrongdoing, their uncooperative behavior aroused suspicion. Even those sympathetic to the South's position found this performance regrettable. At the end of the first day's hearing,

Commissioner Battle reminded the people of Alabama that he had come "as a friend" who believed strongly in "the segregation of the races as the right and proper way of life in the South." But, he chided:

> I fear that the officials of Alabama and of certain of its counties have made an error in doing that which appears to be an attempt to cover up their actions in relation to the exercise of the ballot by some people who may be entitled thereto. The majority of the members of the next Congress will not be sympathetic to the South, and preventive legislation may be passed, and this hearing may be used in advocacy of that legislation.[40]

The Montgomery *Advertiser* concurred, "The refusal of the officials to testify or offer their voter registration records will be construed as an effort to hide something. Would it not have been better, as Governor Battle responded, to fork them over and avoid all commotion?"[41] The obstruction presented by the southern whites also vexed the president. He found their conduct "so reprehensible, because it means . . . showing the American public . . . they can defy the laws of the land when popular opinion in the particular section or locality may support these people."[42]

Unable to secure the desired records voluntarily, the commission then used coercion. On December 11th, two days after the hearing ended, the Justice Department, at the request of the CCR, asked District Judge Frank Johnson to order the registrars of Macon, Barbour, and Bullock Counties to produce their files. Johnson rendered a verdict in which he showed that despite his previous opinion in the *Alabama* case, he did not intend to mutilate the Civil Rights Act. The judge upheld the provision of the statute providing for the inspection of voting records as "an essential step in the process of enforcing and protecting the right to vote . . . considered 'appropriate legislation' within the meaning of Section 2 of the Fifteenth Amendment." Furthermore, in words reminiscent of Judge Waring's a decade earlier, he issued a stern warning to his native state, "The sovereignty of . . . Alabama . . . must yield therefore to this expression of the Congress of the United States, since this expression of Congress, by this Act, was passed in a proper exercise of a power specifically delegated to the Federal Government." [43]

In compliance, the Macon County Board furnished the files, but Circuit Judge George Wallace did not allow inspection of the Barbour and Bullock County records in his custody. When Johnson directed him to grant CCR investigators access to the material, Wallace instead delivered the records to the various grand juries. The government then worked out with the local officials an agreement authorizing its agents to examine the disputed records. On January 12th and 13th, the commission deputies carried out their assignment. Still disturbed by the "dilatory tactics and rather childish conduct," on January 15th the attorney general petitioned Judge Johnson to sentence Wallace for criminal contempt. Since the registration documents had been produced, however, Johnson was inclined to be lenient. He found "that even though it was accomplished through means of subterfuge, George Wallace did comply with the order of this court concerning the production of the records in question." [44]

This episode had a touch of irony, for it was George Wallace who in 1957 had warned congressional lawmakers of the dire consequences to personal liberty in not extending jury trials to criminal contempt cases. Characteristically, Wallace did not show appreciation for Johnson's tolerance. Running for governor in 1962, he called the judge an "integrating, scallywagging, carpetbagging liar." [45]

Meanwhile, on-the-spot perusal of the suffrage lists by the commission agents turned up solid evidence of racial discrimination. Comparing the applications of both whites and blacks, the investigators confirmed the existence of a double standard. In one batch of forms they found that fifty-one Macon County Negroes were required to copy Article II of the United States Constitution, while only three whites had to do the same. From a set of fifteen white-filed applications marked "approved" the agents discovered similar errors that had caused the rejection of black requests for enrollment. After Wallace capitulated, a spot check of the Barbour County records showed that the registrars had overlooked from white applicants mistakes that they did not tolerate from blacks. For example, when asked, "Will you give aid and comfort to the enemies of the U.S. Government or the government of Alabama?" an approved white voter had responded, "No unless necessary [*sic*]." Having handled the applications selectively from July 1956 through April 1958, the board's enrollment boxscore read 607 whites to fifteen Negroes.[46]

While the commission deliberated, the administration showed few signs of becoming actively involved in the civil-rights struggle. The White House had declared a moratorium on the passage of additional legislation. In September 1957 William Rogers had privately revealed, "We do not plan to recommend that the President submit any further proposals to the next session of the Congress, nor do we plan to recommend that he resubmit Part III of the Civil Rights Bill."[47] A few months later he informed Republican congressional leaders of this decision and suggested, "Let some time elapse before asking for more and see how the 1957 items work."[48] But the Civil Rights Division did not vigorously apply the law, and the attorney general took the position that Negroes should make the greater effort to register and file complaints. This wishful thinking did little to comfort frightened Negroes in the South, and nearly a year after the enactment of the statute, the NAACP convention chided the Justice Department for "dragging its feet." The association resolved, "The 1957 measure should be applied so that Negroes in the Deep South could vote without fear or reprisal."[49]

Alarmed at the increased resistance to school integration and equal voting rights in the South, black leaders voiced their concerns directly to the president. Martin Luther King, Jr., the intense young minister who was rapidly gaining stature within the civil-rights movement following his participation in the Montgomery bus boycott and the Prayer Pilgrimage, along with A. Philip Randolph, Roy Wilkins, and Lester Granger of the Urban League, met with Eisenhower and Rogers on June 23, 1958. The delegation presented nine suggestions, among which was a request that the chief executive direct the Justice Department to "protect the right of citizens to register and vote." The group commented that nearly a year had elapsed without the attorney general's bringing a single case despite extensive complaints from Negroes. Roy Wilkins emphasized that when blacks received the franchise they would bring about peaceful change and adjustment in the South. He explained that the "right to vote is the most effective and bloodless way to solve the whole problem." [50]

The president did not seem encouraging. He said he was dismayed that after five years of effort by his administration, black people were more resentful than ever before. Eisenhower wondered if "further constructive action in this field would not only result in more bitterness." Attorney General Rogers offered his rationale for not having the Justice Department prosecute more vigorously. He emphasized that it was "extremely unwise and damaging to institute court action in every individual complaint." Nevertheless, Eisenhower did not specifically reject any of the group's demands. The president thought that each leader showed "reflective thinking," and none of them recommended anything "extreme." Whatever satisfaction the Negro leaders derived from this meeting was symbolic. For several years they had been trying to persuade the chief executive to confer with them as a modest gesture of his concern for the suffering of southern blacks. They had not expected definite promises, and at least they had exhibited their unity. Furthermore, in the future the White House could not declare official ignorance of black goals. [51]

Moral suasion, when backed up by political muscle, soon lifted the prospects for new civil-rights legislation. The 1958 congressional elections brought victories to those considered sympathetic to the cause of equality. Paul Douglas jubilantly asserted that the Democratic triumph gave Congress a "national mandate to push for a civil rights program in the Senate." The returns convinced Democratic chairman Paul Butler that his party could win again in 1960 only by taking "a forth-right and positive stand" on the issue.[52] In a bipartisan mood, NAACP officials optimistically reported, "The chances of new federal civil rights legislation in 1959 were heightened by the election of liberals of both parties to Congress." [53] After ana-lyzing the trend of black voting in the North, a GOP study group inferred that it was worthwhile to "play percentage pol-itics for small gains in predominantly Democratic Negro dis-tricts." Since blacks made up approximately 5 percent of the population of fourteen northern states which held 261 elec-toral votes, Republican policy makers concluded, "In a close nationwide election, the vote of Negroes may well be crucial in determining which party wins the Presidency." [54]

As was the case in 1956 and 1957, translating political sup-port for civil rights into legislative action proved difficult but not impossible. The first test in 1959 came with the liberals' bi-ennial attempt to alter the cloture rule. As in the past, the upper chamber turned back the liberal attempt to convince the Senate to revise its rules by majority vote. The leadership of both. parties opposed the motion to change the controver-sial regulation, and forty Democrats joined twenty Republi-cans to table it, by sixty to thirty-six.[55] However, seventy-two senators, including eight from the South, supported Lyndon Johnson's mild substitute provision that permitted cloture by two-thirds of all those present and voting.[56] This new proce-dure did not really make it easier to choke off filibusters, but its adoption foreshadowed the enactment of some form of civil-rights legislation. Noting that eight Dixie senators ap-proved of this modification, *New York Times* correspondent Russell Baker accurately commented, "The South has moved away from reliance on obstruction and has begun to exert its skills to get the best compromise available. The question is not whether civil rights legislation will be passed but how strong a bill will it be." [57]

To identify himself further with the center of the Demo-cratic party, Lyndon Johnson introduced a civil-rights bill. In mid January the majority leader offered a program that established an independent conciliation service to mediate racial disputes in tense communities, extended the life of the Civil Rights Commission for two years, and provided for federal investigation and penalties in bombing cases. Johnson dealt with the suffrage problem by suggesting that Congress grant the attorney general the right to subpoena documents concerning registration. This section was designed to repair the damage caused by state authorities who refused to cooperate with the Department of Justice in its inquiries. None of these recommendations were really adequate to reverse the growing white recalcitrance in the South, but in presenting them Johnson was acknowledging the strength that the civil-rights advocates had picked up in the Senate.

Having made this overture to the reformers, Johnson watched as his plan quickly came under liberal attack. The ADA scored his four-point bill as "a typical Johnson compromise, scratching the political surface of the civil rights problem and carefully refraining from dragging to its heart school desegregation." [58] Roy Wilkins branded the proposal "a sugar coated pacifier [conceived] to block consideration of effective legislation in this field." [59] Led by Paul Douglas in the Senate and Emanuel Celler in the House, the liberals produced their own four-part version for racial equality. Their bill specifically endorsed the Supreme Court's desegregation decision, furnished federal funds to help aid school systems lacking money because of state laws to thwart integration, empowered HEW to draw up desegregation plans for communities reluctant to do so, and resurrected Title III. Curiously, this proposal omitted any reference to the franchise. Apparently the liberals believed that the Justice Department was adequately equipped to handle the suffrage problem. "Competent administration," Senator Douglas declared, "and enforcement of the Civil Rights Act of 1957 would remove many of the obstacles to voting." He thought that the liberals should focus their energies on securing compliance with the Supreme Court's school-desegregation decisions.[60]

Steering a customary middle course, the president charted

his civil-rights vessel in calmer seas than did the reformers. With Eisenhower as captain, the ship could be expected to make a plodding but steady journey before reaching its destination. In his State of the Union Address, the chief executive promised that the administration would submit a civil-rights program to Congress early in the session.[61] A few days later, on January 15th, Eisenhower divulged to newspapermen that his first priority was:

> to see this problem of voting solved with whatever laws may be necessary. I would like to see extended the life of the Civil Rights Commission. And if this is done . . . new voters themselves . . . will have a greater and finer opportunity to proceed with, you might say, the proper observation of the other rights.[62]

Although the president avoided answering the question as to whether he favored legislation with desegregation, he called school closings a "tragic" circumstance that tarnished America's image abroad.

Discussions within the administration echoed Eisenhower's pronouncements. Attorney General Rogers, Labor Secretary Mitchell, and HEW's Flemming presented to the chief executive a program principally covering voting, obstruction of justice, school shutdowns, and economic assistance for integration. They suggested extending the life of the CCR and requiring the states to preserve all suffrage records pertaining to federal elections for a three-year period, while empowering the attorney general to inspect the material. Rogers desired this latter provision because Alabama was enacting a law enabling local officials to destroy the questionnaires of unsuccessful registration applicants.[63] To combat the outbreak of violence resulting from heightened racial animosities, the White House advisers counseled imposing criminal penalties on persons traveling across interstate lines to avoid prosecution for bombing or setting fire to religious and educational institutions. Also those who wilfully obstructed the carrying out of court orders concerning desegregation or the franchise would go to jail or receive a stiff fine. Finally the administration confidants took a modest stand on the school issue. They proposed authorizing HEW to provide education for the children of military personnel who found that the states closed their school doors to halt integration. Moreover, at the request of the local government HEW would grant financial and technical aid to assist it in developing desegregation plans. In a surprise move the advisers also drafted a modified Title III, permitting the attorney general to seek an injunction upon the complaint of a citizen that he was being denied equal protection and was afraid to sue for fear of reprisal.[64]

The measure delivered to Congress included all of the cabinet members' points except Title III. Apparently, Eisenhower rejected this section, which had always troubled him. Attorney General Rogers explained what probably was the president's thinking, "If we start a great deal of litigation as a result of new legislation . . . it might actually set the cause back. It might harden resistance too much." [65] Predictably in his special message to Congress on February 5th Eisenhower directed the lawmakers' attention to the right to vote, "the keystone of democratic self-government, [that] must be available to all qualified citizens without discrimination." [66] The other legislative items, especially with respect to desegregation, went further than Johnson's program, but not as far as the liberals'. In fact the chief executive summed up his suggestion as "moderate" because of his "belief that only in moderation is to be found the proper atmosphere for government . . . and the private citizen to work together for progress toward solution of problems that are basically human." [67]

Although the suffrage occupied a crucial position in Eisenhower's program, enfranchisement did not figure prominently in the subsequent congressional deliberations. Hardly anyone became excited over the White House's plan to retain state voting files and have the attorney general examine them. The civil-rights advocates, who had omitted any reference to the ballot in their package, routinely endorsed this administration proposal.[68] The main focus of attention at the Senate and House hearings was integration, prompting the *New Republic* to predict that for "the foreseeable future everything is peripheral to school segregation." [69]

The various bills remained in committees throughout the spring and early summer of 1959. As the weather turned hotter, the civil rights proposals were melted down. The Republicans on the House Judiciary Committee joined the southern Democrats to delete Title III, which the administration had not sponsored. The committee shrunk the proposal even further by removing the sections creating an Equal Job Opportunity Commission and authorizing HEW to provide grants-in-aid for promoting desegregation. [70] At least the House group cleared some portions of the measure, whereas its Senate counterpart first watered down the bill and then drowned it. The Subcommittee on Constitutional Rights, which conducted the hearings, dropped every item except those extending the life of the Civil Rights Commission and preserving voting records for three years subject to federal inspection. Once it had reached the full committee, Eastland and his southern companions grabbed this skeleton and refused to release it from their clutches. [71]

By the middle of August, hope faded for passage of civil-rights legislation before Congress adjourned. The hostile House Rules Committee was holding up H.R. 8601, okayed by the Judiciary Committee, and did not intend to let it go. Although President Eisenhower listed the bill as a top priority for the session, conservative Republicans allied with southern Democrats to postpone consideration. As a last resort Celler filed a discharge petition, but getting the required 218 signatures took a good deal of time. [72] In the Senate the liberals tried several futile maneuvers to get a bill onto the floor; however, the leadership decided to carry over the issue until the next session in 1960. On September 14, Johnson and Minority Leader Everett Dirksen worked out an agreement that LBJ dramatically announced to his colleagues, "I serve notice on all members that on or about twelve o'clock on February 15, I anticipate that some Senator will rise in his place and make a motion with regard to the general civil rights question." [73]

Before the lawmakers departed from Washington the CCR had thrust the dilemma of disfranchisement upon their consciousness. The CCR's final report released on September 9, 1959 was the first in-depth analysis of the franchise prepared by the federal government. Evaluating the "right to vote [as] the cornerstone of the Republic, and the key to all other civil rights," the commission attempted to explain why so few Negroes registered in many areas of the Deep South. Major surveys of the suffrage problem previously taken by private organizations, particularly the Southern Regional Council, had attributed disfranchisement both to racist subterfuges and indifference produced by the caste system. The commission's research supported this conclusion, but emphasized outright chicanery as the main obstacle to black voting. According to the *Report*, "Apathy is part of the answer. However, some of the statistics . . . suggest something more than apathy." Such figures showed sixteen counties where Negroes made up a majority of the adult population in 1950, but not a single one was registered. In another forty-nine counties with predominantly black citizens, less than 5 percent of the Negroes had signed up.[74] Having peered behind the numbers through its hearings and on-the-spot investigations, the commission catalogued the discriminatory practices preventing black enfranchisement. The list covered familiar ground: (a) unequal administration of literacy tests, (b) slowdowns by the boards in processing black applications, (c) the voucher system in Alabama, (d) purging by the Citizens' Council in Louisiana, (e) violence, and (f) economic intimidation.[75]

The commision also evaluated the role of the federal government in expanding the suffrage. "In terms of securing and protecting the right to vote," the commission concluded, "the record of the Department of Justice's Civil Rights Division under the Civil Rights Act of 1957 is hardly more encouraging than it was before." Noting that the CRD had initiated only three franchise cases over two years, the *Report* judged that its "legal actions were disappointing in number, nature and results." George Johnson, the former Dean of Howard University Law School, who had replaced Ernest Wilkens after his sudden death, footnoted:

> The total absence of Negroes from the registration rolls or the registration of only a few such [65] counties . . . warrants at least an investigation by the Department of Justice to ascertain whether there are "reasonable grounds" to institute actions for the preventive relief authorized by the statute.[76]

The commissioner implied that Civil Rights Division lawyers should have spent more time in the field than in their offices compiling statutes and digesting state election laws. Privately, the CCR's Staff Director believed the administration was too cautious. Gordon Tiffany thought the departure of Sherman Adams and Maxwell Rabb from the White House staff in 1958 "marked a subtle change in attitudes about civil rights problems" and made these matters "White House orphan[s]." An Eisenhower Republican, Tiffany called upon the president "in carrying out the law [to] give the public impression of conviction and continuing awareness of moral rectitude in the law which [he] must execute." [77]

Agency officials had a good point. Without prodding from within the executive branch, the Civil Rights Division had indeed lagged behind the commission in exhibiting its fervor for freedom. For example, throughout the summer of 1958 the Justice Department had received several complaints that the black residents of Fayette County, Tennessee had been denied the right to register. While the department turned over the case to the FBI, Tennessee Negroes filed their allegations with the CCR. Apparently, the commission's subsequent inquiry stimulated a registration drive during which 600 Negroes signed up. After county Democratic leaders barred these new eligible voters from casting a ballot in the August 1959 primary, the Justice Department finally brought a successful suit against the conduct of the lily-white election.[78]

In assessing responsibility for the Justice Department's mediocre performance, the commission acknowledged the institutional limitations. The *Report* recognized that communities desiring to discriminate against potential voters had a significant advantage because bigoted local authorities were responsible for administering the election statutes. Thus, the "burden of litigation involved in acting against each new evasion of the Constitution, county by county, and registrar by registrar, would be immense." [79]

Convinced that judicial remedies were not working, the commission recommended a bold approach. "The delays inherent in litigation," it advised, "and the real possibility that in the end litigation will prove fruitless because the registrars have resigned, make necessary further remedial action by Congress." [80] The panel proposed the deployment of federal registrars by the president following a commission investigation. When the chief executive received nine or more sworn affidavits alleging racial discrimination by a state registrar, he would hand over these complaints to the CCR for verification. If it substantiated the accusations, the commission would notify the president to designate a federal employee in the area to serve as temporary registrar. This officer would have the power to administer the state electoral laws and sign up qualified citizens to vote only in national elections. The United States registrar would remain until the chief executive determined that his presence was no longer necessary. [81]

The commissioners unanimously agreed that every qualified citizen should cast his ballot, but they were divided over the best method to safeguard the franchise. Five members of the group supported the registrar mechanism, while John Battle disapproved. He believed the laws on the books were sufficient to protect the right to vote and disagreed with his colleagues' suggestion "which would place in the hands of the Federal Government a vital part of the election process so jealously guarded and carefully reserved to the States by the Founding Fathers." [82] The three northerners, however, considered the registrar plan a "stopgap," and wanted to go beyond it. Hannah, Hesburgh, and Johnson advocated a constitutional amendment conferring the suffrage on "every citizen who meets his State's age and residence requirement, and

who is not legally confined at the time of registration." Not
only would this measure eliminate the troublesome literacy
tests, they argued that it would also take away "the occasion
for further direct Federal intervention in the States' administration and conduct of elections." This last prospect did not
sway the three southerners from opposing the idea. Carlton,
Storey, and Battle dissented because they saw "no clear proof
that the other proposed actions will not correct the evil existing." [83] With the commission evenly divided, this proposal did
not get an official endorsement.

Predictably, the *Report* drew a good deal of unfavorable
comment from the segregationist South. Strom Thurmond
blasted it as "obnoxious and vicious." According to Sam Ervin,
the commission's major proposals could not "possibly be reconciled with the fundamentals of our Constitutional and legal
systems." After reading the document, John Sparkman said it
"was inconceivable that this Congress will continue in existence a Commission that asks us to destroy our system of government." The Alabama senator was wrong. When a bipartisan coalition attached to a military appropriations bill a rider
extending the life of the CCR for two years, the Dixie senators
failed to muster nearly enough votes to defeat it. [84]

In contrast to the die-hard senators, a number of southern
moderates accepted the validity of the commission's criticism.
Estes Kefauver applauded the CCR's concern with the suffrage. He informed Chairman Hannah, "I hope the commission will concentrate on this subject . . . and not wander
afield where the result will do nothing but muddy the waters
of progress." His Tennessee colleague Albert Gore also believed that the federal agency had "quite properly concerned
itself" with the right to vote "which should not be denied to
any qualified citizen regardless of race, religion, or economic
condition." Throughout the South others dared to voice these
sentiments. "If a Negro is a citizen," the Greensboro *Daily
News* declared, "he should be treated as any other citizen in his
right to the franchise. What can be done when the race which
controls the political machinery at the local level will not rec-

ognize basic rights?" Although the Lee County Alabama *Bulletin* thought the registrar plan would reintroduce the threat of "carpetbag" rule, it admitted that the "states have failed to act honorably. Alabama has asked for what it is getting. [Its] officials ought to act in good faith in this matter of registering voter applicants regardless of race or color." [85]

The reaction to its report encouraged the commission to pursue this topic in the future. One staff assistant, Harris Wofford, Jr., noted with interest that the "Southern press in criticizing the Commission's recommendations almost unanimously condemned practices which these recommendations are designed to cure. Here it seems to me is the open door. The solid South is split on this issue." He foreshadowed the shift the upcoming civil rights legislation would take away from the "frustratingly slow and complex problem of school desegregation to this clear cut issue of voting rights [that] is politically right and psychologically healthy." [86] Wofford's reasoning reflected the commission's. Speaking for his brethren, Father Hesburgh asserted:

> We are all convinced, after reading the reaction to our *Report* both in the North and South, that our main emphasis during the months to come should be on the essential matter of voting rights. This is a universally recognized problem and even the South understands that state responsibility in the matter of registration and voting of Negroes is the best guarantee of noninterference in states rights on the part of the federal government.[87]

The commission's revelations stimulated the liberals' interest in the right to vote. Previously preoccupied with desegregation, Roy Wilkins now called upon Congress to defend basic rights of Negroes "in the schools and in the voting booths." [88] The experiences of the civil-rights groups confirmed the CCR's conclusion that the 1957 act was not enough to enfranchise blacks. While the NAACP had conducted numerous registration drives, less than 200,000 additional southern Negroes qualified to vote from 1956 through 1960, bringing the total to 1,414,052. These eligible electors still represented only 28 percent of black adults, an increase of 3 percent.[89] This meager gain was disappointing to the association, which had originally hoped that three million Negroes would be able to vote for president in 1960. Hard-core resistance in the rural black belts frequently stymied the suffragists from pursuing their activities, and hence most of the first-time registrants came from the southern cities. Aware that the federal government would have to confront the most defiant counties, congressional reformers introduced bills patterned after the CCR's registrar plan.

Instead of endorsing his commission's suggestion and presenting a united civil-rights front, the president had some doubts about it. In his State of the Union message he reminded Congress, "The Civil Rights Commission has developed additional constructive recommendations. I hope that these will be among the matters to be seriously considered in the current session." [90] At a subsequent news conference, however, the chief executive undercut the CCR's position. Asked whether he agreed with the majority of the commissioners that a law was needed to provide federal registrars, Eisenhower replied, "I don't know—as a matter of fact—I don't even know whether it is constitutional." [91] Privately, the president confided to several Republican advocates of suffrage expansion that he was withholding endorsement of the measure because he had "some real concern about its practicality." [92] Such comments prompted Hubert Humphrey to remark that Eisenhower had

> pulled the rug out from under his own Commission or at least twisted it. It is a tragedy, because this is the one area of civil rights where strong action might have been expected of the President in view of his noble words about practicing the right to vote. But once again after the platitudes there has been nothing to fill the vacuum.[93]

Nevertheless, the *Report* spurred the president to have new franchise legislation prepared, and by the end of January Attorney General Rogers had it ready. Based on the 1957 act, the proposal equipped federal judges with additional weapons to ensure black registration. After the Justice Department filed a successful suit for an injunction, the attorney general would request the court to make a separate finding that there was a "pattern or practice" of disfranchisement. If the judge reached such a conclusion he could select referees to determine whether the Negroes were qualified under state voting laws. Next the presiding jurist could issue the Negroes certificates entitling them to cast a ballot in both state and federal elections. Furthermore, the referee would oversee the polls to make certain that the black enrollees actually were allowed to vote.[94]

Rogers claimed that this device had advantages over the registration procedure. He admitted that the commission's proposal was "probably" constitutional, but the attorney general did not think it would work. He maintained that a Negro enrolled by a federal registrar might never vote, since he did not have a court injunction backing him up. Without such enforcement machinery the registrant's certificate, Rogers concluded, would be "worth just about as much as a ticket to the Dempsey–Firpo fight. It isn't going to be worth a thing." [95] In contrast, the attorney general placed his faith in the referee process, because any state official who presented an obstacle would be punished for contempt of court. As another plus, the administration's suggestion applied to both state and federal elections, whereas the commission's recommendation pertained only to the latter. Moreover, the Justice Department contended that its measure would generate less resistance than the other by guaranteeing black enfranchisement without unduly upsetting traditional state control over the suffrage. Rogers explained that the implementation of the plan:

> would not fragmentize the electoral process. It would leave the election procedures in the states where they have always been. At the same time, it would operate within established judicial procedures to prevent discrimination in all elections as the Constitution of the United States is intended.[96]

The administration's approach disappointed most liberals. They had become convinced as a result of the CCR's findings that the judicial remedies of the 1957 act were unsatisfactory. Joseph Rauh, an official of the Leadership Conference on Civil Rights, commented "that case-by-case adjudication is not the solution of the denial of voting rights in the South. There are just too many denials. There are just too many state officials resisting." [97] Many civil-rights supporters disapproved of the Rogers plan because they feared litigation would deter speedy registration. Senator Douglas complained:

> If we . . . require the applicants first to try to register under a State system which is hostile to them and then deal with these issues upon appeal to the referee, with the findings of the referee in turn appealed to a district federal judge . . . I think we open up illimitable possibilities for delay. [98]

With the experience of enforcing the 1957 act clearly in mind, the liberals shed their illusions that southern jurists could be counted on to extend political equality to Negroes. Harris Wofford noted, "Some of the Federal district judges in the very Black Belt areas of the Deep South which are most involved are southerners who share many of the attitudes of the local officials for whom a substitute is required." He guessed that some of them would refuse to appoint a referee or would select one as biased as the existing registrar. [99]

These civil-rights critics would have to reach an accommodation with the administration. Liberals recognized this political fact of life and considered the best solution to be some combination of the two proposals. Speaking for the majority of the suffragists, Rauh admitted that "they had to bow to Rogers' anti-civil-rights changes by providing that courts would trigger the enrollment process. Once the court had found a pattern or practice of discrimination the subsequent procedure would follow the original registrar plan." [100] At a civil-rights symposium sponsored by Notre Dame Law School on February 14, 1960, legal scholars and lawmakers concurred that after the initial decision was rendered by the judiciary the following "operation of the federal registration machinery was an administrative task that should be conducted by the executive branch of government." In support of this policy, Harris Wofford pointed out that the federal government already employed dual relief in fields such as trade regulation, with antitrust suits and Federal Trade Commission orders.[101] In early February, Senator Kenneth Keating suggested a slightly different merger of the referee and registrar devices. Retaining both plans intact, he left the president with the option of activating either one, depending on the situation.[102]

The attorney general rejected the olive branch offered by the liberals. He reiterated his earlier position that the registrar procedure was not "going to ensure the right to vote. It may ensure you the right to get a certificate, but that is not going to be worth very much." Before the Senate Committee on Rules and Administration conducting hearings on the enrollment plans, Rogers derided Keating's proposed marriage of the two measures as a "shotgun wedding." He believed that the referee measure provided the only practical method of enforcement. Since every administrative agency had to go to the courts to implement its orders, Rogers did not see "why there [was] any particular advantage in doing it first in the administrative agency and then going to court . . . when you have a statute on the books now that permits the United States to be the plaintiff in the case." [103]

Nevertheless, to meet liberal criticism the Justice Department made some technical changes which strengthened the bill. The original measure did not describe the manner in which the hearings would be conducted by the referee nor did it furnish the criteria he would use to evaluate an applicant's qualifications. The reformers advocated *ex parte* proceedings in order to insulate blacks from cross examination by hostile white residents in their community. Recognizing the validity of this suggestion, the department incorporated it into the plan. Furthermore, this revised proposal prescribed a simple test by which black citizens could prove their eligibility. It merely required Negroes to swear that they were qualified to vote under state law and that they had been improperly denied registration by local officials. The blacks still had to meet the literacy requirements, but the customary abuses would be eliminated since the referee administered the examination and sent the results to the judge for his careful review.[104]

In this election year both parties recognized the advantage of passing a civil-rights act. Supporters in the House applied pressure on the Rules Committee to relinquish the measures dealing with the preservation of election records, the extension of the Civil Rights Commission, the bombing of schools and churches, and the emergency education of children of military personnel where desegregation disputes closed public schools. Democrats Emanuel Celler and James Roosevelt had circulated a discharge petition to free H.R. 8601. By mid January 175 congressmen, of whom 145 were Democrats, signed their names to the list, but another forty-three signatures were needed. When the *New York Times* revealed the identities of those who were backing this maneuver, the Democratic leaders taunted their GOP counterparts for failing to assist them.[105] This public disclosure moved Minority Leader Charles Halleck, in the past a foe of the discharge procedure, to comment, "I have told Republican members of the Rules Committee that I favor the bill coming to the floor. It is fair to assume that the President is in favor of the Committee bill." [106] In a similar vein, liberal New York City Republicans Seymour Halpern and John V. Lindsay wrote Eisenhower:

> [We] are concerned about the apparent public posture of the Republican party on the issue. . . . It seems to us that we should make certain that the public is not mislead as to our intentions and desires in respect of this legislation. The important thing is to bring this bill to the floor and that Republicans be in the forefront in doing so.

White House legislative assistants Bryce Harlow and Gerald Morgan agreed that the chief executive "urge the Leadership to bring the civil rights bill to the House and Senate floors for debate." [107] Shortly after on February 18, four Republicans collaborated with three Democrats on the Rules Committee to report the bill out with the stipulation that debate begin on March 10th.

At about the same time the referee plan, in addition to the civil-rights measures introduced the previous year, reached the Senate floor. True to his word, on February 15th Lyndon Johnson guided the omnibus bill into consideration. With very few senators in attendance, the majority leader received unanimous consent to take up House-passed legislation enabling the Army to lease a barracks as a temporary replacement for a burned-down school in rural Stella, Missouri. Johnson announced that civil-rights proposals could be added to this innocuous bill, and Dirksen, who was in complete agreement with the majority leader's strategy, attached the administration's items to it. Managing the legislation in this way, the Texan had shrewdly avoided the roadblock set up by the Senate Judiciary Committee. Furthermore, in accordance with congressional procedure, if the upper chamber approved any of the civil-rights amendments the bill would return directly to the House for reconsideration without a hearing in the Rules Committee.[108] Upset by the majority leader's end run, the southerners came out with the preventive defense of the filibuster.

Johnson used the delay to forge a moderate bill. After a week of leisurely discussion, the majority leader notified his colleagues that on February 29th he would start calling round-the-clock sessions. In this way he hoped to win approval for a compromise bill that appealed to the northerners and that the southerners would not passionately resist. To be sure, several sections, notably those dealing with integration and employment, would probably have to be dropped in order to gather the two-thirds majority for ending a filibuster. Even if cloture failed and the Dixie forces thwarted a vote on the pending amendments, Johnson believed the Senate would still act on civil rights. He guessed that while his colleagues talked themselves hoarse the House would pass the limited bill reported by the Judiciary Committee and send it up for Senate deliberation. Hence, with most of the lawmakers worn out, this minimum program might obtain swift approval.

Both sides prepared for the marathon. Senators limbered up for sleeping on army cots, couches, and in some cases rubdown tables in the Senate office building. Although smaller in number than their opponents, the obstructionists held a definite advantage over the civil-rights battalions. As in 1957, they were guided by Richard Russell. The prototype of a southern gentleman, this taciturn Georgia bachelor, it was said, usually spent quiet evenings at home memorizing Senate rules, a practice that paid off whenever civil-rights legislation was brought up. Divided into three squads of six men each by Russell, every member of the southern team spoke in relays of four hours and then rested for two days. Furthermore, on midnight quorums called by the Dixie troops, their southern comrades remained peacefully asleep while the northerners unhappily had to pull themselves out of bed.[109]

As the endless speeches reverberated throughout the partially filled halls during the first week in March, it became clear that any accord reached would be based on the right to vote. The southerners, as they had done in 1957, displayed the least bitterness toward suffrage legislation and cautiously refrained from condoning racial disfranchisement. Senator Russell placed the referee proposal "way down the line in the order of being obnoxious to me and my associates." [110] Questioned whether he found the provisions of the 1957 act acceptable, B. Everett Jordan from North Carolina admitted, "We could at least live with that system." [111] "Congress has a right to pass legislation to apply the Fifteenth Amendment," The New Orleans *Times-Picayune* grudgingly conceded, "it is specific and not subject to the same stretching and misinterpretation as the Fourteenth." [112] From the North, the *New York Times* expressed the opinion of moderates who favored a settlement centering on the ballot, "While every disability against any citizen is intolerable in a free democracy, the voting disability is the most intolerable of all, and once it has been wiped out the rest will surely follow." [113]

After a week of nonstop conversation, the liberals and Johnson split over when to end the filibuster. The majority leader did not want a cloture vote until after the bill was shaped into a suffrage measure which would win the consent of two-thirds of the Senate. In contrast, the reformers favored closing debate immediately and forcing a showdown on the entire administration program. On March 8th the old Title III was introduced as an amendment to the Dirksen proposal; the liberals did not wait any longer. The parliamentary situation put them in a desperate position. A senator could offer an amendment to the bill, but the southern filibuster prevented a vote directly on the measure. However, the Senate could entertain moves to table it, and these motions were not debatable. If the tabling motion were defeated, the liberals would not triumph, because Title III still had to be voted into the bill, and the southerners would continue to block this effort. But if the Senate successfully voted to table it, the substantive amendment would be dead. Thus, Senators Javits, Clark, and Douglas offered a cloture petition so that the chamber could end the procedural confusion and simply vote on the legislation.[114]

As they provided no competition for the leadership of both parties, the liberals failed in their cloture attempt. They were doomed once Minority Leader Dirksen, one of the bill's sponsor's, threw his support to Johnson. The Illinois Republican did so without White House disapproval. The president declined to get into a fight over the controversial Title III, since he had not recommended it in the first place. In fact, during the time of the debate Eisenhower had been touring Latin America, and when he returned shortly before the vote he did not appear familiar with the Senate events.[115] On March 10th, twenty Republicans joined thirty-three Democrats to defeat cloture. Since less than a majority of those voting had supported the termination of debate, it was no shock that the senators next decided to table Title III by a margin of fifty-five to thirty-eight. Twenty-one Republicans and thirty-four Democrats delivered the fatal blow. Without a presidential endorsement, GOP support for this section fell sharply from what it had been in 1957. That year twenty-five Republicans had favored Title III, compared with ten Republicans three years later. However, Democratic support had increased in that period from thirteen to twenty-eight, with most of the gain from thirteen nonsouthern Democrats elected in 1958. However, their votes could only offset Republican defections.[116]

Losing the cloture battle did not mean an end to reform. The Washington *Post* placed the encounter in its proper perspective, "The defeat of cloture does not mean that the filibuster forces have won. It means only that the final showdown will have to come on proposals that are more moderate than the so-called Part III." [117] To achieve success, Walter Lippmann suggested, "Congress should agree on a bill which deals solely, but sincerely and effectively with the right to vote—what LBJ has wanted them to do from the beginning." [118] At any rate, the majority leader discontinued the prolonged sessions and waited for the House to pass a bill that the Senate could accept with little alteration.

In the House, the Democratic party powerbrokers worked toward a compromise. Speaker Sam Rayburn, the sage of Bonham, Texas, and Johnson's mentor and confidant, set the tone for the debate by appointing Francis E. Walter, a Pennsylvania Democrat, as chairman of the Committee of the Whole. Walter served as head of HUAC and had often cooperated politically with Rayburn and the South. In his present assignment he determined which amendments were germane. Since the liberals hoped to fortify the bill through additions from floor amendments, the presiding officer might make or break their efforts. The only proposal which Walter could not declare out of order, as decided by the Rules Committee, dealt with the referee plan. On March 14th, after several days of discussion, the Pennsylvanian clarified his intention of keeping the omnibus measure in the form designed by the Judiciary Committee. He rejected additions offered by Celler that created a commission on equal job opportunity and funded grants to assist local schools to carry out desegregation. Each time by a wide margin, the House sustained Walter's decision. On a later occasion, amendments to abolish the poll tax in federal elections and to extend the power of the attorney general to obtain Title III injunctions met the same fate.[119]

The moment of truth came over the suffrage measures. John Lindsay offered the original referee plan, and then William McCulloch of Ohio, the Judiciary Committee's ranking Republican, introduced the slightly modified version that detailed the procedure that the court agent would follow. This revision also contained a section that might frighten Negroes from seeking relief. It provided that after a judge found a pattern or practice of discrimination, the black applicant must make another unsuccessful try to register before obtaining a hearing with the referee. This procedure gave the state a fresh opportunity to behave fairly, but failed to take into account that many black southerners who had been intimidated by white men would not care to confront them again.

Dissatisfied with this strictly judicial approach, and concerned that blacks would be afraid to register, Robert Kastenmeier, a Wisconsin Democrat, put forward as a substitute an enrollment-officer plan. Originally conceived by Senator Thomas Hennings of Missouri, this device combined features of the administration's bill with those of the CCR's recommendation. For instance, either a finding of racial disfranchisement by the commission or a successful suit brought by the attorney general under the 1957 act could push the president into selecting federal enrollment officers. These supervisors would then register all Negroes qualified to vote under state law, and the local authorities could challenge these decisions only when the blacks actually voted. Finally, as in the referee program the federal agent inspected the balloting and the vote tabulation.[120]

The final determination on which plan to adopt resulted as much from political considerations as from the relative merits of the judicial or ministerial procedures. Because of the partisan divisions, the southerners held a balance of power and almost wrecked the entire suffrage program. On March 15th the first vote came on the Kastenmeier substitute, and by a vote of 152 to 128, the House accepted it, knocking out the McCulloch version. Observing this teller vote, the *New York Times* reported that enough southerners joined the liberal Democrats to discard the administration plan. This strange coalition next voted 116 to seventy-nine to replace the Lindsay amendment with the Kastenmeier provision. On the final tally, the Dixie ploy became obvious. Taking advantage of the Republicans' distaste for a Democratic bill, the southerners marched behind the GOP congressmen to defeat it, by 170 to 143.[121] The House now had no franchise measure, and the chamber resounded with partisan recriminations. James Roosevelt charged that if the "Republican members had wanted to have a better and more effective voting rights bill they could have had it then and there by supporting the Kastenmeier amendment." On behalf of his GOP colleagues John Lindsay retorted, "[Some] gentlemen from the majority side were very ready to scuttle the whole thing rather than to see a program adopted which happened to have a Republican label on it." [122]

Instead of dwelling on who was to blame, civil-rights proponents of each party united. Led by Emanuel Celler and William McCulloch, the liberals rallied behind a slightly altered administration measure. In fact, they even improved it. James G. O'Hara, a Democrat from Michigan, introduced an amendment that civil-rights lawyers had previously favored, namely, provisional voting. Any black applicant whose registration status had not been determined by the court twenty days prior to an election would have the right to cast a ballot, subject to challenge only at polls. According to O'Hara this method would frustrate white officials who planned on judicial delays to thwart federally certified Negroes from voting.[123]

After approving this section by 188 to 120, the bipartisan coalition repelled all efforts to debilitate the functioning of the referee system. The greatest threat was overcome when the House narrowly defeated, by 137 to 134, an amendment by Homer Budge, a conservative Republican from Idaho, to restrict its operation to federal elections. Finally on March 23rd in the typically sectional division, 172 Democrats and 123 Republicans approved the Celler-McCulloch-O'Hara measure over the opposition of 100 Democrats and twenty-four Republicans. The next day, by a similar breakdown of the vote, the House approved and sent to the Senate a five-point civil-rights bill.[124]

Meanwhile, events in the Senate had indicated that measures bolstering the referee plan could not win approval. Joseph Clark and Jacob Javits introduced a bill as a compromise between the administration's and Henning's offering. Clark, a genteel politician who had served as reform mayor of Philadelphia, was one of the most pungent critics of the Senate's cumbersome procedures and the clique of lawmakers who dominated the upper chamber. Before the Javits-Clark plan went into effect, like the referee proposal, it required a federal district judge to determine that a pattern or practice of discrimination existed. Following this decision, either the court could appoint referees or the president could select registrars. In any case, the provision did not compel a black applicant to make a second attempt to register. Clark recommended this procedure because it allowed

> the Attorney General to have two arrows in his sling—to use the judicial referee proceeding in the hard-core areas where tough opposition could be expected, but also have available the efficacious administrative remedy for other areas where large numbers of disenfranchised [*sic*] citizens could be registered without much opposition expected.[125]

However, Rogers remained adamant and rejected Clark's offer. "As a practical matter," he harshly said of the suggestion, "it would be worthless." [126] The Senate concurred with the attorney general, and on March 24th a bipartisan coalition agreed to table the amendment, by fifty-one to forty-three. Listening to the advice of Rogers and following the lead of Dirksen, twenty-four Republicans united with twenty-seven Democrats. Yet had seven Democrats who occasionally supported civil rights voted with their northern colleagues, they would have changed the result.[127]

The day on which the Javits-Clark measure was shelved, the Senate made its first move to dispose of the House-passed H.R. 8601. With only four members dissenting, the upper chamber affirmed Johnson's motion referring the bill to the Judiciary Committee with instructions to return it not later than March 29th. With his back to the wall, Eastland, who had bitterly opposed this action, chose to conduct hearings. Much of the two-day investigation was spent listening to Attorney General Rogers and his assistant Lawrence Walsh belittle as meaningless all of the plans except the one for referees.[128] Accepting the probable passage of the administration plan, the southerners aimed their fire at its procedures. Sam Ervin complained that barring state registration officials from the *ex parte* deliberations of the referees violated the constitutional guarantee of due process of law. The North Carolinian was not satisfied when Walsh reminded him that if the referee acted incorrectly, "that may be demonstrated to the court." [129]

After the committee ended the hearing, it added a new handicap for many Negroes who wanted to vote. Seven Democrats, mainly from the South, edged five northern Republicans and two Democrats, inserting into the bill a requirement that the interviews held by the referees take place in public and the local registrar have the opportunity to bring along his attorney.[130] Sharing Ervin's concern, Estes Kefauver sponsored this clause, which destroyed the protective safeguard that *ex parte* deliberations provided black petitioners who were partially paralyzed by fear of white intimidation. Although an advocate of enfranchisement, the Tennessee senator also believed, as he had demonstrated in his support of the jury-trial amendment in 1957, that the accused were entitled to definite procedural rights. Also, Kefauver faced a difficult campaign for reelection and his swipe at the administration's measure might soften the criticism of his favorable civil-rights record.[131]

On the Senate floor the liberals quickly pounced on the Kefauver proviso. Disturbed that the presence of unfriendly whites in the referee's chambers would hamper the enrollment process, Kenneth Keating explained, "The applicant would be confronted by the fellow who refused to register him previously and that man's lawyer would be breathing down his neck." [132] The New York senator also reminded his colleagues that the defendant registrars would already have had their day in court in the original trial before the district judge. In response, Kefauver denied that it was his "intention to give State registrars or their attorneys the right to crossexamine, to testify, to harass, to take part in the proceedings, unless the referee called upon them to do so." [133] To be sure, the civil-rights advocates drafted an amendment that clarified Kefauver's stated purpose. Presented by John Carroll of Colorado, the modification ensured, "The applicant shall be heard *ex parte* at such times and places as the court shall direct." [134] The Senate overwhelmingly passed this clarifying section, by sixty-nine to twenty-two.

Fresh from this victory, the liberals failed in their last-ditch effort to win approval of an alternative plan. On behalf of the reformers, Thomas Hennings introduced his enrollment program as a supplement to the referee device. Hennings was an early and committed friend of civil rights and of civil liberties who had dared stand up to the bare-knuckled assaults of Joseph McCarthy. Tireless in his advocacy of measures to extend racial equality, unfortunately the Missouri Senator had a drinking problem that diminished his ability to provide the liberals with active leadership. Unlike Rogers, Hennings, had no doubt that his enrollment method would work, because the federal courts would be authorized to enforce it by issuing injunctions at the request of the Justice Department. "All the Attorney General has to do," Hennings declared, "is to carry out his oath of office with appropriate zeal, industry, and ingenuity." [135] This reasoning was to no avail as the Senate tabled the Hennings amendment, by fifty-eight to twenty-six. Thirty-four Democrats and twenty-four Republicans easily overcame the opposition of twenty-one Democrats and five GOP partisans. Not surprisingly, the lawmakers also tabled a measure suggested by Michigan Democrat Philip Hart to "waive as a requirement of proof before a court or referee . . . the additional burden upon members of the group discriminated against of going to the local boards and again seeking registration." [136]

As predicted by Lyndon Johnson, the final version of H.R. 8601 was moderate. The Senate rejected amendments to restore Title III, to create an equal employment commission, to provide Congressional recognition for the Supreme Court's desegregation decision, and to extend financial assistance to communities integrating their schools. Consequently, on April 8th, except for the token opposition of eighteen southerners, the upper chamber easily adopted the reduced civil-rights bill. This outcome caused Joseph Clark to wryly remark, "Surely in this battle on the Senate floor the roles of Grant and Lee have been reversed. The eighteen implacable defenders of the way of life of the Old South are entitled to congratulations from those of us they have so disastrously defeated." [137]

Led by Johnson, a Republican–southern Democratic coalition aided by some Western Democrats had crushed the reformers' attempts to improve the bill. Sixty-three percent of the Senate Republicans had collaborated with the Dixie bloc on more than half the roll-call votes, compared with 32 percent of the nonsouthern Democrats who had done so. Of those legislators who opposed the anticivil-rights forces more than 75 percent of the time, twenty-five were Democrats and five belonged to the GOP.[138] On procedural questions such as invoking cloture, the reformers could not break the Johnson-Dirksen axis. Moreover, the Department of Justice had consistently rejected the liberals' plea to eliminate the provision necessitating applicants to try again for enrollment by the state registrar. Dazzled by the parliamentary wizardry Johnson and the southerners displayed, together with the administration's reluctance to compromise on the referee proposal, the civil-rights enthusiasts failed. Nevertheless, the liberals did enlarge the White House's suffrage plan. Having accepted it for practical reasons, they helped strengthen the procedure by including provisional voting and *ex parte* hearings.

The referee plan had presented the least common denominator for agreement on a franchise measure. President Eisenhower and his Attorney General William Rogers were tightly bound by their view of the federal system. From their perspective, the referee procedure would not upset the traditional relationship between Washington and the states because it retained the control of county officials over the electoral process. Moreover, Eisenhower and Rogers placed great faith in enlightened southerners to rally behind the rulings of southern-born federal judges and their appointed referees. This conciliatory outlook prevailed, and the final legislative product demonstrated, as Congressman Celler aptly put it, that both "parties are split on the issue of Civil Rights. The fact is simply that there are not enough votes . . . to obtain a really strong bill." [139] After deleting from the measure controversial provisions involving school desegregation and equal employment opportunity, administration spokesmen and Johnson-led Democrats repelled the efforts of the liberals to include a registrar proposal. At the same time, they were true to the spirit of moderation and also upset the attempts of southerners to mutilate the referee format. As a result, the Republicans claimed credit for shaping suffrage legislation and the Democrats preserved party harmony while supporting the principle of enfranchisement; however, both groups benefitted at the expense of the majority of southern Negroes for whom the prospect of acquiring the right to vote remained bleak.

Demoralized after the heat of battle, Negroes and white liberals refused to count their blessings. An embittered Paul Douglas commented that the referee measure "sets up an elaborate obstacle course which the disfranchised Negro in the South must successfully run before he will be permitted to vote at all." [140] The *Nation* evaluated the referee process as "a legal labyrinth beset with booby traps." [141] The bill is a "fraud," NAACP attorney Thurgood Marshall moaned. "It would take two or three years for a good lawyer to get someone registered under this bill." [142] His associate Roy Wilkins seconded this conclusion by stating, "The Negro has to pass more check points and more officials than he would if he were trying to get the U.S. gold reserves in Fort Knox." [143] The Pittsburgh *Courier* predicted that the legislation "will mean exactly NOTHING. It will not mean a STEP FORWARD." [144] Southern spokesmen lent credibility to these interpretations. Strom Thurmond wrote his constituents that the final bill "indicated a pattern of defeat for the NAACP." Allen Ellender called it "a victory for the South," and his fellow Louisianian Russell Long admonished, "Very little will be accomplished . . . if the majority of the white people of the South are determined to frustrate its terms and conditions." [145]

Moderates disagreed. President Eisenhower said he was happy, and William Rogers claimed, "This new law holds forth great promise for substantial and steady progress." [146] Everett Dirksen discerned in the passage of this legislation "a demonstration that by a gradual process we round out the great American dream which was sketched for us 180 years ago." [147] Perhaps through the same rose-colored glasses, the Washington *Post* viewed the bill "from the perspective of American history [as] a significant milestone in the long march toward political equality." [148] Estes Kefauver praised the bill because "to the extent that the Civil Rights Act of 1960 will help guarantee the exercise of this right [to vote] it is in my estimation a helpful and needed piece of legislation." [149]

Each of these contradictory appraisals contained some truth. As was the case with the 1957 Act, law alone would not miraculously enfranchise blacks. Instead, the federal government vigorously had to apply its available resources to stimulate black registration. With this analysis in mind, the participants in the Notre Dame Conference on Civil Rights had predicted that passage of a referee plan would "encourage Negroes to make new or future attempts to register. It may lead the Department of Justice to become far more active in the protection of civil rights." [150] As if to prove the point, William Rogers announced to the United States attorneys that they should count on increased legal action to protect voting rights. As a matter of fact, over the next five months the new chief of the Civil Rights Division, Harold Tyler, initiated four voting cases, one less than the total number presented during the previous two and a half years.[151] In cooperation, Martin Luther King, Roy Wilkins, and A. Philip Randolph formed a "Nonpartisan Crusade to Register One Million New Negro Voters." [152]

The outcome of these efforts, however, would depend a good deal upon the southern federal judges who supervised the referee system. While a few jurists such as Frank Johnson and Skelly Wright, had demonstrated a determination to carry out the law, the general forecast looked cloudy. Only in time could a final judgment be rendered on the educated guess of Jack Peltason, a noted legal scholar, "It is not likely . . . that federal judges will use the 1960 Civil Rights Act in such a fashion as to arouse the ire of Southerners. Judicial decisions here . . . are not likely to make any major departure from the norms of the community." [153]

9

The Suffrage Crusade in the South: The Kennedy Phase

THE CIVIL-RIGHTS FORCES that had helped arouse Congress to enact two pieces of suffrage legislation over the past three years did not intend to relax. In fact, by 1960 the movement was rapidly gaining new recruits who felt restless about the gradual pace toward equality. While the established interracial leaders pressed Washington for laws to deal with unfinished business—school desegregation and equal employment—a younger generations of blacks and their white allies brought the protest movement to the streets. Demonstrators held sit-ins, rode freedom buses, and marched in order to confront directly the Jim Crow system and test the meaning of the Fourteenth and Fifteenth Amendments. The militants organized voter registration drives to force the federal government into vigorously implementing the recently enacted statutes. Because they risked their lives daily to promote enfranchisement, the suffragists expected the Justice Department to guard them against those who might block their efforts. Whoever followed Eisenhower as president inherited the increased power to protect voting rights; his determination to use it over the next crucial years would greatly influence the course of the civil-rights struggle.

By 1960 the black vote figured into the presidential calculations of the major political parties. The strategic location of Negroes in the North had convinced national lawmakers to provide legislative assistance for black southerners. Although since 1936 most Negroes had aligned with the Democrats, fresh trends hinted that the GOP might lure enough of them away to swing an expectedly close election. In six vital cities—Chicago, Cincinnati, Cleveland, Kansas City, New York, and Pittsburgh—Negroes gave less support to Stevenson in 1956 than they had to Truman eight years earlier. Unless the 1960 Democratic candidate received a larger proportion of the black ballots, he had little hope of winning Illinois, Ohio, Missouri, and probably the election. "Neither party can afford to ignore the numerical weight of the Negro vote," Oscar Glantz concluded from the data. "In the next campaign the Democratic candidate will have the responsibility of reversing the changing image of the Democratic party, while the Republican candidate will have the responsibility of enlarging . . . the appeal of the Republican party." [1] With the ever popular Dwight Eisenhower out of the running, the black electorate's backing might furnish the margin of victory.

Although neither nominee for the top office was the first choice of the reformers, each had aided the cause of racial equality. As Democratic senator from Massachusetts, John F. Kennedy had voted for Title III and for amendments strengthening the referee plan. He had not hesitated to applaud the *Brown* opinion, even in unsympathetic Jackson, Mississippi, telling a gathering in 1957, "I accept the Supreme Court decision as the supreme law of the land. . . . We must all agree on the necessity to uphold law and order in every part of the land." [2] However, Kennedy had displeased civil-rights leaders when he lined up behind the jury-trial amendment to the 1957 act. They also were wary because some southerners had boomed him for vice-president in 1956, and Governor John Patterson of Alabama beat Kennedy's campaign drum for the number one spot in 1960. Martin Luther King commented that although the senator displayed "a definite concern" about the plight of Negroes, he did not have a "depthed [sic] understanding" of the problem.[3]

Richard Nixon's civil-rights record compared favorably with that of his Democratic rival. In 1957, Dr. King had thanked Nixon for his "assiduous labor and doubtless courage in seeking to make the Civil Rights Bill a reality."[4] Three years later, Roy Wilkins praised the vice president for "his good record on civil rights." He recalled his ruling on behalf of cloture reform and believed that Nixon had "done something behind the scenes" in active support of the 1960 act.[5] Louis Lautier, veteran political columnist for the *Afro-American,* noted that the vice president and the attorney general were close friends, and suggested that Nixon had spurred Rogers to move vigorously "under the 1960 Act . . . to inspect the voter registration records of election officials" in several Deep South counties where few blacks were enrolled.[6] Despite these laudatory remarks, Richard Nixon remained the liberals' bête noire from his congressional service on the witchhunting HUAC and his association with conservative Republican economic policies.[7]

Kennedy realized that he had some ground to cover before boosting his appeal among black voters. The Massachusetts Democrat appointed to his staff several Negroes, including Louis Martin, former editor of the Chicago *Defender,* and also named Harris Wofford, the liberal assistant to Father Hesburgh, as coordinator of civil rights. Wofford convinced Kennedy that the best chance for progress in this field would come from strong executive conduct.[8] Thus, the candidate repeatedly stressed the Democratic Convention's pledge that a new administration would "use the full powers provided in the Civil Rights Acts of 1957 and 1960 to secure for all Americans the right to vote." He vowed to enforce the existing laws "with vigor and determination" and to see that the franchise was "not denied because of laxity or indifference in the office of the Attorney General."[9] Furthermore, as president, Kennedy promised with the "stroke of a pen" to issue orders eliminating discrimination in federally subsidized housing and in businesses that held government contracts.

Meanwhile, Kennedy did not ignore the need for supplementary legislation. In accordance with his party's platform, he promised to take "whatever action is necessary to eliminate literacy tests and the payment of poll taxes as requirements for voting." [10] If elected, the senator asserted that he would provide Congress with firm leadership and not abandon the civil-rights forces as, he claimed, the retiring chief executive had done. In order to fulfill this pledge promptly, Kennedy named Senator Joseph Clark and Representative Emanuel Celler to "prepare a comprehensive civil rights bill, embodying our platform commitments, for introduction at the beginning of the next session." [11] Besides the suffrage proposals, the program would include a reintroduction of Title III, which Eisenhower had refused to approve.

Nixon presented a slightly different civil-rights package. The GOP standardbearer professed to believe that the federal government had a proper role in preventing abuses of voting procedures, but he did not recommend that Congress completely abolish the literacy test. The vice president contended that this "requirement has been a valid and reasonable one since this Nation was founded. It should be retained." Instead, he suggested a new law that removed the bias in the application of the examination. To this end, he counseled Congress to establish "the completion of six primary grades in an accredited school as prima facie evidence of literacy for voting purposes." [12] Although Nixon refused to sanction a blanket Title III, he did recommend empowering the attorney general to bring suits in "appropriate" school desegregation cases. Otherwise, the nominee ran on a Republican platform that advocated granting aid and technical assistance to schools that attempted to integrate, creating a Commission on Equal Job Opportunity, prohibiting housing discrimination, and revamping Rule 22. [13]

At the same time that they appealed for northern black

votes, both adversaries flirted with the South. Kennedy's running mate, Lyndon Johnson, invited his Dixie neighbors to remain in the Democratic yard. He did not hide the fact that he had guided the passage of two civil-rights bills, but the majority leader campaigned "as the grandson of a Confederate soldier," told a "few homely Texas stories," and reminisced "about his kinship with each state." [14] Pursuing his own southern strategy, on several occasions Nixon journeyed into the Deep South with the message that racial equality was not just a regional problem. The Republican nominee spoke the audiences' language of gradualism when he declared, "Neither of our political parties nor any Administration can expect to solve all at once all problems for all times to come." [15] Committed to the GOP's strong civil-rights plank, Nixon rationalized his own position in terms more acceptable to the southerners. With the Cold War on most minds following the U-2 fiasco and the collapse of the Paris summit conference earlier in the year, he explained that by providing justice for minorities the United States took away from "the Communist leaders any arguments against America and what she stands for." [16] Theodore White, the observant political chronicler, reported that Nixon's theme was well received.[17]

By the final weeks of the hotly contested campaign, prestigious black opinionmakers were leaning toward the young senator from Massachusetts. They believed that a Democratic administration offered Negroes a better deal on civil rights and economic benefits. The *Amsterdam News,* which had endorsed Eisenhower in 1956, criticized the Republicans for failing to speak out on "desegregation, lynchings, appointment of Negroes, opposition to the $1.25 minimum wage, federal aid to education, and medicare for the aged." Since Franklin Roosevelt's first term, impoverished blacks had looked toward Washington for relief of their ills, and they did not appreciate Nixon's theme of returning domestic responsibilities to the states. The Chicago *Defender* called the Republican platform "skimpy and uncertain" on the matter of the "rights of the minority races and the pursuit and accomplishment of these rights through the agency of the Federal Government." [18]

Most black northerners did not seem to allow Kennedy's religion to interfere with their favorable impression of him. Reflecting on the possibility that a Catholic would be elected president, the *Afro-American* tersely noted, "It's about time." [19] An *Amsterdam News* columnist chided some black Protestant ministers in the South who opposed Kennedy because of his church affiliation. "The very thought of this kind of blind, dangerous prejudice," Earl Brown fumed, "should send cold chills down the spine of every Negro in the country." [20] Although the 200,000 member Eastern Baptist Association advised all of its followers to shun Kennedy's candidacy, a poll of the members revealed that they would not adhere to this biased counsel. [21] Also dissenting, Adam Clayton Powell, Jr., a former Democrat for Eisenhower and pastor of the Abyssinia Baptist Church in Harlem, thundered from his pulpit against this kind of "unchristian, un-Godly, and un-American religious bigotry." [22]

In the last days of the battle, an incident occurred that gave each candidate an opportunity to demonstrate his concern for the civil-rights movement. On October 25th Martin Luther King, Jr. was sentenced to four months hard labor in a Georgia jail for a minor traffic-related violation. At the suggestion of Harris Wofford, Kennedy telephoned Mrs. King to offer his sympathy and possible help. The next morning, Robert Kennedy, the nominee's younger brother and campaign manager, on his own initiative interceded with the Democratic state judge who had presided over the case and convinced him to release King on bail pending an appeal. [23] The Kennedy brothers' intervention seemed even more impressive when compared with Nixon's silence on the incident. Although the vice president strongly believed that the black leader was "getting a bum rap," he considered it improper to call the judge. [24] After consulting with Nixon, Attorney General Rogers asked the White House to release a statement that the Justice Department was investigating whether King's constitutional rights had been violated. Unexplainedly, such comforting words never came. [25]

As a result, Kennedy quieted most of the reservations that

Negroes had expressed about his candidacy. The day King stepped out of prison, Reverend Ralph Abernathy, his closest associate, decided to vote Democratic. "I was going to vote for Mr. Nixon, maybe," Abernathy explained, "I hadn't made up my mind. But now I am not going to vote for him." [26] Likewise, Martin Luther King, Sr., a Baptist minister who objected to the senator's religion, put aside his prejudices and announced, "I've got a suitcase of votes, and I'm going to take them to Mr. Kennedy and drop them in his lap." [27] This crucial episode enhanced the affirmative impression that the Massachusetts Democrat had worked so hard to make. James L. Hicks, executive editor of the *Amsterdam News* and an Eisenhower Democrat, placed the drama in the proper perspective, "Kennedy had already SHOWN enough interest in Negroes BEFORE King was jailed, to have enough Negroes around him to tell him WHEN King was jailed that this was a matter which he should speak out on." [28]

John F. Kennedy became president with less than a majority of the nation's popular votes and with few electoral ballots to spare. In such a close election it was difficult, if not impossible, to isolate the single factor that furnished the margin of victory. One of the senator's trusted advisors, Theodore Sorensen, remarked, "[H]ad Kennedy not scored large majorities among . . . Negroes, Jews and union members . . . had he not convinced almost as many Protestants as Catholics who had voted for Eisenhower to switch to him—he would not have won the election." [29] Undoubtedly blacks made up a significant part of the triumphant coalition. An analysis of the returns demonstrated that Negro ballots were enough to give the Democratic contender a winning margin in New Jersey, Michigan, Illinois, Texas, and South Carolina, all states that had supported Eisenhower in 1956. Had the Republican-Democratic division in the black districts of these states broken down in the same way as four years earlier, Richard Nixon would have become the thirty-fifth President. Instead, Kennedy collected an average of 70 percent of the black ballots cast, a 7 percent improvement over the share Stevenson had received. In New York, Pennsylvania, and Minnesota, Negroes helped swell the victor's plurality in the large cities and restored those states to the Democratic ranks. A stunning reversal from the last election came in the swing toward Kennedy by southern blacks. This about-face enabled the senator to hold all but two of the region's traditionally Democratic states where Nixon made inroads on the white electorate.[30]

It was also difficult to pinpoint the exact reasons for Kennedy's popularity among Negroes. One must remember that for nearly twenty-five years, black electors had clearly identified themselves with the party of Franklin Roosevelt. Since Dwight Eisenhower, who had been popular among all groups, was not running, a shift to almost any Democrat might be expected. In fact, although the Massachusetts senator did better than Stevenson had among Negro voters in 1956, he just about equaled the former Illinois governor's share of the black ballots cast in 1952. The King intervention only explained a portion of the return of the Democrats' customary Negro support. Despite Kennedy's assistance to the influential minister, many blacks, particularly in the South, did not clearly perceive the two candidates' differences on the civil-rights issue. After the election, the University of Michigan's Survey Research Center concluded on the basis of its interviews that:

> one set of . . . Negro respondents moves from Republican identification in 1956 to Democratic identification in 1960, justified on civil rights grounds, whereas the other set, attempting the same calculus for the same reasons and with the same information . . . moves from Democratic identification in 1956 to Republican identification in 1960.[31]

It is quite possible that even without the King incident Kennedy would have received the 7 percent gain because of the appeal that the Democratic party's social-welfare programs had for impoverished blacks. Especially after suffering through the recession in the last few years of the Eisenhower administration, most Negroes were anxious to support the party that had brought relief from the Great Depression. As one black Chicago resident told Theodore White, "Mister, they could put a dog at the head of the ticket, and if they called him Democrat I'd vote for him. This hoolarium about civil rights don't mean anything to me—it's the man that puts money into my pocket that counts." [32]

The composition of the Congress elected along with Kennedy did not auger well for the "New Frontier." The Republicans added two senators and twenty-one congressmen; the Democrats still controlled both Houses, but they were ideologically divided. Of the 262 Democratic Representatives in the lower chamber, 101 came from the South, and most of them sided with the GOP on domestic issues. Deprived of an overwhelming mandate, John F. Kennedy did not dare to antagonize unnecessarily the entrenched group of southerners and conservative Republicans who often blocked liberal legislation. As a student of history, Kennedy probably remembered that even Franklin Roosevelt, who had triumphed by a landslide in 1936, could not shatter the "conservative coalition." For a Democratic chief executive interested in racial justice the dilemma was particularly acute; dependent on the powerful southern faction, how could he push for civil-rights legislation without ripping his party asunder and jeopardizing the remainder of his program? Kennedy must have known that Harry Truman spent most of his two terms unable to knock Congress off dead-center. [33]

To break the legislative logjam, Congress had to chop away some of the obstacles that clogged the decisionmaking channels. For nearly a decade, Senate liberals had vainly attempted to alter the cloture rule. When they tried again in January 1961, Majority Leader Mike Mansfield of Montana moved to send the issue to the Committee on Rules and Administration, which he chaired. Kennedy chose not to get involved in this question, and the Mansfield motion was narrowly adopted, by a vote of fifty to forty-six. With Kennedy silent, a dozen Democrats from the border states and the West, along with the predictable southerners, followed their Senate leader to delay reform. [34]

Rather, the chief executive picked the House as the arena for a showdown. Kennedy expected the two southern Democrats and four Republicans to block liberal legislation as they had done in the past by voting against the six northern Democrats on the Rules Committee. After intensive lobbying from the administration and with the active cooperation of Speaker Rayburn, the lower chamber closely accepted a motion, by 217 to 212, to add three members to the committee.[35] The president hoped that the newcomers would join the liberal Democrats to weaken the conservative stranglehold on progressive legislation. In gaining this victory, Kennedy checked the lesser of the two evils haunting civil-rights measures. In 1956 and 1959, the Rules Committee had only been able to delay the strong judiciary bills from reaching the floor, but in the Senate the filibuster had worn away several of the potent items such as Title III.

Regardless of the fate of congressional reform, Kennedy assigned civil rights a low priority on his legislative agenda. He did not care to spend the time or effort on this controversial subject, for fear of sacrificing his liberal economic measures. By going all out on the race issue, the president thought he would solidify the conservative bloc against proposals that benefited those people of low income, including blacks. "If we drive Sparkman, Hill, and other moderate Southerners to the wall with a lot of civil rights demands that can't pass anyway," Kennedy wondered, "then what happens to the Negro on minimum wages, housing, and the rest?"[36] The chief executive believed that legislative action was doomed to fail. He interpreted the partially successful rules fight in a pessimistic manner. "With all of that going for us, with Rayburn's own reputation at stake, with all of the pressures and appeals a new President could make, we won by five votes." The president concluded, "That shows you what we're up against."[37] Moreover, if Kennedy was correct and once Congress failed to respond to the civil-rights forces, he feared that disillusioned blacks would wage their struggle in the streets, and he strained to avoid such a confrontation.

Besides, in 1961, the young president felt little moral urgency to eradicate racial inequality. He based much of his opposition to discrimination on political grounds rather than on deep personal conviction. According to Theodore Sorensen, his trusted confidant, when Kennedy "talked privately about Negroes at all in those days, it was usually about winning Negro votes." [38] Precisely because blacks contributed greatly to his triumph, Kennedy could not ignore their aspirations.

Consequently, he chose a strategy that did not directly challenge southerners in Congress and at the same time relieved some of the pressure exerted by blacks for new legislation. Utilizing the powers of his office, Kennedy demonstrated to Negroes that the federal government cared about them. During his first year as president, he appointed Negroes to high positions, persuaded the Coast Guard Academy to recruit more black candidates, invited civil-rights spokesmen to the White House, named the conscientious Harris Wofford as his special consultant on race relations, and established a subcabinet group to coordinate civil-rights efforts within the executive branch. Although Kennedy moved cautiously, he did send federal marshals to protect the freedom riders from the vicious mob violence they encountered in Alabama. Determined to prove that the interracial travelers had not suffered in vain, the attorney general brought a successful action before the Interstate Commerce Commission to desegregate all rail and bus terminals. In 1962 and 1963, when stubborn governors in Mississippi and Alabama attempted to frustrate court ordered integration of their state universities, the chief executive mobilized troops to get the black students into the classrooms. And, after serving for nearly two years, Kennedy finally found a pen with which to write a decree banning certain types of housing bias.[39]

The Kennedy administration, however, displayed its executive style most consistently in the field of voting rights. The president, as did Eisenhower, relied on extending the franchise to open the way for black advancement. He reasoned that once Negroes cast their ballots they could in time dramatically alter the intransigence of Southern political leaders in all other civil rights measures, shift the balance of political power in several states, and immunize Southern politics from the demagogue whose only campaign cry was "Nigger." [40]

By vigorously implementing the legislation recently placed on the books, the White House had a chance to prove that it could alleviate the suffering of mistreated blacks. Shortly after taking office as attorney general, Robert Kennedy made this intention known, "I have an impression that people in the Department of Justice wanted to do more, but were held back by a general hands off policy in the past. . . . This won't be true in the future." [41]

The Kennedys rallied behind suffrage expansion. At first, they had considered a mild proposal left over from the Eisenhower administration. The Civil Rights Division had suggested "a full scale publicity program sponsored by the Department of Justice . . . to stimulate interest in registration applications by qualified Negroes." [42] However, since the freedom riders had accelerated the pace of black protest, in early 1961 the president discerned that his civil-rights constituency would not be satisfied with a public-relations campaign. Instead, Harris Wofford and Assistant Attorney General Burke Marshall induced several philanthropic agencies to provide the money for organizing massive voter registration drives.[43] This kind of activity did not usually involve large-scale demonstrations, but depended on laborious door-to-door canvassing and establishing citizenship schools.

Lured by the prospect of fresh contributions, the habitually underfinanced civil-rights groups were willing to focus their energies on enfranchisement activities. A series of meetings on June 9, June 16, and July 28, 1961 attracted representatives from the Taconic Foundation, Field Fund, SNCC, SCLC, Congress of Racial Equality, NAACP, National Urban League, SRC, and the National Student Association. The White House sent Marshall and Wofford as observers. All those in attendance completely agreed "that voter registration is a matter of the highest, though not the sole priority." [44] When the foundations expressed their willingness to subsidize a suffrage project, Martin Luther King recommended that the Southern Regional Council assume the responsibility of supervising the field work and disbursing the money to the participants. The interracial council was mainly a research group long concerned with black disfranchisement, and it was an excellent selection to allocate the revenues impartially among organizations that normally competed for scarce dollars. This coordinating agency was prepared to devote full-time attention to the painstaking planning needed to organize voter-registration drives on the precinct and county levels and not be distracted by the "glamour" of direct-action campaigns. Leslie Dunbar, the SRC's executive secretary, reported that he "was deeply impressed by the amiability and harmony of the gathering." [45]

Nevertheless, the suffrage plan sparked some controversy. Some members of SNCC, fast becoming the most militant of the civil-rights groups, distrusted the motive of the national government in promoting voter registration. Coming soon after the sit-ins and freedom rides, these students suspected that the Kennedy administration wanted to "cool off" their militancy and substitute a more sedate form of protest. [46] Another faction within the student committee wholeheartedly believed that blacks could radically improve their lives by participating fully in the southern political process. Even before the foundations offered their money, Robert Parris Moses, a black SNCC field secretary, had been planning a voter-registration program in several counties of the tough Mississippi Delta. A twenty-five-year-old mathematics teacher at a private school in New York City, in 1961 Moses quit his job and thrust himself full time to breaking down the barriers to black enrollment. For Moses, registration campaigns would not only open up the ballot boxes to Negroes, but would also free his people from the mental bondage of the racist caste system. He later reflected:

> You dig into yourself and the community to wage psychological warfare; you combat your own fears about beatings, shootings, and possible mob violence; you stimy [sic], by your mere physical

presence, the anxious fear of the Negro community . . . that maybe you *did* come only to boil and bubble and then burst, out of sight and sound; you create a small striking force capable of moving out when the time comes, which it must, whether we help it or not.[47]

A majority of SNCC agreed with Moses. A young man who joined the movement in southwest Georgia described the emancipationist philosophy:

I consider the work in voter registration . . . to fit within the same context of non violent direct-action as the sit-ins and other forms of protest and demonstration. In many ways it seems to me that the voter registration project is even more significant than other forms of protest. The problem of segregation is being attacked at its core. A new sense of human dignity and self respect is being discovered.[48]

The young activists also discovered that like the freedom rides, participation in voter-registration drives in the Deep South would bring them in direct confrontation with the racist system. Moses had graphically proven this point when he was beaten up by Mississippi whites and arrested by the state police in August 1961.[49] Furthermore, SNCC doubters became less apprehensive once they realized that with white liberals paying the bills, finances usually reserved for suffrage drives could be diverted into mass protest.[50]

The NAACP held some reservations about joining the venture, but for reasons different from those of SNCC. Long concerned with the suffrage front, the association jealously guarded its reputation as the dominant agency conducting voting drives. Roy Wilkins thought that it would be a

disservice . . . and confusing to the public if the NAACP's cooperative joint listing with other groups, some of which thus far have little more than good intentions to offer, should be taken to imply equality as regards their relative importance and potential in the work to be done.

In addition, Wilkins feared that some of the militant groups would divert energy away from the common goal by deploying their forces in other areas. "Recent events have already indicated," he complained, "how voter registration activity can be sidetracked when allied with diversionary efforts." Nevertheless, the NAACP recognized the enormity of the franchise task and concluded "that no bona fide source of help should be excluded." [51] Its last doubts were removed by Leslie Dunbar, who assured Wilkins that the Southern Regional Council did "not think that a 'joint listing' betokens equal importance," and he pointed out that there would be a lesser chance of "sidetracks" if the NAACP shared its wisdom in the mutual enterprise.[52]

The remaining groups were eager to mobilize their legions. Martin Luther King, whose SCLC had sponsored voting drives in the late 1950s, declared, "If we in the South can win the right to vote it . . . will give us the concrete tool with which we ourselves can correct injustice." [53] For James Farmer of the Congress of Racial Equality (CORE), the gains from the undertaking transcended material improvement. "We do not register so much to secure better garbage collection (important as that may be)," he commented, "as to assert our dignity." [54] The Urban League, whose branches in the South had been deprived of community-chest funds as a result of segregationist attacks following the *Brown* decision, could not resist the liberals' tempting financial offer. Although it usually focused on welfare matters, vocational guidance, and disseminating housing and employment information, the league felt justified in promoting registration "from the standpoint of education for citizenship and assisting the Negro community to live up to its full responsibility as good citizens." [55]

Supported by the "big five" of the civil-rights movement, the SRC was prepared to start its operations by the end of March 1962. Wiley Branton, a black Arkansas lawyer who had represented the harassed school children in Little Rock, was appointed director of the Voter Education Project (VEP). While the council created the nonpartisan VEP to stimulate registration, it also aimed to investigate and expose the causes of disfranchisement. Assigned the fieldwork by Branton, each unit conducted a suffrage drive "in such a way as to gather reports which will be submitted to VEP for analysis and study of the methods and techniques used by the organizations, the problems encountered, solutions developed, and results of the program." [56]

To perform its research function, the council designated locations throughout the South where blacks faced both bitter resistance and little opposition. The Congress of Racial Equality ventured into hostile northern Louisiana and rural South Carolina, and SNCC and SCLC set up programs in unfriendly southwest Georgia and Mississippi. In contrast, the NAACP and the Urban League were mainly responsible for canvassing in more receptive Tennessee, Florida, North Carolina, and Virginia cities.[57] Putting aside the normal jurisdictional disputes, the civil-rights groups, with the exception of the Urban League, joined together as the Council of Federated Organizations (COFO) to maximize their strength in Mississippi. With Aaron Henry, head of the state NAACP, as president, and Robert Moses as director, COFO received and disbursed money furnished by the VEP.[58]

The civil-rights shock troops could not advance too far without adequate reinforcement from Washington. Assistant Attorney General Burke Marshall had sat in on the conferences launching the VEP, and while he placed the administration's blessing on the project, he never specifically promised federal protection of the registration workers.[59] According to the SRC's Harold Flemming, who also attended the meetings, "I never heard anybody from the Justice Department say, 'Sure you fellows go out there and we'll give you all the protection you need'." [60] Still, Marshall apparently left the impression that the national government would intervene to safeguard the activists' constitutional rights. "[F]ederal cooperation," Wiley Branton recalled, "without spelling out what that cooperation would be, was implied, and in fact promised." [61] Inside the movement, opinions varied over the definition of "cooperation." The VEP director and Martin Luther King believed that it meant "all steps necessary to protect those rights in danger." [62] Robert Walters, who sat in on the early planning sessions as a spokesman for the National Student Association, understood Marshall to pledge "teams of FBI men, use of all legal devices the Justice Department had available, and any other aid we could reasonably expect." [63] Interpreting the commitment more narrowly, CORE "assumed that the Justice Department will bear expense of suits against registration boards if they are needed," and the NAACP agreed that the "Justice Department might proceed [as it did in the Eisenhower Administration] to bring actions under civil rights statutes." [64] At any rate, the Kennedys had encouraged the interracial groups to engage in voter registration in the first place and they had a moral responsibility to use federal authority on behalf of those entering into the southern battlegrounds.

The men in charge of the Justice Department attempted to fulfill their obligation to the suffrage activists in lawyerlike fashion. While they adhered to the democratic creed of racial equality, neither Robert Kennedy nor Burke Marshall had been identified with the cause of civil rights. Kennedy had made his reputation as a scourge of labor racketeers, and Marshall had reached prominence as a corporate attorney. Not driven by an ideological fervor to wipe out discrimination immediately, they sought to negotiate with recalcitrant southern officials in a calm and rational manner. At the very beginning of his tenure in office the attorney general explained:

> I have had a number of conversations and conferences with the leadership of many of these states where there is a problem. And I have pointed out to them that in a certain county it would appear that the Negroes were discriminated against. In a number of instances they have indicated that they themselves would take steps to insure that the Negro is permitted to register. Where they will take the steps themselves, where we can do it on an amiable basis, this will be done and kept out of the courts; but where steps were not taken by the local authorities or by the states, we, ourselves, will have to move.[65]

Marshall asserted that the Kennedy policy was "to make the federal system in the voting field work by itself through local action, without federal court compulsion." [66]

The Justice Department, however, discovered that many southern officials did not respond to gentlemanly persuasion, and it mounted an offensive. "In Mississippi and parts of Alabama and Louisiana," Burke Marshall lamented, "the size of the Negro population and political factors have made efforts for voluntary compliance fruitless." [67] Rebuffed by local authorities, the Civil Rights Division no longer waited for complaints from blacks in order to go into court, as it had done for so long under Eisenhower; instead, the division prosecuted when the registration data that it had previously compiled showed probable discrimination. At the hearings on his nomination, Marshall had frankly admitted to an unsympathetic James Eastland, "I would expect to file suits in some cases where the investigation was started without a specific complaint." [68] Furthermore, the assistant attorney general doubled the number of voting-rights attorneys on his staff to ten and sent them down South to supervise prosecutions and negotiations. John Doar, an energetic young lawyer hired by the Civil Rights Division during the final months of Republican rule, coordinated the trial work and served as troubleshooter when tense situations threatened to explode.

As the Justice Department representatives observed the situations for themselves, they discovered many instances where litigation was essential before Negroes could vote. Armed with volumes of statistical proof, Civil Rights Division attorneys convinced most federal jurists that deceptive enrollment practices were occurring. "An exhaustive analysis of accepted and rejected applications," Robert Kennedy explained, "enables the court to articulate precisely in its decree the standards by which applications are to be judged by the registrar." [69] In 1962 Judge Frank Johnson of Alabama carefully reviewed the registration documents and concluded that Montgomery officials had applied a double standard, since "1070 white applicants whose applications contained errors were accepted in a five year period compared with only 54 Negroes." [70] That same year, the Fifth Circuit Court of Appeals issued an injunction ordering the registrar of Forrest County, Mississippi, to disregard "insignificant errors and omissions" in the blacks' forms as he had overlooked similar mistakes in the whites'.[71] In 1963 the Justice Department persuaded a District Court in Louisiana that a parish registrar had purged the names of 953 blacks, based on errors also made by 75 percent of the white voters who remained on the lists; the judge ordered that the names be restored.[72]

Perhaps the most notable victory achieved by the federal government resulted in the judicial concept of "freezing." Civil Rights Division attorneys warned that guilty registrars might legally nullify the intent of an injunction against future bias by strictly applying the suffrage procedures to both races. Since most whites and few blacks were enrolled, crafty officials could perpetuate the status quo and not technically violate the law. To forestall this possibility, the Justice Department requested the courts to "freeze" the "requirements to vote which were in effect, to the benefit of others, at the time the Negroes were being discriminated against." [73] Thus, adult blacks would only have to meet the criteria, or lack thereof, that whites had during the period of disfranchisement. To accomplish this, the judiciary had to suspend the administration of literacy tests that had been unequally applied in the past. In a pioneer decision in 1962, Judge Johnson accepted this reasoning and ordered the registrars of Montgomery County, Alabama, to "apply the same standards used by the Board . . . in qualifying white applicants during the period within which the pattern of discrimination is found to exist." [74] Displaying a slight variation of the principle behind freezing, the judiciary struck down the voucher system. In 1963 a Louisiana District Court voided this requirement in counties where blacks had been kept off the suffrage lists, and thus could not get any voters of their race to identify them.[75] Thus, the Kennedy administration had successfully challenged most of the suffrage requirements put on the books by the white South to keep Negroes from registering. Charles Hamilton, after studying the judicial confrontation between 1957 and 1962, concluded, "[T]he federal courts have virtually nullified all possible 'legal' efforts to deter Negro voting." [76]

The government had a tougher time in combating more subtle persecution of blacks. Although the 1957 Civil Rights Act outlawed discriminatory coercion, the Justice Department faced the difficult task of proving that an individual intended specifically to interfere with the right to vote. When a county board of education in Mississippi refused to renew the contract of a black teacher who had participated in a voter registration campaign, the Civil Rights Division charged that this was a racially motivated reprisal. Neither the federal district nor appellate courts, however, found sufficient evidence that the defendants fired the educator because of her extracurricular suffrage activities.[77] In Rankin County, Mississippi, three blacks who came to enroll were severely beaten by the sheriff after he warned them to leave the crowded courthouse. The courts ruled that this brutality was an isolated event and not part of any deliberate plan of disfranchisement.[78] However, most of the harassment occurred daily, and complaints seldom reached the federal judiciary. Civil-rights workers were arrested for a variety of minor offenses such as traffic violations, vagrancy, breach of the peace, and trespassing. It did not matter whether they were convicted, one volunteer lawyer who handled these cases wrote, because the "primary effort is to use arrests and threats of arrest, costly bail, to hamstring voter registration." [79]

Nevertheless, the Civil Rights Division won several cases involving illegal economic pressure. Its attorneys argued the case of Joseph Atlas, a Louisiana farmer who suffered financially because he testified before the Civil Rights Commission in 1961. In retaliation, merchants did not sell him supplies, ginners refused to process his cotton, and grain elevator operators stopped storing his grain. After the government went into court, the defendant businessmen agreed to cease the boycott.[80] In Haywood and Fayette Counties, Tennessee, where the Civil Rights Division had successfully litigated an end to the white primary, landowners evicted all tenants and sharecroppers who registered, and merchants declined to trade with them. At the request of the Justice Department, a federal court of appeals in 1961 enjoined the use of these methods to prevent blacks from signing up.[81] In 1963 landowners in Wilcox County, Alabama, denied a black insurance man, who had led a registration drive, access to his clients renting on their property. The United States Court of Appeals issued a decree prohibiting this "coercion for the purpose of interfering with the right or rights of others whom he represented in exercising their right to register and vote." [82]

Occasionally the Justice Department was able to prevent other serious annoyances. John Hardy, a black Tennessean and SNCC staffer, was one of the first outsiders to infiltrate in Mississippi. During the summer of 1961, Hardy conducted a voter-education school in Walthall County, where none of the 2,490 adult blacks was enrolled. Having accompanied his graduates to the courthouse, Hardy was warned by the registrar, "Get out of here you damn son of a bitch and don't come back in here." As Hardy started to walk out, the registrar, John Q. Wood, whacked him over the head with a pistol. To add insult to injury, the wounded civil-rights worker was arrested for disturbing the peace. John Doar personally managed the case and sought to enjoin the county from bringing Hardy to trial. The government attorney contended that such a pursuit would deter other Negroes, fearing similar consequences, from trying to register. His proposition was first rejected by a District Court, but Doar convinced the Circuit Court of Appeals to issue a restraining order blocking the prosecution, and nearly a year and a half later in April, 1963, the charges were dropped against Hardy.[83]

Sometimes the Civil Rights Division made southern law officers aware that they could not thwart the efforts of civil-rights personnel by arresting them on phony charges. In Terrell County, Georgia, where the department had won its first suit under the 1957 Civil Rights Act, less than fifty blacks were eligible to vote in 1962. Though SNCC field secretaries diligently canvassed the area, they ran up against the stiff opposition of the sheriff and his deputies. In July 1962 Zeke Mathews, "keeper of the peace" for twenty years, locked up two suffragists for vagrancy. The Justice Department quickly asked for an injunction barring prosecution and prohibiting the sheriff and his aides from arbitrarily hindering those engaged in franchise projects. Decisively challenged by Washington, the sheriff modified his behavior. Even before final disposition of the case, a SNCC member happily reported that he and his compatriots were "not really harassed constantly by the police; we have not . . . been stopped for traffic offenses, nor have we even been followed." In January 1964 a federal district court permanently enjoined the defendants from disturbing individuals who promoted registration.[84]

Despite the increased effort and successes, the mass of blacks remained unregistered. After governmental suits in forty-six counties, 37,146 Negroes could vote out of 548,358 black adults who lived in those areas. Overall in 1964, the 2,074,461 Negroes eligible to cast ballots in the South constituted only 40 percent of the black population of voting age, compared to 70 percent of the adult whites. In Mississippi, Alabama, Louisiana, and Virginia less than one-third of the potential enrollees had qualified.[85] Even Marshall deduced that these figures were "not encouraging." [86] Especially in the rural black-belt counties of the Deep South, most of the Negroes still were afraid to make attempts to register. Litigation did not stop whites from exerting economic pressure or prevent local officials from using dilatory tactics to keep blacks off the rolls. The courts generally were too slow in providing relief for those submerged at the bottom of the racial caste system.

The federal judges played a vital role in proving the merits and flaws in the voting-rights statutes. Recommended by the senators of their states and generally committed to the values of their region, the appointed jurists, observed Marshall, "want to do as little as possible to disturb the patterns of life and politics in their community." [87] But other factors reduced the possibilities for obstructionism. Members of the Court of Appeals reflected a broader spectrum of southern opinion and did not feel as directly the pressure to conform as did their brethren sitting on the district benches. Furthermore, the chief judge of the Fifth Circuit Court of Appeals, who presided over most of the cases, was Elbert Tuttle, a jurist committed to "prompt hearings in the district courts, accelerated settlings of appeal in the appellate courts, and temporary relief by way of injunction when the law was clear." [88] As head of the circuit, Tuttle assigned the personnel to review lower-court decisions and often picked colleagues sympathetic with civil rights. Above all, the liberal Supreme Court served as the ultimate arbiter, and the southern judges were sworn to apply its rulings.

Whereas many of the district-court jurists upheld black voting rights, a vocal minority rendered opinions that delayed progress and frustrated the demands of the suffragists. Charles Hamilton classified the jurists into three categories. The "judicial aggressor," like Frank Johnson, cooperated with the Department of Justice and oversaw compliance with his decrees detailing equitable registration methods. The "judicial gradualist," represented by Ben Dawkins of Louisiana, held strong segregationist views; however, after his initial decisions were overturned, he faithfully interpreted the law as the higher courts directed. The "judicial resisters" canceled out the fine performances of their robed brothers. Die-hard white supremacists such as William Harold Cox, Claude Clayton, and Ben Cameron, ignored recent precedents demolishing schemes for disfranchisement and railed against outside agitators. Cox referred to blacks as "niggers" who lined up to register and pushed "people around, acting like a bunch of chimpanzees." He scolded John Doar, "I spend most of my time in fooling with lousy cases brought before me by your Department." [89] Cameron informed the world beyond the Magnolia Curtain how he arrived at a verdict, "It is the universal conviction of the people . . . that the judges who function in this circuit should render justice in individual cases against a background of, and as interpreters of, the ethos of the people whose servants they are." [90] To make matters worse, these jurists presided in Mississippi, where they continuously collided with the civil-rights freedom fighters living among the rural black population and failed to halt the campaign of terror waged against them.

Cox and company used delay as their main tactic to preserve the status quo. On August 11, 1960 the federal government requested the registrar of Forrest County to make his files available for inspection as mandated by the Civil Rights Act passed earlier that year. Theron Lynd refused, and on January 19, 1961 the government asked Cox to force compliance with its demand. Months elapsed without an answer from the judge, and on September 6, 1961, before Cox gave a ruling, the attorney general brought another suit in his court to enjoin Lynd from discriminating against black applicants. Finally, on February 15, 1962 Cox dismissed the proceedings on obtaining the records, and a month later he granted the defense a recess on the campanion action. On April 10th, the United States Court of Appeals, at the instigation of the Civil Rights Division, came to the rescue and issued the desired decree.[91]

In Panola County on October 16, 1961 Judge Clayton had received a request from the Civil Rights Division to restrain the registrar from further discriminatory behavior. Not until March 19, 1963 did the jurist call the case to trial, and after three days he held for the defendant. On May 22, 1964, nearly a year later, the appeals tribunal unanimously vacated Clayton's judgment and delivered the order which the government had sought thirty-two months before.[92] In the interim, blacks had to sit out several elections waiting for the judicially sanctioned blockade of the ballot boxes to be broken. Although the obstructionist judges did not "affect the final outcome of litigation," Burke Marshall perceived, they did "directly and deeply affect its pace." To one commentator the drawn-out maneuvers resembled a "chess game where the appellate court is continually checking the diversionary tactics of the district courts but without a checkmate." [93]

The Kennedy administration, whose voting-rights strategy centered on the judiciary, added to its own frustrations by appointing some of the recalcitrant judges in the first place. The tradition of senatorial courtesy was partly responsible, inasmuch as Kennedy's nominees had to meet the approval of the southern Democratic senators whose preferences were against racial equality. Then they were obliged to run the gauntlet of the Senate Judiciary Committee chaired by James Eastland, a notorious champion of white supremacy. But the president did have some leeway. Within the boundaries imposed by the political system, his advisors screened judicial candidates in order to keep Negrophobes off the bench. Executive assistants quizzed each candidate to gauge whether he would implement the Constitution and Supreme Court decisions. However, the investigative process was not foolproof, and perhaps the administration suspended critical judgment if the denial of an appointment would raise a political storm. Harold Cox, a law-school roommate of Eastland's at "Ole Miss," won the president's okay by telling the attorney general of his intention to uphold the law of the land.[94] Since there was much more civil-rights adjudication during the sixties than the previous decade, Kennedy's poor selections were in a position to do more damage than in previous years. On paper, the assignments made by the president seemed of quality equal to those picked by his Republican predecessor, but if, as one scholar calculated,

> one takes the total number of civil rights cases decided by all the Eisenhower and Kennedy judges in each year and determines the percentage of those cases that favored the Negro plaintiff, the Eisenhower judges have a more liberal record than do the Kennedy judges.[95]

The civil-rights guerilla forces in Mississippi, Louisiana, Georgia, and Alabama evaluated the Justice Department strictly on its ability to shield them from racist terror. It did not really matter to the suffragists that most of the Democratic appointed jurists interpreted the statutes without bias. The movement needed a powerful tool to shatter the chains of white brutality shackling panic-striken Negroes and keeping them from registering. Carver Neblett, a young black SNCC organizer in Southwest Georgia, explained the problem:

> How does one get it across to the people that we are not alone, when all around them white men are killing and getting away? Not only getting away, but also in many cases being promoted. . . . Following the killing of Bobby Hall in Baker County in which Sheriff Claude M. Screws was involved in 1943, Sheriff Screws was elected to the State Senate in 1958. A. B. Henre who is now Mayor of Bronwood killed a Negro 14 years ago. How do you push a meeting when they tell you, "I might be killed, my house may be burned, I may be fired from my job, etc"? [96]

Isolated in the rural areas of the South, the rights workers depended on a vigilant federal government for psychological as well as physical support. "The Justice Department," Charles Sherrod, a SNCC field secretary, stated, "is a magic phrase and in the Deep South holds an unbelievable position of confidence . . . in the minds of the oppressed." [97] Yet, soothing words from Washington were not enough for the beleagured emancipators. Aaron Henry, whose house was fire-bombed on Good Friday, 1963, predicted, "Until the Department of Justice moves in and guarantees the right to life and freedom from police intimidation and hoodlum involvement, Mississippi is not a safe place to live." [98]

Events in Greenwood, Mississippi, revealed the plight of the activists. Since June 1962, SNCC people had encountered severe hostility while canvassing in Greenwood, the seat of Leflore County, where only 2 percent of the adult blacks could vote. White mobs ransacked their office, thugs beat them up, police officers threatened to "bash in" their teeth, and county officials discontinued the distribution of surplus food to over 20,000 Negroes after SNCC's exhortations prompted dozens of blacks to attempt to enroll. At one point in August, the SNCC staff faced so much danger that they decided to tone down their activities for a period of time. When winter came, the group sent out a distress call for food and clothing. As contributions poured in from the North, hundreds of Negroes

gathered the strength and courage to apply again for enrollment. Angry over these developments, on February 28, 1963,
white nightriders blasted shots at a car carrying Randolph
Blackwell, a VEP aide, Robert Moses, and his SNCC partner
James Travis, who was badly wounded.[99]

Officials of the VEP viewed this incident as an opportunity
to prod Washington into safeguarding the workers before
anyone got killed. Wiley Branton commanded all VEP sponsored agencies in Mississippi to descend on Greenwood. On
March 1st he alerted Attorney General Kennedy that the

> campaign will begin immediately. You must anticipate that this
> campaign will be met by violence and other harassment. We are
> notifying you in advance so that you can provide the necessary
> federal protection to prevent violence and other forms of intimi-
> dation against registration workers and applicants.[100]

Branton's warnings came true. During March the COFO
headquarters was set ablaze, eight suffrage protesters were
jailed, several SNCC members and local blacks were shot at,
and the police broke up a peaceful march to the courthouse
by unleashing growling dogs on the demonstrators. On March
29, Branton telegraphed Robert Kennedy:

> LOCAL POLICE HAVE NOT ONLY FAILED TO PROTECT PEOPLE SEEKING
> TO REGISTER BUT NOW USE VIOLENCE AND INTIMIDATION THEM-
> SELVES AGAINST NEGRO CITIZENS ACTIVE IN VOTER REGISTRATION. I
> URGE YOU TO ACT AT ONCE TO RESTORE LAW AND ORDER TO LEFLORE
> COUNTY MISSISSIPPI AND PROTECT THE LIVES AND PROPERTY OF
> NEGRO CITIZENS.[101]

Although the Justice Department came to the side of the
besieged civil-rights platoons, its response did not entirely satisfy them. When first informed of the VEP's plan, Burke Marshall had urged restraint. He preferred that the group postpone its drive until after a pending franchise suit was settled.
If Negroes were frightened away from enrolling during the
campaign, Marshall maintained, they might not make another
attempt when the government won its case. However, the
naked brutality perpetrated in March convinced the assistant

attorney general that Washington had to relieve the anguish immediately. Summoned to the scene, John Doar petitioned the District Court for a decree ordering local officials to release the jailed protestors, to refrain from bullying the workers, and to defend the peaceful marchers from white assaults. At the same time, Doar put his considerable talents to work for mediation of the dispute. He coaxed Greenwood authorities to free the imprisoned crusaders but disappointed the militants by dropping the government's plea for the sweeping injunction. Fearful of increased lawlessness, the Kennedy strategists retreated from their advanced position and successfully concentrated on avoiding a direct confrontation with the racists over the suffrage.[102] The VEP participants, according to Wiley Branton, were "all disappointed in the fact that the Justice Department had withdrawn its application for a preliminary injunction," and believed that "some effort should be made to get additional concessions out of the city." With this goal in mind, the suffragists took their turn at bargaining with the town fathers. They agreed to halt their mass marches in exchange for Greenwood's promise to furnish bus transportation between the VEP building and the courthouse.[103]

This episode did not mitigate the rage toward the federal government that was building in many black activists. James Forman, chairman of SNCC and one of those who had been arrested during the turbulance, hoped that Washington's performance would radicalize Negroes. Although he screamed for the Kennedy administration to protect him and his colleagues he also believed that if it "did not intervene, that inaction would once again prove the government was not on our side, and thus intensify the development of mass consciousness among blacks."[104] He found the situation "somewhat ironic" when federal marshals moved the civil-rights prisoners to the courthouses "in handcuffs and chains," while "upstairs we were all depending upon the Federal government."[105] For the moment Forman was frustrated because the Civil Rights Division had salvaged a slight victory for blacks in Greenwood, yet he was confident that white racism was so pervasive that the Justice Department would fail to curb it somewhere else. He did not have to wait long.

Later that year in Selma, Alabama, the central government once again became entangled between the disfranchisers and the emancipators. Its involvement had begun in 1961, when the Civil Rights Division initiated a suit against the registration board of Dallas County, where Negro residents composed a majority of the population but only 0.9 percent of the eligible voters were black. Besides challenging the tactics of the deceitful enrollment officers, the Justice Department prepared to take action against a more sinister culprit. Sheriff Jim Clark was "preserving order" with his regular corps, an auxiliary citizens' police, and fifty state troopers whom he requisitioned as reinforcement. Since February 1963 Clark and his deputies had arrested SNCC workers on minor charges and occasionally roughed up a few in the jailhouse. One battle-scarred activist described the situation, "Selma is in a state of siege. Everywhere you look you see state policemen or members of the special posse brandishing clubs and cattle prods." [106] By mid 1963 the suffrage case of the Civil Rights Division had not been resolved, but the Justice Department still had faith in judicial solutions. On June 27, it moved to block Clark from intimidating black applicants by arresting them for "unlawful assembly." [107]

However, the SNCC people did not wait for the outcome of the litigation. On October 7th they declared a "Freedom Day," adopted the slogan "One Man–One Vote," and sent some 300 blacks to line up to register at the doors of the courthouse. Across the street, Clark's police arrested two protesters who stood on the steps of the Federal Building and held signs that read, "Freedom Now" and "Register Now for Freedom Now." From their upstairs office windows, Justice Department employees did nothing except take pictures and make notes, while they watched this clear abridgment of constitutional rights occur on federal property. [108]

The civil-rights workers were incensed over the Justice Department's hands-off policy. Because the Kennedy administration was unwilling to tame the southern renegades, SNCC complained, it had "in effect sanctioned and perpetuated a consistent pattern on the part of law enforcement officials . . . inimical to civil rights and liberties." [109] An inscription hanging on the wall of a COFO office in Mississippi cynically displayed the organization's bitterness, "There is a town in Mississippi called Liberty, and there is a Department in Washington called Justice." [110] The "new abolitionists," as Howard Zinn labeled them, argued that the federal government had a moral obligation and the legal authority to shelter them from racist-inspired terror. Many of the militants had grudgingly directed their energies into voter registration, Charles Sherrod contended, because "the Federal Government has placed this as the highest priority as far as change concerning the southern social structure and in regard to the Negro." [111]

As the perils mounted for the civil-rights workers, the adminstration watched their predicament with concern. John Doar, whose on-the-spot investigations made him admire the courage of SNCC's regiments, hoped "they don't get discouraged and stick it out and keep working." [112] The president himself raised the suffragists' expectations of federal intervention. After one violent affair in Mississippi in 1962, Kennedy asserted:

> We shall give every protection that we can to anybody seeking to vote. I commend those who are making the effort to register every citizen. They deserve the protection of the U.S. government, the protection of the states, the protection of the local communities. And if it requires extra legislation and extra force, we shall do that.[113]

When it became clear that many southern officials were sparking the lawlessness, the civil-rights proponents expected the chief executive to fulfill his offer.

However, administration spokesmen denied that Washington could use armed strength in the outlaw communities.

They maintained that the federal system diminished the choices of intervention. Burke Marshall explained most fully this point of view:

> When a civil rights worker engaged in voter registration asks the Justice Department for federal protection he is told that there is no national police force, that federal marshals are only process servers working for the courts, that the protection of citizens is a matter for the local police.[114]

Deputy Attorney General Nicholas Katzenbach, who, backed by United States troops, calmly stared down George Wallace in front of the doors to the University of Alabama in 1963, nevertheless declared that the "Federal Government is ill-equipped to assume responsibility for the performance of ordinary police functions." Instead, he reiterated the familiar Justice Department formula of seeking "the cooperation of State officials in a combined effort to curb violence and maintain order." [115] When the Civil Rights Division did intervene, it fought the battle in the judiciary because, Marshall maintained, the "assertion of federal rights . . . can be realized only through the processes of federal courts, case by case, in an endless chain of litigation." [116]

The men at the Justice Department doubted whether a massive invasion of federal personnel would solve the problem. Nicholas Katzenbach stressed the practical difficulties that deterrence from Washington involved. "Simply in terms of men required," he argued, "it would not be feasible to provide protection by marshals to any substantial number of civil rights workers." [117] He also pointed out that the Justice Department had sent nearly 400 deputy marshals to guard only one man, James Meredith, during his matriculation at the University of Mississippi. Marshall believed that coercion would not produce lasting benefits for the Negroes in the South. He reminded his critics that federal supervision of the registration process worked during Reconstruction "because of the presence of military forces and ceased to work when that force was removed." [118] Marshall feared that a massive display of federal power in the South might produce a harmful backlash. His worry was shared by some of the civil-rights advocates. Paul Douglas thought that the southern lawlessness was a "strong provocation to attempt national police force action." But he asked rhetorically, "Do we wish to institute a national police force which today would claim to enforce individual rights in Mississippi, but which tomorrow might, following a change of public opinion, destroy individual rights in Illinois?" [119] In October 1963 the *New Republic* questioned whether the "mere existence of such a force might make many local communities more rebellious than they now are to uphold law and order." Likewise, the liberal journal was convinced that a shift in responsibility for law enforcement away from the local to the national level, in the long run, "would require the creation of a full fledged national police force." [120] It argued that a radical departure in federal–state relations would augment the power of the FBI, an agency extremely suspicious of militant activities for social change.

Yet other civil-rights proponents considered the Justice Department's policy as a rationalization of timidity. A number of noted law professors concluded that, had the chief executive decided that a federal incursion was politically sound, he possessed the power to authorize it. They reminded the president that two sections of Title 10 of the United States Code enabled him to send armed forces whenever he became convinced that state officials could not safeguard the constitutional rights of American citizens or the courts could not enforce the laws by ordinary proceedings. These legal scholars contended that the president could act in Mississippi and several other southern states, because "violence and combination are . . . so hindering the execution of the laws . . . of the United States as to deny to Negroes . . . rights secured by the Constitution . . . and the civil rights laws of the United States." [121]

Perhaps the Justice Department at the very least could have used its available resources in more imaginative ways. Haywood Burns, who served as a legal volunteer in Mississippi, scoffed at the idea that the FBI was only an investigative unit and not a police force. The famous "G-Men" who had shot it out with bank robbers, tracked down kidnappers, apprehended saboteurs, Communists, car thiefs, and mobsters, Burns noted, could surely arrest violators of federal civil-rights statutes.[122] One Civil Rights Division attorney who, on Freedom Day in 1963, watched the Selma police and state troopers beat up the suffragists, later questioned the policy of the federal government. Richard Wasserstrom, having resigned from the Justice Department to become a dean at Tuskegee Institute, wondered why the FBI did not "pursue civil rights violators with one-half or even one-quarter of the zeal with which it searches out violators of the federal narcotics laws or labor racketeers." He suggested that FBI agents "pose as SNCC workers to see if the charges of police brutality are true." [123] The reformers also argued that since the president had mobilized marshals to defend freedom riders and to keep an eye on school children, he could also post them around key registration and voting places. Clarence Mitchell of the NAACP reasoned that when the Justice Department became aware of potential danger to a suffrage worker, it should send deputies to the scene "so that when somebody tries to hit him over the head . . . with a gun . . . there ought to be the Federal presence there and that could be done under existing law to see that these people are not denied the right to vote." [124]

The administration was willing to intercede on behalf of the distressed suffragists, provided that it could be done through judicial channels. Warned in the summer of 1961 that SNCC's voting drive in McComb would evoke racist retaliations, Burke Marshall responded, "We will have to move immediately [through court orders] to prevent the reprisals which may have to be enforced by Federal Marshals." [125] In October 1962 Aaron Henry and Medgar Evers requested Washington to station marshals as voting registrars in Mississippi, and Lee White, who had replaced Harris Wofford as Kennedy's civil-rights consultant, suggested to Marshall that it would be "desirable one day soon to discuss the entire question of voter registration and what courses of action are open to us in addition to the long, laborious series of court cases." [126] The reevaluation apparently never took place, and the judicial approach continued. In August 1963 the assistant attorney general admitted to an aide of Senator Joseph Clark that the civil-rights acts presumably allowed court protection of voter-registration workers "where a purpose to interfere with voter registration is proved." [127]

Nevertheless, Washington's efforts on behalf of the right to vote did yield a sizable increase in the number of blacks eligible to cast ballots. Merely by filing franchise suits, the Justice Department encouraged many Negroes to attempt to register. Aaron Henry recognized the significance of this "booster effect" and thus urged the federal government to step in "if constitutional rights continued to be violated." [128] The Kennedy administration had also contributed indirectly to increased nonwhite enrollment by promoting the creation of the VEP. Between April 1, 1962 and November 1, 1964, 688,800 Negroes, most of them residing in counties where the VEP sponsored a project, qualified to vote for the first time. During that period, the percentage of adult black registrants throughout the South jumped from 26.8 to about 38. The results varied, however. In Tennessee, Florida, and Texas the drives succeeded in enfranchising a majority of the adult blacks. Approximately two-fifths of the possible black electorate made it on the registration rolls in North Carolina, Virginia, Arkansas, and South Carolina, while less than one-third of the voting-age Negroes enrolled in Louisiana, Alabama, and Mississippi.

Although the VEP spent $609,515.93 on its suffrage campaigns, the size of the expenditure did not ensure success, as is indicated by the data in Table 2. In the hard-core areas, the project received the least return on its investment, or stated another way, each dollar spent there produced fewer enrollees than it did elsewhere. In these provinces, the emancipators could least afford to work alone, and they needed greater cooperation from Washington than it was giving by litigation.

In 1963 the VEP decided that it could no longer afford to

TABLE 2. VOTER REGISTRATION IN THE SOUTH AND ITS COST, 1962–1964

State	Number of Blacks Registered, 1962	Percentage	Number of Blacks Registered, 1964	Percentage	Approximate Increase	VEP Expense	VEP Cost per Applicant
Alabama	68,317	13.4	93,000	19.3	24,683	$59,309.33	$2.40
Arkansas	68,970	34.0	78,000	40.4	9,020	14,303.71	1.58
Florida	182,456	36.8	241,000	51.2	58,544	41,787.50	.71
Georgia	175,573		268,000		92,500	96,893.12	1.04
Louisiana	151,663	27.8	163,041	31.7	13,000	62,937.00	4.84
Mississippi	23,920	5.3	28,500	6.7	4,500	54,595.00	12.13
North Carolina	210,450	35.8	258,000	46.8	47,500	44,389.15	.93
South Carolina	90,901	22.9	139,000	37.3	48,099	94,439.83	1.96
Tennessee	150,896	49.8	218,000	69.4	67,100	39,079.46	.58
Texas	111,014	26.7	375,000	57.7	133,000	50,780.00	.38
Virginia	110,113	24.0	144,000	38.3	33,887	51,001.83	1.59

Source: Pat Watters and Reese Cleghorn, Climbing Jacob's Ladder, Appendix II; "Results of VEP Programs, April 1, 1962–March 31, 1964," VEP MSS., SRC; U.S. Department of Commerce, Statistical Abstract of the United States, 1970 (Washington, D.C., 1970), p. 369.

pour money into the Mississippi Delta, where there was little registration. In reluctantly arriving at this conclusion, Wiley Branton blamed the Justice Department for not getting

> any meaningful decrees from any of the voter suits which have been filed in Mississippi, and we know that until and unless favorable decrees are rendered and then vigorously imposed we will not be able to get any people registered successfully. We are also very concerned about the failure of the federal government to protect the people who have sought to register and vote or who are working actively in getting others to register.[129]

It would be misleading, however, to grade the participants' achievements solely on a quantitative basis. Although toilers in Mississippi, southwest Georgia, and northern Louisiana failed to destroy the tyranny of the registrars, they did loosen the mental knot keeping blacks away from citizenship. As Elizabeth Wyckoff, a SNCC organizer in Georgia, poignantly reported:

> Some people may wonder whether the meager statistical results in registration figures, and the very notable improvement in morale of a small portion of the Negro population is worth the dangers and in many cases the suffering of the SNCC workers and of the local people who are active in the registration effort. But to move from the pragmatic level, many of the Negroes with whom we have been in touch . . . have moved into freedom of the mind, and it is now theirs for life, even if they should never succeed in their efforts to persuade a semi-literate hostile registrar to put their names on a roll. They have learned to live with fear, and to advance.[130]

To show that many nonenrolled Mississippi blacks were interested in obtaining suffrage rights, the enfranchisers had held a mock gubernatorial election in 1963. COFO gave Negroes a chance to cast a symbolic vote for Aaron Henry and his running mate Edwin King, a white chaplain at Tougaloo College. "The freedom ballot will show," Robert Moses stated, "that if Negroes had the right to vote without fear of physical or economic reprisal, they would do so." It really did not matter that their ballots would not count officially; rather, Mississippi Negroes had a dramatic chance to affirm that living in a "closed society" had not destroyed their pride. According to Henry, the act of going to the polls in support of his candidacy would "give the unregistered Negro a feeling of somebodyness." Approximately 80,000 blacks, almost four times the number actually enrolled, marked their preferences at the voting booths set up in churches, schools, poolrooms, and buses.[131] The COFO enterprise was an important step in creating a black political mechanism in Mississippi. Henry was impressed that the

> Freedom Vote Movement gave Negroes an opportunity to build an organization in every nook and cranny of this State. We have an organization now in Mississippi that once we get the vote, we'll be able to direct it. We'll be able to educate to the issues that are involved.[132]

Although the Kennedy administration did more to expand black voting rights than any regime since Reconstruction, it had not done enough to satisfy the most vocal elements of the civil-rights movement. Justice Department attorneys led by the tireless John Doar honeycombed the Deep South tracking down evidence of racial disfranchisement and bringing their findings before the judiciary. However, this small corps of federal lawyers could not adequately cover the approximately 100 counties where bias flourished. And even when they did manage to haul some of the the most bigoted southern officials into court, they often encountered judges whose racism exceeded the accuseds'. Mass enfranchisement required novel departures, but Kennedy strategists were too closely tied to tradition. Like their predecessors in the White House, they viewed the federal system as a huge barrier deterring a massive penetration of the South. Moreover, the Kennedys worried that a large display of force on their part would provoke a bloody backlash in the local communities and anger Dixie politicos in Congress. They conceived of themselves as arbitrators, assuming that they could forestall violence and maintain order by dealing with their adversaries as rational men.

Within the bounds of this policy, the administration still could have taken a bolder approach that it did. A more imaginative use of the FBI and the strategic deployment of federal marshals and specifically trained civilian personnel (not to every county in the South, but to those where they obviously were needed) might have had a sobering effect on officials who thought that they could break the law with impunity. Contrary to Justice Department expectations, the most recalcitrant sheriffs and registrars did not listen to reasonable appeals or even court orders; therefore, they had to be disciplined by a crack of the federal whip. Forceful government protection not only would have reduced the grave risks to the safety of the civil rights workers, but would also have helped restore their waning confidence in the American political system. It was true that some of the militants privately gloated over Washington's frustration. "We were interested," James Forman frankly recalled, "in trying to expose the dirt of the United States and thus alienate black people from the whole system." [133] But others like Robert Moses, one of the most heroic figures which the movement produced, gallantly toiled for suffrage expansion as a means of changing the lives of black southerners by operating within traditional political boundaries. It was not Moses and his SNCC comrades who were subverting the Constitution, but those who viciously harassed and brutalized them. No wonder, then, from inside his Mississippi hell, Moses lamented that COFO was "powerless to register people in significant numbers until . . . the Department of Justice secures for Negroes across the board the right to register." [134] Throughout the Kennedy years the "new abolitionists" persistently hurled this challenge to the liberals in the White House, and the administration's muted response left deep scars on the anxious civil-rights combatants.

10

We Shall Overcome

THE CRIES FOR HELP coming from the civil-rights workers moved President Kennedy, but not in the direction that the besieged preferred. After a slow start, the administration worked overtime in trying to catch up with the advancing civil-rights batallions. The disappointing experiences of the Justice Department before some federal judges and the bitter encounters the suffragists had with white racists convinced the president to request remedial legislation from Congress. Yet when he did answer the agitated demands for suffrage measures, he chose a plan designed to make the existing judicial machinery operate more smoothly.

Initially committed to execution action, President Kennedy tried to put off going to Congress for as long as possible. He declined to endorse a civil-rights package introduced by Emanuel Celler and Joseph Clark in May 1961. Faithfully carrying out the instructions of candidate Kennedy, the two Democratic lawmakers had prepared a program dealing with school desegregation, employment bias, and voting rights.[1] Liberals who remembered his campaign promises criticized the chief executive for failing to back this legislation on Capitol Hill. Roy Wilkins understood that Kennedy did not want to endanger the rest of his New Frontier measures by solidifying the southern Democratic–conservative Republican alliance, but the NAACP executive secretary was certain that this guarded strategy accomplished little. "It did not save the minimum wage bill from gutting and it will not save other legislation," Wilkins complained to the president; "The Southerners and their Northern satellites . . . function whether a civil rights bill is proposed or withheld." [2] After reviewing the record of Kennedy's first 365 days in office, Martin Luther King unhappily concluded that the White House "waged an essentially cautious and defensive struggle for civil rights." [3]

As it had done two years earlier, the Commission on Civil Rights nudged a reluctant national administration into launching a congressional offensive. After finishing a public hearing in New Orleans on September 9, 1961 the CCR informed the nation that blacks in many of the state's parishes "must attempt to register and vote in the face of serious and sometimes insurmountable obstacles." The commission revealed that a few local officials had testified that they did not adhere to a uniform standard in administering the suffrage laws. "Some registrars," the agency reported, "have built a fortress against Negro registration with such procedural impediments as interpretation of the Constitution, identification, calculation of age, and filling in the application blanks." [4]

The commissioners doubted that the recently enacted civil-rights statutes could effectively end these biased practices. Although they praised Burke Marshall's revamped Civil Rights Division for vigorously prosecuting franchise violations, they emphasized that the "Government, under present laws, must still proceed slowly, suit by suit, county by county. Each suit, moreover, is expensive and time consuming and . . . the CRD . . . has not been able to prepare and file all the suits that appear warranted." [5] In order to avert lengthy judicial proceedings, a majority of the commission advised Congress simply to prohibit the application of voter qualifications "other than age, residence, confinement, and conviction of a felony." This recommendation produced a sharp dissent from the two southern members of the CCR, Robert Storey and Robert Rankin, who maintained that the "security and purity of the ballot can be destroyed by permitting illiterates to vote." The panel harmoniously settled its differences by also offering a second plan which forced state registrars to accept completion of six grades of formal education as proof of literacy for voting.[6]

Sensitive to the criticisms of its franchise program, the administration recognized the need for alternative approaches. In 1962 Attorney General Robert Kennedy acknowledged that the suffrage problem "demands a solution which cannot be provided by lengthy litigation on a piecemeal county-by-county basis. Until there is action by Congress, thousands of Negro citizens will continue to be deprived of their right to vote."[7] But President Kennedy did not propose any comprehensive or quick answers. He decided to support a constitutional amendment prohibiting the payment of poll taxes as a requirement for voting in federal elections—an old proposal that had attracted sponsors, including southerners, yearly since the late 1940s. Although the chief executive insisted that this route was the most practical way to avoid the Dixie roadblocks in the Senate, the liberals protested that it would set an unwarranted precedent and was too slow. However, the president's strategy worked. Within two years after Congress had cleared the proposal in September 1962, the necessary thirty-eight states ratified the Twenty-fourth Amendment.[8]

Meanwhile, Robert Kennedy believed that the CCR's sixth-grade literacy suggestion would not raise the same constitutional objections that southerners traditionally had voiced against antipoll-tax bills. The measure drafted by the Justice Department allowed the states to retain the controversial educational exams, whereas it merely created a minimum scholastic standard to measure reading and writing proficiency. "We are saying," Kennedy explained to the Senate Judiciary Committee in March, "that if a State establishes a vague test on the question and says an individual has to be literate and does not establish a particular and specific test—we say that if they [Negroes] completed a sixth-grade education they should be considered literate." To lessen southern antagonism, the attorney general narrowed the coverage of the proposal to federal elections.[9]

Designed as a compromise, S. 2750 naturally did not satisfy either side. Although the liberals approved of the bill, they derided it as inadequate. Joseph Rauh of the ADA admonished, "Congress had taken enough half-hearted steps in the voting field to know now that the final solution to discrimination against Negro voters in any State is direct Federal administration of elections." [10] Other civil-rights advocates claimed that the bill did not completely eradicate the possibility of bias because it still permitted the application of educational requirements to those who had not matriculated to the sixth grade. Erwin Griswold, Dean of Harvard Law School and a recent appointee to the Civil Rights Commission, testified to the Senate Judiciary Committee that the proposal "can only restrict, not eliminate the opportunities available for evasive or dilatory tactics." [11]

The southerners refused to swallow even this mild pill prescribed by the attorney general. They charged that the government already possessed sufficient remedies to cure the problem of disfranchisement. Sam Ervin pointed out that the Civil Rights Division, according to its own press releases, had initiated numerous suits, investigations, and negotiations to obtain relief for blacks seeking to register. Noting that the national legislature had adopted two statutes in the last five years, Ervin declared, "[It] is much too early for Congress to say that [they are] 'insufficient to protect the right to vote'." [12] Besides, the North Carolina senator thought the literacy bill was unconstitutional. No matter how strenuously administration spokesmen denied that the proposal usurped the state's right to determine voting qualifications, Ervin retorted:

These bills do not constitute . . . appropriate legislation, because they do not attempt to prohibit a State's . . . abridging a man's right to vote on account of his race, color, or previous condition of servitude. But they provide a Federal standard or substitute for all the State literacy tests. [13]

As long as Ervin chaired the subcommittee hearings, S. 2750 had a dismal chance of reaching the Senate floor in the regular manner. Consequently, on April 25th Majority Leader

Mike Mansfield of Montana and Republican chief Everett Dirksen tacked the bill on as an amendment to a minor measure passed by the House.[14] The opponents immediately pounced on it and began to filibuster, but they did not have to worry about preserving their stamina, because the civil-rights managers did not insist on calling all-night sessions.

The opponents of the literacy plan focused their attention on the constitutionality of the legislation. Although the southerners delivered the usual states' rights oratory, they cited recent developments that gave credibility to their arguments. Olin Johnston reminded his colleagues that they had selected a constitutional amendment to remove the poll tax. Assuming that both the financial duty and the literacy test were voting requirements, the South Carolinian queried, "How is it then true that those who now assert that voter qualifications can be regulated by Congress by statute were of the opinion . . . that the proper vehicle for this was a constitutional amendment?" [15] Furthermore, the Dixie senators quoted from a unanimous Supreme Court opinion written in 1959 by Justice William O. Douglas upholding the validity of the North Carolina literacy exam. "The ability to read and write," Douglas ruled, "has some relation to standards designed to promote intelligent use of the ballot. A State might conclude that only those who are literate should exercise the franchise." [16]

The bill's proponents thought that they were being consistent. Mansfield explained that he had favored a poll-tax amendment, because the issue concerned federal and state powers in electoral matters. However, the Montana Democrat asserted that the literacy proposal dealt with the "constitutional question of equalization of voting rights of all citizens." Kenneth Keating elaborated on this distinction: "The difference between the poll tax measure and this pending bill is the difference between abolishing interstate bus travel and subjecting such service to reasonable regulation of the ICC." [17] Both senators insisted that S. 2750 did not proscribe the use of written tests, but outlawed discrimination in their application. As the debaters prepared for a showdown, on May 9th President Kennedy expressed his amazement to newspapermen that anyone found the bill unconstitutional: "I've seen these cases of people with college degrees who were denied being put on the register because they supposedly can't pass the literacy test. It doesn't make any sense." [18]

Despite these comments, the administration forces did not push the bill with great urgency, refraining from provoking a bitter clash over a measure that had elicited so little enthusiasm. After two weeks of relaxed discussion, Mansfield and Dirksen presented a cloture petition. They seemed merely to be going through the motions because the civil-rights troops could not even muster a majority in favor of closing debate. On May 9th thirty northern Democrats and thirteen Republicans were overwhelmed by thirty Democrats, seven of whom represented western states and twenty-three members of the GOP who came from all areas of the North. To give those northerners an opportunity to go on record for civil rights, Mansfield moved to table S. 2750. This time sixty-four senators, two-thirds of those voting, decided to keep the literacy bill alive. As part of the majority were four northern Democrats, three of their border state colleagues, and fourteen Republicans who had helped prolong the filibuster. Having cast their obligatory yea ballots, a few days later the "swing" senators rejoined the ranks of the opposition again to defeat cloture, by forty-three to fifty-two.[19] A skeptical *Time* correspondent wrote that the

> Senate debate had all the conviction of a professional wrestling match: everybody played his role for the crowd, but nobody got hurt. . . . Almost as if the whole thing were merely to make propaganda in the North, Kennedy aides made no real effort to push the bill. The Republicans . . . were happy to be co-sponsors, but that was about all.[20]

Having retreated, the Kennedy administration anticipated that the judiciary would remove the compelling need for this type of legislation. By the end of 1961 and early in 1962, the Civil Rights Division had concluded that the county-by-county method of enjoining prejudiced registrars would not produce gains quickly enough. Instead, division lawyers brought litigation challenging the constitutionality of statewide literacy exams. In December 1961 and March 1962 the Justice Department petitioned the federal courts to invalidate the use of "understanding" tests in Louisiana and Mississippi. Its attorneys argued "that the discretion which is vested in the registrars who administer the test render it unconstitutional . . . under the Fourteenth and Fifteenth Amendments." [21]

In 1963 a three-judge panel prohibited Louisiana registrars from applying literacy requirements. The jurists struck down the exam that blacks had to pass but that most whites already on the rolls had not been asked to take.[22] However, state officials were adept at circumventing legal rulings. Ronnie Moore, an experienced CORE worker in Louisiana, reported soon after this decision that little had changed:

> Registrars are still turning Negroes down in large numbers based on the "technical error" technique used traditionally to disqualify Negroes on the application form instead of on the Constitutional tests which no longer can be used according to federal decree.[23]

A year later more bad news came from Mississippi when a different set of federal judges sanctioned the Magnolia State's educational requirements for voting.[24] Thus, the judiciary left the problem of hard-core disfranchisement unsettled.

While Civil Rights Division lawyers were arguing these cases before the courts, President Kennedy considered ways of expediting the judicial process. In a special message on civil rights to Congress in February 1963 the chief executive suggested that the federal courts be required to give top priority to suffrage litigation and proposed legislation empowering judges to grant temporary relief while the cases were pending. According to his plan, jurists could appoint interim referees to enroll qualified Negroes in counties where less than 15 percent of black adults were registered and the attorney general had filed a complaint under the Civil Rights Acts. If the question of an applicant's literacy arose during the court proceeding, Kennedy wanted any person who had completed at least six years of accredited education to be presumed able to read and write. To reduce the "delay in the granting of the franchise . . . particularly in counties where . . . the intent of Congress [was] openly flouted," President Kennedy advocated that no state official be allowed to deny the right to vote because of immaterial errors or omissions on registration applications.[25]

Suffragists found little solace in these proposals. Veterans of the voter-registration drives disparaged the idea of depending on southern district judges to expedite cases and appoint referees, something they had never done in the past. A victim of the Mississippi inferno and Judge Cox's fiery wrath, Robert Moses recounted to the House Judiciary Committee the black peoples' burden:

> They have to go before these judges and they can't get decisions right away. The Negroes . . . don't know anything about what is going on behind the doors in the court. If the judge resists and does not give them a preliminary injunction, as far as they are concerned, the sheriff got away with it.[26]

The SNCC organizer also criticized the administration's literacy provision. He pointed out that many Negroes would still be subjected to the registrars' double standard because they had not made it to the sixth grade. Moses presented statistics showing that in Mississippi the median number of school years completed by blacks age twenty-five or older was 5.1, compared to 9.9 for whites. Council of Federated Organizations chairman Aaron Henry further revealed that most of the segregated black schools in his homestate were nonaccredited, a condition that would have prevented their graduates from qualifying as literate according to the suggested legislation.[27]

Instead, the civil-rights advocates recommended total abolition of literacy tests and urged direct federal supervision of elections. John Roche, national chairman of ADA, called for a "system of Federal registrars after an executive determination that citizens have been denied the right to vote." Henry favored a "National Registration to Vote Act" which established a one-year residency requirement as the only qualification for voting by adults over twenty-one years of age. Drawing upon both suggestions, Roy Wilkins supported "removal of all arbitrary restrictions on the right to vote and authorization of the Federal Government to conduct and supervise all Federal elections." [28]

The reformers revived the CCR's registration plan just as racial storms were swirling throughout the nation in 1963. After white terrorists in Birmingham bombed the headquarters of Martin Luther King, who was leading demonstrations against job bias and segregation in public accommodations, black mobs retaliated on May 12th by throwing rocks and bottles and shouting, "We'll kill you white man, we'll kill you." [29] When a sniper assassinated the NAACP's Mississippi field secretary, Medgar Evers, in Jackson on June 13th, an embittered Clarence Mitchell admonished Congress to hear the

> cry from the people who are in distress, from the people who are victims of mobs, from the people who are being shot when their Government is out busy in Laos . . . and out busy all over the world trying to keep the peace, to come to Mississippi . . . where there are troubles to keep the peace [*sic*]. [30]

At the same time in the North, Negroes were pouring onto the streets to protest employment discrimination and *de facto* school segregation.

Distressed that blacks were losing patience, the president rushed to head off further disturbances by expanding his civil-rights plan languishing in Congress. On June 19th he warned Washington lawmakers, "The result of continued Federal legislative inaction will be continued, if not increased racial strife—causing the leadership on both sides to pass from the hands of reasonable and responsible men to the purveyors of hate and violence.[31] To relieve the tensions, Kennedy submitted to Congress an omnibus bill guaranteeing equal access to public facilities, permitting the Justice Department to seek injunctions desegregating schools, allowing the government to cut off funds to federal programs where discrimination was practiced, and creating a Community Relations Service to aid troubled towns settle racial disputes peacefully. Most of these items, previously considered extreme, overshadowed Kennedy's renewed request for the moderate suffrage provisions that he had first suggested in February.[32]

During the next several months, the Kennedy administration lobbied intensively on Capitol Hill for approval of its bill. The president's delicate task was to lure conservative Republicans away from their southern allies and still satisfy the civil-rights forces. Most of the parliamentary maneuvering concerned not voting rights, but public accommodations, the resurrected Title III, and an FEPC sponsored by the liberals. By the end of October, the chief executive, his brother, and Vice President Johnson had worked out a compromise acceptable to House Republicans, without sacrificing the original intent of the proposal. Although the ballot was not central to the bill, it was involved in the negotiated agreement. To placate GOP leaders William McCulloch and Charles Halleck, the administration eliminated the provision dealing with the appointment of temporary referees and substituted a clause authorizing a special three-judge federal court to hear suffrage cases. The Republicans had objected to the interim referee procedure because it would allow blacks to vote before a final judgment in a suit could be reached. McCulloch contended that the provisional ballots would have to be held in abeyance, and in close elections this situation would have "potentially too unsettling an effect." [33]

John F. Kennedy never lived to see whether a sharply divided Congress would pass the omnibus measure. Scheduled to address the Democratic State Committee in Austin, Texas, on the evening of November 22, he intended to say, "There is no noncontroversial way to fulfill our constitutional pledge to establish justice and promote domestic tranquility, but we intend to fulfill those obligations because they are right." [34] For the past 1,000 days his administration had gradually advanced the frontiers of political and civil equality. But when those deadly shots were fired in Dallas the problem remained, as Burke Marshall once posed it, "Whether the tempo of the civil rights movement has not quickened to such a degree that there is not enough time left." [35]

The fatal bullets left Lyndon Baines Johnson the heavy task of determining if it was too late for the country to live up to its long-delayed promise of freedom and justice for all. A skillful southern politician who had achieved national prominence and still retained the loyalty of his constituents by supporting the mildest of civil-rights bills, Johnson rose to the occasion. With the grief for the martyred president still fresh on November 27th, he instructed Congress:

> No memorial oration or eulogy could more eloquently honor President Kennedy's memory than the earliest possible passage of the civil rights bill for which he fought.

> We have talked long enough in this country about equal rights. We have talked for one hundred years or more. It is now time to write the next chapter—and to write it in the books of law.[36]

President Johnson had come to speak so forcefully for equality because he thought it would liberate both Negroes and his native South. As Johnson had climbed higher up the political ladder and addressed a widened audience, he became aware of the profound distress that racism had caused for blacks. By the time he ran for vice president in 1960, he had confided to a group of liberals that he would meet his "moral obligation to every person of every color skin." [37] Moreover, if the racial caste system were dismantled, Johnson believed that southern whites could free themselves from the practices for which the majority of their countrymen scorned them. In discarding the race issue, Dixie leaders might realistically tackle the economic and social problems of their region unencumbered by the shibboleths of white supremacy. Without such a reunion, a "further embittered South, defiant and implacable," Tom Wicker perceptively has noted, "would be a dead weight on the Democratic party, on the nation, on the so-called 'great society' that Johnson was to make his political goal." [38]

Throughout the fiercely fought battle that led to the passage of the Civil Rights Act of 1964, the franchise issue remained in the background. The voting sections were among the least controversial in the bill, and many suffragists considered them outmoded. Shortly after Kennedy died, the CCR, updating its last report, grimly concluded, "Case by case proceedings, helpful as they have been in isolated localities, have not provided a prompt or adequate remedy for widespread discriminatory denials of the right to vote." [39] The data examined by the agency even convinced its southern members "that without drastic change in the means used to secure suffrage . . . disfranchisement will continue to be handed down from father to son." [40] The need for severe measures was apparent, so the commission unanimously advocated legislation enabling the president to appoint registrars to enroll qualified blacks as voters in federal and state elections and prohibiting officials from rejecting registration applicants for any cause except age, length of residence, or failure to complete six grades of school. If these cures did not heal the wounds of disfranchised blacks, the CCR suggested that Congress invoke Section II of the Fourteenth Amendment to reduce the representation in the House of Representatives of those states perpetuating discrimination against Negroes. [41]

When President Johnson signed the Civil Rights Act into law on July 2, 1964 it did not contain the proposals which the Civil Rights Commission had suggested. Instead, the statute made a sixth-grade education a presumption of literacy if the question were raised in court, permitted the attorney general to litigate franchise suits before a judicial troika, and prevented registrars from denying the right to vote because of slight errors or omissions by applicants on their registration papers. For the moment, liberals put aside their disappointment with these bland provisions and rejoiced over the enactment of the long-awaited clauses dealing with public accommodations, employment, and education.

In his five years as chief executive, Lyndon Johnson fulfilled many of the legislative goals of Negroes. Among the accomplishments was his translation into statutory language of ideas originally conceived during the Truman, Eisenhower, and Kennedy regimes. It is quite understandable that one black leader asserted that Johnson "made a greater contribution to giving a dignified and hopeful status to Negroes in the United States than any President including Lincoln, Roosevelt, and Kennedy." [42] Undoubtedly there was a dramatic change in the situation with respect to the suffrage for blacks, and Johnson played an instrumental role in this transformation.

Yet the president was divided in his thinking about the right to vote. Like the presidents before him, Johnson viewed the enfranchisement of blacks mainly from a legal perspective. His aim was to eliminate the immediate, arbitrary barriers blocking registration and give Negroes a greater strength at the polling place. From this, he believed, "many other breakthroughs would follow, and they would follow as a consequence of the black man's own legitimate power as an American citizen, not as a gift from the white man." [43] Having placed his faith in the ballot to improve the black condition, Johnson was hesitant to encourage Negroes in making other attempts to restructure southern politics. As long as black southerners confined their efforts to prodding Congress to expand the vote they were safe, but when they demanded a share in shaping Democratic party affairs, the president rebuffed them.

The experience of the Mississippi Freedom Democratic Party (MFDP) is a case in point. An instrumentality of COFO, the Freedom Democratic Party sought to provide a forum where blacks could gather in favor of the liberal principles of the national Democratic party. This group, however, rejected the "old politics" and tried to replace it with a system based on participatory democracy. To this end, according to Robert Moses, the MFDP was trying "to teach the lowest sharecropper that he knows better than the biggest leader exactly what is required to make a decent life for himself." John Lewis, chairman of SNCC, asserted that the Freedom Democrats were against "the so-called old guard leadership, where you had had a select few to speak for the Negro people and to make deals." [44] These dissidents did not want to form a third party but strove to gain recognition as the faithful Democrats from Mississippi. Indeed, they tried to imitate their northern counterparts by constructing a coalition of Negroes, labor, and poor whites. As might be expected, few whites dared to join the MFDP, but it still was the only Democratic organization in the Delta State open to both races. [45]

Throughout the long, hot, violence-ridden summer of 1964, Mississippi blacks and white volunteers from the North busily constructed the party machinery. At first, MFDP adherents attempted to participate in the precinct, county, and state conventions of the traditional Mississippi Democratic party. Either barred from attending the meetings or severely limited in their rights when they did get in, the Freedom Democrats decided to challenge the all-white slate of delegates that the regulars had chosen. Following the rules prescribed by the Democratic National Committee, the integrated MFDP chose forty-four delegates, including Edwin King, the white chaplain at Tougaloo College, and twenty-two alternates to attend the national convention in Atlantic City. While the lily-white group refused to commit itself to whomever was nominated, the reformers pledged their loyalty to Lyndon Johnson. [46]

Before making the trip to the New Jersey seashore, the Mississippi suffragists asked the president for help. During the freedom campaign, their staff was intimidated by law-enforcement officers and vigilantes. The treatment ranged from arrests on minor charges to beatings and the slaying of three COFO workers. Because they believed that their constitutional rights were being trampled on, these shocktroopers clamored for protection from Washington. The militants, however, did not insist on an invasion of federal soldiers. The historian, Howard Zinn, an advisor to SNCC, was among those who argued that the president had the authority to dispatch "marshals in civilian dress . . . and prevent the more flagrant constitutional abuses . . . with more effectiveness and less irritation than the presence of uniformed federal forces or even nationalized units of the local National Guard." [47]

Although in early June, Attorney General Robert Kennedy reported to the president that Mississippi "law enforcement officials are widely believed to be linked to extremist anti-Negro activity, or at the very least to tolerate it," the chief executive, like his predecessor, rejected the pleas for direct assistance. On June 17th, four days prior to the savage killing of three suffrage workers, Lee White, Johnson's White House specialist on civil rights, frowned on the request of a student parents' group for federal protection "before a tragic incident takes place." He found it "incredible that those people who are voluntarily sticking their head into the lion's mouth would ask for somebody to come down and shoot the lion." [48]

The president's legal counselors argued against acting in the manner urged by COFO. On July 1st Deputy Attorney General Nicholas Katzenbach confided to the president that he could find "no specific legal objection to sending federal civilian personnel to guard against possible violations of federal law." Nor did he think that Johnson would be prevented from deploying the militia if there were a complete breakdown of law and order. However, for practical reasons, Katzenbach did not recommend such federal intervention. He maintained that the Justice Department did not have enough personnel to do the job, but most important, the deputy attorney general averred, a massive national intrusion would result in displacement of local policemen who were "most crucial . . . in maintaining law and order in a community gripped by racial crisis." [49] Yet, as Robert Kennedy had pointed out earlier that summer, those very law officers were responsible for promoting terror and perverting justice.

When the battle-fatigued delegates of the MFDP arrived in Atlantic City at the end of August, they intended to air their grievances fully. On August 22nd the group's white lawyer Joseph Rauh, a long-time advocate of civil-rights causes, informed the Credentials Committee that the challengers belonged to the only open party in Mississippi, supported the national platform, would sign the loyalty oath, and would actively campaign for Lyndon Johnson. He was followed by Fannie Lou Hamer, a black delegate from James Eastland's home county, who passionately explained to the committee how Negroes in the Magnolia State were treated if they cared to exercise their rights. In Winona the year before, she tearfully recalled, state troopers forced her down in the jailhouse and, "beat my arms until I had no feeling in them. After a while the first man beating my arms grew numb from tiredness. The other man who was holding me was given the blackjack. Then he began beating me." [50] In contrast, spokesmen for the regular contingent denied that the insurgents legally represented the bulk of the registered Mississippi Democrats, and disclaimed that Negroes had been barred from the primaries. Moreover, they refused to bind themselves to support the national platform and the candidates.[51] With such evidence and testimony, the MFDP lined up ten delegations, enough for a floor fight if necessary. John Lewis alerted President Johnson to the importance of the contest, "Without seating the FDP . . . the Democratic party and the Federal government can never become the instruments of justice for all citizens that they claim to be." [52]

The president, however, was more concerned with preserving a harmonious convention than he was with resolving the moral question. Johnson had labored to give Negroes free access to the ballot box, but he would not take another step and help them acquire some power to make decisions within the Democratic party. To do so might have resulted in a mass defection of the southern states. The Tampa *Tribune* explained, "Johnson is realist enough to know that [Mississippi and Alabama] are lost anyway; what was important was to maintain an air of reasonableness which would keep more moderate southerners under the Democratic umbrella." [53] Johnson was well aware that many disgruntled southerners were ready to jump on the bandwagon of the Republican nominee Barry Goldwater, the conservative senator from Arizona who had voted against the Civil Rights Act of 1964. Furthermore, Claude Sitton, an astute *New York Times* correspondent who had reported on the civil-rights struggle in the

South, observed that Johnson, as party unifier, desired "to avoid a precedent that might open the way for similar controversies in the future between contending loyalist factions elsewhere." [54]

If any one man had the power to influence the decision it was Lyndon Johnson. The chief executive knew that a political party did not always respond to the wishes of its presidential leader, as his mentor Franklin Roosevelt had discovered in 1938. In fact, most of the time, it functioned as a loose amalgam of fifty distinct organizations often going their own seperate ways. But quadrennially the party gathered to reaffirm its common identity and rally around its presidential nominee. When a popular incumbent like Johnson was in charge, the faithful usually listened. Theodore White, who since 1960 had made it his business to carefully detail presidential contests, wrote about Atlantic City, "There was no moment when the Convention machinery of Johnson . . . might not have imposed a solution." [55] Had Johnson completely backed the insurgents, the assembled Democrats probably would have assented. Even the chairman of the regular Mississippi faction sardonically admitted that his colleagues "could seat [the FDP] if they wanted to. They could seat a dozen dead dodos brought there in a silver casket and nobody could do anything about it." [56]

Initially, the chief executive desired to have the traditional Mississippians take the loyalty oath and seat the insurgents as nonvoting guests. As sympathy for the FDP grew after Mrs. Hamer's moving presentation, Johnson considered various compromises. One in particular that he thought was a "good idea" had a few of the regulars catching "a virus" and being replaced "as either delegates or alternates by mutual consent with one or two . . . from the Freedom group already present." [57] Perhaps the scheme was too contrived, because the president pursued a more conventional course. With the assembly already one day in session and the White House pressing for a prompt solution, on August 25th the Credentials Committee offered the FDP two at-large seats and named

Aaron Henry and Ed King to take them. Those lily whites who pledged their loyalty would command the state's forty-four votes, while the remainder of the Freedom Democrats would be invited inside the convention hall as nonvoting guests. Furthermore, the committee promised that blueprints would be drawn up in the future to eliminate discrimination in the party apparatus.[58] This plan, stamped with Johnson's seal of approval, satisfied the liberals on the committee who abandoned any idea of writing a minority report, and that evening the full convention delegates accepted the recommendation.

Johnson assigned Senator Hubert Humphrey, whose civil-rights record was flawless, the job of convincing FDP partisans to accept the bargain. The Minnesota senator's staff informed Humphrey's old friend and ADA colleague, Joe Rauh, that unless an agreement were reached, Humphrey would lose his chance to be Johnson's running mate.[59] Charles Diggs, a black congressman from Detroit and a Credentials Committee member who had originally backed the FDP, later explained why he and many other Negro leaders went along with the presidentially sanctioned compromise:

> There is no question in my mind that the package . . . helped the President in his desire to nominate Humphrey. . . . Had a divisive floor fight developed the President probably would have been forced to select as his Number Two man a person less identified with the liberal wing of the party.[60]

Commentators in both the North and South hailed the compromise as a victory for emancipation. Anthony Lewis of the *New York Times* called it "a long step toward ending racism in Southern Democratic politics."[61] The moderate editor of the St. Petersburg *Times* predicted, "The Delta State's political establishment based on a small structure of white voters will never be its same old magnolia self."[62] Paul Douglas, who sat in the Illinois delegation, thought that the FDP had made a strong moral case, but endorsed the agreement because of its assurance that only groups "selected by Democrats, under free and nondiscriminatory procedures, will be seated at future conventions." [63] For the same reasons, two of their staunchest allies, Rauh and Martin Luther King, counseled the Freedom Democrats to yield, but they were ready to approve whatever decision the insurgents made.[64] Had not the liberals believed that a significant change was made, they would not have endorsed the accord.

On August 26th the FDP rejected the offer that it derisively labeled the "back of the bus proposal." Although the partisans had been awarded two seats, they "wanted to vote for Mississippi." The group was particularly irked that the convention had named its two voting delegates. "We must stop playing the game," the Freedom Democrats fumed, "of accepting token recognition for real change and of allowing the opposition to choose a few 'leaders' to represent the people at large." After all, the militants insisted, "That is the way things have been done in Mississippi, too, for a long time." [65]

Nevertheless, the challengers were not irreconcilables. They were prepared to support the plan suggested by Oregon Congresswoman Edith Green to seat the "loyal" Democrats of both delegations.[66] Since many more FDP members than regular would swear their fidelity, the suffragists would have gained the power they had risked their lives for. But Johnson had no desire to alienate the white South from the national concensus he was trying to build. The president's plan did not stop the walkout of the Mississippi and Alabama delegations, but it was something the rest of the Dixie contingent could live with. Wise to the ways of Congress, LBJ realized that the cooperation of powerful southern chairmen was indispensable for the passage of his expensive socioeconomic reform program. To this end, Johnson's forging of the Atlantic City bargain soothed the Dixie solons and added to his political capital in Congress. Although these calculations had no appeal for the FDP, it still vigorously campaigned for the Johnson–Humphrey ticket, while the lily-white faction generally favored Goldwater.[67]

The Republican candidate carried Mississippi and four

other southern states in November, but nearly everywhere else Johnson won in a landslide. Blacks, particularly, gave the Johnson–Humphrey team an overwhelming mandate to fulfill the president's vision of the Great Society. Both the president and his civil rights supporters agreed that extending the franchise appeared next on the emancipation agenda. The chief executive immediately turned his attention to finding the best method for implementing once and for all the ninety-five-year-old guarantee of the Fifteenth Amendment.

Johnson was presented with three choices for legislation. After the Democratic victory, Nicholas Katzenbach, who had replaced Robert Kennedy as attorney general, told the president that he supported a constitutional amendment "to prohibit States from imposing any qualifications or disqualifications for voting in federal or state elections other than (1) age, (2) a short period of residency, (3) conviction of a felony, (4) commitment to a mental institution." Patterned after a suggestion made by the CCR in 1961, the measure discarded the literacy requirement, which the attorney general called the root of much "racially discriminatory manipulation." As his next preference, Katzenbach proposed a bill empowering a federal commission to conduct registration for federal elections. At the bottom of his list was a recommendation authorizing a federal agency to "assume direct control of registration for voting in both federal and state elections in any area where the percentage of potential Negro registrants actually registered is low." [68]

Timing was of great importance to the administration. Lee White liked the substance of Katzenbach's idea, but he thought that during 1965 the attorney general should concentrate on testing the voting provisions of the recently passed Civil Rights Act.[69] Along these lines, a position paper prepared for the president in late 1964 commented: "Some pending court cases brought by the Justice Department may, if we secure the right decisions, minimize the need for a new approach," and suggested deferring any specific changes until 1966.[70] In the event that Johnson might want to act sooner, in

January 1965 Justice Department lawyers started drafting the universal suffrage amendment and began deliberating about a proposal concerning the appointment of registrars for federal elections.[71]

Circumstances in Selma, Alabama altered the timetable and content of the legislative considerations. At the beginning of 1965, Martin Luther King, just back from Oslo, where he had received the Nobel Peace Prize, began a series of demonstrations to protest against racial disfranchisement. After several years of government litigation and intensive canvassing by SNCC, only 353 Negroes, 2.1 percent of the eligible black voters, were enrolled in Dallas County. At that rate, King wryly noted, "it would take about 103 years to register the adult Negroes." [72] The situation had worsened since February 1964, when the state had instituted a new, extremely complicated literacy test. During January 1965 King marched along with SNCC people to the courthouse with hundreds of Negroes desiring to register. The board was open two days a month, and during its office hours only processed a small fraction of the black applicants. The most brutal obstacle to registration was Sheriff Jim Clark and his armed deputies. By the beginning of February, they had arrested over 2,000 protesters, including the Nobel Laureate. Negroes young and old continued to confront the sheriff because, as James Bevel, an SCLC official, remarked, "If we get out and work [for voter registration] Jim Clark will be picking cotton with my father in about two years." [73]

President Johnson monitored the stressful situation. At a news conference on February 4th he asserted that every American "should be concerned with the efforts of our fellow Americans to register and vote in Alabama." When asked whether he would send federal personnel to safeguard the demonstrators' constitutional rights, the chief executive merely stated, "We will use the tools of the Civil Rights Act of 1964 in every State of the Union in an effort to see that the act is fully observed." [74]

However, the demands were increasing daily for new legislation. King posted bail and flew to Washington to confer with the president. On February 9th he suggested to Johnson that any forthcoming bill should cover both federal and state elections and establish automatic machinery to crush the arbitrary power of local officials, prohibit literacy tests, and provide for enforcement by federal registrars. The president was receptive; the Atlanta minister termed the meeting "very successful," and praised Johnson's "deep commitment to obtaining the right to vote for all Americans." [75] A few days later, representatives of the NAACP advised the president that the planned "constitutional amendment would not be a satisfactory approach." [76]

By February 15th, the administration had scrapped its amendment proposal and was drawing up instead a bill modeled along the lines King had sketched. For the remainder of the month, Justice Department lawyers attempted to perfect the measure in order to effectively "prohibit the use of literacy tests under certain circumstances and to create a Federal Registrar System." [77] They had to write a bill that would get through Congress and survive the scrutiny of the courts. In the few weeks that passed while the administration worked feverishly to get the proposal ready, the Republicans chided the president for not acting. In the House they set up a task force to develop strategy for passage of a voting-rights statute. Senate Minority Leader Dirksen, appalled by the viciousness of the Alabama police, told Katzenbach that he was prepared for a "revolutionary" bill if necessary. [78]

In the meantime, the situation in Selma was deteriorating. Despite a recent court injunction banning the use of the February 1964 literacy exam, the Dallas County Board of Registrars still managed to flunk 75 percent of the black applicants. Nor did a court order change Jim Clark's behavior; the sheriff and his men used electric cattle prods on black demonstrators. "Until Sheriff Clark is removed," Martin Luther King asserted, "the evils of Selma will not be removed. He is still beating our people." [79] This form of black-belt justice was not unique, for on February 18th, in neighboring Marion County,

Jimmie Lee Jackson, a young black peacefully marching to the courthouse, was fatally shot by a state trooper.[80]

As the tension rose in Alabama, Johnson thought it prudent not to display the government's full might for a while. The president rejected the pleas of the civil-rights leaders that federal troops or marshals be sent to Selma to preserve law and order. A show of national force, Johnson later wrote, might have made a martyr of Governor George Wallace, "resurrected bitterness between North and South, [and] destroyed whatever possibilities existed for passage of voting rights legislation." [81] The lawyers at the Justice Department again argued that southern officials bore the responsibility for policing the citizens of their states; armed intervention would be taken only as a last resort.

This faith in conciliation would be sorely tested in Selma. Soon after being released from jail, King had announced plans for a Freedom March from Selma to Montgomery; almost immediately Governor Wallace banned all demonstrations on state highways. On Sunday, March 7th, with FBI agents and Justice Department observers scribbling notes on the sidelines, some 525 demonstrators were viciously attacked by state troopers and the Dallas County police as they peacefully crossed the Edmund Pettus Bridge en route to the state capital. The victim of a painful clubbing, John Lewis groaned, "I don't see how President Johnson can send troops to Vietnam . . . and can't send troops to Selma, Alabama." [82] More violence appeared likely when Martin Luther King, who had been in Atlanta on Bloody Sunday, announced his intention of leading a second march in two days. In so doing, King would have to defy a federal court order temporarily restraining the Montgomery pilgrimage.

With little time to lose, President Johnson dispatched federal mediators to avert another gory confrontation in Selma. He sent Leroy Collins, director of the Community Relations Service and former Florida governor, to prevent a reoccurrence of the clash between blacks and the Alabama authorities. The president had a great respect for Collins's style of persuasion. He "is the kind of fellow who glides you across, not shoves you and makes you balk," Johnson remarked.[83] His faith was well placed; on March 9th a few hours before the journey was to begin, Collins, with the assistance of John Doar, arranged an agreement allowing King and his followers to traverse the Pettus Bridge and then stop and pray in front of a heavily armed line of state troopers before turning back.[84] Television cameras recorded the scene for the nation to watch, and Collins and the viewers relaxed as the drama was played out according to the script. That evening, however, an enlistee in the freedom struggle, Reverend James Reeb, a white minister from Boston, was fatally beaten by racist thugs on a Selma street.

In mourning for their fallen comrades, Jimmie Lee Jackson and James Reeb, the marchers planned with even greater determination to begin the demonstration. With them this time would be the power of the federal government, as President Johnson showed that there were times when he would mobilize troops. District Judge Frank Johnson lifted his ban against the crusade, and George Wallace gave the president the necessary justification to protect the marchers. At a meeting with the governor in the White House on March 13th, Johnson firmly lectured Wallace on the duty of permitting peaceful assembly. He bluntly warned the governor that the central government would patrol the court-sanctioned demonstration if the state could not. An adamant Wallace put Johnson to the test. On March 18th, the Alabamian telegraphed the president that he did not have the available resources to ensure the safety of the interracial travelers; so having received the necessary "invitation" the chief executive federalized the Alabama National Guard.[85] No longer did the president feel confined within the normal boundaries of the federal system. In this instance there was an obvious responsibility for making certain that the specific order of a federal court was obeyed.

The outcry in the North following Bloody Sunday added to Johnson's desire to prevent further violence. During the second and third weeks of March, sympathy processions were held in northern cities, religious leaders met with the president and urged him to intervene, and hundreds of prominent whites were pouring into Alabama to join the demonstration. Also, Johnson responded at a time when the radicals were angrily questioning the will of the federal government. In Washington, D.C. on March 11th, militant blacks sat in at the White House, causing a commotion, and SNCC spokesmen were attracting many young blacks with their impassioned rhetoric. According to historian Eric Goldman, who served Johnson as an adviser, the president was very much aware that if Martin Luther King were "discredited by failure, far less responsible Negroes were likely to take over leadership of the civil rights movement." [86]

Amidst the Alabama turbulence, the president went to Capitol Hill to deliver his voting-rights address. On March 15th, in a speech in which Johnson adopted the battle cry of the civil-rights combatants, he told a joint session of Congress and a prime-time television audience, "It is not just Negroes, but it is really all of us, who must overcome the crippling legacy of bigotry and injustice. And we *shall* overcome." [87] He also reprimanded his fellow southerners, "It is wrong—deadly wrong—to deny any of your fellow Americans the right to vote in this country." [88] Impressed by these sentiments, John Lewis, the bruised veteran of the Selma skirmish, praised the address as "historic, eloquent, and more than inspiring." [89]

The administration bill basically satisfied the civil-rights groups. Unhappy with the discretionary court procedures written in the 1957 and 1960 acts, the Justice Department fashioned a measure that provided for an automatic formula to wipe out discrimination. In states and counties where a literacy test was utilized and less than 50 percent of the population had gone to the polls in the 1964 presidential election, the legislation placed a moratorium on all educational requirements for voting. This device caught Alabama, Georgia, Louisiana, Mississippi, South Carolina, Virginia, and parts of North Carolina. When the attorney general received twenty meritorious complaints from residents of these areas or when he exercised his own judgment, he could have the Civil Service Commission assign federal registrars to enroll those who were qualified. The designated locales could free themselves only by proving to a three-judge District Court in Washington, D.C. that they had not sanctioned racial disfranchisement within the past ten years. However, once shown to have deprived their citizens of the right to vote, these governments could not change their electoral procedures for ten years without the prior approval of the federal judiciary in the nation's capital.

By designing these features of the bill, the administration admitted what the reformers had been saying for some time. After years of frustration culminating in Selma, Attorney General Katzenbach declared that the national government was ready to go beyond "the tortuous, often ineffective pace of litigation." [90] The federal-registrar plan followed the suggestion originally made by the Civil Rights Commission in 1959 and annually requested by the suffragists. Moreover, with identical reasoning which SNCC had used in 1963, the attorney general explained to the House Judiciary Committee two years later that the literacy standard had to be suspended as long as it continued to discriminate against "Negroes who for decades have been systematically denied educational opportunity available to the white population." [91] The administration felt confident taking the big step away from depending on the sixth-grade requirement of the 1964 act, because on March 8, 1965, the Supreme Court in *Louisiana v. United States* affirmed the lower-court decision proclaiming the "freezing" concept as a legitimate method to correct past bias. This opinion gave the Justice Department a precedent on which to base the suspension of literacy tests, giving blacks the same opportunity to register as whites. [92]

Although the proposal contained most of the items that the civil-rights groups had recommended, many of the suffragists hoped that the bill would be improved. James Farmer of CORE, James Forman of SNCC, and Martin Luther King found fault with the automatic trigger for not springing on

Arkansas, Texas, Florida, and Tennessee, which did not have literacy tests, but where blacks encountered difficulty in qualifying to vote. They wanted federal registrars stationed in any community "where the people who are not free to register request it," and there was evidence to prove "subversion of the right to vote." [93] The MFDP and SNCC desired a provision for holding new elections within six to nine months after the arrival of federal examiners. They complained that otherwise Negroes might live under racist rule possibly for two more years, and "democracy—in its true meaning of government by the people as distinct from the bill's present thrust of only the right to vote—" would be postponed.[94] Almost all of the liberals agreed that for state elections the measure should forbid the poll-tax payment required in Mississippi, Alabama, Virginia, and Texas.

This minor criticism from within the reform ranks did not lift the spirits of the dejected southerners. Many Dixie senators doubted that they could muster enough manpower to sustain a filibuster against a bill that had sixty-five bipartisan sponsors. Several of them were resigned to the reality that Congress would pass a suffrage statute. Unable to take his customary place as southern leader because he was suffering from emphysema, Richard Russell lamented, "If there is anything I could do, I would do it, but I assume the die is cast." [95] A. Willis Robertson of Virginia moaned about the poor morale of his colleagues, "When the water reaches the second deck, it's every man for himself." [96] From Montgomery, even before the marchers had descended on the city, the conservative *Advertiser* admitted forlornly, "It is almost certain that President Johnson's reconstruction bill will be enacted." [97] This gloom was well founded. On March 18th, sixty-seven senators trounced thirteen southerners and instructed the Judiciary Committee to report back a franchise bill in three weeks. That same day in the lower chamber, Emanuel Celler, convening hearings on the administration measure, declared, "Any filibuster, any undue delay, any stalling, any dragging of the feet would be inexcusable. The bill must be passed quickly." [98]

The Justice Department did not want to tamper with its handiwork. Katzenbach doubted whether a congressional poll-tax ban for state elections would be constitutional, citing the lawmakers' decision three years earlier that an amendment was the proper route to take in outlawing the financial levy for federal contests. On March 24th, the attorney general told the Senate Judiciary Committee that he did not have enough evidence to prove that the poll tax requirement disfranchised blacks exclusively on the basis of race.[99] In addition, he considered it politically wise to keep the controversial repealer out of the legislation. "I have proceeded on the assumption," Katzenbach informed the president, "that the continued support of Senator Dirksen is necessary to assure votes" for cloture.[100] Since the minority leader, whose revolutionary ardor had its limits, opposed the antipoll-tax clause on constitutional grounds, the administration placated him.

Nor did the attorney general approve of suggestions for alternate formulas that might widen the range of the bill. One House version, authored by the GOP maverick John V. Lindsay of New York City, gave the president power to dispatch registrars when the courts failed to settle a suffrage suit within forty days of hearing it. Katzenbach disliked this plan because it depended "too heavily on the judicial process" which, the government had finally concluded, was too cumbersome.[101] But he also rejected suggestions that did not involve litigation. In March, when a bipartisan group of liberal senators offered a bill authorizing the assignment of examiners to any county where less than 25 percent of the Negroes were registered as of November 1964, Katzenbach testified to the congressional committees that it would be difficult to compute such a racial breakdown in enrollment. However, the attorney general was not telling the entire truth, because publicly and privately the Census Bureau acknowledged that with a considerable amount of effort it could calculate the statistics in a reasonable time.[102]

On April 9th, the attorney general lost the opening round in the Senate Judiciary Committee. The group, commanded by a liberal majority, reported S. 1564, which banned the poll tax as a state suffrage requirement and provided for the appointment of registrars in areas where fewer than 25 percent of adult blacks were enrolled. The measure also contained a section sponsored by Dirksen that weakened the proposal. It freed the governments covered by the bill after five years instead of ten if they registered 60 percent of all of their voting-age citizens and no longer blocked Negroes from enrolling. The suffragists worried that county officials could take advantage of this escape clause by increasing the number of eligible white voters alone.[103] The committee's revision did have a modification that the attorney general readily accepted; it provided for use of poll watchers to observe whether the federally listed black voters actually were allowed to cast their ballots.

From April 13th to May 26th, with time out for Easter recess, the Senate debated the legislation. Much of the discussion centered on the poll tax, and in the second match the administration triumphed. On April 30th, following days of deliberation, Mansfield and Dirksen introduced a substitute that deleted from the judiciary bill the antipoll-tax provision and the 60 percent escape clause. The minority leader, who gave up one of his suggestions, explained the art of negotiation to the liberals, "Don't you know that you can bargain and swap a hat for a monkey wrench? When you make a trade, you've got to get a little something." [104] On May 11th, led by Senator Edward Kennedy of Massachusetts, a member of the Judiciary Committee, the suffragists attempted to restore the repealer. They argued that due to the unequal distribution of income between the races in the South, the tax weighed a "far heavier economic burden on Negroes than on whites," and thus Congress had the power to eliminate it under the Fourteenth and Fifteenth Amendments.[105] Forty-nine senators, twenty-four Democrats, including nine northerners, and twenty-five Republicans narrowly defeated the thirty-nine Democrats, three of them from the nonpoll-tax South, and six Republicans who supported the Kennedy proposal.[106]

The close tally indicated that the administration's firm stand meant the difference. Two weeks before the crucial vote, the president explained why he reluctantly rejected the congressional ban, "I have always opposed the poll tax. I am opposed to it now. I have been advised by constitutional lawyers that we have a problem in repealing the poll tax by statute." [107] Eugene McCarthy of Minnesota, who in this instance defected from the liberal camp, admitted that he did so because Katzenbach had written a letter to Mansfield strongly disapproving of the Kennedy approach.[108] However, to soothe the reformers' hurt feelings, the administration agreed to a provision that put Congress on record against the tax and directed the attorney general to challenge its constitutionality in the courts as soon as possible.

Throughout most of the legislative wrangling, the South had let the Mansfield-Dirksen axis fight the liberals. Once the antipoll-tax bloc had been whittled down, the Dixie senators tried to slice the bill further. Much of their legal argument was handled by Sam Ervin, a graduate of Harvard Law School. The North Carolina senator contended that the legislation was an unconstitutional bill of attainder because its automatic formula condemned certain states without a judicial trial. Moreover, he asserted that the measure in punishing past discrimination was an *ex post facto* law.[109] Many scholars, however, disagreed with the learned senator. Bernard Schwartz, later summing up their views, concluded that Ervin's presentation was "amazingly weak from a constitutional point of view . . . [and] would scarcely be made even by a law school neophyte— so contrary is it to all law on the subject." [110]

The floor managers of S. 1564 also disputed Ervin's arguments. Philip Hart of Michigan found the formula to be a reasonable prescription for diagnosing areas practicing racial disfranchisement. He noted that only the six states to which the bill applied shared the following characteristics: (a) fewer voters than the national average had participated in the 1964 presidential election, (b) literacy tests were used, (c) there was a great disparity in enrollment between whites and blacks, and (d) the races were segregated by law.[111] Birch Bayh of Indiana explained why it made sense to deprive these states of the privilege of administering the literacy requirements, "They cannot . . . provide Negro citizens with an inferior education, while at the same time require them to pass a stiff education test as a prerequisite to the exercise of the right to vote." [112] Directing himself to Ervin's *ex post facto* contention, Jacob Javits answered that the purpose of the measure was twofold, "The bill would attempt to do something about accumulated wrongs and the continuance of the wrongs." [113]

The majority of the Senate followed the suffragists' line of thinking. The upper chamber easily defeated southern motions to drop or modify the important sections of the proposal. On May 25th, after a total of about twenty-four hours of actual debate on the bill, seventy senators successfully imposed cloture. As promised, Dirksen delivered a majority of his party in support of the motion. Twenty-three Republicans joined forty-seven Democrats to overwhelm nine GOP conservatives and twenty-one predominately southern Democrats. The next day, the Senate passed S. 1564 by a vote of seventy-eight to eighteen. On this tally, the reformers picked up three southern Democrats from Tennessee and Texas as well as seven northern Republicans. [114] The Senate package contained a provision that Johnson had not sponsored—the 25 percent triggering formula. Otherwise it strongly reflected his wishes, and the president congratulated the Senate for presenting "triumphant evidence of this nation's resolve that every citizen must and shall be able to march to a polling place and vote without fear of prejudice or obstruction." [115]

Meanwhile the companion administration bill, H.R. 6400, was taking a slower route through the inner recesses of the House. On April 5th, after several weeks of hearings, a Judiciary Subcommittee recommended the measure with two important additions: (a) a poll-tax repealer and (b) authorization for judges, in suits initiated by the attorney general, to appoint federal examiners. Not until May 12th did the parent body endorse the modified proposal, and on June 1st, H.R. 6400 was sent to the Rules Committee. Following his usual procedure with respect to civil rights, Chairman Howard Smith tied up the legislation for weeks. Finally, on July 1st, as support grew for a discharge petition circulated by Celler, the Virginian relented and permitted the committee to report the measure to the floor.

When debate commenced on July 6th, the main controversy developed over a GOP substitute. William McCulloch, ranking Republican on the Judiciary Committee, and Gerald Ford, the minority leader from Michigan, had offered a bill that did not have an automatic detonator but instructed the attorney general to assign registrars to any county where he received twenty-five substantiated complaints of racial disfranchisement. Although this measure was designed to encompass more territory than the administration plan, it did not suspend the use of literacy tests, except when the applicant had finished six grades of formal schooling. Furthermore, the GOP version freed the guilty areas from judicial surveillance immediately after they complied with the rulings of the federal examiner. McCulloch preferred his proposal because "without penalizing areas which have done no wrong, it applies firm, considered standards to meet the critical requirements of the present situation." [116] The Republicans denounced the president's choice of formula as "arbitrary." Howard "Bo" Calloway, the lone GOP representative from Georgia, facetiously remarked that the Justice Department might easily have selected

all states which have an average altitude of 100 to 900 feet, an average yearly temperature of 68° to 77° at 7 a.m., average humidity of 80 to 87%, and a coastline of 50 to 400 miles. With this formula we encompass all the Southern states attacked by H.R. 6400, but have the added advantage of including all of North Carolina and excluding Alaska.[117]

Resigned to the passage of a suffrage act, the southerners accepted the McCulloch-Ford suggestion as the lesser of the two evils. Howard Smith mentioned that it lacked "the vengeance and the dripping venom that falls from every paragraph and sentence of the Committee bill." "Vote for the Mc-

Culloch substitute," William Tuck of Virginia pleaded with "every Member opposed to these so-called voting rights bills." Such appeals did not help the Dixie cause. "Why are the southerners supporting the Ford-McCulloch substitute?" asked Peter Rodino, a New Jersey Democrat who sat on the Judiciary Committee. Responding to his own question, he answered that the adoption of the GOP version would result "in an irreconcilable stalemate" in the Conference Committee, and "this is not what those who are genuinely interested in voting rights are seeking." [118] Convinced that Rodino was correct, approximately twenty-five Republicans bolted their party to help defeat the McCulloch–Ford measure on a teller vote, by 215 to 166.

With the main issue settled, the majority of both parties put rhetoric aside and passed H.R. 6400, practically unamended. On July 9th, 112 Republicans and 221 Democrats overwhelmed twenty-four Republicans and sixty-one Democrats. The victors attracted the support of three southern Republicans and thirty-three Dixie Democrats. Hale Boggs, majority whip from Louisiana, spoke for his liberated colleagues, "I love my State. I love the South. I . . . support this bill because I believe the fundamental right to vote must be a part of this great experiment in human progress under freedom which is America." [119] Not quite canceling out the votes of these defectors, eight Republicans and one Democrat from the North lined up with the losers.

The legislative deliberations in the House left some bitter partisan feelings. On July 10th President Johnson thanked the lower chamber for rejecting the GOP leaders' bill which, he claimed, would have "seriously damaged and diluted the guarantee of the right to vote for all times." [120] Upset by this remark, McCulloch and Ford responded that Johnson was a "Lyndon-come-lately" to the cause of civil rights and pointed to his pre-1957 voting record.[121] On July 13th the chief executive candidly conceded that he had made some mistakes in the past, but he promised to furnish leadership for the present and future.[122]

To prove that he was sincere, Johnson pressed the Conference Committee to settle expeditiously the differences between the Senate and House bills. The main source of disagreement again was the poll tax. On July 13th, the president obliquely commented on the disputed requirement, "I have tried to get it repealed every time I had a chance, when I thought I could do it legally." [123] Obviously Johnson did not believe that congressional prohibition was legal, because he had steadily opposed it as a member of Congress. Hence, he asked the attorney general to meet with the conferees. Katzenbach broke the stalemate when he released to the committee a letter describing a conversation that he had had with Martin Luther King. Interested in the speedy enactment of the law, the civil-rights leader endorsed the Senate's version favored by the administration.[124] With the House repealer scrapped, the committee deleted the Senate's 25 percent trigger from the bill.

The negotiated measure, except for some technical changes, closely resembled the administration's original proposal. On August 3rd the House adopted the Conference Report, by 328 to seventy-four. Seven southern Democrats and two northern Republicans reversed the negative votes that they had cast against the previous House bill. The following day, the Senate rallied seventy-nine members against eighteen to approve the compromise. On this tally, one southerner, George Smathers of Florida, switched his vote in favor of the franchise bill.

On August 6th, an excited Lyndon Johnson hurried over to the Capitol Rotunda to sign the Voting Rights Act. In the beautifully decorated room where Abraham Lincoln had written his name on a bill giving freedom to slaves owned by Civil War Confederates, the president placed his signature on what he called "one of the most monumental laws in the entire history of American freedom." [125] No less enthusiastic, John Lewis interpreted this event as a "milestone and every bit as momentous and significant . . . as the Emancipation Proclamation or the 1954 Supreme Court decision" on school desegregation.[126] Those who were aware of the long, episodic struggle to demolish the various obstacles blocking the Negro's right to vote could certainly agree with Johnson as he declared, "Today what is perhaps the last of the legal barriers is tumbling." [127] By putting this final piece into the suffrage puzzle, Lyndon Johnson demonstrated that he had learned quite a bit since the 1940s, when he voted against congressional civil-rights bills and even since 1960, when he had opposed a federal registrar plan similar to the one he was now placing on the statute books.

Many of the black militants, however, wanted more from Johnson than the legal right to cast a ballot. Encouraged by the sweeping legislation the administration had sponsored, they demanded that the president help them immediately purge white-supremacist representatives from Congress. Although the chief executive understood their impatience, he chose instead to liberalize southern politics gradually by implementing the Voting Rights Act.

This controversy had long been brewing. After the Democratic Convention had adjourned in August 1964 the MFDP continued to challenge the legitimacy of the lily-white faction. The insurgents decided to offer candidates to run against the regular Democratic choices in the fall congressional elections. Having acquired the necessary signatures to run as independents, black nominees petitioned the Mississippi Secretary of State, Heber Ladner, to place their names on the November ballot. Ladner insisted, although the law did not so stipulate, that each name on the petitions be certified by the circuit clerks. Unable to get any satisfaction from these county registrars, who had been responsible for keeping blacks off the rolls in the first place, the MFDP staged a mock election.[128] As a result, Fannie Lou Hamer, Annie Devine, and Victoria Gray were chosen to go to the House of Representatives.

Subsequently on November 10th, supporters of the MFDP met in Washington, D.C., to plan a challenge against the seating in the House of the five white Mississippi congressmen. Disgruntled by what they considered a liberal "sell out" at the

Democratic Convention, the black dissidents turned away from some of their old allies. Instead of teaming up with Joseph Rauh, they chose Arthur Kinoy, a member of the left-wing National Lawyers Guild. Because the Freedom Democrats suspected that the lower chamber would "bargain away [the case] in a half hour . . . [and] decide to adopt whatever procedure it feels to suppress the challenge," they selected a course of action to ensure that the issue would receive a full public hearing.[129] According to Title III, Section 210 of the United States Code, the contestants could begin an appeal within thirty days of the election by serving a subpoena on their adversaries. The petitioners would then gather testimony for forty days; their opponents had an equal time to respond; and both groups would deposit their briefs with the Subcommittee on Privileges and Elections. The dissidents did not expect this southern-dominated group to render a favorable report, but they hoped that the weight of the accumulated evidence would sway the rest of the congressmen.[130]

Working with William Kunstler, a radical attorney who had defended many civil-rights volunteers in the southern courts, Kinoy discovered a little-known statute upon which to protest the validity of the Magnolia State elections. In 1870 Congress had enabled Mississippi to resume its representation in Washington, provided the state never change the existing suffrage qualifications and disfranchise any citizen. The MFDP counselors reasoned that Mississippi had violated its pledge by enacting the poll tax and literacy test as suffrage requirements. Legal advisers to the various civil-rights organizations, as well as legal scholars like Mark De Wolfe Howe of Harvard, endorsed this contention.[131]

The liberals, however, divided over the question of seating the challengers in place of the regular Mississippi delegation. Although they backed the ouster of the white representatives, many civil-rights leaders believed that there was no legal precedent to support the seating of the insurgents. Reflecting the views of the ACLU and the NAACP, Leon Shull, the ADA's national director, distinguished the Atlantic City struggle from the Washington encounter, "Convention rules are loose; delegates to conventions may properly take into consideration questions as party loyalty not relevant in elections to Congress." [132] To preserve unity within the reform ranks, the Freedom Democrats stressed that the "basic decision" for Congress to make was whether the 1964 elections were invalid. Moreover, they made it clear that their main objective was "to unseat the present Mississippi congressional delegation and secure new elections in Mississippi under federal supervision." [133]

Since the challenge was an internal problem for the House to decide, the president did not comment on the dispute. But his House spokesman, Majority Leader Carl Albert of Oklahoma, on January 4, 1965 introduced a resolution to swear in the five Mississippi regulars. The leadership reached this decision without the benefit of a full hearing on the matter. Before William Fitts Ryan, a liberal Democrat from New York City, could recommend that his colleagues refuse to give the oath to the Mississippians until a thorough inquiry was conducted, the House ended discussion. By a 226 to 149 tally, the lawmakers voted to consider the Albert motion, and by voice approved the seating of the white contingent. One hundred sixty-one Democrats, including sixty-six from the North, followed Albert, and 115 Republicans lined up behind Gerald Ford to overwhelm the MFDP supporters. Some administration supporters who were looking forward to guiding the president's Great Society programs into law did not want to antagonize powerful southerners more than necessary by favoring an MFDP delegation whose legal claims to the election they found questionable. Emanuel Celler, who voted to seat the regular Mississippi congressmen, preferred to exercise caution in this matter, because it "was most important that Congress be organized in an orderly fashion so that the great measures sent to us by the President could be acted on as quickly as possible." [134]

Having anticipated this outcome, the MFDP carried its fight into Mississippi. Aided by attorneys from the National Lawyers Guild, the challengers conducted their own hearings according to the law. In February and March, they took over 600 depositions filled with the familiar charges of racial bias.[135] Furthermore, the insurgents documented their position from official sources of the federal government. They pointed out that on March 8th the Supreme Court in *U.S. v. Mississippi* ruled that there had been "a common purpose running through the State's legal and administrative history . . . to adopt whatever expedient seemed necessary to establish white political supremacy."[136] In addition, the MFDP noted that after reviewing the testimony presented before its inquiry at Jackson, Mississippi, in mid February, the Commission on Civil Rights concluded two months later:

> The 15th amendment to the United States Constitution commands that no citizen shall be deprived of the right to vote by reason of race or color. This requirement of the Constitution which is binding in every State has, in substance, been repudiated and denied in Mississippi. Since 1875 Negroes in Mississippi have been systematically excluded from the franchise by legislative enactment, fraud and violence.[137]

The Mississippi incumbents, however, did not concentrate their response on the merits of the MFDP's evidence. Rather than convening hearings, they prepared a brief that argued that the Freedom Democrats had no legal standing to make the challenge. William Colmer contended that House precedents required the contestants to be bona fide candidates, and he claimed that the black nominees were not. The Congressman explained that because Hamer, Devine, and Gray had participated in the 1964 Democratic primary, Mississippi law bound them to support the duly elected candidates in November. Therefore, he concluded, the trio could not campaign as independents or make the challenge.[138]

Busy with the deliberations over the Voting Rights Act, the House was in no rush to add the controversial challenge to its agenda. On May 16th the MFDP deposited its 15,000 pages of corroborating materials with the Clerk of the House, Ralph

Roberts. He did not get the voluminous documents printed until July 29th, when he turned over the testimony to the House Administration Committee. Chaired by Omar Burleson of Texas, the group did not begin consideration of the dispute until the waning days of the session. On September 13th and 14th, nine months after the challenge had been filed, the Subcommittee on Privileges and Elections conducted closed hearings for a total of three hours.

On September 15th the Administration Committee rejected the MFDP claims mainly on technical grounds. The panel reasoned that the white delegates had a prima facie right to their seats, because the House had sworn them in the past January. Besides, the passage of the Voting Rights Act had rendered obsolete the question of disfranchisement. With little consolation to the black challengers, the legislators admitted that the "alleged practices complained of . . . in the 1964 Mississippi elections would constitute violations of the new Act if occurring subsequent to its enactment." [139] "Even if the charges of racial exclusion are true," Robert Ashmore, the chairman of the Elections Subcommittee from South Carolina, instructed his fellow lawmakers, "A member of Congress should not, and would not, be held responsible for the wrongful acts of some registration officer back home in his home district who refused to issue certificates to qualified people." [140]

Similarly the Mississippi representatives did not deny that the majority of blacks had encountered racial bias in trying to register, but they refused to accept any responsibility for the discrimination. "I have not stolen any votes," Thomas Abernathy declared on the floor of the House, "I am not charged with any fraud. No charges are made that I or any member of our delegation has failed to comply with the electoral laws, State or Federal." [141] Likewise, Jamie Whitten asserted that his election was not "conducted any differently or under any different circumstances to those . . . held for the past sixty years, and about which there has been no contest in the Congress or elsewhere." [142] William Colmer suggested that if the House condemned Mississippi for violating the compact that readmitted her into the Union, it would have to make a similar ruling against all of the former Confederate states.[143]

The MFDP's allies wanted the final decision postponed until the subcommittee thoroughly investigated the dispute by convening open hearings. Otherwise, John Lindsay argued, the House would be giving "blanket acceptance to Mississippi's election procedures." [144] John Conyers, a black Democrat from Detroit, proposed that his colleagues undertake a detailed examination of the "veritable mountain of uncontradicted . . . and incontrovertible evidence which has been submitted to prove the obvious and well known fact that Negro Americans are and have for decades been barred from voting in Mississippi because of their race." [145]

The majority of the House preferred to let the Voting Rights Act remedy future problems of disfranchisement. Frank Thompson, a liberal Democrat from New Jersey who in this instance supported the Mississippi regulars, predicted that the "record of this debate . . . will constitute a clear precedent that the House of Representatives will no longer tolerate electoral practices in any State or district which violate the legal or constitutional rights of citizens to register, vote, or to become candidates for office." [146] In the opinion of Charles Goodell, a Republican from upstate New York who served on the Administration Committee, the House would "use the power to unseat in the future, if there is corroborative evidence of the violation of the Voting Rights Act of 1965." [147] For the present, however, these two, along with 226 of their colleagues, decided to affirm the credentials of the white Mississippians. On September 17th, eighty-seven Republicans and 141 Democrats, with fifty-four from the North, followed Carl Albert and Gerald Ford to dismiss the protest, while thirty-four GOP partisans and 109 northern Democrats voted to uphold it.[148]

To the insurgents the message was clear. "The dismissal of the Mississippi challenges leaves the almost one million Negro citizens of Mississippi still unrepresented in Congress." [149] If blacks wanted a share of the decisionmaking power in the

South, they would first have to get the majority of the disfranchised on the registration books. But the civil-rights forces did not have to go it alone. At the very moment when the lower chamber was siding with the lily whites, the attorney general was assigning federal examiners to enroll the Negroes long deprived of the vote. In his own style, Lyndon Johnson had started a quiet political upheaval in the South.

Throughout the various suffrage struggles, the president apparently reconciled whatever contradictions he may have discerned between politics and morality. Johnson never deviated from his ultimate goal of extending the right to vote to the mass of southern Negroes, but he was anxious to achieve his objective without stirring up the wrath of the opposition. Unlike the suffrage crusaders filled with burning rage against their racist oppressors, LBJ did not view southern white leaders as evil men whose sin must be painfully exorcised with righteous indignation. Instead, he preferrred to reason, negotiate, and cajole—the famous "Johnson treatment." The Texan presented his ideas for racial change within a highly charged atmosphere where southerners wielded great power in Congress and elected officials in Dixie whipped up popular resistance. Thus, he sought to expand first-class citizenship for southern blacks and, at the same time, convince the white South to make the required adjustments peacefully and permanently. It was a task for a modern day Samson and a Solomon, and no political leader had the strength and wisdom to satisfy both sides completely.

11

Free at Last?

I

ON AUGUST 6TH President Johnson had promised that he would promptly implement the Voting Rights Act. "I pledge," the chief executive proclaimed, "[W]e will not delay or we will not hesitate, or will not turn aside until Americans of every race and color and origin in this country have the same rights as all others to share in the progress of democracy."[1] Within three days, Nicholas Katzenbach had designated nine counties to receive federal examiners. Among those selected by the attorney general were two of the most infamous in Dixie: Dallas (Alabama), and Leflore (Mississippi). By November 1st, federal registrars had set up offices in thirty-two counties located in Alabama, Louisiana, Mississippi, and South Carolina.

Over the first several months the results of the act were striking. In Selma, Alabama, on August 14th, 381 blacks, more than all those who had been able to enroll in the previous sixty-five years, were listed by the federal examiner.[2] A few days earlier Mrs. Ardies Mauldin, a middle-aged black woman from Selma, had proudly stood at the head of the line to obtain her suffrage certificate. After securing the cherished document, she remarked, "It didn't take but a few minutes. I don't know why it couldn't have been like that in the first place." [3] Her achievement tickled Sheriff Jim Clark to comment, "The whole thing's so ridiculous I haven't gotten over laughing at it yet." [4] But his amusement soon ended as he watched thousands of Negroes like Mrs. Mauldin receive a similar welcome from the federal officials; by November, nearly 8,000 black applicants were signed up to vote. Elsewhere, the figures were equally astounding. A week after the examiners descended on the nine counties chosen initially, the number of black registrants had quadrupled from 1,764 to 6,998. In Leflore County, where only 300 had qualified to vote despite the heroic efforts of the SNCC workers during the early sixties, approximately 5,000 black names were added to the franchise rolls less than two months after the examiners had arrived. At the beginning of November, one of about 7,000 Negroes who registered to cast a ballot in Montgomery, Alabama, the birthplace of the Old Confederacy, was a 105-year-old woman who had been born a slave. [5] On the first anniversary of the passage of the Voting Rights Act, an average of 46 percent of adult blacks in the five Deep South states to which examiners had been assigned could vote, thereby doubling the percentage from the year before.

However, this rapid pace did not last. By the end of 1969, the percentage of registered blacks in the examiner states had increased to an average of 60.7, slightly below the 64.8 percent average for the entire South. Enfranchisement was yet to come for some 40 percent of the Negro adults living in Alabama, Mississippi, Louisiana, Georgia, and South Carolina. Although the gap between the number of blacks and whites on the suffrage rolls in the ex-Confederate states was narrowing, many more Negroes had to get on the lists in order to equal the 83.5 percent of whites qualified to vote in 1969. [6]

With the overt legal barriers destroyed, a lack of political consciousness remained a major obstacle on the road toward enfranchisement, and the reasons for it were quite apparent. Political scientists Donald R. Matthews and James W. Prothro

TABLE 3.　Percentage of Adult White
and Black Registrations in the South:
1964 and 1969

	1964		1969	
State	*White*	*Black*	*White*	*Black*
Alabama	69.2	19.3	94.6	61.3
Arkansas	65.6	40.4	81.6	77.9
Florida	74.8	51.2	94.2	67.0
Georgia	62.6	27.4	88.5	60.4
Louisiana	80.5	31.6	87.1	60.8
Mississippi	69.9	6.7	89.8	66.5
North Carolina	96.8	46.8	78.4	53.7
South Carolina	75.7	37.3	71.5	54.6
Tennessee	72.9	69.5	92.0	92.1
Texas			61.8	73.1
Virginia	61.1	38.3	78.7	59.8
Total	73.4	35.5	83.5	64.8

Source: U.S. Department of Commerce, *Statistical Abstract of the United States, 1970* (Washington, D.C., 1970), p. 369.

have demonstrated that an individual's interest in the electoral process varied directly with a feeling of his ability to effect change and the level of his knowledge about public affairs.[7] Many blacks who had been reared with the idea that "politics was white folks' business" could not easily break this deferential pattern of thought. This problem was noticeable. In November 1965, after surveying the considerable gains that the Voting Rights Act had quickly produced, the Commission on Civil Rights observed that the rate of black registration was already declining. "Negroes, who for generations have played no part in the political process of their communities," the CCR commented on the lack of motivation, "cannot be expected suddenly to embrace all of the responsibilities of citizenship."[8] A detailed study appearing in the *Harvard Civil Rights–Civil Liberties Review* a couple of years later made a similar point, "While some very able political leadership has . . . developed, much more political education and experience are necessary before the southern black man will wield his full share of political power." [9]

The Johnson administration believed that much of the obligation for further expanding the suffrage rested on Negro shoulders. Hardly had the ink dried on the page where the president signed the Voting Rights Act when he solemnly advised the suffragists:

> This Act is not only a victory for Negro leadership. This Act is a great challenge to that leadership. It is a challenge which cannot be met simply by protests and demonstration. It means that dedicated leaders must work around the clock to teach people their responsibilities and to lead them to exercise those rights and to fulfill those responsibilities and those duties to their country. [10]

In February 1966 Attorney General Katzenbach underscored this theme to a meeting of the Southern Regional Council, a group that had led the way in sponsoring registration drives in the past. According to Katzenbach, "the most important factor generating enrollment was local organization." Counties that have seen extensive black registration, he declared, "are counties in which registration campaigns have been conducted. In counties without such campaigns, even the presence of examiners has been of limited gain." [11]

The Regional Council, however, reached a slightly different conclusion. Based on research compiled by the VEP in July 1966 the council found that the "highest Negro registration figures" were "in those counties with both federal examiners and VEP assisted programs." Next, the SRC discovered, came counties with federal examiners alone, followed by those with only VEP activities. [12] Thus, when viewed as separate variables, franchise drives were very helpful, but the presence of federal manpower was most crucial.

Hence, the civil-rights groups persistently urged the attorney general to assign examiners to many more counties than he had designated. By mid 1968, federal registrars functioned in only fifty-eight areas out of 185, in which less than 50 percent of the adult blacks were enrolled.[13] The private organizations interested in promoting the suffrage just did not have the resources to invest in all of these hard-core places. In late October 1965 several civil-rights leaders had informed Katzenbach that they experienced more trouble in getting "volunteer help in fall and winter than in summer, and they were short on finances and paid personnel." [14] This situation became particularly acute as the young militants in SNCC, CORE, and SCLC devoted less time to voter registration and more to attacking the capitalist system and the Vietnam War. Even where black organization at the grass-roots level did not exist, the suffragists still believed that federal enrollment officers could have a positive psychological effect in stimulating fearful Negroes to make an attempt to register. "Black people in the South very much prefer going before a federal examiner to going before a local registrar," a VEP official explained. "There is a difference in attitude. There is a difference in setting, for many black people fear and dread the local county courthouse, which for many of them is a symbol of injustice and oppression." [15]

The administration, however, preferred to dispatch examiners only as a last resort. Except for its enforcement of the act during the first months, the Justice Department characteristically sought to rely on voluntary compliance. On September 30, 1965 Attorney General Katzenbach had set forth Washington's guidelines for implementation of the statute, "Our aim . . . is not the widespread deployment of any army of Federal examiners. The purpose, rather, is to insure that every citizen . . . [register] according to normal and fair local procedure." [16] A month later, John Macy, Chairman of the Civil Service Commission, which selected and trained the examiners, reiterated this position. "Massive designations of additional counties by the Attorney General is not the answer," Macy told the president. "While Federal representatives provide efficient voter listing operations in the designated counties, local authorities should be encouraged to achieve maximum compliance." [17] But if the states refused to cooperate, then the executive branch would remedy the problem. John Doar, appointed chief of the Civil Rights Division in 1965, believed that registrars should be assigned mainly "as a means to assure that full opportunities are available for registration where the State fails to meet its responsibilities." [18] In this way, the Justice Department hoped to avoid a massive federal invasion that might have created a hostile white reaction and reduced the advantages brought by the appointment of examiners.

The department stuck with this strategy because it generally produced spectacular results. In the two and one-half years following the passage of the act, the CCR reported, local registrars in the five designated states had signed up 416,000 black citizens to supplement the 150,767 nonwhites listed by the federal examiners. From 1965 to 1969, the average percentage of registered adult blacks leaped in these states from 24.4 to 60.7. Forbidden to administer literacy tests, the county officials were severely hampered in their ability to block Negro enrollment. Furthermore, the presence of federal registrars in nearby locales perhaps prompted the county authorities to carry out the law faithfully, thus averting a similar intrusion into their domains. [19]

There was another reason for the government to follow a careful approach; political considerations may have influenced the Justice Department's conciliatory policy. Upon enactment of the 1965 statute, the attorney general had decided that he would send examiners to counties where there was "past evidence of discrimination." [20] But Katzenbach did not designate Baker and Terrell Counties in Georgia and Sunflower County, Mississippi, until nearly a year after the act went into effect. "Terrible" Terrell had occasioned the original suit under the Civil Rights Act of 1957, and the others had also been involved with federal litigation challenging voting bias. As late as March 1966 there were thirty counties in Mississippi and twenty-nine in Georgia that had not been assigned federal registrars, although less than 25 percent of their adult black population were registered. [21] Several commentators have concluded that the Justice Department acted discreetly in these states because it did not want to risk the political consequences. Pat Watters and Reese Cleghorn speculated that the administration was hesitant to offend James Eastland, chairman of the Senate Judiciary Committee and owner of a plantation in Sunflower County, and Richard Russell of Georgia, the head of the Senate Armed Services Committee. Eastland's committee processed the legislation sponsored by the Justice Department and deliberated on its nominations to the judiciary, whereas Russell's group handled matters vital to the president's military program in Southeast Asia.[22]

Whatever his political motives may have been, Katzenbach did partially respond to the demands made by the suffragists for more registrars. At the beginning of 1966, the SCLC led a series of demonstrations in Birmingham to protest the dilatory tactics that the board of registrars still used against Negroes who wanted to enroll. Subsequently on January 20th the attorney general assigned examiners to Jefferson County. Working six days and nights each week for the next month, the federal agents added about 19,000 Negroes to the rolls; the percentage of blacks qualified to vote jumped in five weeks from 36.1 to slightly over 50.[23] At the same time, Katzenbach circulated a letter among county officials throughout the Deep South, instructing them to extend the regular registration hours and establish temporary offices in black neighborhoods so that registration might be expedited. When some recalcitrant authorities failed to respond affirmatively, the Department of Justice lost its patience and dispatched examiners into an additional twenty-five counties.[24] During July and August 1966, in Terrell, where Negroes had been demanding examiners for about a year, federal personnel enrolled 1,122 blacks, nearly triple the number entitled to vote on the day they arrived.[25]

Yet many suffragists believed that the federal government could do more than send registrars. They wanted Washington to assist them in carrying on nonpartisan voter-education programs. In November 1965 the CCR had recommended that the president begin a campaign to disseminate "information concerning the right to vote and the requirements of registration and [to provide] training and education to foster better understanding of the rights and duties of citizenship and the significance of voting." [26] In May 1968 the commission again suggested that citizenship training be included in the Great Society's adult education projects administered by HEW, the Department of Agriculture, the Department of Labor, and the Office of Economic Opportunity. Aware that private civil-rights groups lacked the resources to finance and supervise voter-registration drives in many needy counties, the CCR warned that the "right to vote will not be realized fully unless the burden of taking affirmative action to encourage registration is shared by the Federal Government." [27]

Attorney General Katzenbach did not think it was "possible or desirable" for the executive branch to promote voter training. The federal government had no budgetary approval for such programs, and in 1967 Congress passed an amendment to the Economic Opportunity Act of 1964 preventing the disbursement of funds or personnel for the administration's war on poverty with respect to "any voter registration activity." [28] Moreover, Katzenbach and his aides perceived the Justice Department's traditional role as limited to removing the legal obstacles to voting. The task of arousing political enthusiasm among blacks customarily belonged to the private agencies. The "only way that political participation can be permanently achieved," the attorney general informed the Taconic Foundation,

> is through many local organizations doing the routine, the drudgery, but step-by-step creating and developing a viable political organization. It seems to me that even if the federal government undertook to accomplish the actual registration of the mass of unregistered Negroes, when the federal government left, there would be little left for the future.[29]

Having chosen not to participate in this way, the Justice Department carried out its decision with excessive caution. A report issued by the CCR in November, 1965, revealed that although the Civil Service Commission had prepared to mail notices of the opening of examiners offices to all residents of the counties where there were offices, the Department of Justice opposed as inappropriate this procedure and any other affirmative effort of the Federal Government to publicize the program in the examiner counties.[30]

One Negro learned about the presence of federal examiners in his county only after hearing about it on a Huntley-Brinkley evening news telecast.[31] Others found out mainly from the civil-rights workers. The attorney general would not even provide the VEP, which the Regional Council revived in 1966, the same kind of informal cooperation that the Kennedy administration had given to it. In late 1965, Katzenbach had "expressed [an] interest in voter registration drives," but he would not "make any commitments of help in getting financial assistance or in other ways." [32]

Nevertheless, the administration's careful approach yielded significant gains. As the majority of adult blacks in the southern states affected by the act succeeded in registering, they elected members of their race to public office. When Lyndon Johnson left the White House in 1969, there were over 120 blacks holding elected posts in the five examiner states. One of the twenty-nine victorious candidates in Mississippi went to Jackson as a representative to the state legislature, breaking an almost century-old tradition of lily-white rule at the capital. In Macon County, Alabama, where the Tuskegee Civic Association had fought a long battle against disfranchisement and political apathy, Negroes elected a black sheriff, the first one since Reconstruction.[33] When blacks had to choose between two white contenders, they naturally rejected the one who had been outspokenly racist in the past. In Dallas County, newly enfranchised blacks made their persistent foe, Jim Clark, pay for his transgressions against them. Several months before his 1966 reelection bid, the incorrigible sheriff had been asked whether he expected the federally registered Negroes to vote; he burst out laughing and replied, "If they can find their way into town." The emancipated Negroes had no difficulty locating the polling places and cast the margin of victory for

Clark's moderate white rival.[34] Although blacks did not win any statewide contests, probably because they did not constitute a majority of the total electorate, they did modify the behavior of white politicians. Where Negroes held the balance of power in close contests, they forced some white candidates, no matter how virulently they had yelled "Nigger" in the past, to abandon their racist oratory.[35]

Ballots alone did not automatically bring political power. Negroes had to mobilize the potential voters into an actual force at the polls. Although blacks might control the political machinery on the county level, because they were outnumbered by whites in every southern state their race's leaders needed to master the difficult lessons of political bargaining, compromise, and negotiation. Moreover, Negroes lacked the financial resources that might be converted into political strength. The Voting Rights Act had broken the major legal blockades hindering access to the ballot box, but it had not attempted to transform the economic system that perpetuated second-class citizenship. As long as blacks depended on whites for employment and credit, many of them did not feel free enough to make an attempt to register and vote.[36]

The Voting Rights Act had only a limited impact on eradicating bigotry from the Democratic party. In May 1968 the CCR asserted, "As a general rule, relatively few Negroes hold responsible party offices even in those states with a substantial Negro population." [37] Contrary to its pledge at the National Convention in 1964, the Democrats had not issued mandatory guidelines instructing state organizations how to encourage black particiaption in the ranks.[38] "Neither national party has yet established," the CCR concluded, "firm or comprehensive requirements providing for the elimination of discrimination in all aspects of party activity or for significant affirmative steps to overcome the effects of past discrimination." [39] Thus, by the time southern Democrats journeyed to Chicago in 1968, less than 1 percent of the members of their state executive committees were black. In Mississippi, where the FDP had worked so valiantly, no Negroes served on either the statewide or county executive committees, but three blacks did manage to integrate the delegation attending the Windy City convocation.[40]

Yet few could doubt the importance that the right to vote had for the southern Negro. As Matthews and Prothro have pointed out, "the administration of justice tends to improve after southern Negroes become active members of the electorate." [41] Nearly a decade after the passage of the Voting Rights Act, a black activist from Alabama declared, "It's no longer standard operating procedure for whites to kill blacks at will. And it's all because of politics." [42] As the percentage of black registrants rose sharply, so did the quality of the services provided to Negro communities. Responding to the demands of the newly enfranchised, local officeholders paved streets, upgraded sanitary conditions, and hired black patrolmen to police ghetto neighborhoods.[43] Moreover, the ballot instilled a feeling of pride in those who had acquired it. One middle-aged Negro looked forward to voting in order "to be a man." [44] Blacks who had spent their entire lives in Dixie without ever hearing a white man call them "Sir" or "Ma'am" swelled with pride when federal examiners addressed them by these courteous titles.[45] Liberated from the fears of the past, an elderly black woman exclaimed, "I'm going to vote now. I'm going to vote because I haven't been able to vote in my sixty-seven years." [46]

II

Going to the polls for the first time, these people were ending a long nightmare and awakening to a brighter morning. At the outbreak of World War II, southern blacks had encountered a variety of obstacles preventing all but a small fraction of them from voting; a quarter of a century later, a majority of adult Negroes were free to cast their ballots. In 1941, white Democratic primaries, poll taxes, literacy tests, and the biased administration of registration procedures, reinforced by white brutality and economic intimidation, kept 95 percent of the adult blacks residing in Dixie off the franchise lists.

Within a generation, most of these barriers had been dismantled, clearing the path to the polling places for nearly
three-fifths of the voting-age blacks. One hundred years after
the end of the Civil War, federal registrars again functioned
in the South as they had during Reconstruction. However,
unlike the initial attempt to grant Negroes their full political
rights, this second effort brought the majority of blacks into
the mainstream of electoral politics with little prospect of the
South reversing this triumph.

During this "Second Reconstruction," as C. Vann Woodward dubbed it, progress came gradually but steadily.[47] In a
departure from the situation following the Civil War, the new
suffragists had to contend with a resurrected South exerting
powerful influence, both within Congress and the dominant
political party. Not only did this circumstance make the recent
achievements all the more remarkable, but it also helped explain why these accomplishments probably would last longer
than those gained over 100 years ago. Though Dixie legislators were able to slow the rate of change, they failed to destroy
the forces of political emancipation. Ultimately on the losing
side of the legislative and court battles, the South could not
logically deride the outcome as illegitimate. Its congressional
representatives had participated in the decisionmaking process,
and southern-born federal court judges had ruled on the suffrage disputes.[48] By 1969, most white southerners reconciled
themselves to black political participation as a fact of life.

The graph in Figure 1 charts the course of black
enfranchisement. The initial spurt in the percentage of southern black registrants occurred from 1944 to 1952. To secure
the ballot required direct action on the part of public agencies
and private groups. In that interval, the Supreme Court delivered a landmark ruling that made possible Negro participation in the most important southern election. This decision
was followed up with registration drives spurred on by returning World War II veterans who were determined to obtain
their citizenship rights. Furthermore, because black citizens
started out on a very low registration base, it could be ex-

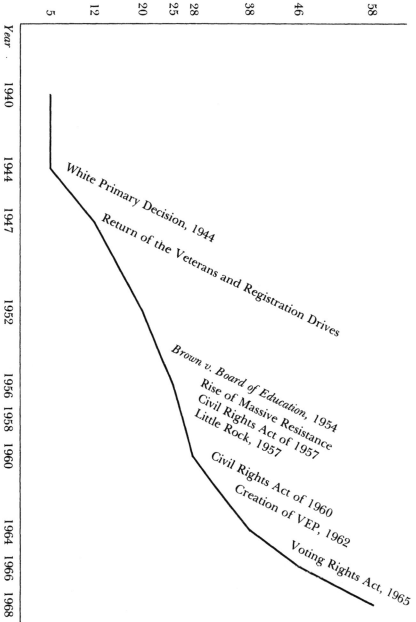

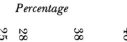

Percentage

58

46

38

28
25
20

12

5

Year · 1940 1944 1947 1952 1956 1958 1960 1964 1966 1968

White Primary Decision, 1944

Return of the Veterans and Registration Drives

Brown v. Board of Education, 1954
Rise of Massive Resistance
Civil Rights Act of 1957
Little Rock, 1957

Civil Rights Act of 1960
Creation of VEP, 1962

Voting Rights Act, 1965

Figure 1. Percentage of voting-age southern blacks registered, 1940–1968. *Source:* D. R. Mathews and J. W. Prothro, *Negroes and New Southern Politics*, p. 18; U.S. Commission on Civil Rights, *Political Participation*, pp. 12–13.

pected that they would enroll in a big burst at the outset of their concerted efforts.

During the Eisenhower regimes, the registration gains began to level off. Although the Republican administration helped put two suffrage laws on the books, it was sluggish in implementing them. The legislation provided for court procedures to safeguard the right to vote, and it needed a vigilant Justice Department to handle the litigation. After the hostile southern white reaction following the *Brown* opinion and the sending of federal troops into Little Rock, Eisenhower worried about inflaming passions further and hesitated to move swiftly.

The greatest rise in enrollment took place between 1960 and 1969. These years were characterized by court opinions favorable to the suffrage, intense voter-registration campaigns, and vigorous enforcement of the federal laws by the executive branch. Whereas the Eisenhower lawyers had moved deliberately, the Kennedy-Johnson attorneys pushed the judiciary far more earnestly. In addition, the Democratic administration cooperated with the civil-rights groups in encouraging them to undertake voter-education projects that stimulated thousands to register. The sharpest percentage increase during this period came after the passage of the Voting Rights Act of 1965. This piece of legislation succeeded so well because it automatically suspended discriminatory voting qualifications and gave the president the authority to send examiners to register Negroes directly. Thus, the statute effectively dealt with the machinations of bigoted southern officials.

In this protracted struggle for enfranchisement, the reformers had labored under serious disadvantages. The federal system consisted of a delicate balance of powers between national and state governments, which often tipped on the side of officials in local communities. Although the Constitution established the right to vote in national elections and the Fifteenth Amendment guaranteed it against racial discrimination in federal and state contests, the states retained a great deal of authority to determine and enforce suffrage requirements. Manufacturing clever devices that made no mention of race, southern politicos were able to prevent blacks from voting. And when the bigots resorted to extralegal schemes and were prosecuted by the federal government, they went into court confident that their white neighbors would serve on the juries, hear the evidence, and acquit them. In the end, however, the federal government extended the limits of national involvement in protecting the ballot and struck down discriminatory voting qualifications, but it moved in an episodic and time-consuming fashion.

Washington's architects of civil-rights strategy cautiously appraised these institutional hazards. Administrations from Franklin Roosevelt through Lyndon Johnson expanded the agenda for suffrage reform, but their officials were held back by conventional perceptions of federal-state relations. Successive presidents and their attorney generals intended to keep community control over law enforcement intact, preferred to work through the courts, and counted on rational appeals and good will to get local officials to obey the law. While definitely pushing forward the frontier of voting rights through legislation and executive action, they also felt an obligation for doing so with a minimum of disruption and in an orderly manner. The federal government was not so callous as to ignore the violence perpetrated against blacks and their white sympathizers, but its policymakers believed that a massive invasion of civilian or military personnel into the South was impractical (not illegal) and sanctioned it only as a desperate last resort. They thought that such action would make martyrs of the civil rights resisters, inflame racial tensions, and harden popular opposition. In the meantime, these considerations made no sense to the civil-rights workers, who knew from brutal experience that a reign of terror had spread into many southern counties where officials would not respond to gentlemanly persuasion but would only yield to superior force.

When suffrage legislation did pass, it was trimmed to suit a variety of political figures. Until the middle of the Kennedy administration, the civil-rights pressure groups and their representatives in Congress did not wield enough influence to mold franchise measures according to their satisfaction. Although most white Americans, particularly in the North, condemned racial inequality after World War II, neither they nor their elected agents felt a moral urgency to tackle the problem without delay. The liberals in both parties were on the fringes of congressional power. They did not have the votes or leadership positions needed to control vital legislation, and organizations like the NAACP and the LCCR did not exert the financial or electoral clout necessary to knock out their opponents. Throughout these years, the suffragists were on the losing side of the numbers game. In the Senate they could count on western Democrats and most northern Republicans to join them in supporting voting-rights measures on a final vote but discovered themselves abandoned when strengthening provisions or cloture resolutions were offered. The occasional allies of the Negro, usually coming from sparsely populated states with few blacks, derived greater rewards for the interests they represented by going along with their temporizing congressional chiefs than by standing firmly alongside of the liberals. Actually on civil-rights issues there were three blocs in Congress, crossing party and sectional lines. Nearly all southern Democrats rejected measures promoting racial equality. The majority of Republicans, about half of the northern Democrats, and a few southerners favored the bills but defected on items like the jury-trial amendment, Title III, and registrar plans. A minority of the GOP and the rest of the northern Democrats consistently supported the strongest proposals. Thus, the civil-rights moderates united with the Dixie lawmakers to eliminate controversial sections from legislation and then joined the liberals to enact whatever remained.

These facts of political life meant that the reformers were able to develop franchise measures and keep public attention on them, but they had to accept bargains that more potent brokers negotiated. Atop the institutional power bases in Congress, the legislative managers prized teamwork as a supreme virtue and scorned the liberals for righteously insisting on holding to their "extreme" positions. The spirit of moderation that pervaded the Eisenhower presidential years in the post-McCarthy period brought forth the first suffrage statutes since Reconstruction and characteristically omitted a valuable provision for federal registrars. Although "Ike" dutifully lined up the GOP behind the civil-rights bills, he showed little enthusiasm for any but the least objectionable suggestions. No match for cautious administration Republicans and Johnson Democrats in 1957 and 1960, the liberals had to wait for the civil-rights constituency to grow and to make an impact on Washington before they could complete their plans.

Meanwhile, of all the measures proposed by the civil-rights advocates, franchise expansion commanded the greatest appeal to the nation and its lawmakers. There was a conservative side to expansion of voting rights that attracted northern politicians, who preferred to see the efforts of the civil-rights troops channeled into "quiet" registration drives rather than into the more provocative freedom rides and mass marches. Moreover, although control of the suffrage was considered a local matter and enfranchisement had produced resistance, white southerners viewed political participation as more acceptable behavior than integration and the equal access to public accommodations. This attitude was reflected in the behavior of some southern congressmen who supported voting-rights bills, but opposed measures promoting other forms of civil equality. Even those Dixie lawmakers who voted against measures to raise the Negroes' citizenship status found voting proposals least objectionable. Besides, they could not easily defend disfranchisement which contravened the democratic ethos.

Southerners were most vulnerable on the franchise issue, but they did not yield without a struggle. Dixie politicos did not merely go through the motions of opposing suffrage bills with the intention of accepting them later in a trade for eliminating the more hated desegregation measures. They instinctively understood that enfranchisement would crack the white-supremacist edifice. When blacks obtained and cast ballots in large numbers, they would shatter the myths perpetuated by whites about Negro apathy and contentment. Furthermore, as a practical matter, southern officials recognized that an outpouring of black voters would endanger their political careers unless they drastically altered their biased ways.

At any rate, time was working against the suffrage restrictionists. Ever since World War II, the civil-rights ranks were slowly accumulating recruits. Added to the lofty wartime pronouncements and the anticommunist rhetoric during the subsequent deep freeze in relations with the Soviet Union, the northward migration of blacks built up the necessary political muscle for breaking the congressional stalemate. From 1940 to 1970, the black population in the North leaped over 400 percent from 2,800,000 to 11,600,000. At the same time, the southern black population grew only slightly from 9,900,000 to 12,000,000. As Negroes migrated above the Mason–Dixon Line, they selectively congregated in strategic locations mainly in the Middle Atlantic, East North Central, and the Pacific Coast (California) states (see Table 4). Here they could use their ballots as a balance of power in close congressional elections, or they might swing their states with large numbers of electoral votes into the winning presidential column. In return, northern blacks pressed both political parties to remedy the ills from which their kinfolk and neighbors still suffered down South.

The unflagging commitment of the interracial coalition furnished another source of strength for enfranchisement. Carrying on the tradition of the abolitionists a century before, blacks and liberal whites joined together in leading the movement for suffrage reform. However, in contrast with the emancipationist coalition of the Civil War period, Negroes played greater leadership roles in the modern struggle for the ballot. The NAACP, which initially headed the challenge against disfranchisement in the twentieth century, garnered talented Negro lawyers to argue its cases in the courts. The voters' leagues, as well as the partisan political clubs, which did

TABLE 4. BLACK POPULATION, 1940 AND 1970

Region	1940	1970
New England	101,509	388,398
Maine, New Hampshire, Vermont, Massachusetts, Rhode Island, Connecticut		
Middle Atlantic	1,268,366	3,953,739
New York, New Jersey, Pennsylvania		
East North Central	1,069,326	3,872,905
Ohio, Indiana, Illinois, Michigan, Wisconsin		
West North Central	350,992	698,645
Minnesota, Iowa, Missouri, North Dakota, South Dakota, Nebraska, Kansas		
South Atlantic	4,698,863	6,423,710
Delaware, Maryland, Virginia, West Virginia, North Carolina, South Carolina, Georgia, Florida		
East South Central	2,780,635	2,597,005
Kentucky, Tennessee, Alabama, Mississippi		
West South Central	2,425,121	3,043,543
Arkansas, Louisiana, Oklahoma, Texas		
Mountain	36,411	180,382
Montana, Idaho, Wyoming, Colorado, New Mexico, Utah, Nevada, Arizona		
Pacific	134,691	1,514,243
Washington, Oregon, California, Alaska, Hawaii		

Sources: U.S. Department of Commerce, *Statistical Abstract of the United States, 1970* (Washington, D.C., 1970), p. 27; *Statistical Abstract . . . , 1971*, p. 27.

so much at the grass roots to stimulate registration, consisted almost entirely of blacks, and the full-time field workers for SNCC, CORE, and SCLC conducting enrollment drives in some of the most hostile areas of the South were predominantly Negroes. Yet whites made a significant contribution to black political freedom by serving as fund raisers, attorneys, lobbyists, and volunteers in the registration drives. Despite the handicaps that the liberal lawmakers in Congress endured, they performed a critical role by drafting legislation and educating their colleagues and the nation to the necessity of enact-

ing it. Furthermore, the presence of whites in the movement
was used to break down southern black fears. One Negro
fieldworker in Georgia explained that the oppressed

> will somehow get used to seeing black and white together as they
> have become used to the separation of the groups. Then too,
> there is the idea that as products of the system, the Negro in the
> South has been trained to react in a certain way to a white man.
> This is well known. The question is what psychological basis is
> there for believing that told by a white man to register, the South-
> ern Negro would go? This statement of probability is based on the
> southern indoctrination that "white is right." Now although we are
> fighting against white supremacy we acknowledge that in the
> minds of the people with which we work it has the ascendancy.
> Our opinion is that we can fight the system with every justifiable
> instrument at our disposal.[49]

By 1960 the technique of confrontation gave blacks an important weapon in the battle for first-class citizenship.
Marches, freedom rides, sit-ins, stand-ins, and wade-ins dramatically exposed the injustices of the southern racist system.
As television cameras recorded the vicious efforts to repress
black protests, sympathy for the abused swelled in the North,
giving the liberals in Congress the crucial public backing for
long-desired legislation. The southern extremists had finally
offended the national conscience. Against the outrages in-
flicted by the "Bull" Connors and Jim Clarks, the nation contrasted the courageous Birmingham children and the fiercely
proud men and women of Selma. When white terrorists attacked the peaceful demonstrators and registration workers
with cattle prods, waterhoses, dynamite, and bullets, Presidents Kennedy and Johnson warned congressmen to settle
legitimate Negro grievances swiftly or a racial conflagration
would erupt. Of course the chief executives, Congress, and
the courts had been plodding toward the goals of enfranchisement and integration over several decades, but the final shove
came after defenseless people were killed and angry blacks
showed increasing signs of taking to the streets in retaliation.
"It is a sorrowful mockery of our principles," Senator Paul

Douglas lamented, "that it required the tragedy of the Birmingham bombings and the Philadelphia, Mississippi murders to pass the Civil Rights Act of 1964 . . . and that it required the atrocities of Selma to invoke the Fifteenth Amendment's instructions." [50]

It is tempting, when looking at the moral dimensions of the franchise struggle, to condemn the nation's elected leaders for moving too cautiously when nothing less than decisiveness and coercion were required. This interpretation becomes even more appealing if one notes the lives destroyed in order to exterminate white supremacy and the callousness exhibited by pernicious southern officials to preserve it. After all, the issue involved specific rights of American citizens, human beings who breathed and bled, and lawmakers should not have deliberated over this question as if they were discussing power dams, tariffs, and farm subsidies. Moreover, liberal chief executives like Truman and Kennedy gave social and economic reforms a higher priority than civil-rights legislation. In this way, they hoped to attract moderate southerners to support progressive legislation that did not have the stigma of race on it. However, modest raises in minimum wages and social-security payments did not lift the bulk of southern Negroes from economic and political bondage.

In so criticizing these public officials, one does not have to assume that they were wicked or insensitive people. After all, the chief executives from Truman through Johnson did extend federal protection for the suffrage in a manner not seen since Reconstruction. Still, why did they move so slowly and require constant pressure before they combatted obvious wrongs? In addition to the structural and political restraints already mentioned, it is important to consider the way in which the lawmakers perceived their roles in wrestling with the problem of racial injustice. The postwar presidents, their assistants, and spokesmen in Congress were politicians and not zealous militants. Conciliators by temperament and profession, they did not share the same moral urgency as the "new abolitionists," whose overriding passion was to purge immediately the racial evils pervasive in the United States. Otherwise, the men in charge would not have been selected to the halls of power in the first place. For them peaceful change according to the rules of the game was axiomatic, and hence they paid careful attention to the hostile conservative faction on Capitol Hill, to the erection of a white backlash, and to defiant southern officials who stirred up trouble at home. Such calculations varied with the quality of presidential leadership. Neither Truman nor Kennedy was particularly adept in dealing with Congress. Eisenhower had the popular appeal but lacked the political finesse; moreover, the two pieces of legislation produced during his White House years testified to his conservative impulses rather than to his farsighted vision. When the right proportions of political skill, principle, and favorable opportunity combined in Lyndon Johnson, he achieved some of twentieth century liberalism's most notable accomplishments.

Because decisionmaking was incremental, the civil-rights proponents developed a crisis mentality. Only successive confrontations seemed to produce corrective governmental responses. The pressure on the militants to continually challenge authority was enormous and often produced battle fatigue. Ironically, for taking this approach dictated by realistic considerations, the activists were condemned by the political establishment and their more moderate civil-rights allies. Warned not to push too quickly for fear of causing white resistance, the radical suffragists had nevertheless learned from bitter experience that the system best responded to internal clashes. At any rate, they faced the perplexing question of what were "legitimate" methods and goals, and this dilemma eventually proved too burdensome for many of them.

As a result, a rupture developed between Washington and the militants. Progress had come in a piecemeal fashion, and many of the young staffers identified with COFO turned off to the traditional political process. The reluctance of the Justice Department to shield them from racist harm and the readiness of Democratic party leaders to compromise the MFDP angered many radicals. Their despair moved them to reject the basic tenets of reform ideology, namely, racial integration and political alliances with white liberals. Alienation spread within the ranks of the movement and helped fracture it. Members of CORE and SNCC embraced black nationalism and black power and withdrew from the biracial coalition leaving behind the NAACP, Urban League, and SCLC. At the same time, the escalating war in Vietnam added Martin Luther King's booming voice in protest against the Johnson administration.

Ironically, the liberals in the 1960s were victims of their own successes. Under the New Frontier and Great Society, southern blacks had enrolled to vote in record numbers, and the statute books were bursting with recently passed civil-rights laws. However, with each new gain Negro aspirations soared higher than Washington could reach to fulfill them. For example, the passage of the Voting Rights Act in 1965 shifted the activists' attention from casting ballots to other features of political influence—party representation, office holding, fund raising, and community organization. Thus, in 1968, when Congress finally enacted legislation enabling the Justice Department to protect civil-rights organizers, many of the former workers were no longer participating in registration drives; they had abandoned the notion that acquisition of the ballot could create meaningful change within the current political and economic structures.

In retrospect it is clear that even without these differences over policy, the franchise struggle was bound to end with some disillusionment. The emancipationists contended that when southern blacks acquired the right to vote they would possess a strong weapon to destroy other racial evils and to guard against future assaults on their freedom. According to this view, the ballot could be stretched a long way to obtain economic and social benefits. However, this faith was too sanguine. Although the suffrage provided a tool for meaningful change, it was only one form of political power. Taking the next step beyond legal enfranchisement, southern blacks had to acquire a greater share of the economic resources so that they could effectively organize the registrants and win representation in crucial governing bodies. The New Frontier and Great Society welfare programs brought some financial relief, but black families residing in Dixie improved their economic position very little and their incomes lagged far behind whites'.[51] Hence, the majority of southern Negroes succeeded in getting their names on the voter rolls, but they still remained trapped in poverty, subject to the coercion of their white employers and landlords. "People in this area," a Negro from Humphreys County, Mississippi, explained in 1969, "don't want to register because they feel they will lose their jobs or will have to move off the plantation with no place to go, or [they feel that] their welfare, social security . . . checks will be cut off because this is what happened in the past." [52]

On balance, a "new day" had dawned for many southern Negroes; but liberals, black and white together, had expected too much of a payoff from enfranchisement. Although there were material and psychological rewards during the 1960s, reformers had optimistically counted on the vote to topple the remaining walls of racism and economic oppression. When the suffrage did not instantly deliver such huge returns, some of the euphoria surrounding the passage of the 1965 Voting Rights Act turned into bitter frustration.[53] Thus, in the period from 1944 to 1969, Negroes in the South had come out of the political desert, but they had not yet entered the promised land.

Notes

1. THE STRANGE CAREER OF BLACK DISFRANCHISEMENT

1. Chilton Williamson, *American Suffrage: From Property to Democracy, 1760–1860* (Princeton: Princeton University Press, 1960), p. 280.

2. Leon F. Litwack, *North of Slavery* (Chicago: University of Chicago Press, 1960), p. 91. The states were Massachusetts, Rhode Island, Maine, New Hampshire, and Vermont. In New York, Negroes could vote if they had a freehold estate worth $250; whites did not have to satisfy this requirement.

3. John Hope Franklin, *Reconstruction: After the Civil War* (Chicago: University of Chicago Press, 1961), p. 86.

4. Ibid., p. 136; Kenneth M. Stampp, *The Era of Reconstruction* (New York: Vintage Books, 1967); Joel Williamson, *After Slavery: The Negro in South Carolina During Reconstruction, 1861–1877* (Chapel Hill: University of North Carolina Press, 1965).

5. William Gillette, *The Right to Vote: Politics and the Passage of the Fifteenth Amendment* (Baltimore: Johns Hopkins University Press, 1969), pp. 26, 27. Enfranchisement referenda passed in Iowa and Minnesota.

6. Ibid., pp. 46–50. For a view that the passage of the amendment resulted more from principle than politics, see LaWanda Cox and John H. Cox, "Negro Suffrage and Republican Politics: The Problem of Motivation in Reconstruction Historiography," *Journal of Southern History* XXXIII (August 1967): 303–330.

7. 18 *United States Code* 241, 242. Richard Claude, *The Supreme Court and the Electoral Process* (Baltimore: Johns Hopkins University Press, 1970), pp. 53–56.

8. Everette Swinney, "Enforcing the Fifteenth Amendment, 1870–1877," *Journal of Southern History* XXVIII (May 1962): 209; Claude, *The Supreme Court*, p. 56.

9. Swinney, "Enforcing the Fifteenth Amendment," p. 206.

10. *United States v. Cruikshank,* 92 U.S. 542 (1876); *United States v. Reese,* 92 U.S. 214 (1876).

11. Claude, *The Supreme Court*, p. 56.

12. W. R. Brock, *An American Crisis* (New York: St. Martin's Press, 1963), pp. 286–287.

13. Claude, *The Supreme Court,* p. 56.

14. John Hope Franklin, " 'Legal' Disfranchisement of the Negro," *Journal of Negro Education* XXVI (Summer 1957): 241.

15. George B. Tindall, *South Carolina Negroes, 1877–1900* (Columbia: University of South Carolina Press, 1952), pp. 69–70.

16. J. Morgan Kousser, *The Shaping of Southern Politics: Suffrage Restriction and the Establishment of the One Party South, 1880–1910* (New Haven: Yale University Press, 1974), pp. 53–54. By 1895, eight of the eleven southern states were using the secret ballot.

17. Chester H. Rowell (compiler), *Digest of Contested Election Cases, 1789–1901* (Washington, D.C.: Government Printing Office, 1901), pp. 384, 393, 457, 459, 470, *Congressional Record,* 51st Congress, 1st Session, pp. 1844 ff.

18. C. Vann Woodward, *The Strange Career of Jim Crow* (2nd rev. ed., New York: Oxford University Press, 1966), p. 54; Carl N. Degler, *Out of Our Past* (rev. ed., New York: Harper and Row, 1970), pp. 228–229. In South Carolina, six Negro Republicans still served in the State House of Representatives in 1892. Rayford W. Logan, *The Betrayal of the Negro* (New York: Collier, 1965), p. 83.

19. Woodward, *Strange Career,* pp. 56–59.

20. George M. Frederickson, *The Black Image in the White Mind: The Debate on Afro-American Character and Destiny, 1817–1914* (New York: Harper and Row, 1971), p. 200; David W. Southern, *The Malignant Heritage: Yankee Progressives and the Negro Question 1901–1914* (Chicago: Loyola University Press, 1968), p. 6; Claude H. Nolen, *The Negro's Image in the South: The Anatomy of White Supremacy* (Lexington: University of Kentucky Press, 1967), p. 57.

21. Vincent P. De Santis, *Republicans Face the Southern Question: The New Departure Years, 1877–1897* (Baltimore: Johns Hopkins University Press, 1959), pp. 196, 198; Logan, *The Betrayal,* p. 71.

22. Richard E. Welch, Jr., "The Federal Elections Bill of 1890: Postscripts and Prelude," *Journal of American History* LII (1965): 511–526.

23. *Cong. Rec.,* 51st Congress, 1st Session, pp. 6553–6554.

24. Quoted in Paul Lewinson, *Race, Class and Party* (New York: Universal Library, 1965), p. 88.

25. Woodward, *Origins of the New South, 1877–1913* (Baton Rouge: Louisiana State University Press, 1951), p. 327.

26. The literature covering the Populists and their relationship with blacks is extensive. For the conclusions reached in this paragraph and the next, I have depended on Jack Abromowitz, "The Negro in the Populist Movement," *Journal of Negro History* XXXVII (July 1953): 257–289; George Crowe, "Tom Watson, Populists, and Blacks Reconsidered," *Journal of Negro History* LV (April 1970): 99–116; Lawrence J. Friedman, *The White Savage* (Englewood, New Jersey: Prentice Hall, 1970); Lawrence C. Goodwyn, "Populist Dreams and Negro Rights: East Texas As a Case Study,"

American Historical Review LXXVI (December 1971): 1435–1456; Jack Temple Kirby, *Darkness At The Dawning: Race and Reform in the Progressive South* (Philadelphia: Lippincott, 1972); Lawrence D. Rice, *The Negro in Texas, 1874–1900* (Baton Rouge: Louisiana State University Press, 1971); Robert Saunders, "Southern Populists and the Negro," *Journal of Negro History* LIV (July 1969): 240–261; and C. Vann Woodward, *Origins of the New South.*

27. George M. Frederickson, *The Black Image in the White Mind*, p. 201; C. Vann Woodward, *American Counterpoint: Slavery and Racism in the North–South Dialogue* (Boston: Little Brown, 1971), Chapter 9; J. Morgan Kousser, *The Shaping of Southern Politics*, passim.

28. V. O. Key, Jr., *Southern Politics in State and Nation* (New York: Vintage Books, 1949), p. 538.

29. Woodward, *Origins of the New South*, p. 332; Albert D. Kirwan, *Revolt of the Rednecks: Mississippi Politics, 1876–1925* (Lexington: University of Kentucky Press, 1951), p. 70. For the contention that many illiterate whites were too embarrassed to take advantage of this clause, see Kousser, *The Shaping of Southern Politics*, p. 60.

30. George S. Stoney, "Suffrage in the South, Part I, The Poll Tax," *Survey Graphic* XXIX (1940): 8–9.

31. *Williams v. Mississippi*, 170 U.S. 213 (1898). Actually this case only indirectly involved the suffrage. Williams, a Negro, had been charged with murder by an all-white grand jury and convicted by a lily-white trial jury. According to Mississippi law, only qualified voters could serve as jurors, and hence, Williams' lawyer argued that because the state constitution denied Negroes the right to vote, it also prevented them from sitting on juries. In effect he maintained, Negroes were not receiving "equal protection of the laws." Richard Bardolph (ed.), *The Civil Rights Record: Black Americans and the Law, 1849–1970* (New York: Crowell, 1970), p. 147.

32. Quoted in Sheldon Hackney, *Populism to Progressivism in Alabama* (Princeton: Princeton University Press, 1969), p. 205. The Supreme Court shielded the Alabama suffrage requirements from attack. In 1903 it heard the case of William Giles, a Negro who had been qualified to vote for twenty years and had been disfranchised by the state constitution. Giles claimed that the registration procedures in Alabama were designed to prevent Negroes from enrolling, and he asked the judiciary to add his name to the lists. The court ruled that it could not provide equity relief for the plaintiff to enforce his political rights. The justices further pointed out that Giles wanted to be enrolled in a registration system that he insisted was tainted with discrimination; how, they asked, "can we make the court a party to the unlawful scheme by accepting it and adding another voter to its fraudulent lists?" *Giles v. Harris*, 189 U.S. 475 (1903); Loren Miller, *The Petitioners* (New York: Pantheon Books, 1966), pp. 158–59.

33. Quoted in Lewinson, *Race, Class and Party*, p. 86. Most of the opposition to the state constitutions came from the poor white counties where

Populist and Republican strength was centered. Their representatives realized that the new procedures would impede the suffrage of poor and illiterate whites as well as blacks. In fact, there is evidence that the white constitutional framers from the black belts had this dual disfranchisement in mind. In this way, they intended to eliminate sources of support for opposing political factions and to preserve Democratic party supremacy. See Kousser, *The Shaping of Southern Politics*, pp. 170, 238, 248.

34. Kirk Porter, *A History of Suffrage in the United States* (New York: Greenwood Press, 1969), p. 224.

35. Quoted in Kousser, *The Shaping of Southern Politics*, p. 76.

36. Thurgood Marshall, "The Rise and Collapse of the 'White Democratic Primary'." *Journal of Negro Education* XXVI (Summer 1957), 249; Woodward, *Origins of the New South*, Chapter 14. The direct primary also gave urban reformers and representatives from poor white counties an opportunity to wrestle power out of the hands of the black-belt planters who dominated party caucuses.

37. Quoted in Gunnar Myrdal, *An American Dilemma* (New York: Harper, 1944), p. 1333, footnotes 13 and 14.

38. Louis R. Harlan, *Booker T. Washington: The Making of a Black Leader, 1856–1901* (New York: Oxford University Press, 1972), pp. 302–303. For the political thought of southern Negro leaders, see August Meier, *Negro Thought in America, 1880–1915* (Ann Arbor: University of Michigan Press, 1963), pp. 40–41.

39. Lewinson, *Race, Class, and Party*, p. 81; Woodward, *Origins of the New South*, pp. 343–344.

40. Virginia Writers' Project, *The Negro in Virginia* (New York: Arno Press, 1969), p. 240.

41. Woodward, *Origins of the New South*, p. 344.

42. Hackney, *Populism to Progressivism*, p. 206. In South Carolina, after the convention, it was reported that 50,000 whites and only 5,500 Negroes were registered. Tindall, *South Carolina Negroes*, p. 88.

43. Woodward, *Origins of the New South*, p. 344. Hackney, *Populism to Progressivism*, p. 206.

44. Myrdal, *An American Dilemma*, p. 949.

45. Vernon Lane Wharton, *Negro in Mississippi, 1865–1900* (New York: Harper Torchbooks, 1965), p. 215.

46. W. E. B. Du Bois, *The Souls of Black Folk* (Chicago: A. C. McClurg, 1903), p. 58.

47. "Declaration of Principles," in: August Meier, Elliot Rudwick, and Francis L. Broderick (eds.), *Black Protest Thought in the Twentieth Century* (2nd ed., Indianapolis: Bobbs-Merrill, 1971), p. 59.

48. James M. McPherson, "The Antislavery Legacy: From Reconstruction to the NAACP," in: Barton J. Bernstein (ed.), *Towards a New Past: Dissenting Essays in American History* (New York: Vintage Books, 1969), pp. 126–137, 148.

49. Allen F. Davis, *Spearheads for Reform: The Social Settlements and the Progressive Movement, 1890–1914* (New York: Oxford University Press, 1967), pp. 94 ff.

50. McPherson, "The Antislavery Legacy," p. 149; Davis, *Spearheads of Reform*, p. 102. Among the fifty-two white signers of the "Call" at least fifteen were former abolitionists or their descendants. Of the thirty-five members of the first steering committee at the conference, eight were social workers. The prime movers behind the conference were Oswald Garrison Villard, grandson of the abolitionist, Mary White Ovington, a social worker and daughter of an abolitionist, and William English Walling and Henry Moskowitz, settlement workers. See also Charles Flint Kellogg, *NAACP, 1909–1920*, Vol. 1 (Baltimore: Johns Hopkins University Press, 1967). For several abolitionists who failed to press the Negro cause, see David Southern, *The Malignant Heritage*, pp. 36 ff.

51. *Guinn v. United States*, 238 U.S. 347, 360 (1915). William B. Hixson, Jr., "Moorfield Storey and the Struggle for Equality," *The Journal of American History* LV (December 1968): 547.

52. Miller, *Petitioners*, pp. 297–298.

53. *Brief of Petitioner, Lane v. Wilson, October Term, 1938*, United States Supreme Court (Washington, 1938). The case was argued by Charles A. Chandler, a black graduate of Yale Law School, and James Nabrit of Howard Law School. Charles A. Chandler to Thurgood Marshall, September 26, 1938, Legal Files D-60, NAACP MSS.

54. *Brief of Respondents, Lane v. Wilson, October Term, 1938, United States Supreme Court* (Washington, 1938).

55. *Lane v. Wilson*, 307 U.S. 268, 275 (1939).

56. During the 1930s the Supreme Court had rendered other favorable rulings for Negro plaintiffs. See *Powell v. Alabama*, 287 U.S. 45 (1932); *Norris v. Alabama*, 294 U.S. 587 (1935), *Missouri ex rel Gaines v. Canada*, 305 U.S. 339 (1938).

57. Lewinson, *Race, Class, and Party*, p. 151.

58. Ralph J. Bunche, "The Political Status of the Negro" (unpublished manuscript for the Carneigie-Myrdal Study of the Negro in America, September 1, 1940) (7 vols.), vol. 5, pp. 1048, 1059.

59. Ibid., p. 1064.

60. For a favorable interpretation of Roosevelt and the Negro, see Leslie H. Fishel, Jr., "The Negro in the New Deal Era," *Wisconsin Magazine of History* XLVIII (Winter 1964): 111–126; Harvard Sitkoff, "Roosevelt and Civil Rights: A Reconsideration," (unpublished paper delivered to the American Historical Association, San Francisco, December 29, 1973). For negative viewpoints, see Baron J. Bernstein, "The New Deal: The Conservative Achievements of Liberal Reform," pp. 263–288, and "America in War and Peace: The Test of Liberalism," pp. 289–321, in: Barton J. Bernstein (ed.), *Towards a New Past* and Raymond Wolters, *Negroes and the Great Depression* (Westport, Connecticut: Greenwood Press, 1970).

61. Bernard Sternsher (ed.), *The Negro in Depression and War: Prelude to Revolution, 1930–1945* (Chicago: Quadrangle Press, 1969), p. 5. This well-balanced volume contains various appraisals of Roosevelt's policy toward Negroes. For an appraisal of the Republican administrations' failure to improve the status of blacks; see Richard B. Sherman, *The Republican Party and Black America: From McKinley to Hoover, 1896–1933* (Charlottesville: University of Virginia Press, 1973), Chapters 6–10.

62. John B. Kirby, "The Roosevelt Administration and Blacks: An Ambivalent Legacy," pp. 267–288, in: Barton Bernstein and Allen J. Matusow (eds.), *Twentieth Century America: Recent Interpretations* (2nd ed., New York: Harcourt Brace Jovanovich, 1972), pp. 270, 272, 278.

63. Myrdal, *An American Dilemma*, pp. 487–488.

64. Bunche, "Political Status of the Negro," vol. 6, pp. 1550–1551.

65. Ibid., p. 1528; Myrdal, *An American Dilemma*, pp. 60–61.

66. Bunche, "Political Status of the Negro," p. 1528.

2. The Rise and Fall of the White Primary

1. J. Morgan Kousser, *The Shaping of Southern Politics* (New Haven: Yale University Press, 1974), p. 208; Paul Casdorph, *A History of the Republican Party in Texas 1865–1965* (Austin: Pemberton Press, 1965), pp. 118, 124; Lawrence D. Rice, *The Negro in Texas*, pp. 98, 113; George Tindall, *The Emergence of the New South 1913–1945* (Baton Rouge: Louisiana State University Press, 1967), p. 167.

2. Melvin James Banks, "The Pursuit of Equality: The Movement for First Class Citizenship Among Negroes in Texas, 1920–1950" (unpublished Ph.D. dissertation, Syracuse University, 1962), p. 298.

3. Charles C. Alexander, *The Ku Klux Klan in the Southwest* (Lexington: University of Kentucky Press, 1965), pp. 125, 127.

4. Ibid., pp. 298, 301. The cases were *Maple v. Marrast*, 84 S.W. 180 (1916); *Walker v. Hopping*, 226 S.W. 146 (1920); *Kay v. Schneider*, 218 S.W. 479 (1920); *Newberry v. United States*, 256 U.S. 323.

5. L. W. Washington to R. W. Bagnall, August 2, 1924, Legal Files D-63, NAACP MSS., Library of Congress (LC).

6. Ibid.

7. William B. Hixson, Jr., "Moorfield Storey and the Struggle for Equality," *The Journal of American History*, LV (December 1968): 533–554.

8. Leonard Dinnerstein, *The Leo Frank Case* (New York: Columbia University Press, 1968), pp. 74–75. In 1913, Leo Frank, a Jewish industrialist who owned a factory in Atlanta, was accused of killing a young Christian girl, Mary Phagan. Frank was tried in an atmosphere of popular hysteria, convicted, and sentenced to death. After the Georgia governor commuted his sentence to life imprisonment in 1915, Frank was kidnapped from jail and hanged by a group of vigilantes.

9. Press Release, April 3, 1925, NAACP MSS, Legal File D-63.

10. Moorfield Storey to Walter White, January 25, 1925; James A. Cobb to Walter White, January 29, 1925, ibid.

11. Banks, "Pursuit of Equality," p. 303.

12. James A. Cobb to Fred C. Knollenberg, April 7, 1926, ibid; *Brief for Plaintiff in Error, L. A. Nixon against C. C. Herndon and Charles Porres, in the Supreme Court, October Term, 1925* (Washington, D.C., 1925).

13. Charles Reznikoff (ed.), *Louis Marshall, Champion of Liberty: Selected Papers and Addresses* (2 vols., Philadelphia: Jewish Publication Society of America, 1957), I, pp. 426, 427, 429, 442.

14. B. Joyce Ross, *J. E. Spingarn and the Rise of the NAACP* (New York: Oxford University Press, 1972), pp. 4, 20.

15. F. C. Knollenberg to Walter White, April 23, 1929, Legal Files D-65, NAACP MSS.

16. *Nixon v. Herndon,* 273 U.S. 536, 541 (1927).

17. Baltimore *Afro-American,* March 12, 1927. James Weldon Johnson erroneously believed that the decision had established the primary as part of the general election system. Press Release, March 8, 1927, Legal File D-64, NAACP MSS.; L. A. Nixon to James Weldon Johnson, March 12, 1927, Legal File D-64, NAACP MSS.

18. *Nixon v. Condon,* 286 U.S. 73 (1932).

19. The association again chose Nixon as plaintiff because he would have a "wonderful psychological affect upon the Court," before which he had previously appeared. F. C. Knollenberg to Walter White, August 20, 1928, Legal File D-64, NAACP MSS.

20. Louis Marshall to W. T. Andrews, January 26, 1929, Legal File D-65, ibid.

21. *Nixon v. Condon,* 34 F. 2d 464, 469 (1929).

22. Frank Cameron to Nathan R. Margold, November 13, 1930, Legal File, D-62, NAACP MSS.

23. *Brief for Petitioner, L. A. Nixon v. James Condon, in the Supreme Court, October Term, 1931* (Washington, D.C., 1931), 18–44.

24. Ibid., pp. 45–49, 53; Reznikoff, *Louis Marshall,* I, p. 458.

25. J. Alston Atkins to James Marshall, October 26, 1931, Legal File D-62, NAACP MSS; *Brief on the Merits in Support of the Petitioner, L. A. Nixon, October Term, 1931* (Washington, D.C., 1931).

26. *Respondent's Brief, October Term, 1931* (Washington, D.C., 1931), 5, 11.

27. *Petitioner's Reply Brief, Nixon v. Condon, October Term, 1931* (Washington, D.C., 1931), 8–9.

28. *Nixon v. Condon,* 286 U.S. 73, 84, 88 (1932).

29. Ibid., 96, 99, 103, 105.

30. William Pickens, "Next Step in Primary Fight," (no date), Legal File, D-63, NAACP MSS.

31. Luther Harris Evans, "Primary Elections and the Constitution,"

Michigan Law Review XXXII (1934), 451–477; "The White Primary in Texas Since *Nixon v. Condon,*" *Harvard Law Review* XLVI (1933), 812–818.

32. Carter Wesley to F. C. Knollenberg, May 30, 1932; L. A. Nixon to R. W. Bagnall, August 3, 1932, Legal File, D-63, NAACP MSS.

33. James Marshall to F. C. Knollenberg, April 18, 1933; Knollenberg to Walter White, October 20, 1932, Legal File, D-63, ibid. The case was *Nixon v. McCann.*

34. El Paso *Herald Post* (no date), clipping in Legal File, D-92, NAACP MSS; F. C. Knollenberg to Walter White, February 8, 1934, ibid. The judge ruled that when the Executive Committee instructed El Paso County Chairmen to exclude Negroes, it was action by the Executive Committee and not the convention that had merely resolved that all whites were qualified to vote.

35. El Paso *Times,* July 13, 1934; L. W. Washington to Walter White, August 6, 1934, Legal File D-92, NAACP MSS.

36. *Nixon v. Herndon* cost $2,909.31, Press Release, March 25, 1927, Legal File, D-64. *Nixon v. Condon* cost $2,879.92. Legal Dept. Memo (no date), Legal File, D-63. *Nixon v. McCann* cost $750.00, F. C. Knollenberg to Walter White, December 28, 1932, Legal File, D-63, ibid.

37. Section 51: "If two or more persons conspire to injure, oppress, threaten or intimidate any citizen in the free exercise or enjoyment of any right or privilege secured to him by the Constitution or laws of the United States, or because of his having exercised the same, or if two or more persons go in disguise on the highway, or on the premises of another, with intent to prevent or hinder his free exercise or enjoyment of any right or privilege so secured, they shall be fined not more than $5,000 and imprisoned not more than ten years, and shall, moreover, be thereafter ineligible to any office, or place of honor, profit, or trust created by the Constitution or laws of the United States." Section 52: "Whoever, under color of any law, statute, ordinance, regulation, or custom, wilfully subjects or causes to be subjected, any inhabitant of any State, Territory, or District to the deprivation of any rights, privileges, or immunities secured or protected by the Constitution and laws of the United States, or to different punishments, pains, or penalties, on account of such inhabitant being an alien, or by reason of his color, or race, than are prescribed for the punishment of citizens, shall be fined not more than $1,000, or imprisoned not more than one year, or both." These clauses are now codified as sections 241 and 242 of Title 18.

38. Charles Houston to Walter White, July 26, 1934, Legal Files, D-92, NAACP MSS.

39. Joseph Keenan to Walter White, December 28, 1934, Administrative File, C-285, ibid. The Texas Supreme Court case was *Bell v. Hill,* 74 S.W. 113 (1934).

40. NAACP to James Farley, March 12, 1934; Emil Hurja to Walter White, September 7, 1934, Administrative File, C-285, NAACP MSS.

41. Charles Houston to Homer Cummings, October 16, 1935. Administrative File, C-286, ibid.; John Thomas Elliff, "The United States Department of Justice and Individual Rights, 1937–1962" (unpublished Ph.D. dissertation, Harvard University, 1967), p. 72.

42. Banks, "Pursuit of Equality," pp. 213, 223.

43. Carter Wesley to Herbert Seligmann, May 20, 1932; Nathan Margold to Charles Houston, March 1, 1932, Legal File, D-63, NAACP MSS.

44. Herbert Seligmann to Carter Wesley, May 26, 1932, Legal File, D-63; J. A. Atkins to Charles Houston, May 12, 1935, Legal File, D-95; Carter Wesley to Thurgood Marshall, December 23, 1946, Box 364, 6 of 7, ibid. Walter White was sensitive to the criticism about the failure to hire black lawyers and had recommended a new policy after *Nixon v. Condon*. White to Arthur Spinarn, January 4, 1933, Legal File, D-63, ibid.

45. Walter White, *A Man Called White* (New York: Viking Press, 1948), p. 88; L. A. Nixon to C. F. Richardson, April 5, 1935, Legal File, D-92, NAACP MSS. The county clerk was a public employee, not a party official. Unable to vote on primary day, Nixon had asked the defendant Townsend for an absentee ballot. His refusal to issue one seemed a clear case of the state assisting the closed contest.

46. *Brief on the Merits for R. R. Grovey, October Term, 1934* (Washington, D.C., 1934), p. 29.

47. Ibid., pp. 14, 17, 26, 32, 35.

48. That same day the court also handed down its ruling in one of the Scottsboro cases, *Norris v. Alabama*, 294 U.S. 587 (1935). The justices decided that a state violated the equal-protection clause of the Fourteenth Amendment by excluding Negroes from serving on juries. For a lively account of the case, see Dan Thomas Carter, *Scottsboro* (New York: Oxford University Press, 1969). The NAACP field secretary William Pickens remarked on the coincidence of the two decisions handed down on the same day: "If one were suspicious of the Court's motives it would look as if they [*sic*] made a trade." Quoted in Thurgood Marshall, "The White Democratic Primary," *Journal of Negro Education* XXVI (Summer 1957): 252.

49. *Grovey v. Townsend*, 295 U.S. 45, 50, 52, 53, 54, 55 (1935).

50. *New Republic* LXXXII (May 8, 1935): 356; Robert L. Hale, *Freedom Through Law: Public Control of Private Governing Power* (New York: Columbia University Press, 1952), p. 340.

51. Charles Houston to Lionel Murphy, July 4, 1935, Administrative Files, C-81, NAACP MSS.

52. James Marshall to Walter White, April 15, 1935, Legal File, D-92, ibid.

53. J. Alston Atkins to Carter Wesley, August 1, 1943, Box 364, 4 of 7; Wesley to Thurgood Marshall, August 18, 1943, Box 364, 6 of 7, ibid.

54. J. Saunders Redding, *Lonesome Road* (Garden City: Doubleday and Co., 1958), pp. 320 ff.

55. For an excellent discussion of this point, see August Meier and Elliot Rudwick, "Attorneys Black and White: A Case Study of Race Relations within the NAACP," *Journal of American History* LXII (March 1976): 913–946. By the time Houston became counsel, Storey and Louis Marshall had died.

56. J. Alston Atkins to Charles Houston, October 8, 1935, Legal File, D-92, NAACP MSS.

57. J. Alston Atkins to Charles Houston, November 11, 1935, Legal File, D-92, ibid.; Banks, "Pursuit of Equality," p. 188.

58. *Crisis* XLII (May, 1935): 145.

59. Charles Houston to Lionel Murphy, July 4, 1935, Administrative File, C-81, NAACP MSS.

60. Charles Houston to J. A. Atkins, November 5, 1935, Legal Files, D-92, ibid.

61. Charles Houston to F. C. Knollenberg, June 9, 1938, Legal File, D-92, ibid.

62. Banks, "Pursuit of Equality," p. 192.

63. Ibid., p. 320; *NAACP Bulletin* I (February, 1941): 3.

64. NAACP *Annual Report,* 1941, p. 25; *Crisis* XLVIII (May 2, 1941): 164.

65. 313 U.S. 299 (1941).

66. Allan P. Sindler, *Huey Long's Louisiana* (Baltimore: Johns Hopkins University Press, 1956), pp. 36–38, 146; Elliff, "U.S. Department of Justice," p. 108; Richard Claude, *The Supreme Court and the Electoral Process* (Baltimore: Johns Hopkins University Press, 1970), p. 32; *Transcript of Record, U.S. v. Classic, October Term, 1940* (Washington, 1940), 3.

67. Jerold S. Auerbach, *Labor and Liberty* (Indianapolis: Bobbs-Merrill, 1966), p. 208; William E. Leuchtenburg, *Franklin D. Roosevelt and the New Deal* (New York: Harper and Row, 1963), p. 242.

68. Robert K. Carr, *Federal Protection of Civil Rights: Quest for a Sword* (Ithaca: Cornell University Press, 1947), p. 260.

69. *Ex Parte Yarbrough,* 110 U.S. 651 (1884).

70. Francis Biddle, *In Brief Authority* (Garden City, N.Y.: Doubleday, 1962), p. 160.

71. *Brief for the United States, in U.S. v. Classic, October Term, 1940* (Washington, D.C., 1940), 11, 34–35.

72. Ibid., 9, 24. For an analysis of Wechsler's role see Claude, *The Supreme Court,* pp. 33 ff.

73. *Brief of Defendants and Appellees, U.S. v. Classic October Term, 1940* (Washington, D.C., 1940), 19, 51.

74. *U.S. v. Classic,* 313 U.S. 299, 339 ff (1941). William O. Douglas, Hugo Black, and Frank Murphy, whom Roosevelt had appointed to the bench in 1939, did not disagree with the idea that primaries were part of the election process; rather, they dissented because they believed that in the absence of specific congressional legislation the language of the criminal statutes was too vague to cover deprivation of the right to vote at primary elections.

75. Leon Ransom to Vance Johnson, September 2, 1941, Box 231, 5 of 5, NAACP MSS. Stone based his conclusion on Article I, Sections 2 and 4, and not on the Fourteenth and Fifteenth Amendments. Article I applies to both private and state action. *U.S. v. Classic,* 318.

76. Minutes, Board of Directors, November 10, 1941, A-4, NAACP MSS.

77. Press Release, "Background of *Smith v. Allwright,*" March 20, 1944, Box 285, 2 of 4, NAACP MSS.

78. The ACLU and the NAACP had a working agreement that the latter group would initiate all cases involving Negro rights. Roger Baldwin to Odis L. Sweedon, February 3, 1938, Legal File, D-60; Jerome Britchey to Walter White, September 1, 1938, Administrative File, C-285, ibid. The National Lawyers Guild and the Workers Defense League also participated as *amici.*

79. Charles Fahy to Francis Biddle, Memo, October 29, 1943, President's Secretary's File, II Departmental Correspondence, Justice Department, Franklin D. Roosevelt Library (FDRL); Francis Biddle to FDR, Memo, October 30, 1943, PSF, FDRL. Herbert Wechsler supported this decision while Criminal Division head Wendell Berge had advocated filing an *amicus* brief. Fahy had replaced Biddle, who was promoted to attorney general in 1941.

80. Fred Folsom, "Federal Elections and the White Primary," *Columbia Law Review* XLIII (November–December, 1943): 1030.

81. *Brief for Petitioner, Smith v. Allwright, October Term, 1943,* (Washington, D.C., 1943), 13, 16. Texas law required all political parties that won 100,000 votes at the previous general election to nominate by direct primary and forbade any candidate defeated in a primary from running in the general election. Since 1859, Democratic nominees had been elected in all major contests except two.

82. Ibid., 21, 26, 29.

83. Carter Wesley to Thurgood Marshall, December 21, 1943; Marshall to Maceo Smith, December 31, 1943, Box 364, 6 of 7, NAACP MSS.

84. J. Woodford Howard, Jr., *Mr. Justice Murphy: A Political Biography* (Princeton: Princeton University Press, 1968), p. 356.

85. Alpheus T. Mason, *Harlan Fiske Stone: Pillar of the Law* (New York: Viking Press, 1956), p. 615.

86. *Smith v. Allwright,* 321 U.S. 649, 660–661 (1944).

87. Ibid., 664.

88. Ibid., 669; Mason, *Harlan Fiske Stone,* p. 617.

89. Chicago *Defender,* May 13, 1944, p. 5.

90. Thurgood Marshall to Mrs. Allan Knight Chalmers, May 8, 1944; Marshall to Sam S. Minter, May 10, 1944, Box 285, 2 of 4, NAACP MSS.

91. William Hastie, "Appraisal of *Smith v. Allwright,*" *Law Guild Review,* V (March–April, 1945): 65–72, 66.

92. Chicago *Defender,* April 15, 1944; *New Republic* CX (April 17, 1944): 517–19; *Nation* CLVIII (April 22, 1944): 470–472; *Commonweal* XXXIX (April 14, 1944): 636; *Newsweek,* XXIII (May 22, 1944): 42.

93. "Editorial Opinion On the White Primary Decision," *Crisis* LI (June, 1944): 186–87, 204. The Jackson *Clarion-Ledger,* Birmingham *Age-Herald,* and Charleston *News and Courier* vehemently denounced the decision.

94. *Time* XLIII (April 17, 1944): 20–21.

95. Thurgood Marshall to Francis Biddle, April 3, 1944, Box 285, 2 of 4, NAACP MSS.

96. Jonathan Daniels to FDR, Memo, September 28, 1944, OF 93, Box 10, FDRL.

97. Quoted in Elliff, "United States Department of Justice," p. 175; Chicago *Defender,* October 7, 1944, p. 18. Biddle said he feared that massive Justice Department intervention on behalf of disfranchised blacks would prompt bigoted whites to ignite a "terrible conflagration" in the South.

98. Thurgood Marshall to A. T. Walden, July 26, 1944, Box 364, 4 of 7, NAACP MSS.

99. Thurgood Marshall to A. T. Walden (no date), Box 338, 2 of 5; Walter White to Thurgood Marshall, June 8, 1944, Box 364, 4 of 7; Thurgood Marshall to William Thomas, September 5, 1944, Box 338, 2 of 5 ibid.

100. Francis Biddle to C. A. Scott, December 1, 1944, Box 364, 4 of 7, ibid.

101. Thurgood Marshall to C. A. Scott, April 18, 1945, Box 364, 4 of 7, ibid., T. Marshall, "The Legal Battle," *NAACP Bulletin* IV (October, 1945): 2 criticizes the Justice Department for neglecting to act, but makes no mention of the fact that the association had acquiesced in that decision.

102. *King v. Chapman,* 62 F. Supp. 639 (1945); *Chapman v. King,* 154 F. 2d 460 (1946).

103. A. T. Walden to Francis Biddle, March 13, 1945, Box 364, 4 of 7, NAACP MSS; Thurgood Marshall to Louis Martin, February 21, 1947, Box 389, 1 of 6, NAACP MSS.

104. Legal Department of Board of Directors, Memo, April 5, 1944, Box 228, 2 of 4; Bertram Hoffman, "Constitutional Law—Exclusion of Negroes from voting at primaries as party or state action," *Marquette Law Review,* XXVIII (1944): 116–119; James D. Barnett, "Constitutional Law—Fourteenth and Fifteenth Amendments—Discrimination Against Race in Primary Elections—Public and Private Agencies," *Oregon Law Review* XXIII (June 1944): 264–269.

105. "Reminiscences of Julius Waties Waring," (2 vols.) Columbia Oral History Collection, II, p. 252.

106. *Brief for Appellee, Clay Rice et al. v. George Elmore, U.S. Circuit Court of Appeals, Fourth Circuit,* (no date), No. 5664, 27.

107. Robert Carter to Harold Boulware, July 10, 1946, Box 389, 1 of 6, NAACP MSS.

108. "Preliminary Memorandum Re: Primaries in South Carolina and Georgia," February 10, 1947, Box 389, 1 of 6; Thurgood Marshall to John

H. McCray, January 22, 1947, ibid.; *Brief for Appellees, Rice v. Elmore*, 7, 8, 13, 14.

109. Fred Folsom to Thurgood Marshall, January 17, 1947, Box 389, 1 of 6; Tom Clark, as Assistant Attorney General, had helped Marshall prepare a complaint in the Atlanta Primary Case, Clark to Marshall, May 19, 1945, Box 364, 4 of 7, NAACP MSS.

110. Julius W. Waring, COHC, II, 256, 257, 270.

111. *Elmore v. Rice*, 72 F. Supp. 516, 527, 528 (1947).

112. In accepting the Republican nomination for Governor of North Carolina, Parker had declared, "The Negro as a class does not desire to enter politics. The Republican party of North Carolina does not desire him to do so. We recognize the fact that he has not yet reached the stage in his development when he can share the burdens and responsibilities of government." For a full account of the episode, see Richard L. Watson, Jr., "The Defeat of Judge Parker: A Study in Pressure Groups and Politics," *Journal of American History* L (September 1963): 213–234.

113. *Rice v. Elmore*, 165 F. 2d 387, 392 (1947).

114. Following this case, South Carolina improvised another exclusionary method. On May 19, 1948 the Democratic convention resolved to limit party membership to whites who automatically qualified to vote in the primaries. On the other hand, blacks could vote in the Democratic contests by presenting their general election certificates and taking an oath to support the social and educational separation of the races. An angry Judge Waring attacked this double standard created to avoid his previous ruling. He issued a permanent injunction to prevent any further discrimination against Negro voting, and Judge Parker affirmed. *Brown v. Baskin*, 78 F. Supp. 933 (1948); *Baskin v. Brown*, 174 F. 2d 391 (1949). For his heroism, Waring subsequently faced "complete ostracism," verbal and physical threats on his life, and an unsuccessful impeachment attempt led by Congressman L. Mendel Rivers. Waring, COHC, II, 309, 327.

115. William Hastie to Thurgood Marshall, July 19, 1947, Box 389, 1 of 6, NAACP MSS. Actually the final demise of the white primary came in 1953. Negroes of Fort Bend County, Texas, appealed to the Supreme Court to declare unconstitutional the primary of the Jaybird Democratic party. This all-white group, organized after the Civil War, held primaries closed to blacks. The victors of these contests customarily became the Democratic party nominees and eventually won county governmental office. The Jaybirds did not conduct their elections under state law, nor did they use state officials or funds. The court, in three separate opinions, outlawed this white primary, because it effectively controlled the electoral choice. Justice Sherman Minton dissented. *Terry v. Adams*, 345 U.S. 461 (1953).

116. *NAACP Bulletin*, V (May 1946).

117. Mary Berry, *Black Resistance, White Law* (New York: Appleton-Century-Crofts, 1971), p. 170.

118. Julia Baxter, "NAACP Conducts Branch Survey on Negro Vote," *NAACP Bulletin,* (October–November 1946), 2; Henry Lee Moon, *Balance of Power* (Garden City: Doubleday, 1948), p. 10; Press Release, August 12, 1948, Box 400, 6 of 6, NAACP MSS.; Pittsburgh *Courier,* August 21, 1948; Charleston *News and Courier,* April 20, 1948; Columbia (South Carolina) *State,* August 11, 1948.

119. Pittsburgh *Courier,* August 21, 1948; Charleston *News and Courier,* August 11, 1948.

120. Press Release, August 12, 1948, Box 400, 6 of 6, NAACP MSS.

121. William Andrews to James Weldon Johnson, March 20, 1929, Legal File D-65, NAACP, MSS.

3. THE POLL TAX MUST GO

1. Chicago *Defender,* January 8, 1944. Exactly how many Negroes were disfranchised by the poll tax is a source of dispute. V. O. Key, *Southern Politics in State and Nation* (New York: Vintage Books, 1949), pp. 617–618, and Frederic D. Ogden, *The Poll Tax in the South* (University, Alabama: University of Alabama Press, 1958), p. 286 figure that the levy alone did not reduce the electorate by more than ten percent; J. Morgan Kousser, *The Shaping of Southern Politics* (New Haven: Yale University Press, 1974), p. 67 contends that the tax cut the black vote by 16–28 percent.

2. Ogden, *The Poll Tax,* pp. 33–36, 41; U.S. Senate, 77th Congress, 2nd Session, Committee on the Judiciary, *Hearings on H.R. 1280,* March 12, 1942, pp. 320–321.

3. Mitchell's statement appears in the U.S. Senate, 77th Congress, 2nd Session, Committee on the Judiciary, *Hearings on H.R. 1280,* p. 88. Henry Lee Moon, "Counted Out-and In," *Survey Graphic* XXVI (January 1947): 79; George C. Stoney, "Suffrage in the South," Part II, *Survey Graphic* XXIX (March 1940): 205.

4. *Congressional Record,* 76th Congress, 3rd Session, Appendix, p. 3332.

5. Franklin D. Roosevelt to Aubrey Williams, March 28, 1938, PPF 200, FDRL.

6. Franklin D. Roosevelt to Brooks Hays, August 31, 1938, PPF 156, FDRL.

7. Frank Freidel, *F.D.R. and the South* (Baton Rouge: Louisiana State University Press, 1965), p. 97.

8. Ibid., p. 98; Pat Harrison to FDR, October 17, 1938, PPF 4069, FDRL.

9. Stephen Early to Mrs. Carl Stafford, February 3, 1939, PPF 156, FDRL. In Tennessee the fight against the tax was led by Jennings Perry, editor of the Nashville *Tennessean.* Perry and his publisher Silliman Evans challenged the levy to break the stranglehold which Memphis's "Boss" Ed Crump had on the conduct of "honest elections." Both a distaste for Crump and a commitment to a free ballot motivated the repealers. Jennings Perry,

Democracy Begins At Home (Philadelphia: J. P. Lippincott, 1944), passim; Jennings Perry, personal interview, Nashville, August 23, 1970.

10. Barry Bingham, "Do All Americans Have the Right to Vote?" reprinted in *Congressional Record*, 76th Congress, 1st Session, Appendix, p. 1558.

11. Roy Wilkins to Walter White, memo November 27, 1939, Box 317, II, 6 of 6, NAACP MSS.

12. Lee Geyer, *Cong. Rec.*, 76th Congress, 3rd Session, Appendix, p. 1531. "The Poll Tax," *Nation* XLIV (March 21, 1942): 329.

13. Virginius Dabney, *Below the Potomac* (New York: Kennikat Press, 1942), p. 120. Ellis Arnall, *The Shore Dimly Seen* (Philadelphia: J. B. Lippincott, 1946) and Brooks Hays, *A Southern Moderate Speaks* (Chapel Hill: University of North Carolina Press, 1959) were primarily concerned with the plight of the poor whites. They did not believe that the abolition of the poll tax would greatly increase Negro voting. This attitude was shared by several deep South newspapers; see Rayford Logan (ed.), *The Attitude of the Southern White Press Toward Negro Suffrage, 1932–1940* (Washington, D.C.: Foundation Publishers, 1940), pp. 4, 5, 45, 46.

14. Quoted in "The Poll Tax," *Nation* XLIV (March 21, 1942): 239.

15. Thomas A. Krueger, *And Promises To Keep; The Southern Conference for Human Welfare, 1938–1948* (Nashville: Vanderbilt University Press, 1967), pp. 17, 25–29; George B. Tindall, *The Emergence of the New South, 1913–1945* (Baton Rouge: Louisiana University Press, 1967), pp. 640–41.

16. Virginia Foster Durr, personal interview, March 19, 1970.

17. Joseph Gelders to Frank Graham, September 20, 1939, Southern Conference for Human Welfare (SCHW) MSS., National Committee to Abolish the Poll Tax (NCAPT) folder, Negro Collection, Atlanta University.

18. Portion of a typewritten manuscript by the vice-chairman of the NCAPT (Mrs. Durr) (no date), SCHW MSS.

19. *Breedlove v. Suttles*, 302 U.S. 277, 283 (1938). Speaking for the unanimous Court, Justice Pierce Butler found no evidence of discrimination, since "payment as a prerequisite is not required for the purpose of denying or abridging the privilege of voting." Rather, paying the tax before registration "undoubtedly served to aid in its collection."

20. Crampton Harris, Typewritten Brief, *Henry Pirtle v. H. B. Brown*, pp. 8, 13, Tray 86, Box 4, George Norris MSS, LC.

21. *Pirtle v. Brown*, 118 F. 2d 218, 221 (1941).

22. Lee Geyer to Virginia Durr, February 2, 1940, NCAPT folder, SCHW MSS, Negro Collection, Atlanta University; Virginia Durr, personal interview, March 19, 1970, Wetumpka, Alabama.

23. *Congressional Record*, 76th Congress, 1st Session, Appendix, p. 4123.

24. Lucy R. Mason to Howard Lee, February 20, 1940, W 11, Southern Conference Educational Fund (SCEF) MSS. David Carliner to Lee Pressman (no date), NCAPT folder, SCHW MSS.

25. George Stoney to Howard Lee, February 13, 1940, W 14, SCEF MSS.

26. The NAACP conceived of the NCAPT as a "clearinghouse." Lee Geyer to Walter White, May 15, 1941, Box 231, 5 of 5, NAACP MSS; Geyer to Judge W. C. Hueston, February 27, 1940, NCAPT folder, Neg. Coll., SCHW MSS.

27. Joseph Gelders to Virginia Durr, August 6, 1940, NCAPT folder, Neg. Coll., SCHW MSS.

28. Eloise Bittel to Joseph Gelders, May 20, 1940; Minutes of the Executive Board Meeting of the SCHW at Washington D.C., August 2, 1941, ibid.

29. Virginia Durr, personal interview, March 19, 1970, Wetumpka, Alabama. Members of both the SCHW and NCAPT included: Virginia Durr, Frank Graham, Mary McLeod Bethune, Jennings Perry, Clark Foreman, and William Hastie.

30. Jennings Perry, personal interview, August 23, 1970, Nashville, Tennessee; V. Durr, interview. During its existence the committee had four executive secretaries: (a) Sylvia Beitscher, (b) Frances Saylor, the daughter of Senator Burton Wheeler, (c) Katherine Shryver, who had worked for the TVA, and (d) Sarah d'Avila, a Vassar-educated social worker involved with the CIO.

31. Address of Mrs. Eleanor Roosevelt before the Southern Electoral Reform League, February 1, 1941, NCAPT folder, SCHW MSS., Neg. Coll., Atlanta University; Virginia Durr to Joseph Gelders (no date), W 16, SCEF MSS, Tuskegee Institute; Eloise Bittel to Joseph Gelders, May 29, 1940, NCAPT folder, SCHW MSS.

32. A. Stoesen, "The Senatorial Career of Claude Pepper" (unpublished Ph.D. dissertation, University of North Carolina, 1964), pp. 77, 107.

33. Virginia Durr to Joseph Gelders (no date), W 16, SCEF MSS; statement of Claude Pepper, U.S. Senate, 77th Congress, 2nd Session, Committee on the Judiciary, *Hearings on H.R. 1024,* July 19, 1941, p. 26. Thurgood Marshall had opposed the wording of the Geyer bill in a memo to the ACLU, March 5, 1940, Box 219, 1 of 5 NAACP MSS.

34. *United States v. Classic,* 313 U.S. 299 (1941); Notes, "Anti-Poll Tax Legislation—Constitutionality," *New York University Law Review* XXI (January 1946): 119; Notes, *"U.S. v. Classic," Illinois Law Review* XXXVI (December 1941): 477, doubted whether the *Classic* decision would apply, since it concerned already qualified voters. On the other hand, Gelders thought that Congress could act to protect the national franchise from state contamination based on the decision in *McCulloch v. Maryland.* Gelders to Frank Graham, September 30, 1939, NCAPT folder, Negro Collection, SCHW MSS.

35. A. T. Mason, *Harlan Fiske Stone: Pillar of the Law* (New York: Viking Press, 1956), p. 589.

36. U.S. Senate, 77th Congress, 2nd Session, Committee on the Judiciary, *Hearings on H.R. 1024,* July 19, 1941, p. 33. Miss Bontecou had worked for the Civil Liberties Unit of the Department of Justice and had also studied the poll tax for the New School For Social Research, *The Poll Tax* (Washington, D.C., 1942).

37. Article 1, Section 4: "The Times, Places, and Manner of holding Elections for Senators and Representatives, shall be prescribed in each State by the Legislature thereof; but the Congress may at any time by Law make or alter such Regulations, except as to the Places of choosing Senators."

38. See the statement of Abram P. Staples, Virginia Attorney General, U.S. Senate, 77th Congress, 2nd Session, Committee on the Judiciary, September 22, 1942, p. 378, and Congressman William Whittington from Mississippi, *Congressional Record,* 77th Congress, 2nd Session, October 12, 1942, p. 8077. Irving Brant responded that Justice Stone had told him that a denial of *certiorari* "means nothing," and he had never heard of *Pirtle v. Brown.* Irving Brant Notes (no date), NCAPT folder, Negro Collection, SCHW MSS.

39. *Crisis* XLIX (September 1942): 299; Chicago *Defender,* September 19, 1942.

40. Chicago *Defender,* November 21, 1942; statement by Communist Party officials William Z. Foster and Robert Minor contrasted with that of Alabama Governor Frank Dixon, who argued that the abolitionist agitation hindered the war effort by dividing the nation. U.S. Senate, 77th Congress, 2nd Session, Committee on the Judiciary, *Hearings on H.R. 1024,* March 14, October 13, 1942, pp. 194, 505.

41. The Kefauver amendment lost by thirty-three to sixty-five. *Congressional Record,* 77th Congress, 2nd Session, p. 6561.

42. Ibid., pp. 6971–6972. The rider passed by thirty-three to twenty, with the Democratic South in opposition. The full measure succeeded by forty-seven to five. The House routinely accepted it, 248 to fifty-three, as nearly all northern Democrats and Republicans backed the bill. Joseph C. Kallenbach, "Constitutional Aspects of Federal Anti-Poll Tax Legislation," *Michigan Law Review* XLV (April 1947): 719, concludes that the 1942 Act had little consequence because of light participation by the armed forces. See also Roland Young, *Congressional Politics in the Second World War* (New York: Columbia University Press, 1956), pp. 83–84.

43. *New York Times,* September 21, 1942, p. 17.

44. "Notes on telephone call with Mrs. Durr," September 16, 1942, Box 239, 2 of 7, NAACP MSS; Louis H. Andrews, Jr., to Burnet Maybank, November 17, 1942, Box 7, "M–Z," Maybank MSS, South Carolina Department of Archives.

45. *Congressional Record,* 77th Congress, 2nd Session, pp. 8132, 8151; John Robsion to Walter White, July 3, 1942, Box 239, 1 of 7, NAACP MSS.

46. *Cong. Rec.,* 77th Congress, 2nd Session, p. 8167; Sam Hobbs to Frank N. Julian, October 26, 1942, Boswell Amendment folder, Hobbs MSS, University of Alabama.

47. North Carolina (1920), Louisiana (1934), and Florida (1937) had previously eliminated the levy. Claude Pepper was the only representative from these states who voted for repeal. After Georgia removed the qualification in 1945, its congressmen continued to oppose federal legislation.

48. *Congressional Record,* 77th Congress, 2nd Session, pp. 8139, 3718A. In 1945, he again voted for repeal, and in 1946 he lost in the Democratic primary.

49. Joining Kefauver were East Tennessee Republicans Reece and Jennings, and Middle Tennessee, anti-Crump Democrats Gore, Priest, and Courtney. No representative from the "Boss's" stronghold in West Tennessee supported the proposal. Ogden, *The Poll Tax,* p. 254.

50. U.S. Senate, 77th Congress, 2nd Session, Committee on the Judiciary, *Report #1662,* October 27, 1942.

51. Ibid.

52. Those named in the warrants included: Kenneth McKellar (Tennessee), Burnet Maybank (South Carolina), Wall Doxey (Mississippi), "Pappy" O'Daniel (Texas), Lister Hill (Alabama), Richard Russell (Georgia), and John Overton (Louisiana). McKellar, who had once recommended that Barkley receive a Supreme Court nomination, refused to speak to the Majority Leader.

53. *Congressional Record,* 77th Congress, 2nd Session, November 19, 1942, p. 8958.

54. NCAPT to FDR, November 20, 1942, Of 1113, FDRL.

55. Presidential News Conference, November 20, 1942, microfilm, 862 (253–254) (Columbia University Library). The president told his secretary that he did not want to comment on the poll-tax filibuster "because of the hot pending legislation at the present time." Privately, he deplored the stalling tactics. FDR to Marvin McIntyre, memo, November 16, 1942, OF 1113, FDRL.

56. Francis Biddle, *In Brief Authority* (Garden City: Doubleday, 1962), p. 198.

57. *Southern Patriot,* I (February–March 1943); *Poll Tax Repealer,* April, 1943.

58. Alan Schaffer, *Vito Marcantonio: Radical in Congress* (Syracuse: University of Syracuse Press, 1966), pp. 117, 132–133; Walter White to Leslie Perry, March 19, 1943, Box 263, 3 of 5 NAACP MSS; memo of long-distance call from William Hastie, March 19, 1943, Box 475, 6 of 6, NAACP MSS; Morris Milgram to Warren Magnuson, March 20, 1943, Box 12, Vito Marcantonio MSS, New York Public Library.

59. Virginia Durr to Walter White, March 18, 1943, Box 263, 3 of 5,

NAACP MSS.; Warren Magnuson to Morris Milgram, March 26, 1943, Box 12, Marcantonio MSS.

60. Conference with Warren Magnuson, March 24, April 20, 1943, Box 263, 4 of 5, NAACP MSS.

61. *Congressional Record,* 78th Congress, 1st Session, pp. 4847–4849, 4860, 4880.

62. February 1943.

63. *New Republic* CVIII (June 7, 1943): 750.

64. U.S. Senate, 77th Congress, 2nd Session, Committee on the Judiciary, *Hearings on H.R. 1024,* October 13, 1942, p. 526.

65. U.S. Senate, 78th Congress, 1st Session, Committee on the Judiciary, *Hearings on H.R. 7,* October 25, 26, November 2, 1943, pp. 1–77 for favorable testimony and pp. 78–100 for Warren's statement.

66. Gessner T. McCorvey to Members of the Alabama Legislature, May 10, 1945, Hobbs MSS.

67. *New York Times,* April 4, 1944.

68. January 8, 1944.

69. George Bender to James Dombrowski, June 9, 1943, W 4, SCEF MSS.

70. Chicago *Defender,* February 5, 1944. The paper reported that the soldiers were not getting their ballots, May 27, 1944.

71. Katherine Shryver to James Dombrowski, February 29, 1944, W 4, SCEF MSS. Washington *Post,* May 15, 1944.

72. "Washington Calling," Washington *Post,* May 15, 1944.

73. James F. Byrnes to FDR, June 1, 1944, PSF Box 58, FDRL. At the convention Henry Wallace thundered that "the poll tax must go," but he went instead, and the convention refused to condemn the tax specifically. Chicago *Defender,* July 29, 1944; Congressman Joseph Gavagan remembered that he received very little support from the White House, possibly because the president felt there were more vital measures to the nation than equal rights. Gavagan, Columbia Oral History Collection, p. 46; Robert A. Garson, *The Democratic Party and the Politics of Sectionalism, 1941–1948* (Baton Rouge: Louisiana State University Press, 1974), pp. 25–26, 110, 118.

74. Irving Brant to FDR, April 10, 1944, OF 1113, FDRL.

75. Presidential News Conference, March 28, 1944, microfilm, #945, Columbia University Library; Conference with Warren Magnuson, April 20, 1943, Box 263, 4 of 5, NAACP MSS; Virginia Durr to Irving Brant, June 7, 1944, NCAPT folder, Negro Collection, SCHW MSS. As early as November, 1942, FDR had suggested privately that "a joint House and Senate resolution be passed urging that the respective states eliminate by their own action the poll tax requirements," Leslie Perry to Walter White, November 20, 1942, Box 239, 1 of 7, NAACP MSS. Garson, *Democratic Party,* p. 68.

76. Jonathan Daniels to Marvin McIntyre, February 4, 1943, Box 29,

Jonathan Daniels MSS, Southern Historical Collection, University of North Carolina.

77. *New York Times*, May 12, 1944; Chicago *Defender*, May 23, 1944.

78. The 1940 Republican presidential nominee, Wendell Willkie, criticized his party for adopting the resolution supporting a constitutional amendment and thereby accepting the states' rights logic. Wendell Willkie, "Citizens of Negro Blood," *Collier's* CXIV (October 7, 1944): 11, 47–49.

79. Katherine Shryver to James Dombrowski, November 20, 1943, W 4, SCEF MSS; Leslie Perry, *NAACP Bulletin* III (June 1944): 3.

80. Charleston *News and Courier*, November 29, 1943; Sam Hobbs to W. H. Brothers and W. D. Gray, May 1, 1945, Hobbs MSS. Louisiana Senator Allen Ellender was quoted as saying, "as long as I have breath, I am not concerned about the amendment because there will never be enough states to ratify it." NAACP Press Release, October 4, 1945, Box 344, 4 of 6 NAACP MSS.

81. Chicago *Defender*, January 15, 1944 and February 12, 1944. The Georgia statute extended the exemption to all those who, if they were in their home counties, could vote in primaries. This predated the outlawing of the white primary. The Mississippi absentee law allowed the election managers to determine the qualifications of all persons seeking to vote under the act. In 1943, the Tennessee Legislature had repealed the tax. However, later in the year the State Supreme Court ruled such an action contrary to the Tennessee Constitution. *Biggs v. Beeler*, 173 S.W. 2d 144 (1943). See also *Saunders v. Wilkins*, 152 F. 2d 235 (1945), for a novel but unsuccessful attempt to get the judiciary to strike down the Virginia poll-tax requirement based on section two of the Fourteenth Amendment.

82. In 1942, Truman had voted to impose cloture, and in 1944, he was absent but paired in favor of it. Actually, the Missouri senator had voted against placing a repealer in the Soldier Vote Bill, but in the final vote, he supported it.

83. *Public Papers of the Presidents of the United States, Harry S. Truman,.1946* (Washington, D.C., 1962), p. 185.

84. Ibid., p. 192.

85. Harry S. Truman to John H. Bankhead, April 13, 1946, Box 465-b, Harry S. Truman Library (HSTL).

86. Katherine Shryver to V. Marcantonio, February 16, 1946, Box 12, Marcantonio MSS; Harry S. Truman to Irving Brant, March 29, 1946, Box 465-B, HSTL.

87. William Carl Berman, *The Politics of Civil Rights in the Truman Administration* (Columbus: Ohio State University Press, 1970), pp. 41 ff.

88. The Subcommittee consisted of Henry Knox Sherrill, Bishop of the Episcopal Church, Sadie T. Alexander, a board member of the National Urban League, Frank Graham, president of the University of North Caro-

lina, John Dickey, president of Dartmouth College, and Francis Matthews, former supreme commander of the Knights of Columbus.

89. Memo to Subcommittee Number One, March 5, 1947; Interim Report of Subcommittee Number One, April 17, 1947; Robert Carr, Memo to Subcommittee Number One, May 2, 1947, all found in the papers of the President's Committee on Civil Rights, Box 16, HSTL; President's Committee on Civil Rights, *To Secure These Rights* (Washington, D.C., 1947), p. 160.

90. Cabell Phillips, *The Truman Presidency: The History of a Triumphant Succession* (New York, 1966), pp. 198, 206. For Truman's miscalculation and subsequent reversals on the civil-rights issue in general, see Richard Kirkendall, "Truman and Domestic Politics: The Election of 1948," pp. 33–54, in: Robert D. Marcus and David Burner (eds.), *America Since 1945* (New York: St. Martin's Press, 1972).

91. *New York Times,* February 28, 1948, p. 7.

92. Sarah d'Avila to Ralph Gamble, July 20, 1947, NCAPT folder, Negro Collection, SCHW MSS.

93. *Congressional Record,* 80th Congress, 2nd Session, pp. 9460–9461.

94. Ibid., p. 9463.

95. Ibid., p. 9480.

96. Earlier, Democrat Sam Hobbs had suggested that the Republican leaders indicated their attitude toward antipoll-tax legislation by "their lackadaisical defense of the filibuster"; Hobbs to Carter Poland, August 6, 1948, Hobbs MSS.

97. *New York Times,* March 11, 12, 16, 1949.

98. Stephen Spingarn to Clark Clifford, March 21, 1949, Box 4, Clifford MSS, HSTL. The attorney general's testimony appeared in the *Congressional Record,* 81st Congress, 1st Session, pp. 10099 ff; Janice Christensen, "The Constitutionality of National Anti-Poll Tax Bills," *Minnesota Law Review* XXXIII (February 1949): 244.

99. James Dombrowski to Jennings Perry, December 6, 1946, W 8, SCEF MSS; Jennings Perry to NCAPT Board members, January 1, 1949, NCAPT MSS, Negro Collection; Katherine Shryver to Frank Graham, February 2, 1946, "Anti Poll Tax Files," Frank Graham MSS, Southern Historical Collection, University of North Carolina.

100. Roger Baldwin to Jennings Perry, January 20, 1949, NCAPT folder, Negro Collection, SCHW MSS.

101. Barry Bingham to Virginia Durr, May 27, 1940, NCAPT, Negro Collection, SCHW MSS. See also Eleanor Bontecou to Frank Graham, May 25, 1942, Folder 124, Graham MSS, Southern Historical Collection, University of North Carolina.

102. K. Shryver to J. Dombrowski, May 1, 1945, W 11, SCEF MSS; Lee Geyer to Walter White, March 24, 1941, Box 231, 5 of 5 NAACP MSS. No matter how much the NCAPT disclaimed the poll tax as a racial issue, it

could not break the connection between the Negro and the franchise question. For example, the Chicago Congressman, Adolph Sabath, announced that he would vote for repeal, because of his appreciation for the support given him by his black constituents. *Congressional Record,* 79th Congress, 1st Session, Appendix, 2835.

103. William S. White, *New York Times,* August 1, 1948, IV, p. 8.

104. Ogden, *Poll Tax,* p. 252; Virginia Durr to Claude Pepper, October 3, 1944, NCAPT folder, Negro Collection, SCHW MSS.

4. THE SOUTH FIGHTS BACK: BOSWELLIANISM AND BILBOISM

1. William P. Mitchell, personal interview, March 24, 1970, Tuskegee, Alabama.

2. Donald S. Strong, *Registration of Voters in Alabama* (University, Alabama: University of Alabama Press, 1956), p. 120.

3. Ibid.; Constance Smith, *Voting and Election Laws* (New York: Oceana Publications, 1960), pp. 65–67. The nonsouthern states with literacy tests in 1960 were Arizona, California, Connecticut, Delaware, Maine, Massachusetts, New Hampshire, New York, Oregon, Washington, and Wyoming.

4. V. O. Key, *Southern Politics in State and Nation* (New York: Vintage Books, 1948), p. 559; Pittsburgh *Courier,* February 2, 1946; Chicago *Defender,* March 3, 1945.

5. Luther P. Jackson, "Race and Suffrage in the South Since 1940," *New South* III (June–July 1948): 8.

6. Tally R. Broady, "Will Two Good White Men Vouch for You?" *Crisis,* LIV (January, 1947): 10. William Mitchell had given the names of two people, one white and one black, who could identify him, and whom the Board knew. However, one man saw the crowded courthouse and left, while the other voucher was not notified that Mitchell had selected him. Mitchell was a physical-therapy technician at the Tuskegee Veterans Hospital. *Mitchell v. Wright,* 69 F. Supp. 698 (1947).

7. Strong, *Registration of Voters,* pp. 14, 54. In Macon County, Alabama, William P. Mitchell spent two years trying to persuade the federal courts to enjoin the Board of Registrars from denying him enrollment. He had to drop the suit when the clerks "discovered" that they had previously registered him. *Mitchell v. Wright,* 154 F. 2d 924 (1946); *Mitchell v. Wright,* 69 F. Supp. 698 (1947). William P. Mitchell, personal interview, March 24, 1970, Tuskegee, Alabama.

8. Pittsburgh *Courier,* May 22, 1948; Key, *Southern Politics,* p. 520.

9. Joseph Matt Britain, "Negro Suffrage and Politics in Alabama Since 1870" (unpublished Ph.D. dissertation, Indiana University, 1958), p. 148.

10. Quoted in Vera Chandler Foster, "Boswellianism, A Technique in the Restriction of Negro Voting," *Phylon* X (March 1949): 33.

11. Chicago *Defender,* February 17, 1945 and April 28, 1945; *Crisis* LIII (February 1946): 40.

12. Gessner McCorvey to Members of the Alabama Legislature, May 10, 1945, Sam Hobbs MSS, University of Alabama; Chicago *Defender,* May 26, 1945.

13. Brittain, "Negro Suffrage in Alabama," pp. 189–90. The vote on the amendment was eighty-four to zero in the House and twenty-seven to three in the Senate. The plan also required "good character" and an understanding of the obligations of good citizenship under a Republican form of government.

14. Committee for Alabama, October 31, 1946, Box 389, 1 of 5, NAACP MSS; Pauline Dobbs to James Dombrowski, February 19, 1945, W 6, SCEF MSS.; Chicago *Defender,* February 17, 1945. For influences on Folsom see William D. Barnard, *Dixiecrats and Democrats, Alabama Politics 1942–1950* (University, Alabama: University of Alabama Press, 1974), pp. 14, 32.

15. Key, *Southern Politics,* pp. 633–34; Speech, Richard T. Rives, April 18, 1946, Hobbs MSS.

16. Key, *Southern Politics,* pp. 36, 634; Committee for Alabama, October 31, 1946, Box 389, 1 of 5, NAACP MSS; Rives Speech, April 18, 1946, Hobbs MSS; Aubrey Williams to Lister Hill, December 8, 1946, Group 58, Box 35, Aubrey Williams MSS, FDRL; "James E. Folsom," *Current Biography* (New York, 1949), pp. 204–206; Foster, "Boswellianism," 30. The Montgomery *Advertiser,* October 4, 1947, had disapproved of the amendment because it would "stir up a Federal hornet's nest."

17. Robert A. Garson, *The Democratic Party and the Politics of Sectionalism, 1941–1948,* (Baton Rouge: Louisiana State University Press, 1974), pp. 218, 289, 314.

18. Foster, "Boswellianism," 28; Anniston (Alabama), *Star,* October 10, 1946; Horace C. Wilkinson, "Argument for Adoption of the Boswell Amendment," *Alabama Lawyer,* VII (October, 1946): 382.

19. Key, *Southern Politics,* p. 633. Birmingham *News,* February 20, 1948.

20. Pittsburgh *Courier,* December 7, 1946, February 7, 1948; Douglas Hunt, Birmingham *News,* February 20, 1948. On the other hand, in one central Alabama county with fewer than 30 percent Negroes, the registrars failed few and paid no attention to the amendment, insisting that "we know how to run our own affairs." Foster, "Boswellianism," p. 31.

21. Chicago *Defender,* January 13, 1945; *NAACP Bulletin* V (October 1946): 1; Pittsburgh *Courier,* October 25, 1947.

22. Thurgood Marshall to William Ming, Jr., November 6, 1946; Marshall to Emory Jackson, September 16, 1947, Box 389, 1 of 5, NAACP MSS; *Davis v. Schnell,* 81 F. Supp. 872 (1949).

23. J. J. Thomas to Thurgood Marshall, March 22, 1949, Box 389, 1 of 5, NAACP MSS.

24. John LeFlore to Emory Jackson, November 12, 1948, LeFlore to

Thurgood Marshall, February 19, 1949, Box 389, 1 of 5, NAACP MSS. LeFlore belonged to the VVA, but the organization refused to renew his membership during the controversy.

25. George Leighton to Thurgood Marshall, August 12, 1948, Robert Carter to John LeFlore, January 3, 1949, Box 389, 1 of 5, NAACP MSS.

26. Chicago *Defender,* November 11, 1944; Pittsburgh *Courier,* February 9, 1946.

27. Pittsburgh *Courier,* October 30, 1948, January 1, 1949.

28. *Davis v. Schnell,* 81 F. Supp. 872 (1949), 876, 878. The court noted that since October, 1947, the board had enrolled 2,800 whites and 104 Negroes, way out of line with their relative proportion of the population; 64 percent white and 36 percent black.

29. Ibid., 877. The Supreme Court affirmed judgment *per curiam,* 336 U.S. 933 (1949); Francis W. Collopy, "Discrimination Against Applicants for the Franchise on the Basis of Race or Color—*Davis v. Schnell,*" *Notre Dame Lawyer* XXIV (Summer 1949): 573.

30. Pittsburgh *Courier,* September 17, 1949; Brittain, "Negro Suffrage in Alabama," p. 196. Folsom's supporters in the Alabama Senate filibustered the bill to death in the last days of the 1949 session, only to see it resurrected and passed at the 1950 meeting. The voters barely approved it by 369 votes, 60,357–59,988.

31. Pittsburgh *Courier,* January 28, 1950, February 18, 1950. The Negro vote did increase from 6,000 in 1947 to over 25,000 in 1952.

32. James T. McCain, "The Negro Voter in South Carolina," *Journal of Negro Education* XXVI (Summer 1957): 360.

33. United States Senate, 79th Congress, 2nd Session, *Hearings Before the Special Committee to Investigate Senatorial Campaign Expenditures,* 1946, (Washington D.C., 1947), pp. 246–252. (Herein cited as *Bilbo Hearings*).

34. Albert D. Kirwan, *Revolt of the Rednecks: Mississippi Politics, 1876–1925* (Lexington: University of Kentucky Press, 1951), pp. 65 ff; Key, *Southern Politics,* p. 232.

35. Key, *Southern Politics,* pp. 241–244.

36. "Hodding Carter," *Current Biography* (New York, 1946), p. 96. Bilbo had written an American of Italian descent a letter with the salutation, "Dear Dago."

37. A. Wigfall Green, *The Man Bilbo* (Baton Rouge: Louisiana State University Press, 1963), p. 101; Theodore G. Bilbo, *Take Your Choice, Separation or Mongrelization* (Poplarville, Mississippi, 1947), p. 95.

38. Roman J. Zorn, "Theodore G. Bilbo, Shibboleths for Statesmanship," J. T. Statler (ed.), *Public Men In and Out of Office* (Chapel Hill: University of North Carolina Press, 1946), p. 277.

39. Bilbo, *Take Your Choice,* p. 288.

40. "Hodding Carter," *Current Biography,* p. 95; Pittsburgh *Courier,* August 31, 1946.

41. Key, *Southern Politics*, p. 497.

42. Jackson *Daily News*, May 28, 1946, as cited in *Bilbo Hearings*, p. 8.

43. Hodding Carter, "The Man From Mississippi—Bilbo," *New York Times Magazine* (June 30, 1946), 12; Jackson *Daily News*, June 23, 1946, *Bilbo Hearings*, p. 7.

44. *Bilbo Hearings*, p. 15, and see p. 393, for Section 244 of the Mississippi Constitution.

45. Drew Pearson, "Washington Merry-Go-Round," Washington *Post*, December 6, 1946; Charles Houston and Thurgood Marshall, *Brief for the National Association for the Advancement of Colored People, in the Matter of the Investigation of the Mississippi Democratic Primary Campaign of Senator Theodore G. Bilbo* (no date), p. 17; Memo to Special Committee to Investigate Senatorial Campaign Expenditures, October 7, 1946, Burnet Maybank MSS.

46. Chicago *Defender*, November 11, 1944; Pittsburgh *Courier*, May 18, 1946.

47. *Bilbo Hearings*, p. 31.

48. Roy Wilkins, "The Negro Wants Full Equality," Rayford Logan (ed.), *What the Negro Wants* (Chapel Hill: University of North Carolina Press, 1944), pp. 131 ff. On the contrary, Bilbo maintained that World War II "and all its great victories will not in any way or in any manner change the views and sentiments of white America on the questions of social equality and intermarriage of the Negro and white race. Bilbo, *Take Your Choice*, p. 67.

49. Statement of Frank J. Spaites, *Bilbo Hearings*, p. 102; *NAACP Bulletin*, V (July 1946), 3.

50. Frederick D. Patterson, "The Negro Wants Full Participation in the American Democracy," Rayford Logan (ed.), *What the Negro Wants*, p. 272.

51. Flier from the All Citizens Registration Committee, Veteran's Division (no date), Grace Townes Hamilton MSS, Negro Collection, Atlanta University. Throughout the South Negro veterans militantly demanded the franchise. In January, 1946, 100 veterans marched through the main streets of Birmingham to the courthouse to register. *Southern Patriot*, March, 1946.

52. Harry Wright, "A Survey of Veterans Services for Negro Voters in Mississippi," *New South* II (March 1947): 10; Bilbo to his opponents, June 16, 1946, in Charles La Follette, Brief, *U.S. v. Bilboism*, Box 475, 2 of 5, NAACP MSS.

53. James Graham Cook, *The Segregationists* (New York: Appleton-Century-Crofts, 1962), pp. 95–96.

54. "The Battle for the Ballot," *Nation* CLXXV (September 27, 1952): 250.

55. Robert Carter to Walter White, July 28, 1946, White to David O. Selznick, September 30, 1946; White to William Hastie, October 2, 1946; Memo for Tentative Budget for Special Committee of NAACP on Contest of Senator Elect Bilbo's Seat (no date), all in Box 475, 2 of 5, NAACP MSS.

56. Bilbo to Clark Foreman, August 13, 1945, W 12, SCEF MSS.

57. Washington *Post,* July 4, 1946; Pittsburgh *Courier,* July 6, 1946.

58. Pittsburgh *Courier,* November 23, 1946.

59. Walter White to David O. Selznick, September 30, 1946, White to Quentin Reynolds, October 14, 1946, Box 475, 2 of 5, NAACP MSS.

60. See comments of William Colmer on outside interference, United States Congress, 80th Congress, 2nd Session, *Memorial Services for Theodore Gilmore Bilbo* (Washington, D.C., 1950), pp. 77–78. Colmer represented Bilbo's Congressional district; Pittsburgh *Courier,* September 28, 1946. In the 1950s Greene was considered an "Uncle Tom" for disapproving of the *Brown v. Board of Education* decision and opposing enactment of federal civil-rights legislation. Cook, *Segregationists,* p. 316.

61. *P.M.,* June 28, 1946; *Congressional Record,* 80th Congress, 1st Session, pp. 8–9; Robert Carter to Daniel Byrd, June 12, 1946, Box 380, 5 of 5, NAACP MSS.

62. *Bilbo Hearings,* "Excerpts from Minutes, 5th Meeting Special Committee to Investigate Senatorial Campaign Expenditures, November 16, 1946," p. 21.

63. *Lane v. Wilson,* 307 U.S. 268 (1939).

64. In 1944 and 1946, the conservative Republican Bridges did vote against the cloture petition that would have ended the filibuster on the antipoll-tax bill. In 1946, Hickenlooper was absent on official business when the vote came up, but he was announced as favoring the petition.

65. *Bilbo Hearings,* pp. 3–6; Robert Carter to Daniel Byrd, July 12, 1946, Box 380, 5 of 5, NAACP MSS.

66. Pittsburgh *Courier,* June 29, 1946.

67. *Bilbo Hearings,* p. 20.

68. Ibid., p. 21; *Crisis* LIV (January 1947): 19; Charles LaFollette to Charles Houston, December 10, 1946, Box 475, 2 of 5, NAACP MSS. Emanuel Bloch and Charles Houston did provide unofficial legal counsel for the witnesses.

69. *Bilbo Hearings,* p. 18.

70. Ibid., pp. 45 ff; Affidavit of Etoy Fletcher, Box 380, 5 of 5, NAACP MSS.

71. *Bilbo Hearings,* pp. 50 ff; *New York Times,* December 3, 1946.

72. *Bilbo Hearings,* pp. 142–48.

73. Ibid., pp. 238–39.

74. Ibid., pp. 80, 138.

75. Ibid., pp. 183, 196, 187, 205.

76. Ibid., p. 209; Charles Houston Report to the NAACP re Bilbo Hearing, December 2, 1946, Box 475, 2 of 5, NAACP MSS.

77. *Bilbo Hearings,* pp. 23, 39, 90, 112, 148–54; Houston Report, ibid.

78. *Newsweek* XXVIII (December 16, 1946): 33. Bilbo had recently had his front teeth extracted, to allow removal of a malignant tumor in the jaw.

79. *Bilbo Hearings,* pp. 333, 342.

80. Ibid., pp. 10, 346, 365, 372.

81. NAACP *Brief,* 32; Washington *Post,* December 6, 1946.

82. For Thomas's views on the one-party basis of Negro disfranchisement, see *Bilbo Hearings,* p. 359; Walter White to David O. Selznick, December 18, 1946, Box 475, 2 of 5, NAACP MSS.

83. Committee to Investigate Senatorial Campaign Expenditures, 80th Congress, 1st Session, *Report on S. Res 224,* (Washington D.C., 1947), pp. 9, 10, 12.

84. Ibid., pp. 16, 18, 19, 21.

85. *New York Times,* January 1, and 3, 1947.

86. *Congressional Record,* 80th Congress, 1st Session, pp. 8–9, 14, 20. Bilbo faced other charges. A Special Committee to Investigate the National Defense Program had reported that the senator had accepted $25,000 in gifts from government contractors. In this matter, a bipartisan group had found Bilbo guilty of misusing his office. However, the challenge against "The Man" focused on the race issue. *New York Times,* January 2, 1947; *Newsweek* XXVIII (December 23, 1946): 23.

87. *New York Times,* January 5, 1947; Pittsburgh *Courier,* January 11, 1947.

88. Bilbo *Memorial,* pp. 77–78; Pittsburgh *Courier,* January 11, 1947, March 13, 1948; Earl M. Lewis, "Negro Voter in Mississippi"; *Journal of Negro Education* XXVI (Summer 1957), 341; Key, *Southern Politics,* p. 640.

89. James W. Silver, *Mississippi: The Closed Society* (New York: Harcourt Brace World, 1966). Jennings Perry, *P.M.,* December 5, 1946; *Crisis* LIV (March 1947): 73; *NAACP Bulletin* V (December 1946), 3; Pittsburgh *Courier,* December 14, 1946.

90. J. A. Rogers, Pittsburgh *Courier,* November 23, 1946.

5. The Suffrage Crusade in the South: The Early Phase

1. Robert K. Carr, *Federal Protection of Civil Rights* (Ithaca: Cornell University Press, 1946), p. 61; Richard Claude, *The Supreme Court and the Electoral Process* (Baltimore: Johns Hopkins University Press, 1970), p. 56. *Ex parte Yarbrough,* 110 U.S. 651 (1884). *James v. Bowman,* 190 U.S. 127 (1903) weakened the *Yarbrough* ruling by holding that the Enforcement Act of 1870 could apply only to state intimidation, not private actions. This decision also made it clear that the prosecution would have to prove that the intimidation was done for racial reasons.

2. John T. Elliff, "The United States Department of Justice and Individual Rights, 1937–1962" (unpublished Ph.D. dissertation, Harvard University, 1967), p. 171.

3. Carr, *Federal Protection,* pp. 106–08. *Screws v. U.S.,* 325 U.S. 91 (1945).

4. Carr, *Federal Protection,* p. 115.

5. Ibid., p. 110; Osmond K. Fraenkel, "The Federal Civil Rights Laws," *Minnesota Law Review* XXXI (March 1947): 307.

6. Carr, *Federal Protection*, pp. 179–80.

7. Turner Smith to Sam Hobbs, October 22, 1946, Hobbs MSS.

8. Robert Carter to Theron Caudle, August 6, 1946, Box 475, 2 of 5, NAACP MSS. After a steady barrage of criticism from the NAACP, the Department of Justice decided in 1947 to prosecute persons accused of violating Negro rights in the 1946 Mississippi primary. The grand jury refused to return indictments. See Elliff, "The United States Department of Justice," p. 223.

9. Memorandum on the Department of Justice by Marian W. Perry, January 15, 1947, Box 475, 2 of 5, NAACP MSS.

10. *NAACP Bulletin* V (July 1946): 1.

11. President's Committee on Civil Rights, *To Secure These Rights* (Washington, D.C., 1947), vii; Elliff, "The United States Department of Justice," p. 236, describes an independent move within the Department to establish a presidential commission. The attorney general had called for a report from the Civil Rights Section on its past activities. Because of its small size, the section responded that it would need two attorneys and weeks of preparation to do the research, in addition to its regular activities. A commission offered the best solution.

12. Memo from Maceo Hubbard to President's Committee on Civil Rights, February 27, 1947, President's Committee on Civil Rights Papers, Harry S. Truman Library (HSTL). Maceo Hubbard, personal interview, November 3, 1970, Washington, D.C.

13. Conference, February 7, 1947, with Robert Carr, Turner Smith, Maceo Hubbard, and Fred Folsom, President's Committee on Civil Rights Papers, HSTL.

14. Tom Clark to Robert Carr, July 10, 1947; Conference, February 7, 1947, President's Committee on Civil Rights Papers, HSTL.

15. Carr, *Federal Protection*, p. 178; President's Committee on Civil Rights, *To Secure These Rights*, pp. 125, 151, 208. The Civil Rights Section had prosecuted 178 cases in eight years.

16. *To Secure These Rights*, p. 156. The committee also suggested increasing the penalty under Section 52 from a $1,000 fine and a one-year prison term to a $5,000 fine and a ten-year jail sentence. In effect, violation of this law would change from a misdemeanor to a felony.

17. Jerold Auerbach, *Labor and Liberty: The La Follette Committee and the New Deal* (Indianapolis: Bobbs-Merrill, 1966).

18. *To Secure These Rights*, p. 103.

19. *Crisis* LIV (March 1947): 73.

20. Minutes, February 6 and 7, 1947, President's Committee on Civil Rights Papers, HSTL. While the committee researched its report, the NAACP was preparing to deliver to the United Nations a petition that criti-

cized the United States' treatment of Negro citizens. W. E. B. Du Bois (ed.), *An Appeal to the World* (New York, 1947).

21. *To Secure These Rights,* p. 100.

22. Harry S. Truman, *Public Papers of the President, 1947* (Washington, D.C., 1948), pp. 311–312. Truman's speech was all the more forceful because he had been advised by David Niles to devote only a few minutes to domestic civil rights. However, the president overruled his advisor and directed most of his address to the question. David Niles to Matthew Connelly, June 16, 1947, Box 2, George Elsey Papers, HSTL.

23. Elliff, "The United States Department of Justice," p. 280; Draft of Civil Rights Bill of 1949, January 27, 1949, Box 3, Clark Clifford Papers, HSTL.

24. Luther P. Jackson, "Race and Suffrage in the South Since 1940," *New South* III (June–July 1948): 17.

25. Quoted in Donald R. Matthews and James W. Prothro, *Negroes and the New Southern Politics* (New York: Harcourt Brace World, 1966), pp. 262–63.

26. Ibid., p. 278.

27. Quoted in Margaret Price, *The Negro Voter in the South* (Atlanta: Southern Regional Council, 1957), p. 59.

28. Henry Lee Moon, *Balance of Power* (Garden City: Doubleday, 1948), pp. 191–92.

29. *NAACP Bulletin,* VI (June, 1947), 2; Alexander Heard, *A Two-Party South?* (Chapel Hill: University of North Carolina Press, 1952), pp. 183, 186.

30. Pittsburgh *Courier,* September 24, 1949.

31. Quoted in Heard, *A Two-Party South?,* p. 186.

32. C. A. Bacote, "The Negro in Atlanta Politics," *Phylon* XXV (December 1955): 346.

33. Anne Mason Roberts, Pittsburgh *Courier,* January 21, 1950.

34. Pittsburgh *Courier,* October 29, 1949; Bacote, "The Negro and Atlanta Politics," 346.

35. Andrew Buni, *The Negro in Virginia Politics, 1902–1965* (Charlottesville: University of Virginia Press, 1967), p. 127; Harold Fleming, "Negro Vote Getter," *Reporter* II (1950): 20; Pittsburgh *Courier,* February 18, 1950; Heard, *A Two-Party South?,* p. 190.

36. Pittsburgh *Courier,* February 23, 1946; Chicago *Sun,* April 18, 1946. In 1950 in Arkansas, 40,000 black ballots cast for the renomination of Governor Sidney McMath were credited with helping him beat the challenge of a Dixiecrat opponent. Pittsburgh *Courier,* August 5, 1950.

37. Frederic Ogden, *The Poll Tax in the South* (University, Alabama: University of Alabama Press, 1958), pp. 100–03.

38. Everett C. Ladd, Jr., *Negro Political Leadership in the South* (Ithaca: Cornell University Press, 1966), p. 60.

39. A. Willis Robertson to Tom Connally, July 27, 1948, Box 104, Tom Connally MSS, LC.

40. Margaret Price, *The Negro Voter in the South* (Atlanta: Southern Regional Council, 1957), p. 40.

41. Emory O. Jackson to Walter White, February 21, 1948, Box 389, 1 of 5, NAACP MSS.

42. Pittsburgh *Courier*, July 8, 1950. Price, *The Negro Voter*, p. 40.

43. Pittsburgh *Courier*, April 13, 1946.

44. Jackson, "Race and Suffrage," p. 20; *New South* VI (September 1951): 7; Moon, *Balance of Power*, p. 188; Buni, *Negro in Virginia*, pp. 148, 158; Pittsburgh *Courier*, November 17, 1951; Price, *The Negro Voter*, pp. 47–48.

45. Quoted in Jessie Gusman, Lewis Jones, Woodrow Hall (eds.), *1952 Negro Year Book* (New York: Wise, 1952), p. 308.

46. *New South* VIII (January 1953): 8.

47. Samuel Lubell, *The Future of American Politics* (Garden City: Doubleday, 1955), Chapter 6; A. Stoesen, "The Senatorial Career of Claude D. Pepper" (unpublished Ph.D. dissertation, University of North Carolina, 1964), pp. 329 ff.

48. Pittsburgh *Courier*, April 9, 1952.

49. "Race and Suffrage Today," *New South* VIII (January 1953): 8.

50. Quoted in *Nation* CLXXV (September 27, 1952): 244. Tillman C. Cothran and William M. Phillips, Jr., "Expansion of Negro Suffrage in Arkansas," *Journal of Negro Education* XXVI (Summer 1957): 291. These two political scientists attributed the diminishing returns to the decreased potential for enrollment as the more motivated Negroes had registered.

51. Quoted in James W. Vander Zanden, *Race Relations in Transition* (New York: Random House, 1965), p. 28.

52. *Negroes and the New Southern Politics*, p. 118.

53. Statement of Michigan Congressman, Charles Diggs, *Congressional Record*, 85th Congress, 1st Session, 8611, 8705. Mississippi led the list of disfranchisers with thirteen counties; Alabama and Louisiana followed with four, Georgia had two, and South Carolina had one.

54. "Race and Suffrage Today," *New South* VIII (January 1953): 4.

55. "Negroes Vote in Mississippi," *Ebony* VII (November 1951): 15.

56. John L. Clark, Pittsburgh *Courier*, September 19, 1953.

57. *Negroes and the New Southern Politics*, p. 154.

58. Pittsburgh *Courier*, March 31, 1951.

59. Memo, Franklin Williams to Henry Moon, October 25, 1948, Box 380, 5 of 5, NAACP MSS; Pittsburgh *Courier*, November 13, 1948. The Negro newspaper gave the story extensive coverage and waged a successful drive to raise $5,000 to relocate Nixon's widow and six children in Florida. April 23, 1949.

60. Pittsburgh *Courier*, June 17, 1950, November 10, 1951. In December 1951 John Lester Mitchell, one of the Negroes trying to register here, was shot through the heart by a deputy sheriff. Later, a coroner's jury called the death "justifiable homicide."

61. Gloster Current, "Martyr for a Cause," *Crisis* LIX (February 1952): 72–81, 133–34.

62. *Newsweek* XXIX (January 7, 1952): 15–16. Moore's activity in the Groveland rape case also had a lot to do with his murder. Three Negroes had been brought to trial and convicted for rape. The Supreme Court ordered a new trial, but the sheriff killed one of the defendants and wounded another. Moore crusaded for the police officer's punishment. For other incendiary incidents during this period see "Battle for the Ballot," *Nation* CLXXV (September 27, 1952): 250–251.

63. Donald S. Strong, "The Future of the Negro Voter," *Journal of Negro Education* XXVI (Summer 1957): 404.

64. Hugh D. Price, *The Negro and Southern Politics* (New York: New York University Press, 1957), p. 106.

65. Elliff, "The United States Department of Justice," p. 377.

66. Numan Bartley, *The Rise of Massive Resistance* (Baton Rouge: Louisiana State University Press, 1970), p. 280, points out that Governors Jim Folsom of Alabama and Earl Long of Louisiana risked their political careers to forge a biracial coalition in the late 1940s and early 1950s. In Mississippi the publicity generated by the Bilbo hearings boosted the courage in Negroes to register. In Florida, legislative attempts to repeal the primary statutes ceased after 1947, and the bitter Pepper-Smathers contest of 1950 with its racial overtones briefly generated black enrollment. Price, *Negro & Southern Politics*, pp. 32–33.

67. In Alabama from 1954 to 1956, the progress in Negro registration did slow down considerably. This was mirrored in Folsom's failure to win election as a Democratic National Committeeman in 1956. He lost to a pro-segregationist by a three-to-one margin. See *Southern School News*, June, 1956. In Georgia, the registration rate had declined after 1947, as the Talmadge-controled legislature passed a law requiring permanent reregistration. Pittsburgh *Courier*, February 5, 1949, July 1, 1950, and March 8, 1950.

68. Pittsburgh *Courier*, March 24, 1951; *Nation* CLXXIV (January 5, 1952): 3–4; John B. Martin, "The Deep South Says Never," Part I, *Saturday Evening Post* CCXXIX (June 15, 1957): 23, 72. For the cases dismantling segregation in higher education and professional studies, see *Sipuel v. Oklahoma*, 382 U.S. 631 (1948); *Sweatt v. Painter*, 339 U.S. 629 (1950); *McLaurin v. Oklahoma State Regents*, 339 U.S. 637 (1950).

69. Robert Sherill, *Gothic Politics in the Deep South* (New York: Grossman Publishers, 1968), p. 46. Hodding Carter, III, *The South Strikes Back* (Garden City: Doubleday, 1959), p. 32; *Crisis* LIII (May 1946): 137.

70. James Graham Cook, *The Segregationists* (New York: Appleton-Century-Crofts, 1962): p. 61.

71. Tom P. Brady, *Black Monday* (Winona, Mississippi: Citizens' Councils of America, 1955), p. 84.

72. House Judiciary Committee, *Hearings on Civil Rights,* February 13, 1957, 85th Congress, 1st Session, p. 1026.

73. Pittsburgh *Courier,* January 7, 1956; Carter, *South Strikes Back,* pp. 126–27.

74. *Citizens' Council,* June, 1956; Bartley, *Massive Resistance,* pp. 200–201; Price, *Negro Voter,* p. 14.

75. Price, *Negro Voter,* pp. 15–16.

76. Jack Mendlesohn, *The Martyrs,* (New York: Harper and Row, 1966), Chapter 1. A coroner's jury ruled that Lee died from "unknown" causes. Neil R. McMillen, *The Citizens' Council* (Urbana: University of Illinois Press, 1971), pp. 216–219.

77. Senate Committee on the Judiciary, *Hearings on Civil Rights,* February 28, 1957, 85th Congress, 1st Session, pp. 421, 434. In August, Lamar Smith was killed on the Brookhaven County Courthouse lawn, according to the NAACP, for failing to remove his name from the voting lists and ceasing all political activity. See NAACP, *Annual Report,* 1955, pp. 9, 24.

78. Quoted in Donald McCoy and Richard T. Reutten, *Quest and Response: Minority Rights and the Truman Administration* (Lawrence: University of Kansas Press, 1973), p. 53.

6. Politics and the Origins of the Civil Rights Act of 1957

1. U.S. Senate, Committee on Armed Services, *Hearings on Universal Military Training,* 80th Congress, 2nd Session, p. 996. In 1952, Eisenhower, the candidate, asserted: "We can no longer afford to hold on to the anachronistic principles of race segregation in the armed service organizations." Quoted in William C. Berman, *The Politics of Civil Rights in the Truman Administration* (Columbus: Ohio State University Press, 1970), p. 204.

2. E. Frederic Morrow, "Reminiscences," pp. 79–80, Columbia Oral History Collection.

3. Dwight D. Eisenhower (DDE) to James Byrnes, July 23, 1957, OF 102-B-3, Eisenhower Library (DDEL).

4. U.S. Senate, *Hearings on Universal Military Training,* p. 998.

5. Ibid., p. 997.

6. E. Frederic Morrow to Sherman Adams, September 20, 1952, OF 138-C-4, DDEL.

7. Berman, *The Politics of Civil Rights,* p. 231. Eisenhower won three southern states: Florida, Texas, and Virginia.

8. Maxwell Rabb, personal interview, October 6, 1970, New York City.

9. E. Frederic Morrow, "Reminiscences," Columbia Oral History Collection.

10. Robert J. Donovan, *Eisenhower: The Inside Story* (New York: Harper, 1956), pp. 156–68; Rabb interview, October 6, 1970.

11. Berman, *Politics of Civil Rights,* pp. 210, 221.

12. Donovan, *Eisenhower*, p. 160. The chief executive made a number of top-level appointments of Negroes, including J. Ernest Wilkens as assistant secretary of labor. Wilkens also served on the Contract Compliance Committee.

13. Adam Clayton Powell, Jr., "The President and the Negro," *Reader's Digest* LXV (October 1954): 61–64.

14. Roy Wilkins, "Address to 2nd Annual Youth Legislative Conference," OF 142-A-5, DDEL.

15. Burnet Maybank to Alvin Tucker, February 15, 1954, "Segregation," Box 2, Maybank MSS.

16. *Public Papers of the Presidents: Dwight D. Eisenhower, 1953*, March 25, 1953, p. 127; Samuel Spencer to DDE, September 20, 1954, OF 142-A-5, DDEL, for a progress report on D.C. school integration.

17. *Public Papers . . . Eisenhower, 1956*, February 8, 1956, p. 741.

18. Ibid., August 8, 1956, pp. 668–669.

19. E. Frederic Morrow, *Black Man in the White House: A Diary of the Administrative Years By the Administrative Officer for Special Projects* (New York: Coward-McCann, 1963), p. 98.

20. Herbert Parmet, *Eisenhower and the American Crusades* (New York: Macmillan, 1972), p. 439; Arthur Larson, *Eisenhower: The President Nobody Knew* (New York: Charles Scribner's, 1968) p. 128.

21. Senate Majority Policy Committee, "Background Reports in Selected Legislative Proposals, 83rd Congress 2nd Session," December, 1953, Box 2, I. Jack Martin MSS, DDEL.

22. LCCR, "Minutes of Steering Committee," February 10, 1953, Box 7, 3 of 5, ADA MSS. Among its members were: AME Church, ACLU, AFL, CIO, American Jewish Committee, American Jewish Congress, American Veterans' Committee, Brotherhood of Sleeping Car Porters, Catholic Interracial Council, CORE, Hotel Restaurant and Bartenders' International Union, Fraternal Order of the Elks, ILGWU, Japanese American Citizens' Committee, National Alliance of Postal Employees, National Baptist Convention, National Bar Association, National Newspaper Publishers Association, Transport Workers' Union, United Steelworkers' Union, Workmens' Circle, Workers' Defense League.

23. Arnold Aronson to John Gunther, February 15, 1955, Box 12, 3 of 5, ADA MSS.

24. For the complaints of the SCEF at the LCCR's restrictive policy, see A. Philip Randolph to Aubrey Williams, July 26, 1956, Group 58, Box 32, Aubrey Williams to James Dombrowski, February 18, 1957, Group 58, Box 38, Williams MSS, FDRL. In March, 1954, James Eastland brought a one-man Senate Internal Security Subcommittee to New Orleans to investigate the alleged Communist ties of the SCEF and particularly its founders: Aubrey Williams, James Dombrowski, and Virginia Durr. *New York Times*, March 17–20, 1954.

25. LCCR "Minutes of Steering Committee," February 10, 1953, Box 7, 3 of 5, ADA MSS.; Memo to the attorney general on "Administrative Action to Improve the Civil Rights Machinery of the Department of Justice," May 1, 1953, Box 7, 3 of 5, ADA MSS.; John T. Elliff, "The United States Department of Justice and Individual Rights, 1937–1962," (unpublished Ph.D. dissertation, Harvard University, 1967), pp. 351 ff.

26. Elliff, "The United States Department of Justice," pp. 376–377.

27. Everett Dirksen to Thomas Stephens, January 1, 1953, OF 102-B-3, DDEL.

28. U.S. Senate, Committee on the Judiciary, *Hearings on S. 1 and 5. 535,* 83rd Congress, 2nd Session, January 26, 1954, p. 14.

29. Ibid., p. 45.

30. LCCR "Minutes of Executive Committee," July 19, 1955, Box 12, 3 of 5, ADA MSS.

31. Ibid.

32. Henry Lee Moon, *Balance of Power* (Garden City: Doubleday, 1948), p. 9.

33. NAACP, *Annual Report,* 1956, p. 8.

34. John Gunther to Arnold Aronson, September 27, 1955, Box 12, 3 of 5, ADA MSS.

35. Hollander to Joseph Rauh and John Gunther, September 26, 1955, Box 7, 3 of 5, ADA MSS.

36. *Public Papers . . . Dwight D. Eisenhower, 1956,* pp. 668–669.

37. "Text of Civil Rights Statement by UAW–CIO Executive Board," October 30, 1955, Box 7, 3 of 5, ADA MSS.

38. John Gunther to Arnold Aronson, September 27, 1955, Box 12, 3 of 5, ADA MSS.

39. Richard Bolling, *House Out of Order* (New York: E. P. Dutton, 1965), p. 176.

40. Clarence Mitchell to Roy Wilkins, December 5, 1955, Box 12, 3 of 5, ADA MSS.

41. *Crisis* LXIII (January 1956), p. 50; Edward Hollander to Hubert Humphrey, February 23, 1956, Box 9, 3 of 5; John Gunther to Richard Bolling, February 24, 1956, Box 8, 3 of 5, ADA MSS.

42. Drew Pearson, "Washington Merry-Go-Round," Washington *Post,* January 12, 1956; Bolling, *House Out of Order,* p. 176.

43. Elliff, "The United States Department of Justice," p. 497; Maceo Hubbard, personal interview, November 3, 1970, Washington, D.C. The voters of Mississippi had ratified a constitutional amendment with a literacy test making it more difficult for Negroes to register than ever before.

44. Herbert Brownell, "Federally-Protected Civil Rights," *Vital Speeches* XXII (November 1, 1955): 45.

45. Sherman Adams, *First Hand Report* (New York: Harper, 1962), p. 45.

46. Donovan, *Eisenhower,* p. 394; J. W. Anderson, *Eisenhower, Brownell and*

the Congress: The Tangled Origins of the Civil Rights Bill of 1956–1957 (University, Alabama: University of Alabama Press, 1964), p. 4.

47. Morrow, *Black Man in the White House,* p. 19; Sherman Adams noted the "widespread speculation about the selection of another Republican candidate for President in 1956." *First Hand Report,* p. 181.

48. The seven states were New York, Illinois, Pennsylvania, Ohio, California, Massachusetts, and New Jersey. The ranges were: New England—80 percent, Middle Atlantic—212 percent, East North Central—250 percent, and Mountain—122 percent. Lawson Purdy, "Negro Migration in the United States," *American Journal of Economics and Sociology* XIII (July 1954): 357–362; "Where Does Negro Voter Strength Lie?" *Congressional Quarterly Weekly* XIV (May 4, 1956): 491–496.

49. "Purists and Progress," *New Republic* CXXXVII (August 12, 1957): 3; Anderson, *Eisenhower, Brownell, and the Congress,* p. 25.

50. "A Legal Mind and a Political Brain," *Time* LXI (February 16, 1953): 61.

51. Ibid.

52. Maxwell Rabb to Howard Pyle, August 8, 1955, OF 142-A-4, Box 731, DDEL.

53. Frederic Morrow to Maxwell Rabb, November 29, 1955, Box 10, Morrow Files, DDEL; Morrow, *Black Man in the White House,* pp. 30, 47. The Emmett Till murder was considered the main outrage by Negroes, Morrow to Sherman Adams, December 16, 1955, OF 138-A-6, DDEL.

54. Sherman Adams to Arthur Minnich, February 11, 1960, Box 24, Adams MSS.

55. Dwight D. Eisenhower, *Waging Peace, 1956–1961* (Garden City: Doubleday, 1956), p. 153.

56. *Public Papers . . . Dwight D. Eisenhower,* 1956, p. 25.

57. Elliff, "The Justice Department," pp. 498–499; Ruth C. Wright, "The Enactment of the Civil Rights Acts of 1866 and 1957" (unpublished Ph.D. dissertation, the American University, 1968), pp. 102–107.

58. Quoted in Elliff, "The Justice Department," p. 428; Gilbert Ware, "The National Association For the Advancement of Colored People and the Civil Rights Act of 1957" (unpublished Ph.D. dissertation, Princeton University, 1962), p. 101a, f.n. 43.

59. Cabinet Minutes, March 9, 1956, Box 8, Sherman Adams MSS; Adams, *First Hand Report,* p. 332.

60. Cabinet Meeting "Excerpt," March 9, 1956, Bureau of the Budget Office Files, Washington, D.C.

61. Wright, "The Enactment of the Civil Rights Acts," pp. 110–111.

62. Office of Staff Secretary, Cabinet Minutes, March 20, 1956, 15 of 15, DDEL, and Adams MSS, Box 8.

63. Cabinet Minutes, March 23, 1956, Box 8, Adams MSS.

64. Adams, *First Hand Report,* p. 333.

65. Bryce Harlow to Adam Clayton Powell, February 24, 1956, OF 142-A-6; DDE to Leroy Collins, March 31, 1956, OF 102-B-3, DDEL. The president could create a commission without congressional approval, but the agency would lack subpoena power. James Reston, "Outlook for Civil Rights," *New York Times*, April 3, 1956.

66. U.S. House of Representatives, Committee on the Judiciary, *Hearings on Civil Rights*, 84th Congress, 2nd Session, p. 65; I. J. Martin to William Knowland, April 9, 1956, Office of Staff Secretary, 15 of 15, DDEL, mentions only the two sections as the program for introduction into Congress.

67. Anderson, *Eisenhower, Brownell, and the Congress*, pp. 41–42. Keating introduced the bill on April 9, and Dirksen submitted it on April 11.

68. U.S. Senate, Committee on the Judiciary, *Hearings on Civil Rights*, 84th Congress, 2nd Session, May 16, 1956, p. 81; *New York Times*, May 25, 1956.

69. Charles Diggs to DDE, June 1, 1956; Bryce Harlow to Gerald Morgan, June 1, 1956; Maxwell Rabb to Gerald Morgan (no date); Bryce Harlow to Charles Diggs, June 7, 1956, OF 102-B-3, DDEL.

70. "Where Does Negro Voter Strength Lie?" *Congressional Quarterly Weekly*, XIV (May 4, 1956): 495; Hugh Scott to Sherman Adams, January 30, 1956, Sherman Adams to Bryce Harlow, February 6, 1956, OF 102-B-3, DDEL.

71. Maxwell Rabb to Sherman Adams, March 30, 1956, Box 29, Howard Pyle MSS, DDEL. Rabb also wrote, "The need . . . is to pinpoint our attentions on this issue on the people who are vitally interested, namely, the Northern Negro."

72. Robert Sherill, *Gothic Politics in the Deep South* (New York: Grossman Publishers, 1968), p. 210.

73. Chicago *Defender*, March 31, 1956.

74. Ibid., March 10, 1956.

75. Emanuel Celler to Robert F. Wagner, Jr., October 23, 1956, Box 454, Celler MSS LC; Bolling, *House Out of Order*, p. 176.

76. Bolling, *House Out of Order*, pp. 179–180.

77. Maxwell Rabb to Bryce Harlow, June 20, 1956, OF 142-A, DDEL.

78. Anderson, *Eisenhower, Brownell, and the Congress*, pp. 95–96. *Congressional Record*, 84th Congress, 2nd Session, pp. 12818–12819. The next day, July 17, Democrat James Roosevelt inserted into the *Record* a letter that he had received from presidential assistant Bryce Harlow, stating Eisenhower's approval of "the various measures proposed by the Attorney General." This letter sent to a Democrat disturbed Keating, who wanted a Republican to get the credit as the spokesman for civil rights. *Congressional Record*, 84th Congress, 2nd Session, pp. 13147–13148; Memo SJS to Bryce Harlow, July 17, 1956, Memo, July 18, 1956, Box 8, Bryce Harlow MSS, DDEL.

79. *Congressional Record*, 84th Congress, 2nd Session, pp. 12923 ff.

80. Ibid., pp. 12918, 13180.

81. Ibid., pp. 12935, 13133, 13176.

82. *Congressional Quarterly Weekly* XIV (July 20, 1956): 877.

83. *Congressional Record*, 84th Congress, 2nd Session, p. 13543.

84. Ibid., p. 13562.

85. Thomas Hennings to David Dubinsky, July 27, 1956, Box 58, Hennings MSS, University of Missouri.

86. Howard E. Shuman, "Senate Rules and the Civil Rights Bill: A Case Study," *American Political Science Review* LI (December 1957): 956; *New York Times,* July 24, 30, 1956; *Congressional Record,* 84th Congress, 2nd Session, pp. 14162 ff., 14216.

87. Rowland Evans and Robert Novak, *Lyndon Johnson: The Exercise of Power* (New York: New American Library, 1966), p. 123. Minority Leader William Knowland supported Johnson's policy.

88. *New York Times,* July 25, 1956.

89. *New York Times,* August 21, 1956; Pittsburgh *Courier,* September 1, 1956; Anderson, *Eisenhower, Brownell, and the Congress,* pp. 121–123.

90. *New York Times,* October 15, 1956; *Congressional Record,* 84th Congress, 2nd Session, p. 13113.

91. Quoted in Robert Bendiner, "The Negro Vote and the Democrats," *The Reporter* XIV (May 31, 1956): 9. Some white liberals were dismayed by Wilkins' criticism of the Democratic party. Joe Rauh wrote the NAACP executive secretary, "It seems to me that the only way to maintain true neutrality when you are criticizing the foulness of the Democratic politicians in the South, is to make clear each time the keen disappointment of Negroes with the leadership given by the President on civil rights." Rauh to Wilkins, September 7, 1956, Box 48, 3 of 5, ADA MSS. See also Ware, "The N.A.A.C.P. and the Civil Rights Act," p. 58.

92. May 31, 1956, p. 10.

93. XLVII (April 9, 1956): 37.

94. *New York Times,* October 13, 1956.

95. Elliff, "The Justice Department," pp. 503–504; Robert Carr concluded that the government could initiate civil action to protect voting rights, *Federal Protection of Civil Rights* (Ithaca: Cornell University Press, 1947), pp. 196–98.

96. U.S. Senate, Committee on the Judiciary, *Hearings on Civil Rights,* 85th Congress, 1st Session, "Statement by Warren Olney III before the Senate Subcommittee on Privileges and Elections, pp. 237 ff. The ADA charged that Olney's testimony "was aimed more at gathering votes in the North than at protecting the right of the Negro to vote in the South." John Gunther to Washington *Post,* October 30, 1956, Box 8, 3 of 5, ADA MSS.

97. November 3, 1956.

98. "For Whom Did Negroes Vote in 1956," *CQW* XV (June 7, 1957): 704–705; Henry Lee Moon, "The 1956 Negro Vote," *Journal of Negro Education* XXVI (Summer 1957): 219 ff. From 1952 to 1956, Eisenhower's share of the black vote rose from 21 percent to 39 percent.

99. *New York Times,* July 18, 1957.

100. Samuel Lubell, "The Future of the Negro Voter," *Journal of Negro Education* XXXVI (Summer 1957): 416.

101. DDE, *Waging Peace,* pp. 153–54.

102. *Time* LXVIII (December 24, 1956): 11.

103. Paul Douglas to Ester Saverson, January 17, 1957, Legislative File, Box 100 R 01, Douglas MSS, Chicago Historical Society.

7. Politics and the Passage of the Civil Rights Act of 1957

1. Cabinet Meeting Minutes, December 31, 1956, Box 8, Sherman Adams MSS; *Public Papers of the Presidents: David D. Eisenhower, 1957,* p. 23.

2. Chicago *Defender,* January 12, 1957.

3. Hubert Humphrey to Joseph Rauh, January 15, 1957, Box 14, 3 of 5, ADA MSS.

4. Warren Olney III, "The Government's Role in Defending Civil Rights," Address for delivery, April 5, 1957, before the Conference of the National Civil Liberties Clearinghouse, Box 8, 3 of 5, ADA MSS.

5. Howard E. Shuman, "Senate Rules and the Civil Rights Bill: A Case Study," *American Political Science Review* LI (December 1957): 959.

6. Ibid.; *New York Times,* January 4, 1957. In 1953 twenty-nine Democrats and forty-one Republicans voted to table the motion, while fifteen Democrats and five Republicans opposed it.

7. *Congressional Quarterly Weekly* XV (January 11, 1957): 389.

8. *New York Times,* January 12, 1957.

9. Cabell Phillips, *New York Times,* January 6, 1957.

10. Rowland Evans and Robert Novak, *Lyndon B. Johnson: The Exercise of Power* (New York: New American Library, 1966): p. 127.

11. U.S. House of Representatives, Committee on the Judiciary, *Hearings on Civil Rights,* 1957, pp. 806, 1187.

12. Ibid., pp. 804–806.

13. Ruth C. Wright, "The Enactment of the Civil Rights Acts of 1866 and 1957" (unpublished Ph.D. dissertation, The American University, 1968), pp. 159–60; Gilbert Ware, "The National Association For the Advancement of Colored People and the Civil Rights Act of 1957" (unpublished Ph.D. dissertation, Princeton University, 1962), p. 77.

14. U.S. Senate, Committee on the Judiciary, *Hearings on Civil Rights, 1957,* pp. 214 ff.

15. Ibid., pp. 7, 40, 215.

16. *New York Times,* May 26, 1957; Press Release, April 1, 1957, Box 191, Olin Johnston MSS.

17. Thomas Hennings to William Langer, April 10, 1957, Box 96, Hennings MSS.

18. Richard Bolling, *House Out of Order* (New York: E. P. Dutton, 1965),

pp. 183–84; *New York Times,* April 9, 1957. Usually the Rules Committee heard the chairman and several members of the committee that reported the bill.

19. John Dingell to Dwight D. Eisenhower (DDE), May 8, 1957, OF 102-B-2, DDEL.

20. I. J. Martin to John Dingell, May 14, 1957, OF 102-B-2, DDEL; *Public Papers . . . Dwight Eisenhower, 1957,* May 15, 1957.

21. John Dingell to DDE, May 20, 1957, I. J. Martin to Dingell, May 24, 1957, OF 102-B-2, DDEL.

22. Gilbert Ware, "The NAACP and the 1957 Civil Rights Act," p. 126. Interestingly, Walter F. Murphy has shown that many of the southern senators who defended jury trials in contempt cases represented states where there was no such procedure required. In fact, Sam Ervin, while he was a judge, rendered decisions denying jury trials for persons who wilfully disobeyed court injunctions. Walter F. Murphy, "Some Strange New Converts to the Cause of Civil Rights," *The Reporter* XVI (June 27, 1957): 13–14.

23. Quoted in Ware, "The NAACP and the 1957 Civil Rights Act," pp. 134–135.

24. *New York Times,* June 11, 1957; Telford Taylor, "Crux of the Civil Rights Debate," *New York Times Magazine* (June 16, 1957): 7.

25. J. W. Peltason, *Fifty-Eight Lonely Men* (New York: Random House, 1961): p. 9.

26. Ibid., p. 11.

27. Paul Douglas, *In the Fullness of Time* (New York: Harcourt, Brace, Jovanovich, 1972), p. 289.

28. Olney, "Government's Role in Defending Civil Rights," Box 8, ADA MSS.

29. *Public Papers . . . Eisenhower,* 1957, p. 105.

30. *New York Times,* June 4, 1957.

31. *Cong. Rec.,* 85th Congress, 1st Session, pp. 9192, 9197.

32. Ibid., pp. 9021, 9203.

33. Herbert Brownell to Clifford Case, May 31, 1957, reprinted in *Cong. Rec.,* 85th Congress, 1st Session, p. 12084.

34. "Call to A Prayer Pilgrimage for Freedom," GF 124-A-1, DDEL. The pilgrimage was officially conceived because Eisenhower would not consent to speak out against the breakdown of law and order in the South. Martin Luther King, Jr., to DDE, January 11, 1957, GF 124-A-1, DDEL; Pittsburgh *Courier,* February 9, 23, April 20, 27, 1957.

35. George Metcalf, *Black Profiles* (New York: McGraw-Hill, 1968), p. 101; Lerone Bennett, Jr., *Confrontation Black and White* (Baltimore: Penguin Books, 1966), p. 145, 313 ff; August Meier, "On the Role of Martin Luther King," *New Politics* IV (Winter 1965): 52–59.

36. Pittsburgh *Courier,* May 25, 1957.

37. Ibid., June 1 and 29, 1957.

38. Among the ten congressmen, three were from Kentucky, two from Oklahoma, one from Tennessee, and five from West Virginia.

39. Roy Wilkins to E. Frederic Morrow, June 17, 1957, Box 10, Morrow Files, DDEL.

40. Shuman, "Senate Rules," 957, 965. At that juncture Olin Johnston was reading leisurely to the Judiciary Committee from a ninety-page brief on arbitrary injunction procedures. Press Release, June 10, 1957, Box 191, Johnston MSS.

41. For an analysis of these motives, see Cabell Phillips, *New York Times*, July 14, 1957; William S. White, *New York Times*, August 18, 1957.

42. Shuman, "Senate Rules," 969; *Cong. Rec.*, 85th Congress, 1st Session, p. 9811. One stranger in the Johnson camp was Wayne Morse of Oregon, an outspoken civil-rights advocate. In this instance he preferred to send the bill to the Judiciary Committee with instructions to report it back within seven days.

43. *Cong. Rec.*, 85th Congress, 1st Session, 9627.

44. Ibid., p. 10771.

45. *Public Papers . . . Eisenhower*, 1957, p. 520.

46. *Cong. Rec.*, 85th Congress, 1st Session, p. 11344.

47. Ibid., p. 11347.

48. Press release, July 9, 1957, Box 191, Johnston MSS.

49. Eisenhower, *Waging Peace*, pp. 156, 158; Washington *Post*, July 11, 1957; Olin Johnston to Roger C. Peace, July 13, 1957, Box 188, Johnston MSS.

50. Eisenhower, *Waging Peace*, p. 158; *Public Papers . . . Eisenhower, 1957*, pp. 505–506.

51. Eisenhower, *Waging Peace*, p. 158.

52. *New York Times*, July 11, 1957.

53. "Voting and Integration," Washington *Post*, July 11, 1957.

54. Tampa *Tribune*, July 22, 1957, Raleigh *News and Observer*, July 16, 1957; Charlotte *Observer*, July 18, 1957. For contrast see New Orleans *Times-Picaqune*, July 19, 1957.

55. *Cong. Rec.*, 85th Congress, 1st Session, p. 10771.

56. *New York Times*, July 11, 1957. *Cong. Rec.*, 85th Congress, 1st Session, p. 11621.

57. Arthur Krock, *New York Times*, July 12, 1957. However Dirksen pointed out correctly that another act, Title 10, Section 333, allowed the president to use the armed forces to remove interferences with the execution of U.S. laws. *Cong. Rec.*, 85th Congress, 1st Session, p. 11218. On July 17th, the president remarked, "I can't imagine any set of circumstances that would ever induce me to send Federal troops . . . into any area to enforce orders of the Federal Court." *Public Papers . . . Eisenhower*, 1957, p. 546.

58. *New York Times*, July 17, 1957.

59. *Public Papers . . . Eisenhower, 1957*, pp. 555–556.

60. *Cong. Rec.*, 85th Congress, 1st Session, p. 12098.

61. "Let's Look at Congress," *U.S. News and World Reports* LXIII (July 26, 1957): 55. The attorney general would have used Title III to prevent individuals from interfering with voluntary attempts by school boards to comply with the Supreme Court decision. Memo, Warren Olney, "Civil Rights Bill and Segregated Education," July 9, 1957, Box 8, Adams MSS.

62. The nonsouthern Democrats who supported the elimination of Title III came from Arizona, Idaho, Montana, Nevada, New Mexico, Oklahoma, Rhode Island, and Wyoming.

63. E. Frederic Morrow to Sherman Adams, July 12, 1957, Box 9, Morrow Files, DDEL.

64. Maxwell Rabb to Janet Simpson, July 18, 1957, GF 2b (8), DDEL.

65. Val Washington to DDE, July 18, 1957, Box 9, Morrow Files, DDEL.

66. *Public Papers . . . Eisenhower, 1957,* p. 547.

67. Atlanta *Constitution*, July 29, 1957; Evans and Novak, *Lyndon B. Johnson*, p. 125; T. Harry Williams, "Huey, Lyndon, and Southern Radicalism," *The Journal of American History* LX (September 1973): 281, pointed out that not "once in [Johnson's] twelve years in the House . . . did he rant about civil rights on the floor or insert in the record an anti-black diatribe, that technique of southern politicians known as 'talking Nigra'."

68. George Reedy to Lyndon B. Johnson (no date—ca. 1957), CR-Box 3, Senate Papers, Lyndon B. Johnson Library (LBJL).

69. George Reedy to LBJ, December 3, 1956, CR-Box 7, LBJL.

70. Harry McPherson, *A Political Education* (Boston: Little Brown, 1972), p. 145. This Johnson assistant recalled how his boss had kept open the lines of communication between the liberals and conservatives, "Once in the cloakroom I heard him tell Douglas, 'If we're going to have any civil rights bill at all, we've got to be reasonable about this jury trial amendment.' Five minutes later, at the opposite end of the room, he advised Sam Ervin to 'be ready to take up the Nigra bill again' that afternoon."

71. Evans and Novak, *Lyndon B. Johnson,* p. 134; Ware, "The NAACP and the Civil Rights Act of 1957," p. 139.

72. Carl A. Auerbach, "Jury Trials and Civil Rights," *New Leader* XL (April 29, 1957): 16–18.

73. Evans and Novak, *Lyndon B. Johnson,* p. 134; Benjamin V. Cohen to Charles H. Slayman, Jr., July 16, 1957, Box 234, Paul Douglas MSS.

74. *Cong. Rec.*, 85th Congress, 1st Session, p. 12532.

75. Quoted in *Congressional Quarterly Almanac* XIII (1957): 563.

76. Estes Kefauver to Spencer Williams, May 25, 1957, Ser. 1, Box 9, Kefauver MSS.

77. *Cong. Rec.*, 85th Congress, 1st Session, p. 11983.

78. Lucius Burch to Kefauver, March 26, 1957; W. Corry Smith to Kefauver, May 31, 1957, Ser. 1, Box 9, Kefauver MSS. Smith, a college roommate and good friend of Kefauver, warned the senator that a majority of

Tennesseans opposed the civil-rights bill and "you should not substitute your feelings for theirs or you won't get reelected."

79. Paul Douglas to Estes Kefauver, June 12, 1957, Ser. 1, Box 9, Kefauver MSS.

80. August 19, 1957.

81. Douglas, *In the Fullness of Time*, p. 289.

82. "Statement of Position of Indiana Civil Liberties Union With Respect to Right to Trial by Jury Pending Civil Rights Legislation" (no date), vol. 41, ACLU MSS, Princeton University.

83. Press Release, May 17, 1957, vol. 41, ACLU MSS. Also, individuals had a full right to appeal to higher courts, a check on arbitrary decisions. One of those members of the ACLU's Board of Directors who opposed the jury-trial amendment was the former district court judge J. Waties Waring of South Carolina. Minutes, Special Board of Directors, April 3, 1957, vol. 41, ACLU MSS.

84. Paul Douglas to John Temple Graves, July 25, 1957, Legislative Files, Box 100 R 04, Douglas MSS; *Cong. Rec.*, 85th Congress, 1st Session, p. 13324.

85. *Cong. Rec.*, 85th Congress, 1st Session, p. 12004.

86. LCCR, "Fact Sheet on H.R. 6127," vol. 41, ACLU MSS.

87. *Cong. Rec.*, 85th Cong., 1st Session, pp. 2813–2818. See also Herbert Brownell, "Protecting Civil Rights," *Vital Speeches* XXIII (August 1, 1957): 622–625.

88. *Cong. Rec.*, 85th Congress, 1st Session, pp. 12148, 12155, 12911.

89. Ibid., p. 13154.

90. Evans and Novak, *Lyndon B. Johnson*, p. 103. When Church campaigned for the Senate in 1956, he faced the stiff opposition of the state's private electric utility. Short on money, the candidate received assistance from Johnson, who persuaded the Senate Democratic Campaign Committee to send funds to Church.

91. C. Vann Woodward, "The Great Civil Rights Debate," *Commentary* XXIV (October 1957): 288. Woodward added, "But evidence of such negotiations is hard to establish, even by historians with access to private archives and years of research at their disposal."

92. Douglas, *In the Fullness of Time*, p. 287.

93. Dwight D. Eisenhower, *Waging Peace*, pp. 155–156; Evans and Novak, *Lyndon B. Johnson*, pp. 130, 137; Douglass Cater, "How the Senate Passed the Civil Rights Bill," *Reporter* XVII (September 5, 1957): 12.

94. Atlanta *Constitution*, August 7, 1957.

95. Montgomery *Advertiser*, August 14, 1957.

96. Idaho *Statesman*, June 25, August 5, 1957. See also Portland *Oregonian*, June 22, 23, 1957, and Seattle *Times*, July 31, 1957.

97. *Cong. Rec.*, 85th Congress, 1st Session, p. 13015; Drew Pearson, "Johnson Worked Votes Miracle," Washington *Post*, August 8, 1957.

98. Quoted in Ware, "NAACP and the Civil Rights Act of 1957," p. 141; Andrew Biemiller to Estes Kefauver, August 1, 1957, Scr. 1, Box 9, Kefauver MSS.

99. *Cong. Rec.*, 85th Congress, 1st Session, p. 13307.

100. Washington *Post*, August 2, 1957. For an editorial opposing the jury-trial amendment, see *Post*, July 28, 1957.

101. Raleigh *News and Observer*, August 3, 1957; Atlanta *Constitution*, July 16, 1957.

102. Dwight D. Eisenhower to James F. Byrnes, July 23, 1957, OF 102-B-3, DDEL. *Cong. Rec.*, 85th Congress, 1st Session, p. 9204, provides a complete listing of the acts which permitted the federal government to obtain injunctions and allowed the issuance of contempt citations without jury trials.

103. *Public Papers . . . Eisenhower, 1957*, p. 573.

104. *New York Times*, August 2, 1957; "Civil Rights Back Stage Drama," *Newsweek* L (August 12, 1957): 25–26.

105. The nonsouthern Democrats represented Delaware, Arizona, Idaho, Massachusetts, Montana, Nevada, New Mexico, Ohio, Oklahoma, Rhode Island, Washington, and Wyoming. The GOP supporters of the amendment came from Arizona, Delaware, Indiana, Kansas, Maine, Maryland, Nebraska, Nevada, North Dakota, and South Dakota.

106. Three of those who followed Eisenhower's lead—Saltonstall, H. Alexander Smith, and Bricker—based their votes on the conviction that the scope of Title III was too broad, while Title IV dealt only with the right to vote with little chance for governmental abuse. *Cong. Rec.*, 85th Congress, 1st Session, pp. 12541, 13003. Smith wrote James B. Carey: "Now that we have limited the bill to the 'right-to-vote', a jury trial would only complicate the situation and I am afraid is a stalling operation to make the 'right-to-vote' ineffective," July 30, 1957, Box 156, Smith MSS.

107. *Cong. Rec.*, 85th Congress, 1st Session, pp. 12087, 13306. In explaining his vote for the amendment, Kennedy said that most of the cases could be handled as civil contempts without juries. Mark Howe and Paul Freund influenced him on this point. He also believed "that the Southerners would have filibustered the civil rights bill if a jury trial amendment were not adopted and that it would have been impossible to obtain cloture." Furthermore, Kennedy thought that with the amendment the civil-rights bill would have appealed to the "progressive elements in the South whom I believe are most important in the eventual attainment of equal rights for Southern Negroes." John F. Kennedy to Herbert Tucker, August 2, 1957, Box 458, Pre-Presidential Papers, John F. Kennedy Library (JFKL); Frederick L. Holborn (FLH) to JFK, July 31, 1957, Box 548, Pre-Presidential Papers, JFKL. For another view of his motives based on presidential ambitions, see "Purists and Progress," *New Republic* CXLVII (August 12, 1957): 4.

108. The additional two Republicans who defected were Margaret Chase

Smith (Maine) and Homer Capehart (Indiana). For LBJ's personal influence on Mrs. Smith, see Evans and Novak, *Lyndon B. Johnson,* p. 128. Along the same line, see Theodore F. Green to Dorothy Hunt, July 31, 1957, Box 890, Theodore Green MSS.

109. *New York Times,* August 3, 1957. Howard Shuman, the legislative assistant to Senator Douglas, who publicly denounced the western senators for making a deal, believed that the arrangement was more subtle than did his boss. "In the Senate, things are done by 'tacit' agreements or understandings rather than outright deals," he wrote to David Mayhew, March 19, 1958, Legislative Files, Box 100 R 01, Douglas MSS.

110. *New York Times,* August 2, 1957.

111. *Public Papers . . . Eisenhower, 1957,* p. 587.

112. The final vote, seventy-two to eighteen, reflected a sectional split. However, there were several important exceptions. Johnson and Ralph Yarborough of Texas, and Smathers of Florida supported the revised bill. Voting against it because he thought it was not strong enough was Wayne Morse of Oregon. The remainder of the opposition consisted of southern Democrats.

113. *New York Times,* August 5, 13, 1957.

114. Ibid., August 11, 1957.

115. Morrow, *Black Man in the White House,* pp. 167–68; Maxwell Rabb to Wilton Persons, August 19, 1957, Box 9, Morrow Files, DDEL; *Congressional Quarterly Weekly* XV (August 23, 1957): 1006; Chicago *Defender,* August 17, 1957.

116. *New York Times,* August 5, 1957; see also the perceptive comments of James Reston on the Republican dilemma, *New York Times,* August 6, 1957.

117. Pittsburgh *Courier,* September 5, 1957; "Meaning of the Civil Rights Bill," *Crisis* LXIV (August–September, 1957): 422–423.

118. Louis Lautier, *Afro-American,* August 24, 1957; Joseph Rauh to *New York Times,* August 28, 1957, Box 9, 3 of 5, ADA MSS.

119. August 17, 1957.

120. August 10, 1957.

121. August 30, 1957, clipping in Box 456, Celler MSS.

122. New York *Amsterdam News,* August 10, 1957; Norfolk *Journal and Guide,* August 10, 1957; Chicago *Defender,* August 31, 1957.

123. *New York Times,* August 10, 15, 16, 1957.

124. Gerald Morgan to DDE, August 16, 1957, Box 6, Gerald Morgan Files, DDEL.

125. *New York Times,* August 22, 1957.

126. Ibid., August 24, 1957.

127. Sam Rayburn to A. J. Marshall, August 31, 1957, Rayburn Library. The majority of both parties backed H.R. 6127; 128 Democrats and 151 Republicans supported the bill and eighty-two Democrats and fifteen Re-

publicans opposed it. Representatives from Tennessee, Kentucky, Oklahoma, and Florida supported the legislation.

128. "Why Was There Not a Filibuster on the Civil Rights Bill?" Report by Senator Olin Johnston, September 12, 1957, Box 188, Johnston MSS.

129. Ibid.; Shuman, "Senate Rules," 974; Richard Rovere, "Letter from Washington," *The New Yorker* XXXIII (August 31, 1957): 76; Atlanta *Constitution*, August 30, 1957.

130. Quoted in Johnston, "Why Was There Not a Filibuster?"

131. *Cong. Rec.*, 85th Congress, 1st Session, p. 12561.

132. Ibid., p. 12287.

133. Ibid., p. 11687.

134. James Reston, "Trial by Jury Versus the Right to Vote," *New York Times*, July 14, 1957.

135. Richard Russell was the speaker. *Cong. Rec.*, 85th Congress, 1st Session, p. 15172.

136. Houston *Post*, August 9, 1957; Montgomery *Advertiser*, August 9, 1957. McPherson, *A Political Education*, p. 148, remembers that Johnson told the liberals who expressed some disappointment with the bill, "It's just the beginning. We've shown that we can do it. We'll do it again, in a couple of years."

137. James M. Burns, *Kennedy: A Political Profile* (New York: Harcourt Brace World, 1960), p. 204. This sympathetic biographer concluded that Kennedy "showed a profile in caution and moderation. He walked a teetering tightrope; at the same time that he was telling liberals of the effectiveness of a bill that included the O'Mahoney provision, he was assuring worried Southerners that it was a moderate bill that would be enforced by Southern courts and Southern juries."

138. August 17, 1957.

139. LXX (September 9, 1957): 24.

140. CLXXXV (August 17, 1957): 62. See also the *New Republic*, CXXXVII (September 16, 1957): 14.

141. Emory O. Jackson to Paul Douglas, August 3, 1957, Legislative Files, Box 100 R 01, Douglas MSS.

142. Paul Douglas to Jean Taft Douglas, June 27, 1957 (1955–1957 correspondence), Douglas MSS.

143. Paul Douglas to William S. White, August 29, 1958, Legislative Files, Box 100 R 01, ibid.

144. Paul Douglas to John A. Morsell, August 22, 1957, Legislative Files, Box 100 R 01, ibid.

145. Dorsey F. Lane, "The Civil Rights Act of 1957," *Howard Law Journal* IV (January 1958): 46.

146. Carl Auerbach, "Is It Strong Enough to Do the Job?" *Reporter*, XCII (September 5, 1957): 14.

147. Kurt W. Melchior to ACLU, October 7, 1957, vol. 41, ACLU MSS. Rowland Watts, Staff Counsel, ACLU to Kurt W. Melchior, November 8, 1957, vol. 41, wrote in reply: "It was difficult for a civil liberties organization to suggest that a jury trial was not *always* the bulwark of liberty. In any event, we agree that the matter is not so critical."

148. *New York Times,* August 6, 1957.

149. Joseph Rauh to *Reporter* XVII (October 3, 1957): 6.

150. Woodward, "The Great Civil Rights Debate," 291.

151. Memo from Roy Wilkins on Civil Rights Bill, August 13, 1957, copy in Box 456, Emanuel Celler MSS.

152. Maxwell Rabb to William R. Ming, Jr., January 14, 1958, GF Box 43, DDEL.

8. JUSTICE DELAYED . . . JUSTICE DENIED

1. U.S. Senate, Committee on the Judiciary, *Hearings: The Nomination of Wilson White,* 85th Congress, 2nd Session (Washington, D.C., 1958), pp. 3 ff.

2. Ibid., p. 45.

3. U.S. House of Representatives, Committee on the Judiciary, Subcommittee No. 5, *Hearings on Civil Rights,* 86th Congress, 1st Session (Washington, D.C., 1959), p. 228.

4. John T. Elliff, "The United States Department of Justice and Individual Rights, 1937–1962" (unpublished doctoral dissertation, Harvard University, 1967), p. 547.

5. U.S. Congress, House Committee on Appropriations, *Hearings: Department of Justice,* 86th Congress, 1st Session (Washington, D.C., 1959), p. 195; Elliff, "United States Department of Justice," p. 548.

6. U.S. Congress, House Committee on the Judiciary, *Hearings on Civil Rights,* 86th Congress, 1st Session (Washington, D.C., 1959), p. 78.

7. U.S. Congress, House Committee on Appropriations, *Hearings: Department of Justice,* 86th Congress, 1st Session (Washington, D.C., 1959), p. 198; U.S. Department of Justice, *Annual Report of the Attorney General* (Washington, D.C., 1958), p. 182. When Wilson White informed the Appropriations Committee of the Division's work in gathering information, Chairman John Rooney exclaimed, "My gosh, I am trying to find out what you have been doing with the taxpayers' money. This statistical business you related is something which I would have expected you had since the days of the Civil Rights Section of the Criminal Division."

8. Margaret Price, *The Negro and the Ballot in the South* (Atlanta: Southern Regional Council, 1959), p. 69; *New York Times,* September 5, 6, and 13, 1958.

9. W. Wilson White to William Rogers, September 1, 1958, GF 138-A-6, DDEL. A few months earlier, Fred Morrow had spoken to White about the Terrell situation and had pessimistically concluded: "The Assistant Attorney

General's coolness and nonchalance about the whole matter disturbed me no end. The Federal Government had no intention of interfering." E. Frederic Morrow, *Black Man in the White House* (New York: Coward-McCann, 1963), pp. 225–226.

10. *U.S. v. James G. Raines et al.,* "Transcript of Record," Supreme Court of the United States, October Term, 1959.

11. *U.S. v. Raines,* 172 F. Supp. 552 (1959); *Race Relations Law Reporter,* 4 (1959), 314 ff.

12. *New York Times,* January 13, 1960. Clarence Mitchell wrote Rogers, January 15, 1960, DDEL: "I attach great significance to your appearance before the Supreme Court. This appearance could leave no doubt about where our Government stood officially on this case because its highest law officer was there in person even though he could have delegated the task to someone else."

13. Brief for the U.S., *U.S. v. James G. Raines et al.,* October Term, 1959.

14. Brief for Appellees, *U.S. v. Raines,* October Term, 1959.

15. *U.S. v. Raines,* 362 U.S. 17, 21, 25, 26 (1960). After this decision, the case was remanded to the District Court for trial. Judge Bootle presided, found for the government, and permanently enjoined the defendants or their successors in office from engaging in discriminatory acts. At the same time, he ordered the four disfranchised blacks placed on the voting rolls. *Race Relations Law Reporter* 5 (1960): 1111–1112.

16. Lewis Jones and Stanley Smith, *Voting Rights and Economic Pressure* (New York: Anti-Defamation League, 1958), pp. 6, 7, and 24; Stokely Carmichael and Charles Hamilton, *Black Power* (New York: Vintage Books, 1967), p. 128.

17. William P. Mitchell, "Eight Year Summary of Registration Efforts of Negroes in Macon County," U.S. Committee on Civil Rights, *Hearings on Voting* (Washington, 1959), pp. 26–29.

18. For a complete account of the gerrymander case, see Bernard Taper, *Gomillion Versus Lightfoot* (New York: McGraw-Hill, 1962); *Gomillion v. Lightfoot,* 364 U.S. 339 (1960), declared that the redistricting for racial purposes violated the Fifteenth Amendment.

19. Montgomery *Advertiser,* July 31, 1957; Warren Olney III, St. John Barrett, Civil Rights Section interview with Charles Gomillion, July 11, 1957; Maxwell Rabb to Sherman Adams, July 12, 1957, Box 43 GF, DDEL.

20. *U.S. v. Alabama,* 171 F. Supp. 720. Johnson added, "Nothing stated in this opinion should be construed to mean that this Court sanctions or will sanction the proposition that registrars are free to resign at will, indiscriminately and in bad faith, and thereby cast off all of their responsibilities and obligations as such officers." One official, Grady Rogers, resigned to run successfully for the Alabama House of Representatives in 1958, and the other, E. P. Livingston, left to serve as Jury Commissioner for Macon County.

21. *U.S. v. Alabama,* 363 U.S. 602 (1960), *per curiam.*

22. Charles V. Hamilton, "Southern Federal Courts and the Right of Negroes to Vote, 1957–1962" (unpublished doctoral dissertation. University of Chicago, 1964), pp. 119 ff.

23. Brief for the United States, *U.S. v. Curtis M. Thomas,* Supreme Court, October Term, 1959.

24. *U.S. v. McElveen,* 177 F. Supp. 335 (1959; 180 F. Supp. 10 (1960); 362 U.S. 58 (1960), *per curiam.*

25. *New York Times,* March 22, 1959.

26. Ibid., August 14, 1959.

27. *Public Papers . . . Dwight D. Eisenhower, 1957,* p. 783.

28. Foster Rhea Dulles, *The Civil Rights Commission: 1957–1965* (Lansing: Michigan State University Press, 1968), pp. 19–22; U.S. Senate, Committee on the Judiciary, *Hearings on the Nominations of the Commission on Civil Rights,* 85th Congress, 2nd Session (Washington, D.C., 1958), p. 6.

29. *Nation* CLXXXVI (January 18, 1958): 42; Washington *Post,* November 9, 1957.

30. Morrow, *Black Man in the White House,* pp. 171–172.

31. Dulles, *Commission on Civil Rights,* pp. 22–24.

32. Quoted in a speech by Harris Wofford Jr., to the City Club of Chicago, November 2, 1959, Box 1, Wilton Persons MSS, DDEL.

33. U.S. Congress, House Committee on Appropriations, *Hearings on the Commission on Civil Rights,* 86th Congress, 1st Session (Washington, D.C., 1959), p. 1199.

34. U.S. Congress, House Committee on the Judiciary, *Hearings on Civil Rights,* 86th Congress, 1st Session (Washington, D.C., 1959), p. 217. Rogers told the committee that the Justice Department had suspended its investigation until after the commission's hearings.

35. U.S. Senate, Committee on the Judiciary, *Hearings on Civil Rights,* 86th Congress, 1st Session (Washington, D.C., 1959), pp. 610–611; U.S. Commission on Civil Rights, *Report* (Washington, D.C. 1959), p. 70.

36. U.S. Commission on Civil Rights, *Hearings, 1959,* (Washington, D.C., 1959), pp. 75, 104.

37. Ibid., p. 116

38. Ibid., pp. 52, 59.

39. Ibid., pp. 156, 166, 177, 182.

40. Ibid., pp. 206–207.

41. Quoted in U.S. Commission on Civil Rights, *Report,* p. 85.

42. *Public Papers . . . Dwight D. Eisenhower, 1958,* p. 859.

43. *In re Wallace, Race Relations Law Reporter* IV (1959): 104, 108.

44. Ibid., p. 121.

45. Quoted in Robert Sherrill, *Gothic Politics in the Deep South* (New York: Grossman Publishers, 1968), p. 280.

46. Commission on Civil Rights, *Hearings,* p. 301; *Report,* pp. 87, 89.

47. William Rogers to Sherman Adams, September 17, 1957, DDEL.

48. Cabinet Meeting Minutes, December 4, 1957, Box 8, Sherman Adams MSS.

49. *New York Times,* July 10, 1958 and January 16, 1959. When Rogers maintained that the Division had not received written accusations from Negroes, Clarence Mitchell objected: "I know they have had complaints because I have submitted them myself." U.S. Senate, Committee on the Judiciary, *Hearings on Civil Rights* (Washington, D.C., 1959), pp. 295–296.

50. "Memo for the Files, re: Negro leaders, June 24, 1958," OF 142-A, DDEL.

51. Ibid.; L. D. Reddick, *Crusader Without Violence: A Biography of Martin Luther King, Jr.* (New York: Harper, 1959), pp. 223–225. Wilkins, one of the most conciliatory in the group, changed his tone toward the president after Eisenhower refused to speak out against the arrest of Martin Luther King in Montgomery later that year. Roy Wilkins to Fred Morrow, September 4, 1958, Box 10, Morrow MSS., DDEL.

52. *New York Times,* November 8 and 9, 1958.

53. NAACP, *Annual Report, 1958,* p. 53; *New York Times,* December 31, 1958. The Democrats gained thirteen new Senate seats for a total of sixty-two. The freshmen came from California, Connecticut, Indiana, Maine, Michigan, Minnesota, Nevada, New Jersey, Ohio, Utah, West Virginia (two), and Wyoming. The Republicans added Keating of New York and Scott of Pennsylvania, supporters of civil rights in the House. In the House, the Democrats gained forty-seven seats for a total of 282.

54. The study was prepared by the Research Division of the Republican National Committee and extracts from it appear in the *Congressional Quarterly Weekly,* XVII (January 23, 1959): pp. 117–118. For an opinion that the Republicans were not doing enough to attract the support of Negroes at the grass roots, see Fred Morrow to Gerald Morgan, November 10, 1958, Box 10, Morrow MSS., DDEL.

55. *New York Times,* January 10, 1959. Of the fifteen newly elected Democratic senators, eight went along with the majority leader.

56. Ibid., January 13, 1959. The southerners were Ervin, Jordan, Holland, Smathers, Kefauver, Gore, Yarborough, and Johnson.

57. Ibid., January 14, 1959.

58. Ibid., January 21, 1959.

59. *Congressional Quarterly Weekly* XVII (January 30, 1959): 152.

60. Paul Douglas to William A. Hahn, October 3, 1958, Legislative Files, Box 100 R 01, Douglas MSS; Meeting of the Executive Committee of the LCCR, April 16, 1958, 3 of 5, Box 9, ADA MSS.

61. *Public Papers . . . Dwight D. Eisenhower,* 1957, p. 17.

62. Ibid., p. 22.

63. Brief for the United States, *U.S. v. Alabama,* October Term, Supreme Court (Washington, D.C., 1959).

64. Wilton Persons Memo to the President, January 28, 1959, Box 1, Persons MSS, DDEL. They also recommended the establishment of a Commission on Equal Job Opportunity Under Government Contracts to replace the existing President's Committee on Government Contracts.

65. U.S. Senate, Committee on the Judiciary, *Hearings on Civil Rights* (Washington, D.C., 1959), pp. 223 ff.

66. *Public Papers . . . Eisenhower, 1959*, p. 165.

67. Dwight Eisenhower to C. A. Scott, March 11, 1959, OF 102-B-3, DDEL.

68. U.S. Senate, Committee on the Judiciary, *Hearings on Civil Rights* (Washington, D.C., 1959), pp. 172 ff.

69. *New Republic* CXL (March 30, 1959): 4. The hearings did touch upon voting rights. See U.S. Senate, Committee on the Judiciary, *Hearings on Civil Rights* (Washington, D.C., 1959), pp. 519–520, 571, 612; U.S. Congress, House Committee on the Judiciary, *Hearings on Civil Rights* (Washington, D.C., 1959), pp. 553, 783.

70. U.S. Congress, House Committee on the Judiciary, *Report to Accompany H.R. 8601*, 86th Congress, 1st Session, (Washington, D.C., 1959), p. 3. Left intact were provisions concerning obstruction of court orders, bombing of educational and religious structures, extension of the CCR, the preservation of federal election records, and the education of children of military personnel.

71. *New York Times*, June 18, July 11, and August 4, 1959; *Congressional Quarterly Weekly* XVII (July 17, 1959), p. 983.

72. *New York Times*, August 24 and 27, 1959; *Public Papers . . . Eisenhower, 1959*, pp. 578, 598.

73. *Cong. Rec.*, 86th Cong., 2nd Sess., p. 3389. In desperation the liberals tacked on civil-rights amendments to a bill providing subsidies for southern peanut growers. The southerners allowed their cherished bill to die rather than to swallow the civil-rights poison.

74. U.S. Commission on Civil Rights, *Report*, p. 52.

75. Ibid., pp. 99 ff.

76. Ibid., pp. 131–132.

77. Gordon Tiffany, "Report to the President and to the Commission on Civil Rights From the Staff Director, 1958–1960," OF 102-B-3-A, DDEL. Fred Morrow asserted in his diary that Max Rabb was "perhaps the only one in the White House Staff who showed deep personal concern about the plight of the Negro." *Black Man in the White House*, p. 223.

78. Elliff, "The Justice Department," pp. 585–586. Even then the Civil Rights Division acted within narrow bounds, its lawyers discussed the possibility of also attempting to ensure the participation of blacks in future elections. However, they concluded that by "trying to accomplish too much, we may end up by accomplishing nothing at all." As a result, the government later had to file suits to enjoin economic intimidation by white landlords

against black farmers. For details see Charles Hamilton, "Federal Courts and Negro Voting Rights," pp. 228 ff.

79. U.S. Commission on Civil Rights, *Report,* p. 133.

80. Ibid., p. 140.

81. Ibid., pp. 141–142.

82. Ibid.

83. Ibid., pp. 143, 145. In addition, the CCR unanimously agreed on a proposal that Congress require that all states preserve their voting records for five years.

84. *Congressional Quarterly Weekly* XVII (September 11, 1959): 1126, 1246.

85. Estes Kefauver to John Hannah, October 5, 1959, Series 5h, Box 1, Kefauver MSS; *Cong. Rec.,* 86th Congress, 2nd Session, p. 19531; Greensboro *Daily News,* September 9, 1959; Lee County *Bulletin,* February 2, 1960.

86. Speech to the City Club of Chicago, Box 1, Persons MSS, DDEL.

87. Theodore Hesburgh to Dwight Eisenhower, October 19, 1959, OF 102-B-3-A, Box 431, DDEL.

88. *New York Times,* November 8, 1959.

89. Donald Matthews and James Prothro, *Negroes and the New Southern Politics* (New York: Harcourt Brace World, 1966), p. 18; NAACP, *Annual Report,* 1960, p. 37.

90. *Public Papers . . . Eisenhower, 1960,* p. 14.

91. Ibid., pp. 26–27.

92. Ed McCabe Memo for Ann Whitman, January 20, 1960, Box 18, Gerald Morgan Files, DDEL. To add to the confusion, in his January 19 Budget Message, Eisenhower called the commission's recommendations for protecting the right to vote "constructive" and hoped they "will also be earnestly considered by Congress." *Public Papers,* p. 105.

93. U.S. Senate, Committee on Rules and Administration, *Hearings on Federal Registrars,* 86th Congress, 2nd Session, (Washington, D.C., 1960), p. 112.

94. At a press conference on January 26th Eisenhower announced that the attorney general would soon reveal a new plan. The president did not specifically describe it because he did not want to be misunderstood. "It is somewhat technical . . . a legalistic amendment," Eisenhower hesitated, "that would be difficult to describe in detail." *Public Papers . . . 1960,* pp. 125–126. He probably remembered that his confusion about some provisions of the 1957 Act had embarrassed him.

95. U.S. Senate, Committee on Rules and Administration, *Hearings on Federal Registrars,* p. 358.

96. Ibid., pp. 334 ff.

97. Ibid., p. 120.

98. Quoted in Harris Wofford, Jr., "Notre Dame Conference on Civil Rights: A Contribution to the Development of Public Law," *Notre Dame Lawyer* XXXV (May 1960): 343; *Cong. Rec.,* 86th Congress, 2nd Session, p. 3693.

99. Wofford, "Notre Dame Conference on Civil Rights," 342–343.

100. "Meeting on Civil Rights February 26, 1960," Box 2W(B), Joseph Clark MSS.

101. Harris Wofford, "Notre Dame Conference on Civil Rights," p. 344. *Cong. Rec.*, 86th Congress, 2nd Session, pp. 3889, 3895.

102. U.S. Senate, Committee on Rules and Administration, *Hearings on Federal Registrars*, p. 368.

103. Ibid., pp. 363 ff.

104. Wofford, "Notre Dame Conference on Civil Rights," pp. 346, 350; *Cong. Rec.*, 86th Congress, 2nd Session, pp. 3877–3878. *New York Times*, February 10 and 19, 1960. The attorney general did not adopt another of the critics' suggestions. The administration bill gave the right to challenge the qualifications of individuals registered by the referee up to ten days after the court received his report. The civil-rights advocates believed that the correct time for challenges came on election day after the registrant had cast his ballot. In this way, no amount of pre-election legal maneuvers by the state could tie up the Negroes from voting.

105. Daniel M. Berman, *A Bill Becomes A Law: The Civil Rights Act of 1960* (New York: Macmillan, 1962), p. 90.

106. *New York Times,* January 7, 1960.

107. Seymour Halpern and John Lindsay to Dwight Eisenhower, January 25, 1960, OF 102-B-3, DDEL; Harlow Memo was attached to the Halpern-Lindsay letter; Dwight Eisenhower to Seymour Halpern and John Lindsay, January 26, 1960. Eisenhower wrote, "I feel . . . that it is inappropriate for a President to intrude into strictly procedural questions in either body of Congress," but privately the White House applied some pressure. *Newsweek* LV (February 19, 1960): 26; Washington *Post*, February 18, 1960.

108. Berman, *Bill Becomes A Law*, p. 58.

109. See *New York Times*, July 3, 1957, and January 22, 1971, for Russell's obituary; *Time* LXXXV (March 14, 1960): 19.

110. Washington *Post*, March 1, 1960. The next day Russell stated that any idea of compromise was "furthest on earth from my mind."

111. *Cong. Rec.*, 86th Congress, 2nd Session, p. 4450.

112. March 3, 1960.

113. *New York Times*, March 2, 1960.

114. Roy Wilkins and Arnold Aronson to Estes Kefauver, March 5, 1960, Box 1, Series 1, Kefauver MSS; Berman, *Bill Becomes A Law*, pp. 82–83; *Cong. Rec.*, 88th Congress, 2nd Session, pp. 4909–4911.

115. *New York Times*, March 8, 1960. As Eisenhower returned home from the tour he asked Halleck, "You got the filibuster broken yet?" The newspaper reported that those along the receiving line laughed because the delay was in the Senate, not in the House.

116. James L. Sundquist, *Politics and Policy* (Washington, D.C.: Brookings Institution, 1968), p. 49.

117. March 11, 1960.

118. Ibid., March 17, 1960.

119.. Berman, *Bill Becomes A Law*, p. 99. *Cong. Rec.*, 86th Congress, 2nd Session, pp. 5477, 5479, 6297, 6308.

120. *Cong. Rec.*, 86th Congress, 2nd Session, pp. 5644 ff.

121. *New York Times*, March 16, 1960.

122. *Cong. Rec.*, 86th Congress, 2nd Session, p. 5770.

123. Ibid., p. 5755.

124. The final package included: (a) criminal penalties for obstruction of desegregation orders, (b) criminal penalties for crossing interstate lines to avoid prosecution for the destruction of any building, (c) a requirement that state officials preserve federal election records for two years and make them available to the attorney general for inspection, (d) federally subsidized education for children of military personnel in areas where local schools had closed to avoid desegregation, and (e) federal referees.

125. *Cong. Rec.*, 86th Congress, 2nd Session, p. 5870; Joseph Clark to the Washington *Post*, March 13, 1960, Box 2-W(a), Clark MSS.

126. William Rogers to Everett Dirksen, March 22, 1960, in *Cong. Rec.*, 86th Congress, 2nd Session, p. 6265.

127. The seven Democrats were Hayden (Arizona), Frear (Delaware), Anderson and Chavez (New Mexico), Kerr (Oklahoma), Green (Rhode Island), and Kefauver (Tennessee).

128. U.S. Senate, Committee on the Judiciary, *Hearings on H.R. 8601*, 86th Congress, 2nd Session (Washington, D.C., 1960), p. 23.

129. Ibid., p. 41.

130. Kefauver, Johnston, Ervin, McClellan, Eastland, O'Mahoney, and Carroll outnumbered Hart, Hennings, Dirksen, Hruska, Keating, and Cotton.

131. Joseph Bruce Gorman, *Kefauver: A Political Biography* (New York: Oxford University Press, 1971), pp. 315, 328, 329, 337–338. *Newsweek* LV (April 23, 1960): 38.

132. *Cong. Rec.*, 86th Congress, 2nd Session, p. 7040.

133. Ibid., p. 7026.

134. Ibid., p. 7137.

135. U.S. Senate Committee on the Judiciary, *Report to Accompany H.R. 8601, Part 2*, p. 9; *Cong. Rec.*, 86th Congress, 2nd Session, p. 7223. Donald J. Kemper, *Decade of Fear: Senator Hennings and Civil Liberties* (Columbia: University of Missouri Press, 1965), pp. 214–215.

136. *Cong. Rec.*, 86th Congress, 2nd Session, p. 7225. Twenty-seven Democrats and twenty-four Republicans whipped the twenty-seven Democrats and eleven Republicans who favored the Hart bill.

137. Ibid., p. 7769.

138. *Congressional Quarterly Weekly* XVIII (May 6, 1960): 773.

139. Emanuel Celler to Irving J. Panzer, April 1, 1960, Box 460, Celler MSS.

140. *Cong. Rec.*, 86th Congress, 2nd Session, p. 7805.

141. *Nation* XCX (April 23, 1960): 345.

142. *New York Times,* April 22, 1960.

143. *Congressional Quarterly Weekly* XVIII (May 6, 1960): 763.

144. Pittsburgh *Courier,* April 23, 1960.

145. *Congressional Quarterly Weekly* XVIII (May 6, 1960): 763; *Cong. Rec.,* 86th Congress, 2nd Session, p. 7808.

146. *New York Times,* April 6 and 22, 1960.

147. *Cong. Rec.,* 86th Congress, 2nd Session, p. 7808.

148. Washington *Post,* April 9, 1960.

149. Estes Kefauver to J. B. Avery, May 5, 1960, Ser. 1, Box 9, Kefauver MSS.

150. Wofford, "Notre Dame Conference on Civil Rights," p. 354.

151. Elliff, "The Justice Department," p. 550.

152. Washington *Post,* April 5, 1960; *New York Times,* September 15, 1960.

153. Jack Peltason, *Fifty-Eight Lonely Men* (New York: Random House, 1961), p. 253.

9. THE SUFFRAGE CRUSADE IN THE SOUTH: THE KENNEDY PHASE

1. Oscar Glantz, "The Negro Voter in Northern Industrial Cities," *Western Political Quarterly* XIII (December 1960): 1010.

2. Quoted in Harry Golden, *Mr. Kennedy and the Negroes* (New York: Fawcett World Library, 1964), p. 130.

3. Arthur Schlesinger, Jr., *A Thousand Days* (Boston: Houghton-Mifflin, 1965), p. 928; *Afro-American,* June 11, 1960. Roy Wilkins displayed the liberals' ambivalence concerning Kennedy. On May 29, 1958 he wrote the senator that Negroes were disturbed "because, while they know that logic and tradition would seem to dictate that you could not be in the Dixiecrat camp, you are hailed by the Dixiecrat leaders of South Carolina, Georgia, and Mississippi, which along with Alabama, are the 'worst' states on the Negro question." However, on October 19, 1958, with Kennedy up for reelection, the NAACP executive secretary commended him to the Massachusetts Citizens' Committee for Minority Rights because his "record taken as a whole . . . must be regarded as one of the best voting records on civil rights of any Senator." Pre-Presidential Papers, Box 497, John F. Kennedy Library (JFKL).

4. Quoted in L. D. Reddick, *Crusader Without Violence* (New York: Harper, 1959), p. 206.

5. *New York Times,* June 21, 1960. See the *Afro-American,* May 28, 1960, for another view.

6. *Afro-American,* June 25, 1960.

7. Writing in the *Nation* at the outset of the campaign Henry Lee Moon pointed out that Nixon was more conservative fiscally than was Kennedy, "not an asset among people needing change." But he balanced this liability

with the fact that the vice president, unlike the Democrat, was not associated with any of the southern racists. "The Negro Voter," *Nation* CLXXXI (September 17, 1960): 155–157.

8. Schlesinger, *Thousand Days*, pp. 928–929.

9. Richard Bardolph (ed.), *The Civil Rights Record* (New York: Crowell, 1970), p. 360; U.S. Senate, Committee on Commerce, *Speeches, Remarks, Press Conferences, and Statements of Senator John F. Kennedy* (Washington, D.C., 1961), pp. 147, 432, 1012.

10. U.S. Senate, Committee on Commerce, *Speeches, Remarks of Kennedy,* pp. 449–450.

11. Ibid., p. 69.

12. U.S. Senate, Committee on Commerce, *Joint Appearances of Senator John F. Kennedy and Vice President Richard M. Nixon* (Washington, D.C., 1961), p. 450.

13. Bardolph, *Civil Rights Record*, pp. 360–361. The vice president also alerted his listeners in the North to the fact that a Republican victory would make his running mate, Henry Cabot Lodge, presiding officer of the Senate. In this capacity, he would make crucial decisions, as Nixon had favorably done, with respect to civil-rights legislation. Nixon further asserted that Lyndon Johnson, as a senator, had voted against his rulings to allow bills to bypass the Judiciary Committee and to permit the Senate by majority vote to change the cloture procedure at each new session. See U.S. Senate, Committee on Commerce, *The Speeches, Remarks, Press Conferences, and Study Papers of Vice President Richard M. Nixon* (Washington, D.C., 1961), p. 694.

14. Theodore Sorensen, *Kennedy* (New York: Harper, 1965), pp. 211–212.

15. *Afro-American*, October 8, 1960.

16. U.S. Senate, Committee on Commerce, *Speeches . . . Nixon*, pp. 266, 275, 297, 303.

17. Theodore White, *The Making of the President 1960* (New York: Atheneum, 1961), pp. 324–326.

18. *Amsterdam News*, October 29, 1960; Chicago *Defender*, October 29, 1960. The *Defender* also complained that when Lodge had proposed appointing a Negro to the Cabinet, Nixon had ignored the suggestion.

19. *Afro-American*, August 13, 1960.

20. *Amsterdam News*, September 3, 1960.

21. Ibid.

22. Chicago *Defender*, October 8, 1960.

23. White, *Making of the President 1960*, pp. 385 ff; Theodore Sorensen, "Election of 1960," in Arthur Schlesinger, Jr. and Fred Israel (eds.), *History of Presidential Elections, 1789–1968* (New York: McGraw-Hill, 1971), p. 3466.

24. Richard M. Nixon, *Six Crises* (Garden City: Doubleday, 1962), p. 362.

25. Ibid., p. 363. The announcement which Deputy Attorney General Lawrence Walsh prepared, read, "It seems to be fundamentally unjust that a

man who has peacefully attempted to establish his right to equal treatment free from racial discrimination be imprisoned on an old, unrelated and relatively insignificant charge, driving without a license. Further, it is important that the nations of the free world understand that this is not the action of the U.S. government. Accordingly, I have asked the Attorney General to take all proper steps to join with Dr. King in an appropriate application to vacate this sentence." "Suggested Statement Prepared by Lawrence E. Walsh, 10/31/60," OF 142-A-4, DDEL. Publicly, Nixon informed the press that he had "no comment." White, *Making of the President 1960*, p. 378.

26. *Afro-American*, November 5, 1960.

27. White, *Making of the President*, p. 387. On the eve of the election, the senator reminded Philadelphia's black ghetto dwellers that Nixon had issued a "no comment" statement. "If that is what you want, you can have him," he shouted. See U.S. Senate, Committee on Commerce, *Speeches . . . Kennedy*, p. 829.

28. *Amsterdam News*, November 5, 1960. One pre-election survey showed that Negroes were going to vote Democratic even before the King episode. In Detroit, 39 percent of the Protestant population were black. A survey conducted less than two weeks prior to the 1960 election showed that of the Protestant Truman voters who had switched to Eisenhower only 23 percent of the whites would return to the Democratic party, while for Negroes the return to the Democratic party was 63 percent. See Roberta S. Sigel, "Race and Religion as Factors in the Kennedy Victory in Detroit, 1960," *Journal of Negro Education* XXXI (Fall 1962): 444.

29. Sorensen, *Kennedy*, p. 245.

30. Nixon carried Virginia and Florida. White, *Making of the President*, pp. 387, 424, 430; Richard Scammon, "How Negroes Voted," *New Republic* CXLIII (November 21, 1960): 8, 9.

31. Angus Campbell, et al., *Elections and the Political Order* (New York: Wiley, 1966), p. 234.

32. White, *The Making of the President*, p. 424.

33. Ibid., pp. 432–433. In 1960, southern Democrats in the House voted against the position taken by a majority of their northern partisans on 40 percent of all roll-call votes. An average of seventy-three southerners joined the conservative Republicans. Helen Fuller, *Year of Trial* (New York: Harcourt Brace World, 1962), p. 71.

34. James L. Sundquist, *Politics and Policy: The Eisenhower, Kennedy, and Johnson Years* (Washington, D.C.: Brookings Institution, 1968), p. 255. On the Republican side, eighteen senators led by Everett Dirksen joined the thirty-two Democrats.

35. Fuller, *Year of Trial*, p. 77. Sorensen, *Kennedy*, pp. 380 ff.

36. Sorensen, *Kennedy*, p. 534.

37. Ibid., p. 382.

38. Ibid., p. 529.

39. For an incisive elaboration of the Kennedy strategy see Harris Wofford, Memorandum to President-Elect Kennedy on Civil Rights—1961, December 30, 1960, Box 21, 1960 Campaign Files, Robert F. Kennedy MSS. Personal interview with William Taylor, October 28, 1970, Washington, D.C. In March, 1961, Joe Rauh made the case for new civil-rights legislation, but the president replied, "No, I can't go for legislation at this time. I hope you have liked my appointments. I'm going to make some more, and Bobby will bring voting suits." Schlesinger, *Thousand Days*, p. 931. Sorensen, *Kennedy*, chapter 18.

40. Sorensen, *Kennedy*, pp. 537, 538.

41. Fuller, *Year of Trial*, p. 116; as a candidate, Kennedy had remarked to some of his civil-rights supporters that his attorney general would "hire a corps of lawyers and prepare cases against the disfranchisement of the Negroes in the South." Golden, *Mr. Kennedy and the Negroes*, p. 187.

42. Elliff, "Justice Department and Civil Liberties," p. 653.

43. Ibid. The publicity campaign was to accompany the department's legal efforts and consisted of placing placards on Post Office walls urging citizens to register. Fred Dutton to JFK, October 5, 1961; William Taylor to Fred Dutton and Harris Wofford, October 30, 1961, OF 374, JFKL.

44. Leslie Dunbar to the Southern Regional Council Executive Committee, July 31, 1961, Voter Education Project Files, SRC Headquarters. August Meier and Elliot Rudwick, *CORE: A Study of the Civil Rights Movement 1942–1968* (New York: Oxford University Press, 1973), pp. 173, 174.

45. Dunbar to SRC Executive Committee, July 31, 1961, VEP Files.

46. Howard Zinn, *SNCC* (Boston: Beacon Press, 1964), pp. 58–59.

47. Bob Moses to Chicago Friends of SNCC, February 27, 1963, VEP Files, SRC. For a biographical sketch of Moses, see Zinn, *SNCC*, and Jack Newfield, *A Prophetic Minority* (New York: New American Library, 1966), pp. 74 ff.

48. John O'Neal to Wiley Branton, December 11, 1962, VEP Files, SRC.

49. SNCC Executive Secretary James Forman recalled: ". . . working on voter registration was indeed a dangerous thing in the South and those working on it would get all the direct action they needed once they ran up against Southern sheriffs." *The Making of Black Revolutionaries* (New York: Macmillan, 1972), p. 235.

50. Louis Lomax, *The Negro Revolt* (New York: Harper, 1963), p. 248.

51. Roy Wilkins to Leslie Dunbar, October 17, 1961, VEP Files, SRC.

52. Leslie Dunbar to Roy Wilkins, November 10, 1961; Wilkins to Dunbar, November 22, 1961, VEP Files, SRC.

53. Quoted in Schlesinger, *Thousand Days*, p. 935.

54. Memo from James Farmer to Stephen Courier, August 1961, VEP Files, SRC.

55. Lester Granger to Stephen Courier, August 14, 1961, VEP Files, SRC.

56. "First Annual Report of the Voter Education Project of the Southern Regional Council, April 1, 1962–March 31, 1963," VEP Files, SRC.

57. "First Status Report, VEP, September 20, 1962," "Grants and Quantitative Results of the VEP Programs During the First Half of Fiscal Year 1963;" "Results of VEP Programs, April 1, 1962–March 31, 1964," VEP Files, SRC. The NAACP drew tougher duty in Fayette and Haywood, Tennessee, while SCLC worked in easier localities in Virginia, and CORE operated in several cities in Florida. James Forman wrote that in 1962, Roy Wilkins voiced opposition to SNCC's intention to concentrate on the rural South. The NAACP secretary, according to Forman, believed that the activities should be carried on in urban areas. *Making of Black Revolutionaries,* p. 266.

58. Wiley Branton to Aaron Henry, September 5, 1962, VEP Files, SRC.

59. Louis Lomax first revealed that should "Negroes encounter trouble as they attempt to register, the Justice Department will close in . . . and not only clear the path to the voting booth but provide protection for Negroes who register and vote." *Negro Revolt,* pp. 250, 253. Meier and Rudwick, *CORE,* maintain that Robert Kennedy promised "that Justice Department personnel, including FBI teams, would provide all possible aid and cooperation," p. 173. For a similar interpretation, see Pat Watters and Reese Cleghorn, *Climbing Jacob's Ladder* (New York: Harcourt Brace World, 1967), p. 47.

60. Quoted in Victor Navasky, *Kennedy Justice* (New York: Atheneum, 1971), p. 118. Fleming added that a promise of protection "may have been understood. But Burke was scarcely one to overstate these things." Personal interview with Maceo Hubbard, October 26, 1970, Washington, D.C. Hubbard, a black Justice Department lawyer who attended some of the meetings, said no federal protection was guaranteed.

61. Personal interview with Wiley Branton, October 21, 1970, Washington, D.C.

62. Ibid.; Helen Fuller, *Year of Trial,* p. 133; Navasky, *Kennedy Justice,* p. 207.

63. Robert Walters to Richard Rettig and Tim Jenkins, June 16, 1961; Edward Hollander Papers, copy supplied courtesy of August Meier and Elliot Rudwick.

64. "Schedule of Estimated Annual Expenses, CORE Voter Registration Program," August 17, 1961, VEP Files, SRC.

65. U.S. Congress, House of Representatives, Committee on Appropriations, *Hearings,* 89th Congress, 1st Session, p. 21.

66. Burke Marshall, *Federalism and Civil Rights* (New York: Columbia University Press, 1964), p. 23; Navasky, *Kennedy Justice,* p. 163.

67. Marshall, *Federalism and Civil Rights,* p. 24.

68. U.S. Senate, Committee on the Judiciary, *Hearings on the Nomination of*

Burke Marshall, 89th Congress, 1st Session, pp. 4, 5. It was Marshall's predecessor, Harold Tyler, who had begun initiating cases in the South without a formal complaint. Golden, *Mr. Kennedy and the Negroes,* pp. 142–143. Alan Lichtman, "The Federal Assault Against Voting Discrimination in the Deep South, 1957–1967," *Journal of Negro History* LIV (October 1969): 346–367.

69. U.S. Department of Justice, *Attorney General Reports,* 1962, p. 166.

70. *U.S. v. Penton,* 212 F. Supp. 193 (1962). For a handy and detailed compendium of the important lower-court cases, consult Donald Strong, *Negroes, Ballots, and Judges* (University, Alabama: University of Alabama Press, 1968).

71. *U.S. v. Lynd,* 301 F. 2nd 818 (1962).

72. *U.S. v. Wilder,* 222 F. Supp. 749 (1963).

73. Charles V. Hamilton, "Southern Federal Courts and the Rights of Negroes to Vote, 1957–1962" (unpublished doctoral dissertation, University of Chicago, 1964), pp. 205–206.

74. *U.S. v. Penton,* 212 F. Supp. 193 (1962); "Federal Protection of Negro Voting Rights," *Virginia Law Review* LI (1965): 113 ff; "Freezing Voter Qualifications to Aid Negro Registration," *Michigan Law Review* LXIII (March, 1965): 938. For a complete account of another case which confirmed the principle of freezing, *U.S. v. Duke,* F. 2nd 759 (1964), see Frederick M. Wirt, *The Politics of Southern Equality* (Chicago: Aldine, 1970).

75. *U.S. v. Ward,* 222 F. Supp. 617 (1963), *U.S. v. Manning,* 205 F. Supp. 172 (1962).

76. Hamilton, "Southern Judges," p. 264.

77. *U.S. v. Board of Education of Green County, Race Relations Law Reporter* VII (1962) 770.

78. *U.S. v. Edwards, Race Relations Law Reporter* IX *(RRLR)* 800 (1964).

79. Peter R. Treachant, "Louisiana Underlaw," in: Leon Friedman (ed.), *Southern Justice* (New York: Pantheon, 1965), pp. 57–79; Marvin Braiterman, "Harold and the Highwaymen," in: Friedman (ed.), *Southern Justice,* pp. 88–104, for a tragicomic account of the situation.

80. U.S. Department of Justice, *Attorney General Reports,* 1961. The case was *U.S. v. Deal.* Atlas never did manage to register. Strong, *Negroes, Ballots, and Judges,* p. 11.

81. *Attorney General Reports, 1961.* The cases were *U.S. v. Beaty, U.S. v. Barcroft,* and *U.S. v. Atkeison.*

82. *U.S. v. Bruce,* 353 F. 2nd 475 (1965). By the time the case was settled, the insurance company had transferred its agent to another part of the state. Strong, *Negroes, Ballots, and Judges,* p. 13.

83. *U.S. v. Wood,* 295 F. 2nd 772 (1961).

84. Jack Chatfield to Wiley Branton, December 11, 1962; VEP Files, SRC; *U.S. v. Matthews, et al., RRLR,* IX (1964), 225; Atlanta *Constitution,* January 28, 1964.

85. "Federal Protection of Negro Voting Rights," *Virginia Law Review* LI

(1965): 1195–1196; Watters and Cleghorn, *Climbing Jacob's Ladder*, Appendix II.

86. Marshall, *Federalism and Civil Rights*, p. 24.

87. Ibid., p. 31.

88. Elbert P. Tuttle, "Equality and the Vote," *New York University Law Review* XLI (April 1966): 264. Tuttle's liberal brethren were John Minor Wisdom of Louisiana, Richard T. Rives of Alabama, and John R. Brown of Texas.

89. Charles V. Hamilton, *The Bench and the Ballot: Southern Federal Judges and Black Voters* (New York: Oxford University Press, 1973), chapters 5, 6, 7; Navasky, *Kennedy Justice*, pp. 244, 248–249. Cox did find discrimination against Negroes in Clarke County, but he did not interpret this as part of a pattern or practice. Since only one black, the school principal, had qualified to vote during the past thirty years, the Court of Appeals reversed Cox's finding, which it called "clearly erroneous." See Gerald M. Stern, "Judge William Harold Cox and the Right to Vote in Clarke County, Mississippi," in: Friedman (ed.), *Southern Justice*, p. 172.

90. Quoted in Strong, *Negroes, Ballots, and Judges*, p. 71.

91. Hamilton, *Bench and Ballot*, pp. 126–136, when the Justice Department offered statistics to show that only twenty-five of 7,495 adult blacks were enrolled in Forrest County, Cox retorted, "I think the Court should take judicial notice of the illiteracy that is prevalent among the colored people, and I do know . . . the intelligence of the colored people don't [*sic*] compare ratio wise to white people. I mean that is just a matter of common knowledge. Mentioning figures like that to me wouldn't mean a thing in the world without something to go along with it."

92. Wirt, *Politics of Southern Equality*, pp. 93, 102 ff.

93. Marshall, *Federalism and Civil Rights*, p. 31; Donald P. Kommers, "The Right to Vote and Its Implementation," *Notre Dame Lawyer* XXXIX (June 1964): 391.

94. Navasky, *Kennedy Justice*, pp. 48, 244, 250–251. Kennedy appointed four other resisters: (a) E. Gordon West (Louisiana), (b) Robert Elliot (Georgia), (c) Clarence Allgood (Alabama), and (d) Walter Gewin (Alabama). Sorensen, *Kennedy*, p. 532, points out that the president also appointed five black federal judges in the North, including Thurgood Marshall.

95. The quotation is from a study done by Mary Curzan, cited in Navasky, *Kennedy Justice*, p. 270.

96. Carver Neblett to Wiley Branton, December 11, 1962, VEP Files, SRC.

97. "Southwest Georgia Voter Registration Project" (no date), VEP Files, SRC.

98. Aaron Henry to Robert Kennedy, April 14, 1963, VEP Files, SRC.

99. Zinn, *SNCC*, pp. 82–91; Jack Minnis, "Notes on Telephone Conversations with Samuel Block, August 8, 14, and 17, 1962," VEP Files, SRC;

"Surplus Commodity Program in Mississippi and Leflore County," prepared by Dick Gregory, April 4, 1963, VEP Files, SRC. Since 1955, the U.S. Department of Agriculture had given Mississippi surplus foods. Each county decided whether it wanted the produce and had to pay for the cost of storage and distribution. About 75–90 percent of the recipients in Mississippi were Negroes.

100. Wiley Branton to Robert Kennedy, March 1, 1963, VEP Files, SRC.

101. Wiley Branton to Robert Kennedy, March 29, 1963, VEP Files, SRC. Martin Luther King, about to embark on his crusade in Birmingham, also demanded federal intervention in Greenwood. King to Robert Kennedy, March 27, 1963, VEP Files, SRC.

102. Watters and Cleghorn, *Climbing Jacob's Ladder,* pp. 60–62.

103. Wiley Branton, "Chronology of Events Following the Shooting of James Travis in Leflore County, Mississippi on February 28, 1963," Entry for April 4, VEP Files, SRC. *New York Times,* April 6, 1963. In part the rebels accepted the compromise, because they had some doubts that the government would be able to obtain an injunction allowing people to parade in large numbers. Furthermore, on March 20, the Leflore County Board of Supervisors voted to resume, for one month, a full-scale food distribution program; see SNCC News Release, March 20, 1963, VEP Files, SRC. Yet by January, 1964, only 281 Negroes, or 1.6 percent of the black population, had managed to register to vote. U.S. Commission on Civil Rights, *Voting in Mississippi* (Washington, D.C., 1965), p. 71.

104. Forman, *Making of Black Revolutionaries,* p. 302.

105. Ibid.

106. SNCC, "Special Report: Selma, Alabama," September 26, 1963, VEP Files, SRC.

107. U.S. Senate, Committee on the Judiciary, *Hearings on Voting Rights* (Testimony of Nicholas Katzenbach), 89th Congress, 1st Session, pp. 10–11; SNCC, Special Report: Selma, Alabama," September 26, 1963, VEP Files, SRC; Zinn, *SNCC,* chapter 8.

108. Howard Zinn, "Registration in Alabama," *New Republic* CXLIX (October 26, 1963): 11–12. See Burke Marshall's reply, *New Republic* CXLIX (November 16, 1963): 29–30. For photographs of the incident, see Lorraine Hansberry (ed.), *The Movement* (New York: Simon and Schuster, 1964), pp. 62–63.

109. "Complaint of Robert Moses, *et al.* Against Robert F. Kennedy and J. Edgar Hoover," filed in the U.S. District Court for Washington, D.C., and reprinted in U.S. Congress, House of Representatives, Committee on the Judiciary, *Hearings on Civil Rights,* 1963, 88th Congress, 1st Session, pp. 1280–1283.

110. Quoted in Wirt, *Politics of Southern Equality,* p. 82.

111. U.S. Congress, House of Representatives, Committee on the Judiciary, *Hearings on Civil Rights, 1963,* 88th Congress, 1st Session, p. 1252.

112. Quoted in Barbara Carter, "The Fifteenth Amendment Comes to Mississippi," *Reporter* XXVIII (January 17, 1963): 23.

113. *Public Papers of the President, John F. Kennedy, 1962* (Washington, D.C., 1963), pp. 676–677.

114. Burke Marshall, *Federalism and Civil Rights,* p. 5. Robert Kennedy told the House Judiciary Committee: "Neither the Federal Bureau of Investigation nor the marshals are a national police department in the United States. Our authority in these matters is limited." U.S. Congress, House of Representatives, Committee on the Judiciary, *Hearings on Civil Rights,* 1963, 88th Congress, 1st Session, p. 1430.

115. Nicholas Katzenbach to John V. Lindsay, July 30, 1964, as reprinted in the *Cong. Rec.,* 88th Congress, 2nd Session, pp. 18661–18662.

116. Marshall, *Federalism and Civil Rights,* p. 5. A sign on Marshall's desk reflected his dilemma: "Blessed Are the Peacemakers, for they catch hell from both sides." Wirt, *Politics of Southern Equality,* p. 87.

117. Nicholas Katzenbach to Lyndon Johnson, July 1, 1964, Hu2 St24, Box 26, LBJL.

118. Marshall, *Federalism and Civil Rights,* p. 30.

119. Paul Douglas to Steve Antler, October 23, 1964, Legislative Files, Box 100 R 04, Douglas MSS.

120. *New Republic* CXLIX (October 26, 1963): 3.

121. *Cong. Rec.,* 88th Congress, 2nd Session, p. 15646; "Notre Dame Conference on Congressional Civil Rights Legislation—A Report," *Notre Dame Lawyer* XXXVIII (June 1963): 444.

122. Haywood Burns, "The Federal Government and Civil Rights," in Friedman, *Southern Justice,* p. 238. Navasky, *Kennedy Justice,* pp. 52 ff, has noted Robert Kennedy's zealous and innovative use of the FBI to battle organized crime, compared with his sluggishness in pushing the agency into the civil-rights field.

123. Richard A. Wasserstrom, "Federalism and Civil Rights," *University of Chicago Law Review* XXXIII (Winter 1966): 413.

124. U.S. Congress, House of Representatives, Committee on the Judiciary, *Hearings on Civil Rights, 1963,* 88th Congress, 1st Session, p. 1264. From September, 1957 to August, 1965, the Civil Rights Division dispatched marshals in sixteen situations concerning freedom rides, twenty-six incidents involving school desegregation, and twice during incidents dealing with voter registration. Lichtman, "Federal Assault Against Voting Discrimination," p. 362.

125. Burke Marshall Memo to Byron White, July 14, 1961, Burke Marshall Papers, Box 1, JFKL.

126. Lee White to Burke Marshall, October 22 and 29, 1962, OF Box 374, JFKL.

127. Burke Marshall to Harry Schwartz, August 10, 1963, Box 2w(A), Joseph Clark MSS.

128. Hamilton, *The Bench and the Ballot*, p. 220.

129. Wiley Branton to Aaron Henry and Robert Moses, November 12, 1963, VEP Files, SRC.

130. Elizabeth Wyckoff to Wiley Branton, December 11, 1962, VEP Files, SRC.

131. *Student Voice* (SNCC), September 11, 1963; "Make Believe Vote," *Newsweek* (October 28, 1963): 23; Jeannine Herron, "Underground Election," *Nation* CXCVII (December 7, 1963): 387–389; Watters and Cleghorn, *Climbing Jacob's Ladder*, p. 67.

132. Transcript of Aaron Henry Interview with Martha M. Roberts (no date), VEP Files, SRC.

133. Forman, *Making of Black Revolutionaries*, p. 265.

134. Robert Moses, "Report on Mississippi Voter Registration Project," December 5, 1962, VEP Files, SRC. For evidence that Moses welcomed Justice Department success more than failure, see Forman, *Making of Black Revolutionaries*, p. 306, and Barbara Carter, "The Fifteenth Amendment," p. 23.

10. WE SHALL OVERCOME

1. *New York Times*, May 9, 1961. The suffrage proposals eliminated poll taxes and literacy tests as requirements for voting in federal elections. Joseph Clark expressed his disappointment to the president but understood Kennedy's political difficulties. Joseph Clark, "Oral History," John F. Kennedy Library (JFKL).

2. Roy Wilkins to Harris Wofford, April 5, 1961, Box 11, Harris Wofford Files, JFKL.

3. Martin Luther King, Jr., "Fumbling on the New Frontier," *Nation* CXCIV (March 3, 1962): 190–193.

4. United States Commission on Civil Rights, *Report on Voting* (Washington, D.C., 1961), p. 71. U.S. Commission on Civil Rights, *Hearings Held in New Orleans, Louisiana* (Washington, D.C., 1961), pp. 229 ff. When put to the test by the commissioners, the registrar of Plaquemines Parish could not correctly compute her age in years, months, and days. She admitted to failing blacks for making similar errors.

5. CCR, *Voting*, p. 100.

6. Ibid., pp. 139, 140.

7. U.S. Senate, Committee on the Judiciary, *Hearings on Literacy Tests*, 87th Congress, 2nd Session (Washington, D.C., 1962), p. 264.

8. Burke Marshall to Lee White, February 19, 1962, Box 1 (Chronological File), JFKL; Burke Marshall, memo for the president, "Constitutionality of Poll Tax Legislation" (no date), Box 1, Lee White Files, JFKL. While Marshall believed that the Fifteenth Amendment authorized Congress to remove poll-tax payments by statute, he noted that Senator Holland of Florida, the original proponent of the measure, was "particularly opposed to

the statutory method." Thus, the assistant attorney general suggested that if "pressing for a statute would result in nothing being done, we should clearly indicate that we think an amendment is also appropriate."

9. U.S. Senate, Committee on the Judiciary, *Hearings on Literacy Tests,* pp. 271, 292.

10. Ibid., p. 454.

11. Ibid., pp. 118–119.

12. Ibid., p. 28.

13. Ibid., pp. 226–227.

14. *Congressional Record,* 87th Congress, 2nd Session, p. 7167. This was H.R. 1361, "for the relief of James M. Norman."

15. Senate Judiciary Committee, *Hearings on Literacy Tests,* p. 45.

16. *Lassiter v. Northampton County Board of Elections,* 360 U.S. 45, 51 (1959). For the rebuttal that Lassiter did not prevent reasonable congressional action to eliminate discriminatory administration of literacy exams and to ensure the purity of federal elections, see Donald P. Kommers, "The Right to Vote and its Implementation," *Notre Dame Lawyer* XXXIX (June 1964): 408; Kathryn M. Werdegar, "The Constitutionality of Federal Legislation to Abolish Literacy Tests," *George Washington Law Review* XXX (April 1962): 741; Douglas Maggs and Lawrence Wallace, "Congress and Literacy Tests: A Comment on Constitutional Power and Legislative Abnegation," *Law and Contemporary Problems,* XXXVII (Summer 1962): 523.

17. *Congressional Record,* 87th Congress, 2nd Session, pp. 7170, 7797.

18. *Public Papers of the Presidents, John F. Kennedy, 1962* (Washington, D.C., 1963), pp. 382–383.

19. *Congressional Record,* 87th Congress, 2nd Session, pp. 7365, 7835. The Democratic senators who switched were: Bible and Cannon (Nevada), Monroney (Oklahoma), Gore and Kefauver (Tennessee), Byrd (West Virginia), and McGee (Wyoming). The Republicans were: Williams (Delaware), Capehart (Indiana), Miller (Iowa), Carlson and Pearson (Kansas), Morton (Kentucky), Curtis and Hruska (Nebraska), Case and Mundt (South Dakota), Bennett (Utah), Aiken and Prouty (Vermont), and Wiley (Wisconsin).

20. *Time* LXXIX (May 18, 1962): 16. Asked to comment on the cloture attempts, Kennedy told the press: "Senator Mansfield is trying . . . but if we don't succeed, if the Senate doesn't succeed . . . then of course there is no use saying you're for it because it won't ever come up." *Public Papers . . . 1962,* pp. 382–383. The lessons that Kennedy derived, according to Theodore Sorensen, were that the bill could not pass without virtually unanimous support, and a filibuster would kill most of his other legislative proposals, including those for better housing and jobs which would help Negroes. Theodore Sorensen, *Kennedy* (New York: Harper, 1965), p. 533.

21. John T. Elliff, "The United States Department of Justice and Individual Rights, 1932–1962" (unpublished doctoral dissertation, Harvard Univer-

sity, 1967), pp. 663–665. In July, 1960, Philip Marcus, an Anti-Trust Division attorney on loan to the Civil Rights Division, drafted a complaint attacking the constitutionality of registration procedures in Mississippi and Alabama. Philip Marcus, Memo to Attorney General Robert Kennedy, January 25, 1961, Burke Marshall Files, Box 20, JFKL.

22. *U.S. v. Louisiana,* 225 F. Supp. 353 (1963).

23. Ronnie Moore to Wiley Branton, May 13, 1964, VEP Files.

24. *U.S. v. Mississippi,* 229 F. Supp. 925 (1964).

25. *Public Papers, Kennedy, 1962,* pp. 222–223.

26. U.S. Congress, House of Representatives, Committee on the Judiciary, *Hearings on Civil Rights,* 88th Congress, 1st Session (Washington, D.C., 1963), pp. 1253–1254.

27. Ibid., p. 1340. Moses told the Committee: "Since Mississippi has provided a separate and unequal education and many black adults have been deprived of schooling, this country has an inescapable obligation either to register those people or to provide a massive adult education program for them so that they can attain this degree of literacy that you stipulated they have to have in order to vote," p. 1256.

28. Ibid., pp. 1242, 1347, 2172.

29. Lerone Bennett, *Before the Mayflower* (Baltimore: Penguin Books, 1966), p. 340.

30. House Judiciary Committee, *Hearings, 1963,* p. 1353.

31. *Public Papers, Kennedy, 1963,* p. 484. On June 11, Kennedy had told a nationwide television audience, "The fires of frustration and discord are burning in every city. We face . . . a moral crisis. It cannot be met by repressive police action. It cannot be left to increased demonstrations in the streets. It cannot be quieted by token moves or talk." *Public Papers,* p. 469.

32. The president was under great pressure to act from the liberals of his party. In January 1963 Senators Hubert Humphrey, Joseph Clark, Paul Douglas, Philip Hart, and Harrison Williams informed Kennedy "that many Democratic members of the Senate Class of 1958 believe strongly that their reelection in 1964 will be materially affected by the Democratic civil-rights record compiled by the 88th Congress. We agree." Letter to John F. Kennedy, January 8, 1963, Box 2w(c), Joseph Clark MSS.

33. "Differences Between Administration's February and June, 1963 Voting Proposals and Title I of the Civil Rights Act of 1964" (no date), Box 3, Lee White Files, Lyndon Baines Johnson Library (LBJL). Before this provision was deleted, the Justice Department had considered it "far more important practically than the literacy provision." Nicholas Katzenbach to Emanuel Celler, August 13, 1963, Box 465, Celler MSS.

34. *Public Papers, Kennedy, 1963,* p. 896.

35. Burke Marshall, *Federalism and Civil Rights* (New York: Columbia University Press, 1964), pp. 37–38.

36. *New York Times,* November 27, 1963.

37. "Notes on Senator Johnson's remarks to Clarence Mitchell and other delegates to January 13–14, 1960 Legislative Conference on Civil," Box 13 (Civil Rights), Senatorial Papers, LBJL.

38. Tom Wicker, *JFK and LBJ: The Influence of Personality Upon Politics* (Baltimore: Penguin Books, 1969), p. 176.

39. U.S. Commission on Civil Rights, *Report* (Washington, D.C., 1963), p. 13.

40. Ibid., p. 30.

41. Ibid., pp. 28, 29, 67.

42. Clarence Mitchell, "Oral History," LBJL.

43. Lyndon Baines Johnson, *The Vantage Point* (New York: Holt Rinehart Winston, 1971), p. 161.

44. Lerone Bennett, Jr., "SNCC: Rebels With A Cause," *Ebony* XX (July 1965): 148; Andrew Kopkind, "Seat Belts for Mississippi's Five," *New Republic* CLIII (July 24, 1965): 17–18.

45. Stokely Carmichael and Charles V. Hamilton, *Black Power* (New York: Vintage Books, 1967), p. 89; Leslie Burl McLemore, "The Freedom Democratic Party and the Changing Political Status of the Negro in Mississippi" (unpublished Master's Thesis, Atlanta University, 1965), pp. 42–44, 49, 55.

46. Len Holt, *The Summer That Didn't End* (New York: William Morrow, 1965), pp. 156, 162–163.

47. Quoted in Noel Day to Clifford Alexander, June 9, 1964, Box 5, Lee White Files, LBJL.

48. Robert F. Kennedy to Lyndon B. Johnson, June 5, 1964, Box 1, FG 135; Lee White to Lyndon Johnson, June 17, 1964, Box 55, Hu 2–7, LBJL.

49. Nicholas Katzenbach to Lyndon B. Johnson, July 1, 1964, Box 26, Hu 2 ST 24, LBJL. Katzenbach admitted the president could invoke Title 10, Sections 332 and 333 of the United States Code permitting military action when state law enforcement had broken down. He noted that it was hard to dispute "the group of law professors which has publicly taken issue with the statement . . . that there was no adequate legal basis for federal law enforcement in Mississippi." For the legal scholars' argument and Katzenbach's public response see *Congressional Record*, 88th Congress, 2nd Session, pp. 15645, 18651. After the Mississippi killings, the record of the FBI in voter intimidation cases noticeably improved. For an insightful discussion of the entire problem, see John Doar and Dorothy Landsberg, "The Performance of the FBI in Investigating Violations of Federal Laws Protecting the Right to Vote, 1960–1967," JFKL.

50. Holt, *Summer That Didn't End*, pp. 168–169.

51. Jackson *Clarion Ledger*, August 22, 1964.

52. John Lewis to Lyndon B. Johnson, August 19, 1964, Box 27, Hu 2 ST 24, LBJL.

53. Tampa *Tribune*, August 27, 1964.

54. *New York Times*, August 27, 1964. The Atlanta *Constitution*, August 26,

1964, crowed that the South was treated with respect, and contended that any votes granted to the FDP were "based solely on special circumstances and set no precedent."

55. Theodore White, *The Making of the President 1964* (New York: Atheneum, 1965), p. 277. The author, as did *New York Times* reporter Anthony Lewis, thought that the MFDP's legal case was not strong. White called it "absurd." They did, however, recognize the appeal of the moral argument. *New York Times*, August 27, 1964.

56. Quoted in Holt, *Summer That Didn't End*, p. 178.

57. Memo typed by Juanita Roberts describing the suggestion, August 24, 1964, PL 1 ST 24, LBJL; McLemore, "The Freedom Democratic Party," p. 64.

58. *New York Times*, August 26, 1964.

59. Anne Cooke Romaine, "The Mississippi Freedom Democratic Party Through August, 1964" (unpublished Ph.D. dissertation, University of Virginia, 1969), pp. 312, 316. Walter Reuther was flown in by LBJ and he took the same line. Reuther was president of the UAW, which hired Rauh as counsel.

60. Charles Diggs to Elizabeth Hirshfeld, September 21, 1964, Box 4, MFDP MSS, Martin Luther King Library Center (MLKC).

61. *New York Times*, August 27, 1964.

62. Nelson Poynter, St. Petersburg *Times*, August 26, 1964.

63. Paul Douglas to Russell W. Nash, September 22, 1964, Legislative Files, Box 100 R 04, Douglas MSS.

64. Martin Luther King told Ed King, "Being a Negro leader, I want you to take this, but if I were a Mississippi Negro, I would vote against it." Romaine, "The Mississippi Freedom Democratic Party," p. 279. Bob Moses and James Forman advocated rejection of the deal. James Forman, *Making of Black Revolutionaries* (New York: Macmillan, 1972), pp. 389 ff.

65. "Position Paper September 20, 1964, Reasons for rejection of Atlantic City Compromise," Box 24, MFDP MSS; "Freedom Primer No. 1: The Convention Challenge and the Freedom Vote," pp. 7–8; "Minutes of the Executive Committee for MFDP, September 13, 1964," Box 23, MFDP MSS, MLKC.

66. Carmichael, *Black Power*, p. 92. John Lewis, Personal Interview with Author, March 12, 1970, Atlanta, Georgia.

67. For Johnson's concerns about dealing with Congress, see Eric F. Goldman, *The Tragedy of Lyndon Johnson* (New York: Dell, 1969), pp. 306–309. On the lily whites see Jackson, *Clarion Ledger*, August 26, 1964.

68. Nicholas Katzenbach to Lyndon Johnson (no date), Box 3, Lee White Files, LBJL.

69. Lee White Memo to Lyndon Johnson, November 18, 1964, Box 22, Hu 2/mc; Lee White to Bill Moyers, December 30, 1964, Box 3, Lee White Files, LBJL.

70. "Position Paper on Civil Rights" (no date), filed by Ramsey Clark at the Justice Department on February 5, 1965, Box 3, Hu 2, LBJL.

71. "Justice Department Weekly Legislative Report to Lawrence O'Brien," January 11 and 18, 1965, Box 8 (Reports on Pending Legislation), LBJL. In his January 4th State of the Union message Johnson said, "I propose that we eliminate every remaining obstacle to the right to vote." *Public Papers of the Presidents of the United States: Lyndon B. Johnson, 1965* (2 vols., Washington, D.C., 1965), I, p. 5.

72. Martin Luther King, Jr., "Civil Right No. 1—The Right to Vote," *New York Times Magazine* (March 14, 1965): 21–27.

73. *New York Times,* January 4 and February 4, 1965.

74. *Public Papers, Johnson, 1965,* I, p. 139.

75. *New York Times,* February 10, 1965; David L. Lewis, *King: A Critical Biography* (New York: Praeger, 1970), p. 269.

76. Justice Department Status Report on Pending Legislation, February 15, 1965, Box 9, LBJL.

77. Justice Department Status Report on Pending Legislation, March 1, 1965, Box 9, LBJL.

78. Neil McNeil, *Dirksen: Portrait of a Public Man* (New York: World Publishing, 1970), p. 252; *New York Times,* January 24, 27, 1965.

79. *New York Times,* February 11, 1965.

80. Jack Mendelsohn, *The Martyrs* (New York: Harper, 1966), chapter VII.

81. Lyndon B. Johnson, *Vantage Point,* p. 162.

82. Quoted in *New Republic* CLII (March 20, 1965): 5.

83. Quoted in Eric F. Goldman, *Tragedy of Lyndon Johnson,* p. 370.

84. Fred Miller to George W. Culbertson, April 15, 1965, Leroy Collins MSS, University of South Florida. This eyewitness account reported that King and his SCLC advisers agreed "not to use force during this march and after they were stopped they asked for a few minutes to sing and pray." Leroy Collins, Oral History, University of South Florida, courtesy of Julia Chapman. King denied that he had made any deal with the federal mediators, but he told District Judge Johnson that he never intended to defy the injunction and walk all the way to Montgomery. He said that he did not want to risk the loss of any lives. Martin Luther King, Jr., "Behind the Selma March," *Saturday Review* XLVIII (April 3, 1965): 16; *New York Times,* March 12, 1965. One of LBJ's speech writers, Horace Busby, suggested that if the president were asked at a news conference if a bargain had been made, he should deny it and say: "Neither they on the scene or any of us in Washington knew what would happen until it happened, but I do think Governor Collins and Mr. Doar were extremely helpful, and I am proud of them for the very effective way in which they conducted themselves in a tense and delicate situation." Weekly Report on Developments in the Department of Justice to Jack Valenti and Jack Rosenthal, March 10, 1965, Box 3, Horace

Busby Files, LBJL. When asked about the negotiations, on March 13, all LBJ would publicly say 'was that Collins was among those present in Selma "working to keep the peace and enforce the law." *Public Papers, Johnson, 1965,* I, p. 274. John Doar has recently denied that any deal was worked out with King, and has claimed that he did not know what the minister would do until he actually halted the march in front of the Alabama State troopers. John Doar interview, August 27, 1973, New York City, courtesy of Mark I. Gelfand.

85. *Public Papers, Johnson, 1965,* I, pp. 296–297; Goldman, *Tragedy of Lyndon Johnson,* pp. 371–373. But the troops were not around on March 25th, when three nightriders shot and killed a white volunteer from Detroit, Mrs. Viola Liuzzo. Mendelsohn, *Martyrs,* chapter IX.

86. Goldman, *Tragedy of Lyndon Johnson,* p. 370.

87. *Public Papers, Johnson, 1965,* I, p. 284.

88. Ibid., p. 282.

89. John Lewis to Lee White, April 20, 1965, Box 47, Sp 2–3, 1965/Hu 2-7 (March 15, 1965), LBJL.

90. U.S. Congress, House of Representatives, Committee on the Judiciary, *Hearings on Voting Rights,* 89th Congress, 1st Session (Washington, D.C., 1965), p. 9.

91. Ibid., p. 16.

92. *Louisiana v. U.S.,* 380 U.S. 145 (1965). U.S. Senate, Committee on the ciary, *Hearings on Voting Rights,* 89th Congress, 1st Session (Washington, D.C., 1965), p. 100; "Federal Protection of Negro Voting Rights," *Virginia Law Review* LI (1965): 1204, demonstrates the government's debt to the federal judiciary.

93. James Farmer, James Forman, Martin Luther King, and Lawrence Guyot (MFDP), Memo, February 27, 1965, Box 71, LE/NU 2-7, LBJL.

94. House of Representatives, Committee on the Judiciary, *Hearings, Voting Rights, 1965,* pp. 521, 525–526.

95. Quoted in MacNeil, *Dirksen,* p. 255.

96. *Newsweek* LXV (May 10, 1965): 39. A Gallup poll taken from March 18, 1965, to March 23, 1965, revealed that 49 percent of those polled from the South endorsed a suffrage bill, 37 percent disapproved of it, and 14 percent had no opinion. Seventy-six percent of the national sample favored franchise legislation. George H. Gallup (ed.), *The Gallup Poll* (3 vols., New York: Greenwood Press, 1972), III, 1933–1934.

97. Montgomery *Advertiser,* March 17, 1965. See also Birmingham *News,* March 13, 1965.

98. House Judiciary Committee, *Hearings, Voting Rights,* p. 1.

99. Senate Judiciary Committee, *Hearings, Voting Rights,* p. 153.

100. Nicholas Katzenbach to Lyndon Johnson, May 21, 1965, Box 2, Henry Wilson Files, LBJL.

101. Justice Department Memo to Lee White, March 5, 1965, Box 3, Lee

White Files, LBJL; House Judiciary Committee, *Hearings, Voting Rights,* p. 390.

102. Senate Judiciary Committee, *Voting Rights,* pp. 179, 593; Bureau of the Budget Memo for Lee White, December 17, 1964, Box 3, Lee White Files. Moreover, Katzenbach had enthusiastically backed the 15 percent plan in 1963.

103. *New York Times,* April 10, 1965.

104. MacNeil, *Dirksen,* p. 256.

105. *Congressional Record,* 89th Congress, 1st Session, 9919, 9924, 10039. Republican Clifford Case of New Jersey reminded the minority leader that he had supported a poll-tax repeal bill in 1947. At that time Dirksen had declared, "A poll tax is not a qualification, but it is a restriction."

106. The three "nonpoll-tax" southerners were: Bass (Tennessee), Gore (Tennessee), and Long (Louisiana). A fourth southerner, Yarborough (Texas), joined them. The six Republicans were Boggs (Delaware), Case (New Jersey), Fong (Hawaii), Javits (New York), Kuchel (California), and Smith (Maine).

107. *Public Papers, Johnson, 1965,* I, p. 453.

108. *Congressional Record,* 89th Congress, 1st Session, 9930–9931, 10075. Vance Hartke, Democrat of Indiana, emulated McCarthy and voted with the administration. The antipoll-tax advocates also lost Edward Long of Missouri, an original sponsor of the amendment. Other nonsouthern Democrats against the repealer were: Hayden (Arizona), Bible (Nevada), Anderson and Montoya (New Mexico), Mansfield (Montana), and Monroney (Oklahoma).

109. Ibid., 9272.

110. Bernard Schwartz, *Statutory History of the United States: Civil Rights* (New York: McGraw-Hill, 1970), II, 1469–1472. For example, the attorney general had pointed out that the *ex post facto* concept applied to criminal, not civil, cases. Furthermore, the legislation was not a bill of attainder because the states could petition the judiciary if they wanted to escape coverage. Senate Judiciary Committee, *Hearings Voting Rights,* 1965, p. 61.

111. *Congressional Record,* 89th Congress, 1st Session, 9795.

112. Ibid., p. 8481.

113. Ibid., p. 8295.

114. The three southern Democrats were: Bass and Gore (Tennessee), and Yarborough (Texas).

115. *Public Papers, Johnson, 1965,* I, p. 581. The Senate bill contained an amendment sponsored by Senators Robert Kennedy and Jacob Javits of New York, specifying that a person could not be deprived of the right to vote because of an inability to read or write in English if he demonstrated that he had successfully completed the sixth grade in an American-flag school that was conducted in a language other than English. This provision would apply mainly to the Puerto Rican population centered in New York City.

116. *Congressional Record,* 89th Congress, 1st Session, 15653–15654.

117. Ibid., 15723. The administration's trigger sprang on Alaska, which had a literacy test and where less than 50 percent of the eligible voters had turned out in November, 1964. The reason was not racial discrimination, but cold weather and geographical isolation.

118. Ibid., pp. 15642, 15721, 16219.

119. Ibid., p. 16222.

120. *Public Papers, Johnson, 1965,* II, p. 731.

121. *New York Times,* July 13, 1965.

122. Ibid., July 14, 1965; Goldman, *Tragedy of Lyndon Johnson,* p. 392.

123. *Public Papers, Johnson, 1965,* II, p. 741.

124. *New York Times,* August 8, 1965. The Conference Committee also accepted the Senate provision that allowed non-English speaking citizens with six years of schooling to vote.

125. *Public Papers, Johnson, 1965,* II, p. 842.

126. John Lewis to Lyndon Johnson, August 6, 1965, Box 55, Hu 2-7, LBJL.

127. *Public Papers, Johnson, 1965,* II, p. 842.

128. William M. Kunstler, *Deep in My Heart* (New York: William Morrow, 1966), pp. 324–326.

129. "FDP Meeting, November 10, 1964," MFDP Files, Box 4, MLKC. Rauh, as a member of the Democratic National Committee continued to work for party reform.

130. The subcommittee was chaired by Robert Ashmore of South Carolina. The other southerners were: Watkins Abbitt (Virginia), Joe Waggonner (Louisiana), Sam Gibbons (Florida), Carl Perkins (Kentucky), and John Davis (Georgia). The parent House Committee on Administration, however, consisted of ten southerners out of twenty-five members.

131. Mark De Wolfe Howe Memo, December 22, 1964, Box 4; Leon Shull to ADA National Officers, December 19, 1964, Box 3; Marshall Krause (Northern California ACLU) to "Dear Friend," January 11, 1965, Box 3, MFDP MSS, MLKC; "Memo on Lobbying," June 10, 1965, Box 4, MFDP MSS, MLKC.

132. Shull to ADA National Officers, December 19, 1964, Box 3, MFDP MSS, MLKC.

133. Mike Thelwell to Cooperating Groups for the Challenge, December 24, 1964, Box 4, MFDP MSS, MLKC; Dr. George Wiley to All CORE Chapters, April 7, 1965, Series 1, Box 8, Folder 9, CORE MSS.

134. Emanuel Celler to I. Roodenko, July 21, 1965, Box 469, Celler MSS; Celler to "Dear Friend," January 1965, Box 469, Celler MSS.

135. Kunstler, *Deep in My Heart,* pp. 340 ff.

136. 380 U.S. 128 (1965).

137. U.S. Commission on Civil Rights, *Voting in Mississippi* (Washington, D.C., May 18, 1965), p. 59.

138. *Congressional Record,* 89th Congress, 1st Session, p. 24286.

139. Ibid., pp. 24263, 24264; Jackson *Clarion Ledger,* September 17, 1965. The committee also mentioned that there were not enough disputed black votes to have changed the outcome of the election.

140. Ibid., p. 24264.

141. Ibid., p. 24284.

142. Ibid., p. 24288. Apparently he forgot about the case of Theodore Bilbo before the Senate in 1947.

143. Ibid., p. 24286.

144. Ibid., p. 24272.

145. Ibid., p. 24273.

146. Ibid., p. 24278.

147. Ibid., p. 24264.

148. Albert made one concession to the liberals. He offered an amendment that struck from the resolution language stating that the Mississippi congressmen were "entitled to their seats as Representatives." In accepting the Albert proposal, the House merely dismissed the challenges without condoning discriminatory practices. Ibid., p. 24290.

149. MFDP Press Release (no date), Charles Sherrod Papers, Box 3, MLKC. For a balanced appraisal of the challenge, see Hanes Walton, Jr., *Black Political Parties* (New York: Free Press, 1972), pp. 107–113.

11. FREE AT LAST?

1. *Public Papers of the Presidents, Lyndon B. Johnson, 1965,* II, p. 843.

2. John W. Macy, Jr. to Lyndon Johnson, August 16, 1956, Hu 2–7, LBJL.

3. Remarks of Vernon E. Jordan, Jr., Director of the VEP, to the National Civil Liberties Clearing House, March 21, 1969, Washington, D.C., VEP Files.

4. Quoted in Eric Goldman, *The Tragedy of Lyndon Johnson* (New York: Dell, 1969), p. 393.

5. John W. Macy to Lyndon Johnson, November 1, 1965, Hu 2–7, Box 55, LBJL; L. Thorne McCarty and Russell B. Stevenson, "The Voting Rights Act of 1965: An Evaluation," *Harvard Civil Rights–Civil Liberties Review,* III (Spring 1968): 370–371; United States Commission on Civil Rights, *The Voting Rights Act . . . the first months* (Washington, D.C., 1965), pp. 37–39.

6. McCarty and Stevenson, "The Voting Rights Act," 372. The figures on black registration in the other southern states were: Tennessee, 71 percent; Texas, 63 percent; Florida, 62.5 percent; Virginia, 50 percent.

7. Donald R. Matthews and James W. Prothro, *Negroes and the New Southern Politics* (New York: Harcourt Brace World, 1966), chapter 10.

8. U.S. Commission on Civil Rights, *The Voting Rights Act,* p. 35.

9. McCarty and Stevenson, "The Voting Rights Act," 394.

10. *Public Papers of the Presidents, Lyndon Johnson, 1965,* II, 843.

11. Nicholas Katzenbach, "A Lesson in Responsible Leadership," *New South* XXI (Spring 1966): 50. On November 2, 1965, the attorney general privately emphasized to several civil-rights leaders the "importance of . . . organization at the local level because the problem is not merely the number of Negroes registered but of continuing to get these people actively participating in politics for the first time in their lives." Katzenbach Memo for the President, November 2, 1965, Hu 2-7, Box 55, LBJL.

12. VEP, "The Effects of Federal Examiners and Organized Registration Campaigns on Negro Voter Registration," July 1966, VEP Files.

13. U.S. Commission on Civil Rights, *Political Participation* (Washington, D.C., 1968), pp. 155-156. Of these counties, seventy-six were in Georgia, thirty-two in Alabama, twenty-seven in North Carolina, twenty-five in South Carolina, sixteen in Mississippi, and nine in Louisiana.

14. Katzenbach Memo for the President, November 2, 1965, Hu 2-7, Box 55, LBJL; John Macy reported the same thing, Memo to the President, November 1, 1965, Hu 2-7, Box 55, LBJL.

15. Vernon Jordan, Speech to the Civil Liberties Clearing House, March 21, 1969, VEP Files.

16. U.S. Commission on Civil Rights, *The Voting Rights Act,* p. 43.

17. John Macy to Lyndon Johnson, November 1, 1965, Hu 2-7, Box 55, LBJL.

18. U.S. Commission on Civil Rights, *Political Participation,* p. 155, footnote 6.

19. U.S. Commission on Civil Rights, *Political Participation,* p. 12; McCarty and Stevenson, "The Voting Rights Act," 371; Richard Claude, *The Supreme Court and the Electoral Process* (Baltimore: Johns Hopkins University Press, 1970), p. 123. In Arkansas, Florida, North Carolina, and Tennessee (the figures for Texas were incomplete) the average percentage of adult blacks registered during this same period increased from 51.9 to 62.3. In Virginia, which was required to suspend its literacy tests, but did not receive examiners, the percentage rose from 38.3 to 55.6.

20. Nicholas Katzenbach to William L. Taylor, December 4, 1965, Box 3, Lee White Files, LBJL.

21. Pat Watters and Reese Cleghorn, *Climbing Jacob's Ladder* (New York: Harcourt Brace World, 1967), p. 262.

22. Ibid.; McCarty and Stevenson, "The Voting Rights Act," 383.

23. August Meier, "The Dilemmas of Negro Protest Strategy," *New South* XXXI (Spring 1966): 13; Katzenbach, "A Lesson in Responsible Leadership," 57.

24. McCarty and Stevenson, "The Voting Rights Act," 377.

25. Watters and Cleghorn, *Climbing Jacob's Ladder,* p. 259.

26. U.S. Commission on Civil Rights, *The Voting Rights Act,* p. 4.

27. U.S. Commission on Civil Rights, *Political Participation,* p. 186.

28. U.S. Commission on Civil Rights, *Political Participation,* p. 186. The commission called upon Congress to repeal this amendment.

29. Ibid., pp. 156–157.

30. U.S. Commission on Civil Rights, *Voting Rights Act,* p. 36. For Katzenbach's reply to this report see his letter to William L. Taylor, Commission Staff Director, December 4, 1965, Box 3, Lee White Files, LBJL.

31. U.S. Commission on Civil Rights, *Voting Rights Act,* p. 36.

32. Nicholas Katzenbach to Lyndon Johnson, November 2, 1965, Hu 2–7, Box 55, LBJL.

33. U.S. Commission on Civil Rights, *Political Participation,* p. 16. Of the elected officials twenty-four were in Alabama, twenty-nine in Mississippi, thirty-seven in Louisiana, twenty-one in Georgia, and eleven in South Carolina.

34. Eric Goldman, *Tragedy of Lyndon Johnson,* p. 393.

35. McCarty and Stevenson, "Voting Rights Act," 373–374.

36. U.S. Commission on Civil Rights, *Political Participation,* p. 167. The Commission pointed out that Negroes in the South still were subject to some discriminatory practices by local registrars. Also, states were able to dilute the Negro vote by gerrymandering election districts. For another view that blacks continued to be thwarted in their attempts to enroll and vote, see Charles V. Hamilton, *The Bench and the Ballot* (New York: Oxford University Press, 1973), pp. 240–241.

37. U.S. Commission on Civil Rights, *Political Participation,* p. 134.

38. In 1967, the Democratic National Committee did make some nonbinding suggestions. It recommended that state organizations "undertake minimal affirmative efforts by publicizing . . . party meetings, party office selection procedures, and qualifications for party office, but it is not suggested that State party organizations take such steps as specifically inviting Negro Democrats to party meetings or undertaking voter registration campaigns in Negro communities," the CCR reported. *Political Participation,* p. 133.

39. Ibid., p. 173.

40. Georgia was the only southern state where blacks served on the Democratic Executive Committee. By 1968, the MFDP had collapsed. Many of the COFO organizers had deserted the state, disillusioned with politics. The interracial delegation that attended the convention was put together by labor organizers, white liberals, and the NAACP. Charles N. Fortenberry and F. Glen Abney, "Mississippi: Unreconstructed and Unredeemed," in: William C. Havard (ed.), *The Changing Politics of the South* (Baton Rouge: Louisiana State University Press, 1972), p. 494.

41. Matthews and Prothro, *Negroes and the New Southern Politics,* pp. 479–480.

42. Quotation is from Dr. John Cashin, the head of the all-black National Democratic Party of Alabama. *New York Times,* September 19, 1973, 33.

43. McCarty and Stevenson, "The Voting Rights Act," 374.

44. Matthews and Prothro, *Negroes and New Southern Politics,* p. 481.

45. U.S. Commission on Civil Rights, *The Voting Rights Act,* p. 21.

46. Goldman, *The Tragedy of Lyndon Johnson,* p. 393.

47. C. Vann Woodward, *The Strange Career of Jim Crow* (2nd rev. ed., New York: Oxford University Press), pp. 8–9.

48. Kenneth Vines, "Courts and Political Change in the South," *Journal of Social Issues* XXII (January 1966): 59–62.

49. Charles Sherrod, "An Analysis," December 11, 1962, VEP Files.

50. Paul Douglas to Alberta Dannells, April 8, 1965, Legislative Files, Negro Rights, Box 100 R 01, Douglas MSS.

51. Herman P. Miller, *Rich Man, Poor Man* (New York: Crowell, 1971), p. 77. In 1959, the median income of southern blacks was 46 percent that of whites; in 1968, it was 54 percent.

52. "Transcript of the Testimony of Vernon E. Jordan, Jr., Subcommittee on Constitutional Rights, Senate Judiciary Committee, February 25, 1970," VEP Files.

53. For a discussion of the limited payoff of the franchise, see William R. Keech, *The Impact of Negro Voting* (Chicago: Rand McNally, 1968).

Bibliography

MANUSCRIPT COLLECTIONS

Adams, Sherman. Papers, Dartmouth College Library.
American Civil Liberties Union. Papers, Princeton University Library.
Americans for Democratic Action. Papers, Wisconsin Historical Society.
Bureau of the Budget. Office Files, Washington, D.C.
Busby, Horace. Files, Lyndon B. Johnson Library.
Celler, Emanuel. Papers, Library of Congress.
Clark, Joseph. Papers, Pennsylvania Historical Society.
Collins, Leroy. Papers, University of South Florida Library.
Congress of Racial Equality. Papers, Wisconsin Historical Society.
Connally, Tom. Papers, Library of Congress.
Daniels, Jonathan. Papers, Southern Historical Collection, University of North Carolina.
Douglas, Paul H. Papers, Chicago Historical Society.
Eisenhower, Dwight David. Papers, Dwight D. Eisenhower Library.
Elsey, George. Papers, Harry S. Truman Library.
Harlow, Bryce N. Files, Dwight D. Eisenhower Library.
Hennings, Thomas. Papers, University of Missouri Library.
Hobbs, Sam. Papers, University of Alabama Library.
Johnson, Lyndon Baines. Papers, Lyndon B. Johnson Library.
Johnston, Olin. Papers, University of South Carolina Library.
Kefauver, Estes. Papers, University of Tennessee Library.
Kennedy, John F. Papers, John F. Kennedy Library.
Kennedy, Robert F. Papers, John F. Kennedy Library.
Marcantonio, Vito. Papers, New York Public Library.
Marshall, Burke. Files, John F. Kennedy Library.
Martin, I. Jack. Files, Dwight D. Eisenhower Library.
Maybank, Burnet. Papers, South Carolina Department of Archives.
Mississippi Freedom Democratic Party. Papers, Martin Luther King Library Center.
Morgan, Gerald. Files, Dwight D. Eisenhower Library.
Morrow, E. Frederic. Files, Dwight D. Eisenhower Library.
Nash, Phileo. Files, Harry S. Truman Library.

National Association for the Advancement of Colored People. Papers, Library of Congress.
National Committee to Abolish the Poll Tax. Papers, Negro Collection, Atlanta University.
Nixon, L. A. Papers, Lyndon B. Johnson Library.
Norris, George. Papers, Library of Congress.
Persons, Wilton. Files, Dwight D. Eisenhower Library.
President's Committee on Civil Rights. Records, Harry S. Truman Library.
Rayburn, Sam. Papers, Sam Rayburn Library.
Rogers, William P. Files, Dwight D. Eisenhower Library.
Roosevelt, Franklin D. Papers, Franklin D. Roosevelt Library.
Sherrod, Charles. Papers, Martin Luther King Library Center.
Siciliano, Rocco. Files, Dwight D. Eisenhower Library.
Smith, H. Alexander. Papers, Princeton University Library.
Southern Christian Leadership Conference. Papers, Martin Luther King Library Center.
Southern Conference Educational Fund. Papers, Tuskegee Institute Library.
Southern Conference for Human Welfare. Papers, Tuskegee Institute Library.
Spingarn, Stephen. Files, Harry S. Truman Library.
Truman, Harry S. Papers, Harry S. Truman Library.
United States Commission on Civil Rights. Files, Washington, D.C.
Voter Education Project. Files, Offices of the Southern Regional Council.
White, Lee. Files, Lyndon B. Johnson Library.
White, Lee. Files, John F. Kennedy Library.
Williams, Aubrey. Papers, Franklin D. Roosevelt Library.
Wilson, Henry. Files, Lyndon B. Johnson Library.
Wofford, Harris. Files, John F. Kennedy Library.

Unpublished Materials

Anderson, Robert Lee. "Negro Suffrage in Relation to American Federalism, 1957–1963." Doctoral dissertation, University of Florida, 1964.
Banks, Melvin James. "The Pursuit of Equality: The Movement for First Class Citizenship Among Negroes in Texas, 1920–1950," Doctoral dissertation, Syracuse University, 1962.
Berman, William Carl. "The Politics of Civil Rights in the Truman Administration," Doctoral dissertation, Ohio State University, 1963.
Brittain, Joseph Matt. "Negro Suffrage and Politics in Alabama Since 1870." Doctoral dissertation, Indiana University, 1958.
Bunche, Ralph J. "The Political Status of the Negro," Memorandum for the Carnegie-Myrdal Study, The Negro in America, September 1, 1940.
Elliff, John Thomas. "The United States Department of Justice and Individ-

ual Rights, 1932–1962." Doctoral dissertation, Harvard University, 1967.

Hamilton, Charles V. "Southern Federal Courts and the Right of Negroes to Vote, 1957–1962," Doctoral dissertation, University of Chicago, 1964.

Hazel, David W. "The National Association for the Advancement of Colored People and the National Legislative Process," Doctoral dissertation, University of Michigan, 1957.

McLemore, Leslie Burl. "The Freedom Democratic Party and the Changing Political Status of the Negro in Mississippi," Master's Essay, Atlanta University, 1965.

Romain, Anne Cooke. "The Mississippi Freedom Democratic Party Through August 1964," Doctoral dissertation, University of Virginia, 1969.

Sitkoff, Harvard. "Roosevelt and Civil Rights: A Reconsideration." Paper delivered to the American Historical Association, San Francisco, December 29, 1973.

Stoesen, A. "The Senatorial Career of Claude Pepper," Doctoral dissertation, University of North Carolina, 1964.

Sullivan, Donald Francis. "The Civil Rights Programs of the Kennedy Administration: A Political Analysis," Doctoral dissertation, University of Oklahoma, 1965.

Sulzner, George Theodore, III. "The United States Commission on Civil Rights: A Study of Incrementalism in Policy-Making," Doctoral dissertation, University of Michigan, 1967.

Ware, Gilbert. The National Association for the Advancement of Colored People and the Civil Rights Act of 1957." Doctoral dissertation, Princeton University, 1962.

Whitaker, Hugh Stephen. "A New Day: The Effects of Negro Enfranchisement in Selected Mississippi Counties," Doctoral dissertation, Florida State University, 1965.

Wright, Ruth Cowart. "The Enactment of the Civil Rights Acts of 1866 and 1957," Doctoral dissertation, The American University, 1968.

PUBLIC DOCUMENTS

All of the following, unless otherwise noted, were published at various dates by the Government Printing Office in Washington, D.C.

Brief for Appellees, United States against James G. Raines, in the United States Supreme Court, October Term, 1959. Washington, D.C., 1959.

Brief for the National Association for the Advancement of Colored People, In The Matter of The Investigation of the Mississippi Democratic Primary Campaign of Senator Theodore G. Bilbo, Special Committee To Investigate Senate Campaign Expenditures, 1946. U.S. Senate, 79th Congress (no date).

Brief for Petitioner, Lonnie Smith against S. E. Allwright, in the United States Supreme Court, October Term, 1943. Washington, D.C., 1943.

Brief for Petitioner, L. A. Nixon against James Condon, in the Supreme Court, October Term, 1931. Washington, D.C., 1931.

Brief for Plaintiff in Error, L. A. Nixon against C. C. Herndon and Charles Porres in the Supreme Court, October Term, 1925. Washington, D.C., 1925.

Brief for United States, United States against Alabama, in the Supreme Court, October Term, 1959. Washington, D.C., 1959.

Brief for the United States, in United States against Patrick Classic, in the United States Supreme Court, October Term, 1940. Washington, D.C., 1940.

Brief for the United States, United States against James G. Raines, in the United States Supreme Court, October Term, 1959. Washington, D.C., 1959.

Brief for the United States, United States against Curtis M. Thomas in the United States Supreme Court, October Term, 1959. Washington, D.C., 1959.

Brief of Petitioner, Lane against Wilson, in the Supreme Court, October Term, 1938. Washington, D.C., 1938.

Brief of Respondents, Lane against Wilson, in the United States Supreme Court, October Term, 1938. Washington, D.C., 1938.

Brief on the Merits for R. R. Grovey, in the Supreme Court, October Term, 1934. Washington, D.C., 1934.

President's Committee on Civil Rights. *To Secure These Rights.* 1947.

Public Papers of the Presidents: Dwight D. Eisenhower (8 vols.), 1958–1962.

Public Papers of the Presidents: Lyndon B. Johnson (3 vols.), 1964–1965.

Public Papers of the Presidents: John F. Kennedy (3 vols.), 1962–1964.

Public Papers of the Presidents: Harry S. Truman (8 vols.), 1961–1966.

U.S. Commission on Civil Rights. *Hearings on Voting, Montgomery, Alabama,* 1959.

U.S. Commission on Civil Rights. *Hearings in New Orleans, Louisiana,* 1961.

U.S. Commission on Civil Rights. *Hearings in Jackson, Mississippi,* 1965.

U.S. Commission on Civil Rights. *Political Participation,* 1968.

U.S. Commission on Civil Rights. *Report,* 1959.

U.S. Commission on Civil Rights. *Report, Voting I,* 1961.

U.S. Commission on Civil Rights. *Voting in Mississippi,* 1965.

U.S. Commission on Civil Rights. *The Voting Rights Act . . . the first months,* 1965.

U.S. Congress. *Congressional Record,* 1942–1965.

U.S. Congress. *Memorial Services for Theodore Gilmore Bilbo,* 80th Congress, 2nd Session, 1950.

U.S. Department of Commerce. *Statistical Abstract of the United States, 1970,* 1970.

U.S. Department of Commerce. *Statistical Abstract of the United States, 1971,* 1971.

U.S. Department of Justice, Attorney General. *Annual Report for the Fiscal Year Ended June 30, 1958,* 1958.

U.S. Department of Justice, Attorney General. *Annual Report for the Fiscal Year Ended June 30, 1959,* 1959.

U.S. Department of Justice, Attorney General. *Annual Report for the Fiscal Year Ended June 30, 1960,* 1960.

U.S. Department of Justice, Attorney General. *Annual Report for the Fiscal Year Ended June 30, 1961,* 1961.

U.S. Department of Justice, Attorney General. *Annual Report for the Fiscal Year Ended June 30, 1962,* 1962.

U.S. Department of Justice, Attorney General. *Annual Report for the Fiscal Year Ended June 30, 1963,* 1963.

U.S. Department of Justice, Attorney General. *Annual Report for the Fiscal Year Ended June 30, 1964,* 1964.

U.S. Department of Justice, Attorney General. *Annual Report for the Fiscal Year Ended June 30, 1965,* 1965.

U.S. Department of Justice, Attorney General. *Annual Report for the Fiscal Year Ended June 30, 1966,* 1966.

U.S. House of Representatives, Committee on Appropriations. *Hearings on the Department of Justice,* 86th Congress, 2nd Session, 1960.

U.S. House of Representatives, Committee on Appropriations. *Hearings on the Department of Justice,* 86th Congress, 1st Session, 1959.

U.S. House of Representatives, Committee on Appropriations. *Hearings on the Commission on Civil Rights,* 86th Congress, 1st Session, 1959.

U.S. House of Representatives, Committee on the Judiciary. *Hearings on Civil Rights,* 85th Congress, 1st Session, 1957.

U.S. House of Representatives, Committee on the Judiciary. *Hearings on Civil Rights,* 86th Congress, 1st Session, 1959.

U.S. House of Representatives, Committee on the Judiciary. *Hearings on Voting Rights,* 86th Congress, 2nd Session, 1960.

U.S. House of Representatives, Committee on the Judiciary. *Hearings on Civil Rights,* 88th Congress, 1st Session, 1963.

U.S. House of Representatives, Committee on the Judiciary. *Hearings on Voting Rights, H.R. 6400,* 89th Congress, 1st Session, 1965.

U.S. Senate, Committee on Armed Services. *Hearings on Universal Military Training,* 80th Congress, 2nd Session, 1948.

U.S. Senate, Committee on Commerce. *Report: Speeches, Remarks, Press Conferences, and Statements of Senator John F. Kennedy,* 87th Congress, 1st Session, 1961.

U.S. Senate, Committee on Commerce. *Report: Speeches, Remarks, Press Conferences and Statements of Vice-President Richard M. Nixon,* 87th Congress, 1st Session, 1961.

U.S. Senate, Committee on the Judiciary. *Report 1662,* 77th Congress, 2nd Session, 1942.

U.S. Senate, Committee on the Judiciary. *Hearings on H.R. 1024, Poll Taxes,* 77th Congress, 2nd Session, 1942.

U.S. Senate, Committee on the Judiciary. *Hearings on H.R. 7 Poll Tax,* 78th Congress, 1st Session, 1943.

U.S. Senate, Committee on the Judiciary. *Hearings on Civil Rights,* 84th Congress, 2nd Session, 1956.

U.S. Senate, Committee on the Judiciary. *Hearings on Civil Rights,* 85th Congress, 1st Session, 1957.

U.S. Senate, Committee on the Judiciary. *Hearings on the Nomination of the Members of the Commission on Civil Rights,* 85th Congress, 2nd Session, 1958.

U.S. Senate, Committee on the Judiciary. *Hearings on the Nomination of W. Wilson White,* 85th Congress, 2nd Session, 1958.

U.S. Senate, Committee on the Judiciary. *Hearings on Civil Rights,* 86th Congress, 1st Session, 1959.

U.S. Senate, Committee on the Judiciary. *Report 1205,* 86th Congress, 2nd Session, 1960.

U.S. Senate, Committee on the Judiciary. *Hearings on the Nomination of Burke Marshall,* 87th Congress, 1st Session, 1961.

U.S. Senate, Committee on the Judiciary. *Hearings on Literacy Tests and Voter Requirements in State and Federal Elections,* 87th Congress, 2nd Session, 1962.

U.S. Senate, Committee on the Judiciary. *Hearings on Civil Rights: The President's Program,* 88th Congress, 1st Session, 1963.

U.S. Senate, Committee on the Judiciary. *Hearings on Voting Rights: S. 1564,* 89th Congress, 1st Session, 1965.

U.S. Senate, Committee on Rules and Administration. *Hearings on Federal Registrars,* 86th Congress, 2nd Session, 1960.

COURT CASES

Baskin v. Brown, 174 F. 2d 391 (1949).

Biggs v. Beeler, 173 S. W. 2d 144 (1943).

Breedlove v. Suttles, 302 U.S. 277 (1938).

Brown v. Baskin, 78 F. Supp. 933 (1948).

Chapman v. King, 1954 F. 2d 460 (1946).

Davis v. Schnell, 81 F. Supp. 872 (1949).

Elmore v. Rice, 72 F. Supp. 516 (1947).

Ex parte Yarbrough, 110 U.S. 651 (1884).

Giles v. Harris, 189 U.S. 475 (1903).

Gomillion v. Lightfoot, 365 U.S. 339 (1960).

Grovey v. Townsend, 295 U.S. 45 (1935).

Guinn v. United States, 238 U.S. 347 (1915).

Hannah v. Larche, 363 U.S. 420 (1960).

Harper v. Virginia State Board of Elections, 383 U.S. 663 (1966).

James v. Bowman, 190 U.S. 127 (1903).

King v. Chapman, 62 F. Supp. 639 (1945).

Lane v. Wilson, 307 U.S. 268 (1939).

Larche v. Hannah, 117 F. Supp. 816 (1959).

Lassiter v. Northampton County Board of Elections, 360 U.S. 45 (1959).

Louisiana v. United States, 380 U.S. 145 (1965).

Mitchell v. Wright, 69 F. Supp. 698 (1947).

Mitchell v. Wright, 154 F. 2d 924 (1946).

Newberry v. United States, 256 U.S. 323.

Nixon v. Condon, 286 U.S. 73 (1932).

Nixon v. Herndon, 273 U.S. 536 (1927).

Pirtle v. Brown, 118 F. 2d 218 (1941).

Rice v. Elmore, 1965 F. 2d 387 (1947).

Saunders v. Wilkins, 152 F. 2d 235 (1945).

Screws v. United States, 325 U.S. 91 (1945).

Smith v. Allwright, 321 U.S. 649.

South Carolina v. Katzenbach, 383 U.S. 301 (1966).

Terry v. Adams, 345 U.S. 461 (1953).

United States v. Alabama, 171 F. Supp. 720 (1959).

United States v. Alabama, 362 U.S. 602 (1960).

United States v. Classic, 313 U.S. 299 (1941).

United States v. Cruikshank, 92 U.S. 542 (1876).

United States v. Duke, F. 2d 759 (1964).

United States v. Louisiana, 225 F. Supp. 353 (1963).

United States v. Lynd, 301 F. 2d 810 (1962).

United States v. McElveen, 177 F. Supp. 355 (1959).

United States v. Mississippi, 229 F. Supp. 925 (1964).

United States v. Mississippi, 380 U.S. 128 (1965).

United States v. Penton, 212 F. Supp. 193 (1962).

United States v. Raines, 172 F. Supp. 552 (1959).

United States v. Reese, 92 U.S. 214 (1876).

United States v. Wood, 295 F. 2d 772 (1963).

Williams v. Mississippi, 170 U.S. (1898).

BOOKS

Adams, Sherman. *First Hand Report,* Harper, New York, 1961.

Alexander, Charles C. *The Ku Klux Klan in the Southwest,* University of Kentucky Press, Lexington, 1965.

Anderson, J. W. *Eisenhower, Brownell, and the Congress, The Tangled Origins of the Civil Rights Bill of 1956–1957,* University of Alabama Press, University, 1964.

Arnall, Ellis, *The Shore Dimly Seen,* Lippincott, Philadelphia, 1946.

Auerbach, Jerold S. *Labor and Liberty,* Bobbs-Merrill, Indianapolis, 1966.

Bardolph, Richard (ed.). *The Civil Rights Record,* Crowell, New York, 1970.

Barnard, William D. *Dixiecrats and Democrats: Alabama Politics, 1942–1950,* University of Alabama Press, University, 1974.

Bartley, Numan V. *The Rise of Massive Resistance,* Louisiana State University Press, Baton Rouge, 1970.

Bennett, Lerone, Jr. *Before the Mayflower,* Penguin Books, Baltimore, 1966.

Bennett, Lerone, Jr. *Confrontation Black and White,* Penguin Books, Baltimore, 1965.

Berman, Daniel M. *A Bill Becomes A Law,* 2nd ed., Macmillan, New York, 1966.

Berman, William C. *The Politics of Civil Rights in the Truman Administration,* Ohio State University Press, Columbus, 1970.

Bernstein, Barton J. *Towards A New Past: Dissenting Essays in American History,* Vintage Books, New York, 1969.

Berry, Mary. *Black Resistance White Law,* Appleton-Century-Crofts, New York, 1971.

Biddle, Francis. *In Brief Authority,* Doubleday, Garden City, 1962.

Bilbo, Theodore G. *Take Your Choice: Separation or Mongrelization,* Dream House, Poplarville, Miss., 1947.

Bolling, Richard. *House Out of Order,* Dutton, New York, 1965.

Brady, Tom P. *Black Monday,* Winona, Mississippi: Citizens' Councils of America, 1955.

Brock, W. R. *An American Crisis,* St. Martin's Press, New York, 1963.

Buni, Andrew. *The Negro in Virginia Politics, 1902–1965,* University of Virginia Press, Charlottesville, 1967.

Burns, James MacGregor. *John Kennedy: A Political Profile,* Harcourt Brace and World, New York, 1960.

Campbell, Angus, et al. *Elections and the Political Order,* Wiley, New York, 1966.

Carmichael, Stokely, and Hamilton, Charles V. *Black Power,* Vintage, New York, 1967.

Carr, Robert K. *Federal Protection of Civil Rights: Quest for a Sword,* Cornell University Press, Ithaca, 1947.

Carter, Dan T. *Scottsboro,* Oxford University Press, New York, 1969.

Carter, Hodding, III. *The South Strikes Back,* Doubleday, Garden City, 1959.

Casdorph, Paul. *A History of the Republican Party in Texas 1865–1965,* Pemberton Press, Austin, 1965.

Claude, Richard. *The Supreme Court and the Electoral Process,* Johns Hopkins Press, Baltimore, 1970.

Congressional Quarterly Service. *Revolution in Civil Rights,* Congressional Quarterly Service, Washington, D.C., 1965.

Cook, James Graham. *The Segregationists,* Appleton-Century-Crofts, New York, 1962.

Dabney, Virginius. *Below the Patomac,* Kennikat, New York, 1942.

Dalfiume, Richard. *Desegregation of the U.S. Armed Forces: Fighting on Two Fronts, 1939–1953,* University of Missouri Press, Columbia, 1969.

Davis, Allen F. *Spearheads for Reform: The Social Settlements and the Progressive Movement, 1890–1914,* Oxford University Press, New York, 1967.

Degler, Carl N. *Out of Our Past,* rev. ed., Harper, New York, 1970.

De Santis, Vincent P. *Republicans Face the Southern Question: The New Departure Years, 1877–1897,* Johns Hopkins University Press, Baltimore, 1959.

Dinnerstein, Leonard. *The Leo Frank Case,* Columbia University Press, New York, 1968.

Donovan, Robert J. *Eisenhower: The Inside Story,* Harper, New York, 1956.

Douglas, Paul H. *In the Fullness of Time,* Harcourt Brace Jovanovich, New York, 1971.

Du Bois, W. E. B. *The Souls of Black Folk,* McClurg, Chicago, 1903.

Du Bois, W. E. B. (ed.). *An Appeal To The World,* NAACP, New York, 1947.

Dulles, Foster Rhea. *The Civil Rights Commission: 1957–1965,* University of Michigan Press, Ann Arbor, 1968.

Eisenhower, Dwight D. *Waging Peace, 1956–1961,* Doubleday, Garden City, 1965.

Elazar, Daniel. *American Federalism: A View from the States,* Crowell, New York, 1972.

Evans, Rowland, and Novak, Robert. *Lyndon B. Johnson: The Exercise of Power,* New American Library, New York, 1966.

Evers, Charles. *Evers,* World, New York, 1971.

Forman, James. *Sammy Younge, Jr.,* Grove Press, New York, 1968.

Forman, James. *The Making of Black Revolutionaries,* Macmillan, New York, 1972.

Franklin, John Hope. *Reconstruction: After the Civil War,* University of Chicago Press, Chicago, 1961.

Frederickson, George M. *The Black Image in the White Mind: The Debate on Afro-American Character and Destiny 1817–1917,* Harper and Row, New York, 1971.

Freidel, Frank. *FDR and the South,* Louisiana State University Press, Baton Rouge, 1965.

Friedman, Leon (ed.). *Southern Justice,* Pantheon, New York, 1965.

Fuller, Helen. *Year of Trial: Kennedy's Crucial Decisions,* Harcourt Brace World, New York, 1962.

Gallup, George H. (ed.). *The Gallup Poll* (3 vols.), Greenwood Press, New York, 1972.

Garfinkel, Herbert. *When Negroes March,* Atheneum, New York, 1969.

Garson, Robert A. *The Democratic Party and the Politics of Sectionalism, 1941–1948,* Louisiana State University Press, Baton Rouge, 1974.

Gillette, William. *The Right to Vote: Politics and the Passage of the Fifteenth Amendment,* Johns Hopkins University Press, Baltimore, 1969.

438   BIBLIOGRAPHY

Golden, Harry. *Mr. Kennedy and the Negroes,* Fawcett World Library, New York, 1964.

Goldman, Eric F. *The Tragedy of Lyndon Johnson,* Dell, New York, 1969.

Gorman, Joseph Bruce. *Kefauver: A Political Biography,* Oxford University Press, New York, 1971.

Green, A. Wigfall. *The Man Bilbo,* Louisiana University Press, Baton Rouge, 1963.

Guzman, Jessie P., et al. *Negro Year Book, 1952,* Wise, New York, 1952.

Hackney, Sheldon. *Populism to Progressivism in Alabama,* Princeton University Press, 1969.

Hale, Robert L. *Freedom Through Law,* Columbia University Press, New York, 1952.

Hamilton, Charles V. *The Bench and the Ballot: Southern Federal Judges and Black Voters,* Oxford University Press, New York, 1973.

Hansberry, Lorraine. *The Movement,* Simon and Schuster, New York, 1964.

Harlan, Louis R. *Booker T. Washington: The Making of a Black Leader, 1856–1901,* Oxford University Press, New York, 1972.

Havard, William C. (ed.). *The Changing Politics of the South,* Louisiana State University Press, Baton Rouge, 1972.

Hays, Brooks. *A Southern Moderate Speaks,* University of North Carolina Press, 1959.

Heard, Alexander. *A Two Party South?* University of North Carolina Press, Chapel Hill, 1952.

Herbers, John. *The Lost Priority: What Happened to the Civil Rights Movement in America,* Funk and Wagnalls, New York, 1970.

Hirshson, Stanley P. *Farewell to the Bloody Shirt: Northern Republicans and the Southern Negro, 1877–1893,* University of Indiana Press, Bloomington, 1962.

Holt, Lee. *The Summer That Didn't End,* William Morrow, New York, 1965.

Howard, J. Woodford, Jr. *Mr. Justice Murphy: A Political Biography,* Princeton University Press, 1968.

Johnson, Lyndon B. *The Vantage Point: Perspectives of the Presidency, 1963–1969,* Holt Rinehart Winston, New York, 1971.

Jones, Lewis, and Smith, Stanley. *Voting Rights and Economic Pressure,* Anti-Defamation League, New York, 1958.

Keech, William R. *The Impact of Negro Voting,* Rand McNally, Chicago, 1968.

Kellogg, Charles Flint. *NAACP,* Johns Hopkins Press, Baltimore, 1967.

Kemper, Donald J. *Decade of Fear: Senator Hennings and Civil Liberties,* University of Missouri Press, 1965.

Kennedy, Stetson. *Southern Exposure,* Doubleday, Garden City, 1946.

Key, V. O. *Southern Politics in State and Nation,* Vintage Books, New York, 1949.

Kirby, Jack Temple. *Darkness At the Dawning: Race and Reform in the Progressive South,* Lippincott, Philadelphia, 1972.

Kirwan, Albert D. *Revolt of the Rednecks: Mississippi Politics, 1876–1925,* University of Kentucky Press, Lexington, 1951.

Kousser, J. Morgan. *The Shaping of Southern Politics: Suffrage Restriction and the Establishment of the One Party South, 1880–1910,* Yale University Press, New Haven, 1974.

Krueger, Thomas A. *And Promises to Keep: The Southern Conference for Human Welfare, 1938–1948,* Vanderbilt University Press, Nashville, 1967.

Kunstler, William M. *Deep in My Heart,* William Morrow, New York, 1966.

Ladd, Everett C. *Negro Political Leadership in the South,* Cornell University Press, Ithaca, 1966.

Larson, Arthur. *Eisenhower: The President Nobody Knew,* Charles Scribner's, New York, 1968.

Leuchtenburg, William E. *Franklin D. Roosevelt and the New Deal,* Harper, New York, 1963.

Lewinson, Paul. *Race, Class, and Party,* Universal Library, New York, 1965.

Lewis, Anthony. *Portrait of a Decade,* Random House, New York, 1964.

Lewis, David L. *King: A Critical Biography,* Praeger, New York, 1970.

Litwack, Leon F. *North of Slavery,* University of Chicago Press, Chicago, 1961.

Logan, Rayford (ed.). *The Attitude of the Southern White Press Toward Negro Suffrage, 1932–1940,* Foundation Publishers, Washington, D.C., 1940.

Logan, Rayford. *The Betrayal of the Negro,* Collier, New York, 1965.

Logan, Rayford (ed.). *What the Negro Wants,* University of North Carolina Press, Chapel Hill, 1944.

Lokos, Lionel. *House Divided: The Life and Legacy of Martin Luther King, Jr.,* New Rochelle, New York: Arlington House, 1968.

Lomax, Louis. *The Negro Revolt,* Harper, New York, 1963.

Longaker, Richard P. *The Presidency and Individual Liberties,* Cornell University Press, Ithaca, 1961.

Lubell, Samuel. *The Future of American Politics,* rev. ed., Doubleday, Garden City, 1955.

McCord, William. *Mississippi: the long, hot summer,* Norton, New York, 1965.

McCoy, Donald, and Reutten, Richard T. *Quest and Response: Minority Rights and the Truman Administration,* University of Kansas Press, Lawrence, 1973.

McGovney, Dudley O. *The American Suffrage Medley,* University of Chicago Press, Chicago, 1949.

McMillen, Neil R. *The Citizens' Council: Organized Resistance to the Second Reconstruction, 1954–64.* University of Illinois Press, Urbana, 1971.

MacNeil, Neil. *Dirksen: Portrait of a Public Man,* World, New York, 1970.

McPherson, Henry. *A Political Education,* Little Brown, Boston, 1972.

Marshall, Burke. *Federalism and Civil Rights,* Columbia University Press, New York, 1964.

Mason, Alpheus T. *Harlan Fiske Stone: Pillar of the Law,* Viking Press, New York, 1956.

Matthews, Donald R., and Prothro, James W. *Negroes and the New Southern Politics,* Harcourt Brace World, New York, 1966.

Meier, August. *Negro Thought in America, 1880–1915,* University of Michigan Press, Ann Arbor, 1963.

Meier, August, and Broderick, Francis (eds.). *Black Protest Thought in the Twentieth Century,* 2nd ed., Bobbs-Merrill, Indianapolis, 1971.

Meier, August, and Rudwick, Elliot. *CORE: A Study of the Civil Rights Movement, 1942–1968,* Oxford University Press, New York, 1973.

Mendelsohn, Jack. *The Martyrs,* Harper, New York, 1966.

Metcalf, George R. *Black Profiles,* McGraw-Hill, New York, 1968.

Miller, Herman P. *Rich Man, Poor Man,* Cornell, New York, 1971.

Miller, Loren. *The Petitioners,* Pantheon Books, New York, 1966.

Moon, Henry Lee. *Balance of Power: The Negro Vote,* Doubleday, Garden City, 1948.

Morrow, E. Frederic. *Black Man in the White House,* Coward-McCann, New York, 1963.

Murphy, Paul L. *The Constitution in Crisis Times, 1918–1969,* Harper, New York, 1972.

Muse, Benjamin. *Ten Years of Prelude: The Story of Integration Since The Supreme Court's 1954 Decision,* Viking Press, New York, 1964.

Muse, Benjamin. *The American Negro Revolution,* University of Indiana Press, Bloomington, 1968.

Myrdal, Gunnar. *An American Dilemma,* Harper, New York, 1944.

NAACP. *Annual Reports,* 1944–1957.

National Committee to Abolish The Poll Tax. *Labor's Stake in Abolishing the Poll Tax,* Washington, D.C., 1947.

Navasky, Victor. *Kennedy Justice,* Atheneum, New York, 1971.

Newfield, Jack. *A Prophetic Minority,* New American Library, New York, 1966.

New School for Social Research, *The Poll Tax,* Washington, D.C., 1942.

Nixon, Richard M. *Six Crisis,* Doubleday, Garden City, 1962.

Nolen, Claude H. *The Negro's Image in the South: The Anatomy of White Supremacy,* University of Kentucky Press, Lexington, 1967.

Ogden, Frederic D. *The Poll Tax in the South,* University of Alabama Press, University, 1958.

Parmet, Herbert S. *Eisenhower and the American Crusade,* Macmillan, New York, 1972.

Parsons, Talcott, and Clark, Kenneth (eds.). *The Negro American,* Beacon Press, Boston, 1965.

Patterson, James. *Congressional Conservatism and the New Deal,* University of Kentucky Press, Lexington, 1967.

Peltason, J. W. *Fifty-Eight Lonely Men: Southern Federal Judges and School Desegregation*, Random House, New York, 1961.

Perry, Jennings. *Democracy Begins At Home*, Lippincott, Philadelphia, 1944.

Phillips, Cabell. *The Truman Presidency: The History of a Triumphant Succession*, Macmillan, New York, 1966.

Porter, Kirk H. *A History of Suffrage in the United States*, Greenwood Press, New York, 1969.

Price, Hugh D. *The Negro and Southern Politics: A Chapter of Florida History*, New York University Press, 1957.

Price, Margaret. *The Negro and the Ballot in the South*, Southern Regional Council, Atlanta, 1959.

Price, Margaret. *The Negro Voter in the South*, Southern Regional Council, Atlanta, 1957.

Reddick, L. D. *Crusader Without Violence: A Biography of Martin Luther King, Jr.*, Harper, New York, 1959.

Redding, J. Saunders. *Lonesome Road*, Doubleday, Garden City, 1958.

Reznikoff, Charles (ed.). *Louis Marshall Champion of Liberty, Selected Papers and Addresses*. Jewish Publication Society of America, Philadelphia, 1957.

Rice, Lawrence D. *The Negro in Texas, 1874–1900*, Louisiana State University Press, Baton Rouge, 1971.

Ross, B. Joyce. *J. E. Spingarn and the Rise of the NAACP*, Oxford University Press, New York, 1972.

Rowell, Chester A. (compiler). *Digest of Contested Election Cases, 1789–1901*, Government Printing Office, Washington, D.C., 1901.

Schaffer, Alan. *Vito Marcantonio: Radical in Congress*, Syracuse University Press, 1966.

Schlesinger, Arthur M., Jr. *A Thousand Days*, Houghton-Mifflin, Boston, 1965.

Schlesinger, Arthur M., Jr. (ed.). *History of American Presidential Elections, 1789–1968* (4 vols.), McGraw-Hill, New York, 1971.

Schwartz, Bernard. *Statutory History of the United States: Civil Rights*, McGraw-Hill, New York, 1970.

Sherman, Richard B. *The Republican Party and Black America 1896–1933*, University of Virginia Press, Charlottesville, 1973.

Sherrill, Robert. *Gothic Politics in the Deep South; Stars of the New Confederacy*, Grossman, New York, 1968.

Shoemaker, Don (ed.). *With All Deliberate Speed*, Harper, New York, 1957.

Silver, James W. *Mississippi: The Closed Society*, Harcourt Brace World, New York, 1966.

Sindler, Allan P. (ed.). *Change in the Contemporary South*, Duke University Press, Durham, North Carolina, 1963.

Sindler, Allan P. *Huey Long's Louisiana*, Johns Hopkins Press, Baltimore, 1956.

Smith, Constance E. *Voting and Election Laws,* Oceana Publications, New York, 1960.

Sorensen, Theodore. *Kennedy,* Harper, New York, 1965.

Southern, David W. *The Malignant Heritage: Yankee Progressives and the Negro Question 1901–1914,* Loyola University Press, Chicago, 1968.

Stampp, Kenneth. *Era of Reconstruction,* Vintage Books, New York, 1967.

Sternsher, Bernard (ed.). *The Negro in Depression and War: Prelude to Revolution, 1930–1945,* Quadrangle, Chicago, 1969.

Strong, Donald S. *Negroes, Ballots, and Judges,* University of Alabama Press, University, 1968.

Strong, Donald S. *Registration of Voters in Alabama,* University of Alabama Press, University, 1956.

Sundquist, James L. *Politics and Policy: The Eisenhower, Kennedy, and Johnson Years,* Brookings Institute, Washington, D.C., 1968.

Sutherland, Elizabeth (ed.). *Letters From Mississippi,* McGraw-Hill, New York, 1965.

Taper, Bernard. *Gomillion Versus Lightfoot,* McGraw-Hill, New York, 1962.

Tindall, George B. *The Emergence of the New South, 1913–1945,* Louisiana State University Press, Baton Rouge, 1967.

Tindall, George B. *South Carolina Negroes, 1877–1900,* University of South Carolina Press, Columbia, 1952.

Vander Zanden, James. *Race Relations in Transition,* Random House, New York, 1965.

Virginia Writers' Project. *The Negro in Virginia,* Arno Press, New York, 1969.

Walton, Hanes, Jr. *Black Political Parties,* Free Press, New York, 1972.

Watters, Pat, and Cleghorn, Reese. *Climbing Jacob's Ladder,* Harcourt Brace World, New York, 1967.

Wharton, Vernon Lane. *The Negro in Mississippi, 1865–1890,* Harper, New York, 1965.

White, Theodore H. *The Making of the President 1960,* Atheneum, New York, 1961.

White, Theodore H. *The Making of the President 1964,* Atheneum, New York, 1965.

White, Walter. *A Man Called White,* Viking Press, New York, 1948.

Wicker, Tom. *JFK and LBJ: The Influence of Personality Upon Politics,* Penguin Books, Baltimore, 1969.

Williamson, Chilton. *American Suffrage: From Property to Democracy, 1760–1860,* Princeton University Press, 1960.

Williamson, Joel. *After Slavery: The Negro in South Carolina During Reconstruction,* University of North Carolina Press, Chapel Hill, 1969.

Wirt, Frederick M. *Politics of Southern Equality,* Aldine, Chicago, 1970.

Wolters, Raymond. *Negroes and the Great Depression: The Problem of Economic Recovery,* Greenwood Press, Westport, Connecticut, 1970.

Woodward, C. Vann. *Origins of the New South, 1877–1913,* Louisiana State University Press, Baton Rouge, 1951.

Woodward, C. Vann. *Reunion and Reaction,* Little Brown, Boston, 1951.

Woodward, C. Vann. *The Strange Career of Jim Crow,* 2nd rev. ed., Oxford University Press, New York, 1966.

Zinn, Howard. *SNCC,* Beacon Press, Boston, 1964.

ARTICLES

Anthony, Paul. "Pro Segregation Groups' History and Trends," *New South* XII (January 1957): 4–10.

Auerbach, Carl A. "Is It Strong Enough to Do the Job?" *Reporter* XVII (September 5, 1957): 13–15.

Auerbach, Carl A. "Jury Trial and Civil Rights," *New Leader* XL (April 29, 1957): 16–18.

Bacote, Clarence A. "The Negro in Atlanta Politics," *Phylon* 15 (December 1955): 333–350.

Bacote, Clarence A. "The Negro Voter in Georgia Politics Today," *Journal of Negro Education* XXVI (Summer 1957): 307–318.

Barnett, James D. "Constitutional Law—Fourteenth and Fifteenth Amendments—Discrimination against Race in Primary Elections," *Oregon Law Review* XXII (June 1944): 264–269.

Bennett, Lerone, Jr. "SNCC: Rebels With a Cause," *Ebony* XX (June 1965): 146–153.

Bernhard, Berl I. "The Federal Fact Finding Experience—A Guide to Negro Enfranchisement," *Law and Contemporary Problems* XXVII (Summer 1962), pp. 468–480.

Bernstein, Barton J. "The New Deal: Conservative Achievements of Liberal Reform," in: *Towards a New Past,* Barton J. Bernstein (ed.), Vintage Books, New York, 1969: 263–288.

Bernstein, Barton J. "America in War and Peace: The Test of Liberalism," in: *Towards a New Past,* Barton J. Bernstein (ed.), Vintage Books, New York, 1969: 289–321.

Bickel, Alexander M. "Civil Rights: The Kennedy Record," *New Republic* CXLVII (December 15, 1962): 10–16.

Broady, Tally R. "Will Two Good White Men Vouch For You?" *Crisis* LIV (January 1947): 10, 17.

Brownell, Herbert. "Federally Protected Civil Rights," *Vital Speeches* XXII (November 1, 1955): 44–47.

Bullock, Henry Allen. "Expansion of Negro Suffrage in Texas," *Journal of Negro Education* XXVI (Summer 1957): 369–377.

Callopy, Francis W. "Constitutional Law—Elections—Discrimination against Applicants For the Franchise on the Basis of Race or Color—*Davis v. Schnell,*" *Notre Dame Lawyer* XXIV (Summer 1949): 571–574.

Carter, Hodding. "Chip on Our Shoulder Down South," *Saturday Evening Post* CCIXX (November 2, 1946): 18.

Carter, Hodding. "The Man from Mississippi—Bilbo," *New York Times Magazine* (June 30, 1946): 12.

Carter, Barbara. "The Fifteenth Amendment Comes to Mississippi," *Reporter* XXVIII (January 17, 1963): 20–24.

Cater, Douglass. "How the Senate Passed the Civil Rights Bill," *Reporter* XVII (September 5, 1957): 9–13.

Christensen, Janice. "The Constitutionality of National Anti-Poll Tax Bills," *Minnesota Law Review* XXXIII (February 1949): 217–221.

Cothran, Tilman C., and Phillips, William M., Jr. "Expansion of Negro Suffrage in Arkansas," *Journal of Negro Education* XXVI (Summer 1957): 287–296.

Cox, LaWanda, and Cox, John H. "Negro Suffrage and Republican Politics: The Problem of Motivation in Reconstruction Historiography," *Journal of Southern History* XXXIII (August 1967): 303–330.

Current, Gloster. "Martyr for a Cause," *Crisis* LIX (February 1952): 72–81.

Cushman, Robert E. "The Texas 'White Primary' Case—*Smith v. Allwright*," *Cornell Law Quarterly* XXX (September 1944): 66–76.

Ervin, Sam, Jr. "Literacy Tests For Voters: A Case Study in Federalism," *Law and Contemporary Problems* XXVII (Summer 1962): 481–494.

Evans, Luther Harris. "Primary Elections and the Constitution," *Michigan Law Review* XXXII (1934): 451–477.

Fenton, John H. "The Negro Voter in Louisiana," *Journal of Negro Education* XXVI (Summer 1957): 319–328.

Fishel, Leslie H., Jr. "The Negro in the New Deal Era," *Wisconsin Magazine of History* XLVIII (Winter 1964): 111–126.

Fleming, Harold C. "The Federal Executive and Civil Rights, 1961–1965," in: *The Negro American,* Talcott Parsons and Kenneth Clark (eds.), Beacon Press, Boston, 1965.

Fleming, Harold C. "Negro Vote-Getter," *Reporter* II (March 28, 1950): 18–20.

Folsom, Fred G., Jr. "Federal Elections and the 'White Primary'," *Columbia Law Review* XLIII (November–December, 1943): 1026–1035.

Fortenberry, Charles N., and Abney, F. Glenn. "Mississippi: Unreconstructed and Unredeemed," in: *The Changing Politics of the South,* William C. Havard (ed.), Louisiana State University Press, Baton Rouge, 1972.

Foster, Vera Chandler. " 'Boswellianism': A Technique in the Restriction of Negro Voting," *Phylon* X (March 1949): 26–37.

Fraenkel, Osmond K. "The Federal Civil Rights Laws," *Minnesota Law Review* XXXI (March 1947): 301–327.

Frank, John P., and Munro, Robert F. "The Original Understanding of 'Equal Protection of the Laws'," *Columbia University Law Review* L (February 1950): 131–169.

Franklin, John Hope. " 'Legal' Disfranchisement of the Negro," *Journal of Negro Education* XXVI (Summer 1957): 241–248.

Glantz, Oscar. "The Negro Voter in Northern Industrial Cities," *Western Political Quarterly* XIII (December 1960): 999–1010.

Gomillion, Charles G. "The Negro Voter in Alabama," *Journal of Negro Education* XXVI (Summer 1957): 281–286.

Good, Paul. "Beyond the Bridge," *Reporter* XXXII (April 8, 1965): 23–26.

Hamilton, Charles V. "Southern Judges and Negro Voting: The Judicial Approach To the Solution of Controversial Social Problems," *University of Wisconsin Law Review,* 1965 (Winter 1965): 71–102.

Hamilton, Charles V. "Blacks and the Crisis in Political Participation," *The Public Interest* XXIV (Winter 1974): 188–210.

Hamilton, Howard. "The Negro Recovers the Ballot," *National Bar Journal* VII (December 1949): 422–425.

Hastie, William H. "Appraisal of *Smith v. Allwright,*" *Law Guild Review* V (March–April, 1945): 65–72.

Heron, Jeannine. "Underground Election," *Nation* CXCVII (December 7, 1963): 387–389.

Hill, Herbert. "Southern Negroes at the Ballot Box," *Crisis* LXI (May 1954): 261–266.

Hixson, William B., Jr. "Moorfield Storey and the Struggle for Equality," *The Journal of American History* LV (December 1968): 533–554.

Hoffman, Bertram. "Constitutional Law—Exclusion of Negroes From Voting at Primaries as Party or State Action," *Marquette Law Review* XXVIII (1944): 116–119.

Horsky, Charles A. "The Supreme Court, Congress, and the Right to Vote," *Ohio State Law Journal* XX (Summer 1959): 549–556.

Irving, Florence B. "The Future of the Negro Voter in the South," *Journal of Negro Education* XXVI (Summer 1957): 390–399.

Jackson, Luther P. "Race and Suffrage in the South Since 1940," *New South* III (June–July 1948): 1–26.

Kallenbach, Joseph C. "Constitutional Aspects of Federal Anti-Poll Tax Legislation," *Michigan Law Review* XLV (April 1947): 717–722.

Katzenbach, Nicholas. "A Lesson in Responsible Leadership," *New South* XXI (Spring 1966): 55–60.

Kenworthy, John and Kenworthy, E. W. "The 'Understanding Neorger' and His Right to Vote," *Reporter* XXX (March 26, 1964): 32–34.

King, Martin Luther, Jr. "Behind the Selma March," *Saturday Review* XLVIII (April 3, 1965): 16–18.

King, Martin Luther, Jr. "Civil Rights No. 1—The Right to Vote," *New York Times Magazine* (March 14, 1965): 21–27.

King, Martin Luther, Jr. "Fumbling on the New Frontier," *Nation* CXCIV (March 3, 1962): 190–193.

Kirby, John B. "The Roosevelt Administration and Blacks: An Ambivalent Legacy," in: *Twentieth Century America: Recent Interpretations,* Barton J.

Bernstein and Allen J. Matusow (eds.), 2nd ed., New York: Harcourt Brace Jovanovich, 1972.

Lewis, Anthony. "The Professionals Win Out Over Civil Rights," *Reporter* XXII (May 26, 1960): 27–30.

Lewis, Earl M. "The Negro Voter in Mississippi," *Journal of Negro Education* XXVI (Summer 1957): 329–350.

Lichtman, Allan. "The Federal Assault Against Voting Discrimination in the Deep South, 1957–1967," *Journal of Negro History* LIV (October 1969): 346–367.

Lubell, Samuel. "The Future of the Negro Voter in the United States," *Journal of Negro Education* XXVI (Summer 1957): 408–417.

Lytle, Clifford M. "The History of the Civil Rights Bill of 1964," *Journal of Negro History* LI (October 1966): 275–296.

McCain, James T. "The Negro Voter in South Carolina," *Journal of Negro Education* XXVI (Summer 1957): 359–361.

McCarty, L. Thorne, and Stevenson, Russell B. "The Voting Rights Act of 1965: An Evaluation," *Harvard Civil Rights–Civil Liberties Review* III (Spring 1968): 357–411.

McGill, Ralph. "Civil Rights for the Negro," *Atlantic Monthly* CLXXXIV (November 1949): 64–66.

McGill, Ralph. "If the Southern Negro Got the Vote," *New York Times Magazine* (June 21, 1959): 5.

McPherson, James M. "The Antislavery Legacy: From Reconstruction to the NAACP," in: *Towards a New Past,* Barton J. Bernstein (ed.), Vintage Books, New York, 1969, 126–157.

Maggs, Douglas B., and Wallace, Lawrence G. "Congress and Literacy Tests: A Comment on Constitutional Power and Legislative Abnegation," *Law and Contemporary Problems* XXVII (Summer 1962): 510–536.

Marshall, Thurgood. "The Rise and Collapse of the 'White Democratic Primary'," *Journal of Negro Education* XXVI (Summer 1957): 249–254.

Martin, John Barlow. "The Deep South Says Never," *Saturday Evening Post* CCXXIX (June 15, 1957): 23–25.

Matusow, Allen J. "From Civil Rights to Black Power: The Case of SNCC, 1960–1966," in: *Twentieth-Century America: Recent Interpretations,* Barton J. Bernstein and Allen J. Matusow (eds.), 2nd ed., Harcourt Brace Jovanovich, New York, 1972.

Meier, August. "The Dilemmas of Negro Protest Strategy," *New South* XXI (Spring 1966): 1–18.

Meier, August. "On the Role of Martin Luther King," *New Politics* IV (Winter 1965): 52–59.

Meier, August, and Rudwick, Elliot. "Attorneys Black and White: A Case Study of Race Relations within the NAACP," *Journal of American History* LXII (March 1976): 913–946.

Minter, Sam. "Constitutional Law—Primary Elections—State Function

Within the Fifteenth Amendment," *Texas Law Review* XXII (1944): 498–500.

Moon, Henry Lee. "Counted Out and In," *Survey Graphic* XXXVI (January 1947): 8–10.

Moon, Henry Lee. "The Negro Voter in the Presidential Election of 1956," *Journal of Negro Education* XXVI (Summer 1957): 219–230.

Moon, Henry Lee. "The Negro Voter," *Nation* CXCI (September 17, 1960): 155–157.

Moon, Henry Lee. "The Southern Scene," *Phylon* XVI (December 1955): 351–358.

Murphy, Walter F. "Some Strange New Converts to the Cause of Civil Rights," *Reporter* XVI (June 27, 1957): 13–15.

Nabrit, James, Jr. "The Future of the Negro Voter in the South," *Journal of Negro Education* XXVI (Summer 1957): 418–423.

Newton, J. G. "Expansion of Negro Suffrage in North Carolina," *Journal of Negro Education* XXVI (Summer 1957): 351–358.

Note. "Anti-Poll Tax Legislation—Constitutionality," *New York University Law Review* XXI (January 1946): 113–119.

Note. "Federal Protection of Negro Voting Rights," *Virginia Law Review* LI (1965): 1053–1212.

Note. "Freezing Voter Qualifications To Aid Negro Registration," *Michigan Law Review* LXIII (March 1965): 932–938.

Note. "*U.S. v. Classic*," *Illinois Law Review* XXXVI (December 1941): 475–478.

Note. "The White Primary in Texas Since *Nixon v. Condon*," *Harvard Law Review* XLVI (1933): 812–818.

"Notre Dame Conference on Civil Rights Legislation—A Report," *Notre Dame Lawyer* XXXVIII (June 1963): 430–446.

Powell, Adam Clayton, Jr. "The President and the Negro," *Reader's Digest* LXV (October 1954): 61–64.

Purdy, Lawson. "Negro Migration in the United States," *American Journal of Economics and Sociology* XIII (July 1954): 357–362.

"Race and Suffrage Today," *New South* VIII (January 1953): 1–8.

Roady, Elston E. "The Expansion of Negro Suffrage in Florida," *Journal of Negro Education* XXVI (Summer 1957): 297–306.

Rovere, Richard. "Letter From Washington," *The New Yorker* XXXIII (August 31, 1957): 68–78.

Scammon, Richard. "How Negroes Voted," *New Republic* CXLIII (November 21, 1960): 8–10.

Shuman, Howard E. "Senate Rules and the Civil Rights Bill: A Case Study," *American Political Science Review* LI (December 1957): 955–975.

Sigel, Roberta S. "Race and Religion as Factors in the Kennedy Victory in Detroit, 1960," *Journal of Negro Education* XXXI (Fall 1962): 436–447.

Sitkoff, Harvard. "Harry Truman and the Election of 1948: The Coming of

Age of Civil Rights in American Politics," *Journal of Southern History* XXXVII (November 1971): 597–616.

Stoney, George C. "Suffrage in the South," Parts I and II, *Survey Graphic* XXIX (January–February; March–April, 1940): 5–9, 163–167.

Strong, Donald. "The Future of the Negro Voter in the South," *Journal of Negro Education* XXVI (Summer 1957): 400–407.

Swinney, Everette. "Enforcing the Fifteenth Amendment, 1870–1877," *Journal of Southern History* XXVII (May 1962): 202–218.

"Theories of Federalism and Civil Rights." *Yale Law Journal* LXXV (May 1966): 1007–1052.

Tuttle, Elbert P. "Equality and the Vote," *New York University Law Review* (April 1966): 245–266.

Valien, Preston. "Expansion of Negro Suffrage in Tennessee," *Journal of Negro Education* XXVI (Summer 1957): 362–368.

Vines, Kenneth N. "Courts and Political Change in the South," *Journal of Social Issues* XXII (January 1966): 59–62.

Wasserstrom, Richard A. "Federalism and Civil Rights," *University of Chicago Law Review* XXXIII (Winter 1966): 411–413.

Watson, Richard L., Jr. "The Defeat of Judge Parker: A Study in Pressure Groups and Politics," *Journal of American History* L (September 1963): 213–234.

Welch, Richard E., Jr. "The Federal Elections Bill of 1890: Postscripts and Prelude," *Journal of American History* LII (December 1965): 511–526.

Werdegar, Kathryn Mickle. "The Constitutionality of Federal Legislation to Abolish Literacy Tests," *George Washington Law Review* XXX (April 1962): 723–743.

"Where Does Negro Voter Strength Lie?" *Congressional Quarterly Weekly*, XIV (May 4, 1956): 491–496.

Wilkins, Roy. "Future of the Negro Voter in the United States," *Journal of Negro Education* XXVI (Summer 1957): 424–431.

Wilkinson, Horace C. "Argument for Adoption of the Boswell Amendment," *Alabama Lawyer* VII (October 1946): 380–385.

Williams, T. Harry. "Huey, Lyndon, and Southern Radicalism," *Journal of American History* LX (September 1973): 256–293.

Willkie, Wendell. "Citizens of Negro Blood," *Collier's* CXIV (October 7, 1944): 11, 47–49.

Wofford, Harris, Jr. "Notre Dame Conference on Civil Rights: A Contribution to the Development of Public Law," *Notre Dame Lawyer* XXXV (May 1960): 328–367.

Woodward, C. Vann. "The Great Civil Rights Debate," *Commentary* XXIV (October 1957): 283–291.

Zinn, Howard. "Registration in Alabama," *New Republic* CXLIX (October 26, 1963): 11–12.

INTERVIEWS AND ORAL HISTORIES

Branton, Wiley. Interview, October 21, 1970, Washington, D.C.

Clark, Joseph. Oral History, John F. Kennedy Library.

Clark, Ramsey. Interview Courtesy of Mark I. Gelfand, September 14, 1973, New York City.

Collins, Leroy. Oral History, University of South Florida Library.

Doar, John. Interview Courtesy of Mark I. Gelfand, August 27, 1973, New York City.

Durr, Virginia Foster. Interview, March 19, 1970, Wetumpka, Alabama.

Gavagan, Joseph. Oral History, Columbia University.

Hesburgh, Theodore. Oral History, John F. Kennedy Library.

Hubbard, Maceo. Interview, November 3, 1970, Washington, D.C.

Lewis, John. Interview, March 12, 1970, Atlanta, Georgia.

Mitchell, Clarence. Oral History, Lyndon B. Johnson Library.

Mitchell, William P. Interview, March 24, 1970, Tuskegee, Alabama.

Morrow, E. Frederic. Oral History, Columbia University.

Perry, Jennings. Interview, August 23, 1970, Nashville, Tennessee.

Rabb, Maxwell. Interview, October 6, 1970, New York City.

Taylor, William. Interview, October 28, 1970, Washington, D.C.

Waring, J. Watties. Oral History, Columbia University.

Wilkins, Roy. Oral History, John F. Kennedy Library.

Index

Contemporary American History Series
William E. Leuchtenburg, *General Editor*

Lawrence S. Wittner, *Rebels against War: The American Peace Movement, 1941–1960,* 1969.

Davis R. B. Ross, *Preparing for Ulysses: Politics and Veterans during World War II,* 1969.

John Lewis Gaddis, *The United States and the Origins of the Cold War, 1941–1947,* 1972.

George C. Herring, Jr., *Aid to Russia, 1941–1946: Strategy, Diplomacy, the Origins of the Cold War,* 1973.

Alonzo L. Hamby, *Beyond the New Deal: Harry S. Truman and American Liberalism,* 1973.

Richard M. Fried, *Men against McCarthy,* 1976.

Steven F. Lawson, *Black Ballots: Voting Rights in the South, 1944–1969,* 1976.

About the Author

Steven F. Lawson is professor of history at Rutgers, The State University of New Jersey. He received his Ph.D. in history from Columbia University in 1974. He is the author of *Black Ballots: Voting Rights in the South, 1944–1969* (1976); *In Pursuit of Power: Southern Blacks and Electoral Politics, 1965–1982* (1985); *Running for Freedom: Civil Rights and Black Politics in America Since 1941* (1997); and *Debating the Civil Rights Movement* (with Charles M. Payne, 1998).